Engineering Asset Management Review

Volume 4

Engineering Asset Management Review (EAMR) is published under the auspices of the International Society of Engineering Asset Management (ISEAM). Engineering Asset Management focuses on life-cycle management of the physical assets required by a private or public firm, for the purpose of making products, and/or for providing services in a manner that satisfies various business performance rationales. In exploring the wide ranging issues involved in the management of engineered assets constituting our built environment, EAMR takes a broad view of the inter- and multi-disciplinary approach which combines science, engineering, and technology principles with human behavior and business practice. *Indexed in Scopus.*

Adolfo Crespo Márquez · Turuna Seecharan ·
Georges Abdul-Nour · Joe Amadi-Echendu ·
Jay Lee
Editors

Case Studies in Digital Transformation

Integration of Digital Technologies to Enhance Asset Management Processes

Springer

Editors
Adolfo Crespo Márquez
Department of Industrial Management
University of Seville
Seville, Spain

Georges Abdul-Nour
Department of Industrial Engineering
University of Quebec
Trois-Rivières, QC, Canada

Jay Lee
Department of Mechanical Engineering
Industrial AI Center
University of Maryland, College Park
College Park, MD, USA

Turuna Seecharan
Department of Mechanical and Industrial Engineering
University of Minnesota Duluth
Duluth, MN, USA

Joe Amadi-Echendu
Graduate School of Technology Management
University of Pretoria
Pretoria, South Africa

ISSN 2190-7846 ISSN 2190-7854 (electronic)
Engineering Asset Management Review
ISBN 978-3-032-05591-0 ISBN 978-3-032-05592-7 (eBook)
https://doi.org/10.1007/978-3-032-05592-7

This Springer imprint is published by the registered company Springer Nature Switzerland AG
The registered company address is: Gewerbestrasse 11, 6330 Cham, Switzerland

Preface I

The global asset management research and industry communities are undergoing a profound transformation due to the impact of digital transformation. As industries increasingly embrace the potential of digital technologies, the way organizations approach the management, maintenance, and optimization of their engineering assets is fundamentally evolving. *Case Studies in Digital Transformation—Integration of Digital Technologies to Enhance Asset Management Processes*, the fourth volume of the Engineering Asset Management Review (EAMR), delves into this pivotal moment in asset management's development.

With the advent of digital technologies, such as the Internet of Things (IoT), artificial intelligence (AI)/machine learning (ML), big data analytics, and cloud computing, have reshaped how assets are monitored, analyzed, and maintained. These technologies not only enable more efficient asset tracking but also empower data-driven decision-making, predictive maintenance, lifecycle optimization, and risk management for improved resilience.

The case studies and research presented in this volume explore the real-world applications of these technologies in diverse contexts, from manufacturing and energy to transportation and infrastructure. Each study highlights the challenges faced, the solutions implemented, and the tangible benefits realized through the integration of digital tools into asset management processes. The interdisciplinary nature of these contributions—spanning engineering, data science, and business management—underscores the importance of collaboration in unlocking the full potential of digital transformation in asset management. As organizations continue to leverage digital transformation for improved operational efficiency, reliability, and sustainability, the insights gathered in this volume will serve as a valuable resource for asset managers, engineers, data scientists, and decision-makers seeking to navigate this evolving landscape.

We hope that this collection of case studies in this special volume will inspire further innovation and collaboration, driving the ongoing digital transformation of asset management in creating a new body of knowledge and practices toward more interdisciplinary, interconnected, and intelligent community.

December 2024

Dr. Jay Lee
Clark Distinguished Professor
and Director of Industrial AI Center
University of Maryland
College Park, MD, USA

Preface II

The fourth volume of the Engineering Asset Management Review (EAMR), entitled: *Case Studies in Digital Transformation—Integration of Digital Technologies to Enhance Asset Management Processes*, explores a critical juncture in the evolution of asset management, where the integration of digital transformation technologies, data-driven decision-making, and innovative frameworks converge to address complex challenges in engineering systems. This volume presents a carefully curated selection of research and case studies that reflect the interdisciplinary nature and practical relevance of these advancements across industries.

A Dynamic Landscape for Engineering Asset Management: Organizations worldwide face unprecedented challenges in managing critical assets amidst growing demands for efficiency, sustainability, and resilience. The integration of digital technologies such as the Internet of Things (IoT), machine learning, digital twins, and advanced data analytics provides opportunities to enhance asset lifecycle management while fostering innovation. The chapters in this volume collectively represent diverse approaches to leveraging these technologies in real-world applications, offering both theoretical and practical insights.

Contributions from CongrEGA'24: Many of the chapters in this volume originate from works presented at *CongrEGA'24*, held in Lisbon in July 2024. This event, which brought together leading academics, industry experts, and policymakers, served as a platform for sharing innovative ideas and best practices in engineering asset management. With a special focus on digital transformation and sustainability, *CongrEGA'24* emphasized the importance of interdisciplinary collaboration to tackle the pressing challenges of our time. The papers presented during the congress have been refined and extended to align with the objectives and high standards of this publication, ensuring that they contribute significantly to the advancement of the field.

Structure and Thematic Overview: This volume is organized into five thematic parts that guide the reader through the multifaceted world of digital asset management:

1. *Digital Transformation and Value Creation in Asset Management*: This part examines how digital strategies create new value paradigms, addressing sustainability, urban resilience, and long-term asset performance. It includes contributions that span industries such as agriculture, urban infrastructure, and construction.
2. *Data-Driven Asset Management and IoT Applications*: Highlighting the power of data, this part focuses on real-time asset monitoring, predictive maintenance, and decision-making enabled by IoT and digital integration. Case studies demonstrate practical applications and the tangible benefits of these technologies.
3. *Case Studies and Implementation Frameworks*: Bridging theory and practice, these chapters present case studies on implementing international standards such as ISO 55001 and BIM-powered solutions. The part underscores the challenges and successes encountered during the digital transformation journey.
4. *Specialized Topics and Emerging Applications*: Exploring niche areas, this part delves into machine learning techniques, statistical modeling, and the use of lean methodologies to optimize asset performance and lifecycle management.
5. *Business and Organizational Perspectives*: Concluding the volume, this part addresses the organizational aspects of asset management, including strategies for aligning business objectives with technological advancements and the role of data in decision-making.

Looking Forward: This volume serves as a valuable resource for academics, practitioners, and policymakers navigating the rapidly changing landscape of asset management. It highlights the need for collaborative approaches, interdisciplinary thinking, and a commitment to sustainability to ensure the resilience of critical asset systems.

Acknowledgments: We extend our deepest gratitude to the authors for their contributions, the reviewers for their rigorous evaluations, and the *CongrEGA* community for fostering a global dialogue on engineering asset management. Finally, we are honored to have Prof. Jay Lee, a pioneer in smart manufacturing and digital transformation, introduce this volume with a thought-provoking foreword.

We hope that the insights presented in this volume inspire readers to innovate, adapt, and excel in the field of asset management.

Seville, Spain — Adolfo Crespo Márquez
Duluth, USA — Turuna Seecharan
Trois-Rivières, Canada — Georges Abdul-Nour
Pretoria, South Africa — Joe Amadi-Echendu
College Park, USA — Jay Lee

Contents

Digital Transformation and Value Creation in Asset Management

New Value Perspective for Value Creation with Social Priceless Assets Through Digital Transformations

Amir Farmanesh, Joaquín Ordieres-Meré, Antonia Pacios Álvarez, and Ángel Paris Loreiro

Abstract This paper investigates the potential of digital transformation (DT) in enhancing the management and value of public assets that are currently under-managed due to limited information and their inherent social value. Focusing on regions where these assets are in high demand, the lack of effective management not only wastes time but also contributes to environmental pollution and endangers public safety. To address these challenges, we explore two pivotal use cases: the management of handicapped parking and reserved load/unload spaces, and Public primary emergency response services. The first use case employs a smart monitoring system to track usage patterns and demands, thereby facilitating better asset management and decision-making. The second use case introduces and propose IoT emergency response management system that digitalizes communications and management of emergency response services through mobile applications, wearable devices and sensors, cloud computing, and machine learning models. This system allows individuals to contact public safety answering points (PSAP) and request emergency services via their mobile devices, providing critical information such as location, personal health data, real-time health monitoring streamed by wearable devices and sensors, and real-time data like image, video and direct communication like live voice or video. Furthermore, AI models trained on historical and incoming data analyze this information to assist PSAP agents and provide recommendations. This system not only ensures faster and more accurate responses during emergencies but also collects comprehensive data—including voice, text, events, images, and videos—throughout the incident. Such data is crucial for ongoing analysis

A. Farmanesh · J. Ordieres-Meré (✉) · A. Pacios Álvarez · Á. Paris Loreiro
Universidad Politécnica de Madrid, Madrid, Spain
e-mail: j.ordieres@upm.es

A. Farmanesh
e-mail: amir.farmanesh@alumnos.upm.es

A. Pacios Álvarez
e-mail: antonia.pacios@upm.es

Á. Paris Loreiro
e-mail: angel.paris@upm.es

A. Crespo Márquez et al. (eds.), *Case Studies in Digital Transformation*, Engineering Asset Management Review 4, https://doi.org/10.1007/978-3-032-05592-7_1

and process improvement, supporting future decision-making, training first responders, and enhancing AI models for predictive analytics. In addition to improving emergency service speed and efficiency, which enhances public satisfaction, this system also advances and improves management of the emergency response service as a public asset by optimizing resource management and allocation, providing comprehensive statistics and insights that aid in process and managerial decision-making. This work underscores the transformative power of digital solutions in managing public assets and enhancing public safety, highlighting the organizational implications and the necessary adjustments in change management strategies.

Keywords Digital transformation · Asset management · Management of priceless assets · Integrated emergency response system · Smart parking

1 Introduction

This paper aims to explore the capacity of digital transformation (DT) to increase the value of public assets that currently lack management or have limited oversight, often due to insufficient available information and the communal aspect of the asset (Lafioune et al., 2023).

There are multiple cases of application that fall within the scope defined as the objective of this study. To illustrate a few of them, without intending to be restrictive, we will outline one related to mobility and another concerning emergency healthcare.

For the first example, the rising prevalence of private car usage in urban regions, driven by rapid economic growth, outdated policies, and subsidies, stands as a primary factor contributing to the global concern of car parking in transportation and traffic management. The absence of effective management of downtown parking spaces in cities with high demand leads to inefficient utilization of parking areas and illegal vehicle parking. This situation causes wasted time and effort, exacerbating traffic congestion (Parmar et al., 2020).

A significant 35% loss in productive time was recorded due to the search for parking spots. Statistics from the USA indicate that this wasted time costs drivers approximately $345 in fuel expenses. The requirements for parking, including for autonomous vehicles, must be carefully examined (Usharani & Karmel, 2022).

Emergency management and response service play a pivotal role in ensuring public safety and security (Firoozabadi et al., 2017), a fact underscored by the approximately 320 million emergency calls received annually across the European Union (NENA, 2013). This staggering number highlights the essential need for comprehensive and efficient emergency response systems capable of effectively managing a wide array of unpredictable situations that demand quick action. Effective emergency management not only necessitates the timely provision of aid but also requires the strategic allocation of resources to ensure that interventions are proportionate to the severity and specific needs of each incident.

The decisions made by Public Safety Answering Point (PSAP) staff are central to the effectiveness of these emergency response efforts. These decisions are substantially informed by comprehensive, real-time data that includes the nature of the emergency and ongoing situational updates. The depth and accuracy of this data are critical as they enable PSAP agents to make better-informed decisions and provide targeted, useful recommendations to citizens requiring emergency aid. For example, the integration of video call technology has become increasingly crucial in certain medical emergencies, where immediate advice from experts can mitigate the need for broader intervention, thereby streamlining resource allocation and reducing both costs and operational strain.

Based on the emergency call handling chain (Fig. 1), the process of prioritizing emergencies is also significantly enhanced by the quality of information received by the PSAP. While not all emergencies necessitate the fastest response, all require the most effective and intelligent response—where resources are allocated efficiently and appropriately based on actual needs rather than a one-size-fits-all approach. This strategic prioritization is supported by the ongoing digital transformation within emergency services, including the adoption of innovative technologies such as IoT-enabled wearable sensors, machine learning models, and real-time data analytics. These advancements help to enhance the accuracy and efficiency of emergency responses.

Moreover, the continuous digitalization of emergency management systems, such as the use of Machine learning models to analyse incoming data from various sources—including voice, video, and direct communication from IoT devices—plays a crucial role in optimizing the responses of emergency services. This technology allows for the dynamic assessment of situations as they evolve, ensuring that PSAP staff can make the most informed decisions possible. The goal is to create a more

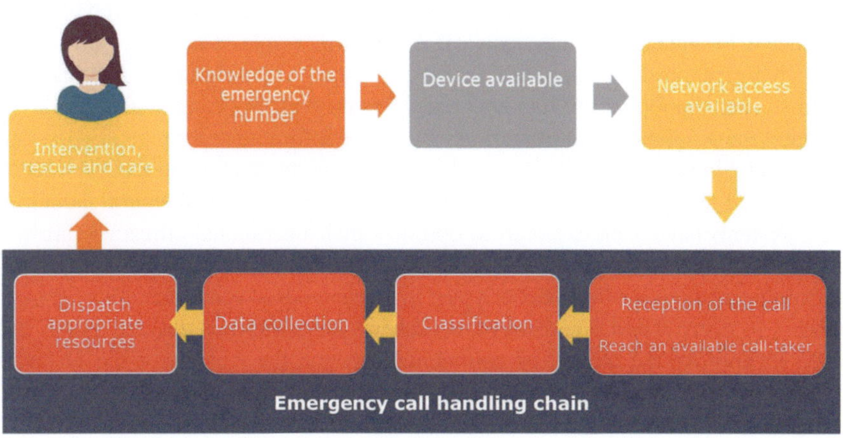

Fig. 1 Emergency call handling chain *Source* (EENA, 2020)

resilient and responsive emergency management ecosystem that not only reacts more adeptly to crises but also anticipates and prepares for potential challenges through better data utilization and technological integration.

2 Literature Review

Smart parking research has been conducted by different authors proposing alternative layers of technology (Usharani & Karmel, 2022), with different alternatives focused on cloud-based solutions (Yun & Yuxin, 2010). Most of the contributions presents the generic concept of using cloud-based intelligent car parking services in smart cities as an important application of the Internet of Things (IoT) paradigm (Ji et al., 2014).

Many works have addressed the location at convenient places proposing solutions based on radar technology (Tiwari & Singh, 2016). It is ideal for outdoor detection over long distances, this solution becomes particularly relevant as European nations increasingly embrace electric shared cars to combat emission pollution. Given this trend, it becomes imperative to regulate recharging stations located around parking areas. To optimize their utilization, radar sensors are installed to deter unauthorized vehicles from occupying these spaces. Once a car parks in one of these spaces, the radar sensor can ascertain whether the vehicle has connected to the charger.

Other proposals include wireless ultrasonic sensor is powered by the wireless network to collect the information through high-frequency ultrasound waves (Jeon et al., 2014). However, a more integrative proposal is required, covering a variety of use cases, from street parking to handicap parking places, load/unload special areas, or even construction & demolition containers placed at the street, among others.

Given the critical importance of emergency response, extensive research has been conducted to enhance the efficiency of emergency response centers, particularly through digital transformation. Studies have focused on how digital technologies can improve each component of the emergency response chain (Yang et al., 2013). For instance, the development of Emergency Response Information Systems (ERISs) has been pivotal in supporting first responders by enhancing their situational awareness, thereby facilitating better decision-making. Furthermore, the architectural models of these systems have been explored to optimize their operational efficacy (Turoff & Chumer, 2004).

Significant attention has also been paid to the methods of communication between citizens in distress and emergency dispatchers. Research includes the use of live video to improve the quality of communication and the efficacy of the response (Bergstrand & Landgren, 2009), exemplified by the Norwegian helicopter emergency medical service (HEMS) which demonstrates that video communication can significantly improve dispatch precision, serving as a promising tool for complex emergency medical communication center (EMCC) operations (Ulvin et al., 2023).

Additionally, the technological and deployment architectures of such communications have been examined, including cloud services, machine-to-machine communications, and ad hoc networks (Gonzalez et al., 2017). These studies highlight the versatility and adaptability of modern emergency communication systems to various technological advancements.

The breadth of topics within emergency management has led to numerous innovative applications of IoT technologies. These technologies enhance emergency response and management by facilitating the digitalization of traditional systems, such as monitoring real-time health data through wearable devices and sending various types of data like images, videos, and direct voice or video communication (Damaševičius et al., 2023). A qualitative study involving 100 emergency medical communication center calls revealed that the effective assessment of emergency calls by emergency medical dispatchers (EMDs) plays a vital role in identifying critical medical conditions and providing essential instructions, although barriers such as contradictory information, unclear primary problems, or poor call structure can impact the quality of emergency call assessments (Lindström et al., 2014).

In countries with a unified emergency number, like the 112 in Europe, there is broad agreement on the benefits of a single number for handling all emergencies within a country or even internationally (MARIN & Pop, 2009).The integration of artificial intelligence (AI) and machine learning models at PSAP centers also highlights a significant shift towards more data-driven emergency response management. These models, trained on historical and real-time data, can analyze emergency requests and provide valuable recommendations to PSAP operators. They process and analyze both labeled and unlabeled data, including images, videos, and voice recordings, thereby enhancing the decision-making capabilities of PSAP agents and reducing error rates and operational costs (Aleksandra et al., 2024).

These initiatives are part of a broader movement towards leveraging advanced technology to improve emergency response systems, ensuring that citizens can quickly and efficiently access emergency services.

3 Methodology

The design principles adopted in this research were shaped by the contributions of (De Sordi, 2021; Gregório et al., 2021; Peffers et al., 2007; Venable et al., 2017). Their design approach encompasses a structured methodology involving problem identification, objective definition, solution development and evaluation, and ultimately, result communication. This method is instrumental in guaranteeing that the resultant artifacts are effective, beneficial, and pertinent to the requirements of stakeholders within a given context. The context may include people, businesses, organizations, and existing technologies that are relevant to the problem. The Design science methodology also helps to identify any potential limitations or challenges that may need to be considered when developing an artifact.

There is a need for a more thorough conceptualization of wearable data within the complex semantic framework of industrial processes. This is especially crucial for understanding interactions between discrete equipment states and human operators, with the goal of reducing discrepancies in comprehending the entire process flow (Ordieres-Meré & Ortega-Mier, 2024).

The methodology for the proposed IoT-based emergency response management system is designed to streamline the response process by integrating real-time health monitoring and efficient communication technologies. This system aims to enhance traditional emergency services by enabling the monitoring of critical health metrics via smart wearable devices. It leverages a robust mobile and cloud infrastructure to ensure seamless information flow.

4 System Architecture

The two proposed use cases involve significant digital transformation efforts aimed at enhancing the value of the proposed adaptations. In the first use case, the transformations are more apparent, as it primarily focuses on technology integration and procedural changes, with most information flow managed by devices and third parties. In contrast, the second use case presents a higher level of complexity, as it necessitates extensive integration between human operators, technological services, and individuals under considerable stress. Consequently, a more detailed analysis will be conducted for this use case, examining various aspects such as User Interface, Tools, Response Team Interface, and Communication Schemas, among others.

The system architecture is delineated into four main tiers: User Interface, Cloud Services, PSAP Dashboard and Response Team Interface, each playing a pivotal role in the emergency response process (Fig. 3).

4.1 User Interface

4.1.1 Mobile Application

The mobile application serves as the primary interface for the emergency response system, enabling users to quickly access emergency services and communicate effectively with Public Safety Answering Points (PSAPs). This app allows users to send multimedia information—voice, text, images, and videos—and to input essential personal data like blood group or age, enhancing the PSAP's capability to deliver tailored and swift responses.

Integrated with wearable devices, the application tracks and sends real-time health metrics, such as heart rate and blood oxygen levels, to the PSAP. This integration facilitates informed decision-making in emergencies by providing up-to-date health data. Furthermore, the app features an emergency activation protocol that, upon user activation, automatically transmits the user's location and vital data, aiding in rapid response deployment.

App development by using Google's Flutter framework, makes the application support both Android and iOS platforms with a single codebase, which simplifies maintenance and accelerates development cycles. Flutter's ability to compile into native code enhances app performance, crucial for tasks requiring real-time processing. Its comprehensive support for internationalization also ensures the app's usability across diverse global audiences (Windmill, 2020).

4.1.2 Wearable Devices

Wearable devices in proposed emergency response system play a crucial role by continuously monitoring vital health metrics such as heart rate and blood oxygen levels, crucial during emergencies. Equipped with sensors, these devices, including smartwatches and fitness bands, employ Bluetooth Low Energy (BLE) technology to transmit data seamlessly to users' smartphones, which in turn send it to Public Safety Answering Points (PSAPs). This real-time health data allows PSAP operators to make quick, informed decisions, provide accurate medical advice, and better coordinate emergency responses.

In emergencies where the user cannot initiate a request, the application can autonomously detect conditions like heart attacks using vital metrics and automatically communicate the emergency to PSAPs along with the user's location and streaming health data. This functionality is pivotal for individuals who may be incapacitated or unable to activate emergency protocols themselves, such as with systems that detect falls or strokes (Bat-Erdene & Saver, 2021).

4.1.3 Connectivity Technology

Most wearables utilize Bluetooth technology to connect to a nearby smartphone, facilitating the transfer of collected data to mobile apps and then to emergency services. The use of Bluetooth low energy technology enhances the communication range and reduces power consumption, which is critical for maintaining the device's operational efficiency over longer periods (Zhang et al., 2014).

4.1.4 Health Monitoring Technologies

Technology	Description	Metric measured
Photoplethysmography (PPG) (Rodriguez-Labra et al., 2021)	PPG sensors use a light-based technology to detect blood volume changes in the microvascular bed of tissue. They employ pulse oximetry to measure various cardiovascular parameters by analyzing light absorption	Heart rate, blood oxygen saturation (SpO_2), heart rate variability
Accelerometers and Gyroscopes (Constant et al., 2021)	These motion sensors measure acceleration and rotational forces, respectively, to monitor the user's orientation and movement across multiple axes	Steps taken, fall detection, physical activity level, sleep patterns, orientation changes
Temperature Sensors (Eisenkraft et al., 2023)	These sensors measure the skin or device surface temperature using thermistors or infrared sensors, with newer models employing a double sensor technique for precise measurements	Skin or body temperature, which can indicate fever, exertion levels, or environmental effects on the body
Bioimpedance Sensors (Namkoong et al., 2024)	Bioimpedance sensors assess body tissue resistance to small electrical currents, which varies with the tissue's water content, affecting conductivity	Hydration levels, respiratory rate, body composition parameters such as fat and muscle mass
ECG (Electrocardiogram) (Prajapati & Darji, 2022)	ECG sensors measure the heart's electrical activity through electrodes on the skin, detecting changes associated with the heart's electrophysiologic activities during each heartbeat	Heart rhythm, heart rate, detailed heart activity that can indicate arrhythmias or ischemic episodes

4.2 Cloud Services

Cloud computing plays a main role in our IoT emergency response management system, enhancing its operational efficiency and scalability. As a central hub for data management and communication, cloud services aggregate and distribute data from user devices, sensors, and first responders, streamlining the management of emergency responses.

4.2.1 Centralized Data Management

Cloud platforms act as the nerve center for emergency systems, facilitating the rapid and efficient transfer of information necessary for coordinating responses during dynamic and large-scale emergencies (Qiu et al., 2014). Centralized data management ensures that all information is readily accessible to PSAP centers and response teams, enhancing the speed and efficiency of dispatch management and real-time tracking of emergency teams (Palmieri et al., 2016).

4.2.2 Communication and Data Storage

The cloud infrastructure supports robust communication networks by acting as a server that connects mobile applications, PSAPs, and response teams, enabling seamless and continuous communication across all platforms. It handles all forms of communication, including text, voice, and video, ensuring robust and secure peer-to-peer connectivity via WebRTC or similar technologies. Additionally, cloud computing offers scalable storage solutions that adjust dynamically to the volume of data generated during emergencies, ensuring that data handling remains efficient even during peak times (Qiu et al., 2014).

4.2.3 Machine Learning Integration

The integration of AI and machine learning models within cloud platforms is crucial for analyzing historical and real-time data to predict incident severity and optimize response strategies. These models provide PSAP agents with actionable insights, aiding in rapid and informed decision-making. For instance, AI capabilities allow for the analysis of video feeds and health metrics to assess the urgency and specifics of an incident, significantly enhancing the decision-making process (Palmieri et al., 2016).

4.2.4 Benefits of Cloud Computing

Cloud services not only support enhanced decision-making through real-time data analytics but also offer scalability and flexibility, adjusting resources to match the demands of emergency situations. This adaptability ensures cost-effective operation across various conditions. Additionally, cloud platforms are designed to meet stringent security and compliance standards, which is crucial for protecting sensitive health and personal data in emergency management scenarios (Chen, 2020).

4.3 PSAP Agent Interface (Dashboard)

The PSAP agent's interface features a comprehensive dashboard that displays real-time data, incoming alerts, and ongoing emergencies, all connected directly to the cloud for immediate data accessibility.

4.3.1 Real-Time Alert Monitoring

Dispatchers receive instant alerts with essential data points highlighted, including the type of emergency, user location, and health vitals. The integration of advanced dispatch systems with real-time data visualization significantly reduces response times and enhances decision-making capabilities, improving the overall efficiency of emergency responses (Repanovici et al., 2022).

4.3.2 Health Data Visualization

The dashboard allows dispatchers to monitor real-time health data, enabling quick, informed decisions during critical situations. This capability is crucial for effective resource management and prioritization in emergencies (Repanovici et al., 2022).

4.3.3 Resource Allocation and Live Tracking

Cloud integration facilitates dynamic resource allocation and real-time tracking of emergency teams, crucial for deploying the most appropriate resources quickly and efficiently (Gardett et al., 2016).

4.3.4 Tools and Technology

Technologies like WebRTC are essential for maintaining continuous communication with both the distressed user and response teams, ensuring seamless coordination for timely and effective responses (Repanovici et al., 2022).

4.4 Response Team Interface

The response team interface connects to the cloud, providing real-time access to emergency case details, navigation, and continuous health updates.

4.4.1 Real-Time Updates

The interface continually refreshes as new data arrives from the PSAP or directly from users' devices, including updates on the user's condition, location, and potential route hazards.

4.4.2 Inter-team Communication

Supports effective coordination among response teams and external communication with the PSAP and the distressed user. Direct communication is facilitated by WebRTC, enabling voice and video communications that provide clear instructions and additional information for rapid response (Aedo et al., 2011).

4.4.3 Development Technology and Data Access

Like the user app, the responder's app is developed using Flutter to ensure consistency across platforms and reduce development time. Real-time communication technologies like WebRTC enhance the speed and accuracy of information exchange during emergencies (Carreras-Coch et al., 2022).

- Advanced Tracking and Navigation: Real-time GPS tracking via platforms like Google Maps API aids in efficient navigation and route planning, ensuring rapid and safe arrival at destinations.
- Data Streaming and Event Handling: Technologies such as Apache Kafka and RabbitMQ support high-volume data streaming and real-time event handling, essential for managing complex workflows and maintaining situational awareness among all parties involved.

4.5 Machine Learning Models in Emergency Response Management

4.5.1 Supervised Learning for Labeled Data

Supervised learning is integral to training models on labeled data within our IoT emergency response management system, helping predict outcomes and optimize decision-making during emergencies. Labeled data in this context often includes historical records of emergency calls with details like response times and incident specifics, which are used to train models to recognize patterns and anticipate needs during similar future events.

Model Selection: For categorical outcomes such as resource type needed or urgency level, classification models like Logistic Regression, Support Vector

Machines (SVM), and Random Forests are used. SVM, for example, is chosen for its effectiveness in high-dimensional spaces typical in emergency data, which may include diverse inputs such as text descriptions, location data, and initial vital signs (Noble, 2006). These models are adept at handling the binary classifications needed to determine immediate life-threatening situations or multi-class scenarios like categorizing types of emergencies.

4.5.2 Deep Learning for Multimedia Data

Deep learning is utilized for analyzing complex data types like images, videos, and audio from emergency scenes, which are crucial for assessing situations and aiding in emergency classification.

- Convolutional Neural Networks (CNN): CNNs are particularly effective for processing image and video data to analyze visual information from emergency scenes, such as traffic accidents or surveillance footage. This analysis helps classify the type of emergency and the severity of the situation.
- Recurrent Neural Networks (RNN) and LSTMs: For audio and sequential data, LSTMs, a type of RNN, are suitable due to their ability to process time-series information efficiently. These models are crucial for interpreting emergency calls or other audio inputs, providing insights that are vital for timely and appropriate responses.

4.5.3 Practical Application and System Integration

Machine learning models are deployed within the cloud framework of the emergency response management system, ensuring they are accessible and operable in real-time. These models continually analyze incoming data from IoT devices and user inputs, enhancing the system's predictive capabilities. For example, models can analyze incoming video and audio to quickly assess emergency scenes and suggest immediate actions to PSAP agents, improving response times and outcome effectiveness.

Continuous Learning and Adaptation: The system incorporates mechanisms for continuous learning, where machine learning models are periodically updated with new data reflecting recent emergencies, enhancing their accuracy and relevance. This adaptive approach ensures the system evolves in response to changing patterns and emergency scenarios, maintaining high performance and reliability.

Integration with Dispatch Systems: Machine learning insights are integrated directly into PSAP's dispatch systems, providing dispatchers with real-time recommendations and predictive analytics. This integration supports dynamic resource allocation and helps dispatchers make informed decisions swiftly, ultimately enhancing the overall efficiency of emergency management operations.

5 Results

Using the public space to deploy and maintain smart devices create significant challenges, related to theft, vandalism, and other non-regular behaviours, and attending to the adopted framework and the use case capabilities, several data flows need to be integrated. On one side bay occupancy information, connected with geographic position. In addition, it is important to collect information related to vehicle user. To reconciliate both data flows two different sensors need to be deployed in a way that no energy demands need to be fulfilled.

The next step is to create the logic behind the hardware deployment. Such logic requires that every user of a parking bay detected by Fig. 2 (left) must self-register the bay usage Fig. 2 (right). The same logic can be implemented for disabled parking places or for the control of construction waste containers placed at the street.

The magnetic sensor placed in the robust case communicate changes (vehicle presence/absence) by means of Lora WAN technology (Aldahdouh et al., 2019; James & Nair, 2017). By means of these technology signals can reach around 1 km

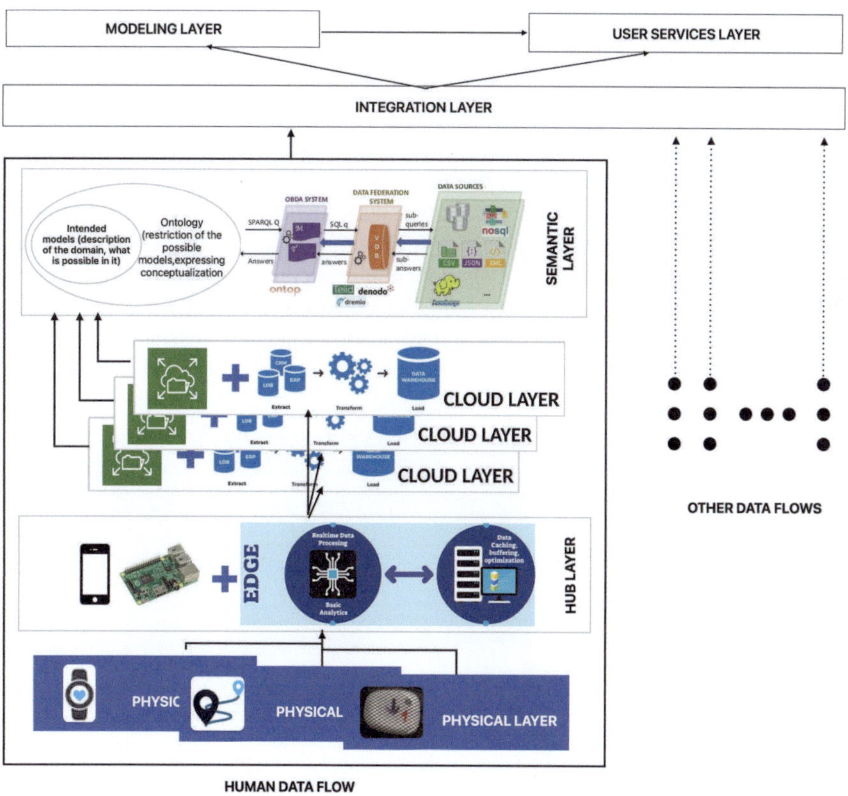

Fig. 2 Adopted framework, *Source* Ordieres-Meré & Ortega-Mier, 2024

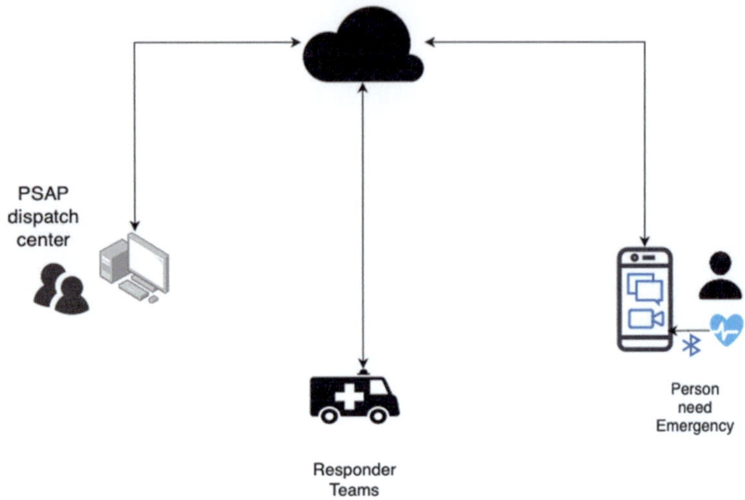

Fig. 3 System architecture

of distance to reach a gateway node usually placed at the outdoor lighting system, making it possible to send the information to the cloud (Siagian & Fernando, 2020). Parallel to the vehicle detection the user must self-register through the cellphone the presence, by scanning the QR, which includes the reference to the geographic position as well as the reference to its corresponding magnetic sensor (Fig. 4).

When the user operates properly, s/he will indicate once the plate reference or the code provided by the municipal license in the case of waste containers temporary placed at the street. In this way not only finer control of the assets can be implemented without extra demand of human operators, but increased efficiency for police officers is reached when a vehicle is detected, and no registration happens in a time boundary of five minutes of each other.

Fig. 4 Hardware components for the defined configuration. Left: magnetic sensor for vehicle presence placed at the center of the parking bay. Right: QR label to be placed at the sidewalk in parallel to the magnetic sensor

Different rules can be automatically derived from the microservice oriented cloud platform, including usage of different type of parking bays, implementing different policies, per geographic sector. Implementation of fees, better tracking of municipal rules is also possible.

The deployment of the emergency response system introduced specific challenges associated with digital technology reliance in critical public services. One of the fundamental requirements for the system's operation is that users must possess a smartphone equipped with internet connectivity. This requirement introduces a barrier to access, as the system's efficacy is contingent upon the user's ability to install and operate the emergency response application. While this setup leverages the widespread availability of smartphones to facilitate immediate communication with Public Safety Answering Points (PSAPs), it also restricts the system's accessibility to those without the necessary technology or reliable internet service. This challenge is particularly pronounced in regions with digital divides or areas with inconsistent mobile network coverage. Addressing these issues involved strategic planning around system outreach and education to ensure widespread adoption and understanding of the application's functionality. Additionally, efforts were made to optimize the app's data usage to accommodate users with limited data plans or those in areas with lower bandwidth availability.

The system was designed to automate and optimize the flow of critical information between emergency callers and response units. This included the implementation of GPS for precise location tracking and multimedia capabilities that allowed for transmitting live images and videos from the scene as well as the text and voice messages. Like how vehicle presence is detected through magnetic sensors in the smart parking system, the emergency response system utilizes mobile GPS data combined with inputs from users through a dedicated mobile application to accurately assess and categorize the nature of emergencies.

Utilizing a combination of advanced cloud computing solutions and on-ground IoT devices, the emergency response system ensured that data regarding the emergency—such as location, type of emergency, and live video feeds—were quickly relayed to the appropriate emergency services. This technological integration resulted in a significant improvement in response times, with preliminary data indicating a reduction in time from emergency call to service dispatch.

Emergency system users are required to interact with the system primarily through a mobile application, which guides them through the process of reporting an emergency. This process includes verification steps like the self-registration required in the smart parking system, ensuring that all relevant details are accurately captured. The application automatically transmits data about the emergency and the user's location while providing the option for the user to supplement this with additional information, such as medical specifics, like how users in the parking system provide vehicle details.

The implementation of the emergency response system not only enhanced the efficiency of emergency services but also significantly improved the management of emergency situations, leading to faster and more effective responses. Additionally, the system's ability to provide continuous and reliable communication between the caller and emergency services has been pivotal in improving the overall quality of emergency management, akin to the enhanced asset management observed with the smart parking system.

6 Discussion

The suggested solution not only enhances control over asset utilization but also offers an expanded knowledge base. This includes easily summarizing the average usage of parking bays throughout the day, on weekends, and so forth, on a per-street basis. Similarly, detailed information can be provided for disabled parking spots and areas with loading/unloading restrictions. Analysing general bay usage yields insights into rotation, quantity, and average vacancy duration, facilitating ongoing policy enhancements. These improvements can be measured cost-effectively through key performance indicators (KPIs) derived from the new layer of information.

Furthermore, an aspect of even greater social significance is ensuring compliance with regulations governing disabled parking spots and designated load/unload times. This entails verifying that vehicles parked in disabled bays correspond to authorized license plates and users, and that the duration of loading operations aligns with permitted time frames. Additionally, the diversity of users can be readily assessed in aggregated terms.

Similarly, the deployment of the emergency response system significantly enhances public safety management by providing quick and reliable communication links between citizens in distress and emergency services. This system utilizes digital technologies to ensure that accurate and comprehensive data regarding the nature and location of emergencies is promptly available to dispatchers and responders. Such capabilities markedly improve the efficiency and effectiveness of emergency responses, crucially reducing response times and improving outcomes.

By leveraging real-time data and advanced analytics, the emergency response system also supports ongoing improvements in emergency management policies and practices. For instance, the detailed data collected can inform more effective resource allocation, emergency planning, and training programs for emergency personnel. This parallels the enhancements seen in smart parking management, where data-driven insights lead to better asset utilization and compliance enforcement.

Moreover, just as smart parking solutions ensure compliance with parking regulations, the emergency response system helps maintain compliance with safety protocols and standards, providing a critical framework for assessing and responding to emergencies. It ensures that every call for help is efficiently processed and matched with appropriate emergency services, thereby safeguarding community welfare.

7 Conclusions

This study presents a proposal for bolstering the monitoring of invaluable public assets, entailing moderate initial investment and minimal operational costs. Leveraging a high degree of integration as per the adopted framework, the system can generate high-quality, real-time information. This data can enhance the efficacy of punitive measures to enforce established regulations and facilitate the adaptive re-planning of specific locations based on observed usage patterns.

The current level of information collected by municipalities does not support the kind of strategic planning facilitated by regular monitoring of key performance indicators (KPIs). However, with a moderate investment, which includes the installation of sensors and light gateways on-site, as well as QR codes on sidewalks for physical hardware, and the implementation of a microservice system to process the generated data, a powerful yet cost-effective information system can be established. Given the manageable additional effort for management, anticipated changes can be minimized, thus reducing resistance to change. Nevertheless, there will be a need to reallocate resources and acquire new skills to effectively utilize the gathered information.

The system's management presents challenges as it necessitates reallocating additional IT services. Besides the demands of change management, there's a need to furnish users with additional information to counterbalance the potential negative perception of a swift and efficient punitive system. Hence, efforts should focus on not only societal education but also enhancing the perceived value for individuals, thereby addressing both aspects effectively.

Similarly, the emergency response system represents a critical enhancement in how emergency services interact with the public. By enabling constant, real-time communication and accurate location services, the system significantly improves the efficiency and effectiveness of emergency response operations. This integration not only supports faster and more informed decision-making but also allows for immediate action in critical situations, thereby potentially saving lives. The system's capability to transmit comprehensive data including video, images, voice, and text to Public Safety Answering Points (PSAPs) enhances the quality of information available to emergency operators. This richer data context helps in making more informed decisions quickly and provides a more complete set of documented data which is invaluable for post-event analysis and continuous improvement of emergency response services. Crucially, the connection is persistent, ensuring that updates can be continuously sent and received, allowing first responders to receive real-time updates about the evolving situation before they arrive at the location.

The combined impact of both systems—smart parking and emergency response—demonstrates the power of digital technologies in transforming public asset management and emergency services. Both systems illustrate how moderate investments in technology can lead to significant improvements in service delivery and operational efficiency.

The system's management of both parking and emergency response scenarios presents challenges, particularly in the need for continuous IT support and adaptation to evolving technologies. The dual requirement of managing both assets and emergency responses necessitates a robust change management strategy, underpinned by ongoing training and education to ensure all stakeholders understand and can effectively use the new systems.

Additional research is necessary to further develop these technologies and to ensure that they can meet the demands of modern urban environments comprehensively. This holistic approach is essential to ensure effectiveness and efficiency across all dimensions of the system, and future studies should focus on refining the integration of these technologies to enhance their benefits further.

References

Abadi, M., Barham, P., Chen, J., Chen, Z., Davis, A., Dean, J., Devin, M., Ghemawat, S., Irving, G., Isard, M., Kudlur, M., Levenberg, J., Monga, R., Moore, S., Murray, D. G., Steiner, B., Tucker, P., Vasudevan, V., Warden, P., & Zheng, X. (2016). TensorFlow: A system for large-scale machine learning. In *Proceedings of the 12th USENIX Symposium on Operating Systems Design and Implementation*, OSDI 2016.

Aedo, I., Díaz, P., Bañuls, V. A., Canós, J.-H., & Hiltz, S. R. (2011). *Information Technologies for Emergency Planning and Training*.

Aldahdouh, K. A., Darabkh, K. A., Al-Sit, W., et al. (2019). A survey of 5G emerging wireless technologies featuring LoRaWAN, Sigfox, NB-IoT and LTE-M. *International Conference on Wireless Communications Signal Processing and Networking (WiSPNET), 2019*, 561–566.

Aleksandra, S., Robert, K., Klaudia, K., Dawid, L., & Mariusz, S. (2024). *Artificial Intelligence in Optimizing the Functioning of Emergency Departments; a Systematic Review of Current Solutions. 12*(1), e22. https://doi.org/10.22037/aaem.v12i1.2110

Bat-Erdene, B. O., & Saver, J. L. (2021). Automatic acute stroke symptom detection and emergency medical systems alerting by mobile health technologies: A review. In *Journal of Stroke and Cerebrovascular Diseases* (Vol. 30, Issue 7). https://doi.org/10.1016/j.jstrokecerebrovasdis.2021.105826

Bergstrand, F., & Landgren, J. (2009). *Using live video for information sharing in emergency response work. 6*(3), 295. https://doi.org/10.1504/IJEM.2009.031567

Burges, C. J. C. (1998). A tutorial on support vector machines for pattern recognition. *Data Mining and Knowledge Discovery*, *2*(2). https://doi.org/10.1023/A:1009715923555

Carreras-Coch, A., Navarro, J., Sans, C., & Zaballos, A. (2022). Communication technologies in emergency situations. In *Electronics (Switzerland)* (Vol. 11, Issue 7). https://doi.org/10.3390/electronics11071155

Chappuis, V. N., Deham, H., Cottet, P., Gartner, B. A., Sarasin, F. P., Niquille, M., Suppan, L., & Larribau, R. (2021). Emergency physician's dispatch by a paramedic-staffed emergency medical communication centre: sensitivity, specificity and search for a reference standard. *Scandinavian Journal of Trauma, Resuscitation and Emergency Medicine*, *29*(1). https://doi.org/10.1186/s13049-021-00844-y

Chen, Y. (2020). *IoT, cloud, big data and AI in interdisciplinary domains. 102*, 102070. https://doi.org/10.1016/j.simpat.2020.102070

Constant, N., Cay, G., Ravichandran, V., Diouf, R., Akbar, U., & Mankodiya, K. (2021). Data analytics for wearable IoT-based telemedicine. In *Wearable Sensors* (pp. 357–378). Elsevier. https://doi.org/10.1016/B978-0-12-819246-7.00013-9

Damaševičius, R., Bacanin, N., & Misra, S. (2023). *From Sensors to Safety: Internet of Emergency Services (IoES) for Emergency Response and Disaster Management, 12*(3), 41. https://doi.org/10.3390/jsan12030041

EENA. (2013). *Next Generation 112 Long Term Definition.*

EENA. (2020). *Emergency call handling service chain description.* EENA.org

Eisenkraft, A., Goldstein, N., Fons, M., Tabi, M., Sherman, A. D., Ben Ishay, A., Merin, R., & Nachman, D. (2023). *Comparing body temperature measurements using the double sensor method within a wearable device with oral and core body temperature measurements using medical grade thermometers—a short report. 14*, 1279314. https://doi.org/10.3389/fphys.2023.1279314

Firoozabadi, S. M. K., Soleimani, G., Amiri, M., & Moradian, M. (2017). *Review of Emergency Response Methods in Disaster Management, Dispatch and Control of Forces in Emergencies, 11*(3).

Friedman, J. H. (2001). Greedy function approximation: A gradient boosting machine. *Annals of Statistics, 29*(5). https://doi.org/10.1214/aos/1013203451

Gardett, I., Clawson, J., Scott, G., Barron, T., Patterson, B., & Olola, C. (2016). Past, present, and future of emergency dispatch research: A systematic literature review. *Emergency Medicine Journal, 33*(9). https://doi.org/10.1136/emermed-2016-206139.13

Gonzalez, E., Peña, R., Avila, A., Vargas-Rosales, C., & Munoz-Rodriguez, D. (2017). A systematic review on recent advances in mhealth systems: deployment architecture for emergency response. In *Journal of Healthcare Engineering* (Vol. 2017). https://doi.org/10.1155/2017/9186270

Gregório, J., Reis, L., Peyroteo, M., Maia, M., Mira da Silva, M., & Lapão, L. V. (2021). The role of design science research methodology in developing pharmacy eHealth services. *Research in Social and Administrative Pharmacy, 17*(12), 2089–2096. https://doi.org/10.1016/J.SAPHARM.2021.05.016

Hochreiter, S., & Schmidhuber, J. (1997). Long short-term memory. *Neural Computation, 9*(8). https://doi.org/10.1162/neco.1997.9.8.1735

James, J. G., & Nair, S. (2017). Efficient, real-time tracking of public transport, using lorawan and rf transceivers. *TENCON 2017–2017 IEEE Region 10 Conference*, pp. 2258–2261.

Jeon, S., Kwon, E., & Jung, I. (2014). Traffic measurement on multiple drive lanes with wireless ultrasonic sensors. *Sensors, 14*(12), 22891–22906. https://doi.org/10.3390/S141222891

Ji, Z., Ganchev, I., O'Droma, M., Zhao, L., & Zhang, X. (2014). A cloud-based car parking middleware for IoT-based smart cities: design and implementation. *Sensors, 14*(12), 22372–22393. https://doi.org/10.3390/S141222372

Krizhevsky, A., Sutskever, I., & Hinton, G. E. (2017). ImageNet classification with deep convolutional neural networks. *Communications of the ACM, 60*(6). https://doi.org/10.1145/3065386

Lafioune, N., Desmarest, A., Poirier, É. A., & St-Jacques, M. (2023). Digital transformation in municipalities for the planning, delivery, use and management of infrastructure assets: Strategic and organizational framework. *Sustainable Futures, 6*, Article 100119. https://doi.org/10.1016/J.SFTR.2023.100119

Lindström, V., Heikkilä, K., Bohm, K., Castrèn, M., & Falk, A.-C. (2014). *Barriers and Opportunities in Assessing Calls to Emergency Medical Communication Centre–a Qualitative Study., 22*(1), 61. https://doi.org/10.1186/s13049-014-0061-3

Marin, G., & Pop, D.-P. (2009). The European emergency number 112. *Journal of Information Systems & Operations Management, 3*, 173–184.

Namkoong, M., McMurray, J., Branan, K., Hernandez, J., Gandhi, M., Ida-Oze, S., Cote, G., & Tian, L. (2024). *Contact Pressure-Guided Wearable Dual-Channel Bioimpedance Device for Continuous Hemodynamic Monitoring., 9*(3), 2301407. https://doi.org/10.1002/admt.202301407

NENA. (2013). *NENA NG9-1-1 Transition Plan Considerations Information Document.*

Noble, W. S. (2006). What is a support vector machine? In *Nature Biotechnology* (Vol. 24, Issue 12). https://doi.org/10.1038/nbt1206-1565

Ordieres-Meré, J., & Ortega-Mier, M. A. (2024). Challenges in Industry 5.0: Human behavior integration. *Manufacturing.*

Palmieri, F., Ficco, M., Pardi, S., & Castiglione, A. (2016). *A Cloud-Based Architecture for Emergency Management and First Responders Localization in Smart City Environments., 56*, 810–830. https://doi.org/10.1016/j.compeleceng.2016.02.012

Parmar, J., Das, P., & Dave, S. M. (2020). Study on demand and characteristics of parking system in urban areas: A review. *Journal of Traffic and Transportation Engineering (English Edition), 7*(1), 111–124. https://doi.org/10.1016/J.JTTE.2019.09.003

Peffers, K., Tuunanen, T., Rothenberger, M. A., & Chatterjee, S. (2007). A design science research methodology for information systems research. *Journal of Management Information Systems, 24*(3), 45–77. https://doi.org/10.2753/MIS0742-1222240302

Prajapati, P. H., & Darji, A. D. (2022). *Hardware Efficient Low-Frequency Artifact Reduction Technique for Wearable ECG Device., 71*, 1–9. https://doi.org/10.1109/TIM.2022.3208262

Qiu, M., Ming, Z., Wang, J., Yang, L. T., & Xiang, Y. (2014). *Enabling Cloud Computing in Emergency Management Systems., 1*(4), 60–67. https://doi.org/10.1109/MCC.2014.71

Repanovici, R. M., Nedelcu, Șerban, Tarbă, L. A., & Busuioceanu, S. (2022). *Improvement of Emergency Situation Management through an Integrated System Using Mobile Alerts. 14*(24), 16424. https://doi.org/10.3390/su142416424

Rodriguez-Labra, J. I., Kosik, C., Maddipatla, D., Narakathu, B. B., & Atashbar, M. Z. (2021). *Development of a PPG Sensor Array as a Wearable Device for Monitoring Cardiovascular Metrics., 21*(23), 26320–26327. https://doi.org/10.1109/JSEN.2021.3064219

Sebillo, M., Vitiello, G., Paolino, L., & Ginige, A. (2016). *Training Emergency Responders through Augmented Reality Mobile Interfaces., 75*(16), 9609–9622. https://doi.org/10.1007/s11042-015-2955-0

Siagian, P., & Fernando, E. (2020). LoRaWAN intelligent outdoor smart street lighting. In *2020 IEEE International Conference on Communication, Networks and Satellite (Comnetsat)*, pp. 198–203.

De Sordi, J. O. (2021). DSR as an innovation accelerator strategy. *Design Science Research Methodology*, 1–5. https://doi.org/10.1007/978-3-030-82156-2_1

Spjeldnæs, T. B., Nilsen, K. A. V., Myrmel, L., Sørnes, J.-O., & Brattebø, G. (2023). *Calling for help: I need you to listen–A qualitative study of callers' experience of calls to the emergency medical communication centre. 31*(1), 94. https://doi.org/10.1186/s13049-023-01161-2

Tiwari, V. K., & Singh, V. (2016). Study of internet of things (IoT): A vision, architectural elements, and future directions.*International Journal of Advanced Research in Computer Science. EBSCOhost*. https://openurl.ebsco.com/EPDB%3Agcd%3A3%3A7865907/detailv2?sid=ebsco%3Aplink%3Ascholar&id=ebsco%3Agcd%3A121071482&crl=c

Turoff, M., & Chumer, M. (2004). *The Design of a Dynamic Emergency Response Management Information System (DERMIS).*

Ulvin, O. E., Skjærseth, E. Å., Krüger, A. J., Thorsen, K., Nordseth, T., & Haugland, H. (2023). Can video communication in the emergency medical communication centre improve dispatch precision? A before–after study in Norwegian helicopter emergency medical services. *BMJ Open, 13*(10). https://doi.org/10.1136/bmjopen-2023-077395

Usharani, S., & Karmel, A. (2022). *Smart Parking System and Its Applications*, pp. 75–99. https://doi.org/10.1007/978-981-19-2184-1_4

Venable, J. R., Pries-Heje, J., & Baskerville, R. L. (2017). Choosing a design science research methodology. In *ACIS 2017 Proceedings*. https://aisel.aisnet.org/acis2017/112

Windmill, E. (2020). *Flutter in Action.* Manning Publications.

Yang, L., Yang, S. H., & Plotnick, L. (2013). *How the Internet of Things Technology Enhances Emergency Response Operations., 80*(9), 1854–1867. https://doi.org/10.1016/j.techfore.2012.07.011

Yun, M., & Yuxin, B. (2010). Research on the architecture and key technology of Internet of Things (IoT) applied on smart grid. In *2010 International Conference on Advances in Energy Engineering, ICAEE 2010*, pp. 69–72. https://doi.org/10.1109/ICAEE.2010.5557611

Zhang, T., Lu, J., Hu, F., & Hao, Q. (2014). Bluetooth low energy for wearable sensor-based healthcare systems. *IEEE Healthcare Innovation Conference (HIC), 2014*, 251–254. https://doi.org/10.1109/HIC.2014.7038922

A Roadmap for Digital Transformation in the Architecture, Engineering, Construction, and Operations Industry: A Survey and Industry Analysis

Seyed Mohammad Hossein Seyedi Rezvani, Maria João Falcão Silva, and Nuno Marques de Almeida

Abstract The Architecture, Engineering, Construction, and Operations (AECO) industry lags in digital adoption despite its potential to enhance productivity and efficiency. This study develops a roadmap for digital transformation within the AECO sector, informed by both a thorough literature review and a survey of industry practitioners across various geographical regions and project types. The research examines challenges hindering digital progress, including low research and development spending, resistance to change, and a skills gap in digital technologies. The study investigates how digitalization challenges differ across various company sizes and project types, including residential buildings, infrastructure, and specialized infrastructure. The proposed roadmap outlines key steps for successful digital adoption, encompassing strategic planning, technology selection, skills development, and process optimization. Emerging technologies like Artificial Intelligence (AI), Virtual Reality (VR), and digital twins are explored for their potential to revolutionize construction practices and enhance productivity. Insights from this research provide a practical guide for AECO stakeholders to overcome barriers to digital adoption and accelerate their digital transformation journey, leading to improved efficiency, collaboration, and sustainability within the industry.

Keywords Construction industry · Digitalization · Technology adoption · Productivity growth · Business practices

S. M. H. S. Rezvani (✉) · N. Marques de Almeida
Civil Engineering Research and Innovation for Sustainability (CERIS), Instituto Superior Técnico, Universidade de Lisboa, Lisboa, Portugal
e-mail: seyedi.rezvani@tecnico.ulisboa.pt

N. Marques de Almeida
e-mail: nunomarquesalmeida@tecnico.ulisboa.pt

M. J. F. Silva
Laboratório Nacional de Engenharia Civil, Lisboa, Portugal
e-mail: mjoaofalcao@lnec.pt

A. Crespo Márquez et al. (eds.), *Case Studies in Digital Transformation*, Engineering Asset Management Review 4, https://doi.org/10.1007/978-3-032-05592-7_2

1 Introduction

The digital revolution has transformed many industries, leading to significant gains in efficiency, productivity, and innovation. However, the construction industry, which includes Architecture, Engineering, Construction, and Operations (AECO), remains one of the least digitalized sectors (Autodesk University, 2024). This lack of digital adoption has major consequences for productivity, which remains low compared to other industries. Despite recognizing the potential benefits of digital tools and technologies, the AECO industry faces productivity challenges, lagging behind other sectors in terms of output per worker and project completion times.

A 2024 report by Autodesk highlights several barriers to digital adoption in the construction industry. According to the report, 42% of companies identify a digital skills gap as a significant barrier, 39% cite cost concerns, and 34% point to a lack of budget allocated to technology (Autodesk University, 2022). Additionally, the report emphasizes the importance of digital transformation for addressing these challenges and driving growth. Key priorities for improving digital adoption include tracking various success measures, selecting a digital champion to lead technology initiatives, assessing AI readiness, and building a supportive digital ecosystem.

Compared to industries like automotive and aerospace, which invest around 3.5 to 4.5% of their revenues in Research and Development (R&D), the construction industry spends less than 1% (Autodesk University, 2022). This difference becomes even more significant when considering that only 6% of construction companies use digital planning tools. This highlights a critical digital gap that limits the industry's ability to benefit from technological advancements (McKinsey, 2023).

Furthermore, another report discusses trends and barriers related to the digitization of construction (Autodesk & Deloitte, 2024). Economic and regulatory factors are driving investment in construction technology, with high investor optimism and increasing venture capital funding (PlanRadar, 2023). However, customer fragmentation, low margins, and challenges with technology adoption and scaling remain significant obstacles. To overcome these barriers, the report suggests strategies such as pursuing a large addressable market, achieving product-market fit, building scalable revenue models, and focusing on customer success (Autodesk University, 2022).

Several factors contribute to the construction industry's slow adoption of digital technologies (Autodesk University, 2024). These include traditionally low spending on R&D, a general resistance to change within the industry, and the complexity and geographic spread of construction projects. This paper aims to shed light on these challenges and explore strategies to close the digital and productivity gap in the AECO sector. By examining how more digitally advanced industries operate, we aim to find practical ways for the construction industry to embrace digital transformation.

We will also investigate the specific reasons behind the digital gap in construction, comparing its current practices with those of other industries. Through this comparison, we will identify key areas for improvement and suggest web-based digital tools and strategies that could drive change. The insights and conclusions from this study will offer valuable guidance for overcoming the barriers that have long prevented the AECO industry from becoming more digitalized and productive.

2 Literature Review

2.1 Systematic Literature Review

The main search criteria for this study focus on peer-reviewed articles and reviews related to construction and digital technologies, ensuring the inclusion of high-quality, scholarly sources published in journals and written in English. The search strategy specifically uses the keywords "construction," "digital," and "technology" to capture relevant research. It excludes studies related to some unrelated keywords, as well as those from subject areas unrelated to the core focus, such as arts, medicine, chemical engineering, biochemistry, chemistry, psychology, agriculture, neuroscience, health, dentistry, pharmacy, nursing, immunology, and physics (Autodesk University, 2024). This approach aims to provide an overview of the current state and advancements in digital technology adoption within the construction industry, highlighting practical and theoretical insights while avoiding minor topics. The focus is on final-stage publications to ensure the inclusion of completed and fully vetted research.

Figure 1 presented shows a notable trend in the volume of scholarly documents related to construction and digital technologies over several decades. Starting with minimal publications in the early 1960s and sporadic outputs through the 1970s and 1980s, there was a gradual increase in the 1990s.

The momentum accelerated from the 2000s onwards, reflecting growing interest and advancements in digital technologies within the construction industry. Particularly striking is the exponential rise in publications from 2019 to 2024, where the year 2023 recorded the highest number of documents at 647 by mid-year, indicating a robust and expanding field of research. This trend underscores the increasing

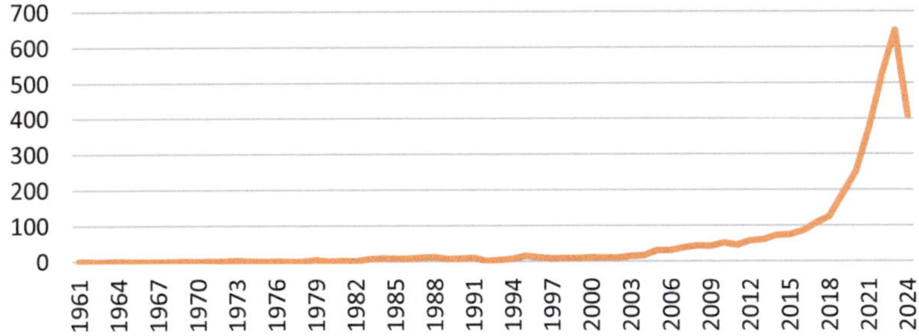

Fig. 1 Publication trend count in time

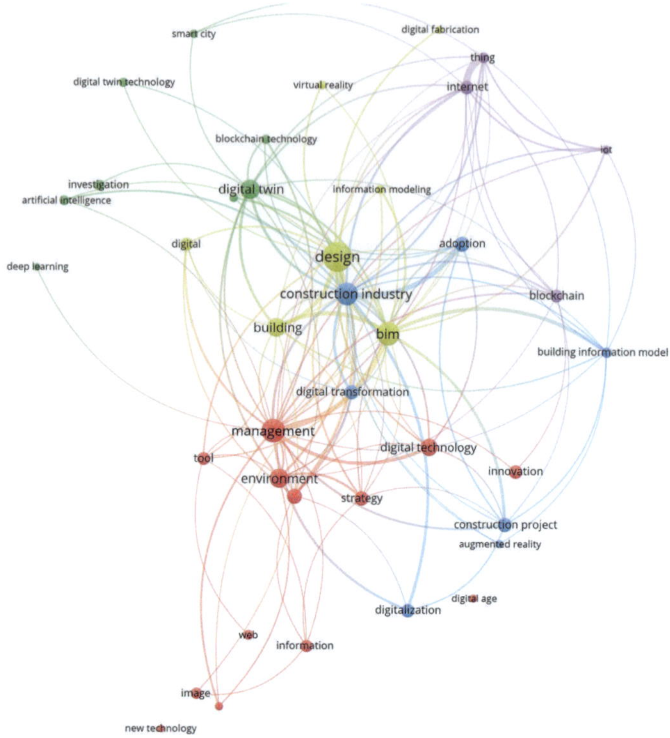

Fig. 2 VOS network visualization

significance of digital technologies in construction practices and the corresponding academic interest and investment in understanding and improving these innovations.

Figure 2 VOS network visualization provides a view of the digital landscape in the AEC industry. This network can be understood through five interconnected clusters, each representing different aspects of the industry's digital transformation

The first cluster, which we can call "Traditional and Foundational," includes terms like architecture, environment, and management. These concepts form the backbone of the AECO industry and have been discussed in literature for a longer time, with average publication years around 2017–201. This cluster connects to others by providing the foundational knowledge upon which digital innovations are built.

The second cluster, "Emerging Technologies," focuses on cutting-edge advancements such as artificial intelligence, deep learning, and digital twins. With recent average publication years of 2021–2022, this cluster represents the frontier of technological adoption in the AECO industry. It links closely with the third and fifth clusters, showing how these technologies are being applied and integrated into industry practices.

The third cluster, "Industry Application," bridges the gap between traditional concepts and new technologies. It includes terms like adoption, construction industry, and digital transformation. With publication years around 2020–2022, this cluster reflects the current state of digital technology implementation in construction.

The fourth cluster centers on "BIM and Design," highlighting the role of Building Information Modeling in modern construction processes. This cluster, with publication years around 2019–2021, shows how BIM has become a cornerstone of digital transformation in the AECO industry.

The fifth cluster, "IoT and Blockchain," represents data-centric technologies that are gaining traction in construction. With recent publication years of 2021–2022, this cluster indicates growing interest in using Internet of Things (IoT) devices and blockchain for improved data management and security in construction projects.

Figure 3 shows emerging topics in the field, which are clearly visible through the overlay visualization. Digital twin technology, with an average publication year of 2022.8, stands out as a key area of current research and development.

Artificial intelligence and deep learning also show high recency, indicating their growing importance in the industry. The ongoing process of digital transformation remains a central theme, reflecting the industry's continued efforts to adopt and integrate new technologies.

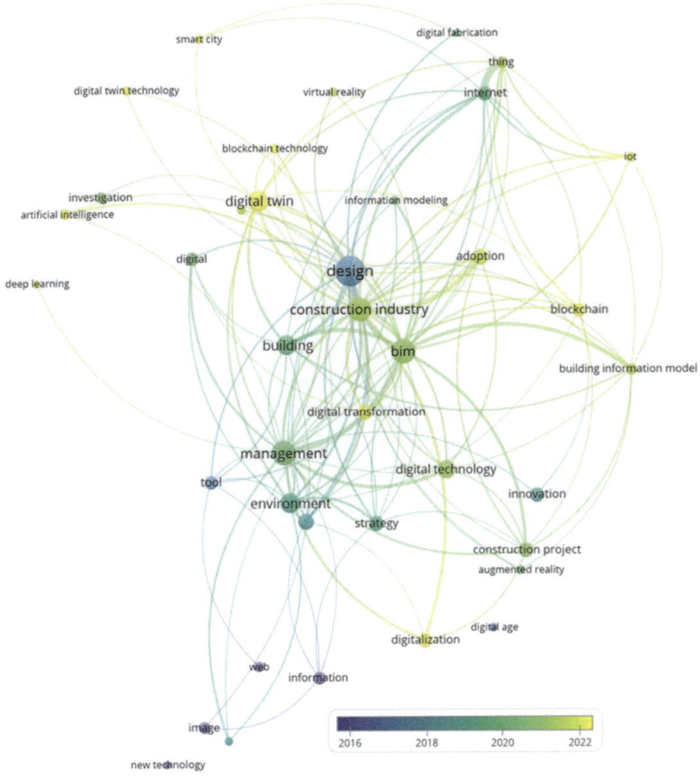

Fig. 3 VOS overlay visualization

The network reveals how the AECO industry is progressing from traditional practices towards more advanced technological applications. The central position of the "Industry Application" cluster underscores the focus on practical implementation of digital technologies, serving as a bridge between established methods and innovative solutions.

While terms like BIM, management, and design still show high occurrence weights, signifying their enduring importance, the recent publication years of topics in the "Emerging Technologies" and "IoT and Blockchain" clusters point to the future direction of the industry's digitalization efforts.

In conclusion, this VOS network visualization offers valuable insights into the complex interplay of traditional practices, current industry applications, and emerging technologies in the AECO sector. It highlights the industry's ongoing journey of digital transformation, showcasing both the established cornerstones and the exciting new frontiers of construction technology.

2.2 *Challenges to Digitalization in the AECO Industry*

The AECO industry faces challenges in its journey towards digitalization. One of the primary hurdles is the inherent complexity of AECO projects. These projects are often unique and intricate, making it hard to create standard processes or implement digital solutions that work across different projects (Musarat et al., 2024). This complexity acts as a roadblock, slowing down the adoption of new digital tools and platforms in the industry (Omari et al., 2023).

Another major issue is the noticeable skills gap within the AECO workforce. Many professionals in the field lack the necessary knowledge and experience to effectively use digital technologies (Van Tam et al., 2024). This shortage of digital skills makes it difficult for companies to fully leverage new technologies, even when they are available.

Closely related to the skills gap is the problem of data silos and interoperability. The AECO industry struggles with integrating data from different software systems and stakeholders (Bajpai & Misra, 2022). When data is fragmented and systems can't "talk" to each other, it becomes hard for teams to work together effectively and share information seamlessly.

The culture of the AECO industry itself presents another challenge. The sector is known for being cautious and risk-averse (Omari et al., 2023; Van Tam et al., 2024). This careful approach, while sometimes beneficial, can slow down the adoption of new technologies. Companies often prefer to stick with tried-and-tested methods rather than experimenting with innovative digital solutions, even if these new approaches could potentially bring significant benefits (Yousif et al., 2021).

Lastly, the regulatory environment in the AECO industry can sometimes hinder digital innovation. Strict regulations and compliance requirements, while necessary for safety and quality, can make it difficult to introduce new digital technologies (Bajpai & Misra, 2022; Van Tam et al., 2024). Updating these regulatory frameworks to accommodate digital innovation while maintaining necessary standards remains an ongoing challenge for the industry.

These challenges are interconnected, each one influencing and sometimes amplifying the others (Begić et al., 2022). Overcoming them will require a coordinated effort from all stakeholders in the AECO industry, from individual professionals to large companies and regulatory bodies. By addressing these issues, the industry can move towards a more digitally enabled future, potentially unlocking significant improvements in efficiency, collaboration, and innovation.

2.3 Emerging Technologies Revolutionizing the AECO Industry

The AECO industry is undergoing a transformative shift driven by the integration of cutting-edge technologies (see Fig. 4). These advancements promise to enhance efficiency, productivity, safety, and sustainability across the sector. As the industry embraces digitalization, a suite of emerging technologies, ranging from Artificial Intelligence and Virtual Reality to 3D Printing and Blockchain, are transforming traditional practices. This section explores the potential of these technologies to reshape the AECO landscape, highlighting their applications, benefits, and the challenges that must be navigated to achieve widespread adoption (Yevu et al., 2021; Braun et al., 2022).

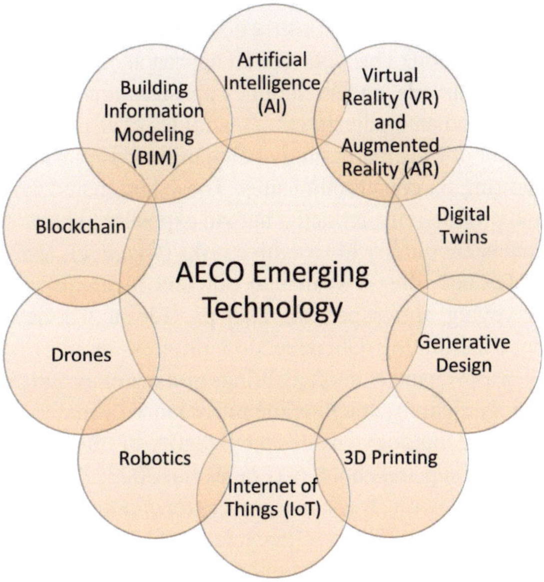

Fig. 4 Emerging technologies in the AECO industry

Artificial Intelligence (AI) is poised to revolutionize the AECO industry by automating a myriad of repetitive tasks, including design analysis, code compliance, and scheduling. AI-powered generative design tools can develop innovative and efficient design solutions, significantly enhancing productivity and creativity in architectural and engineering processes (Barjuei et al., 2024).

Virtual Reality (VR) and Augmented Reality (AR) technologies are transforming the way designers, engineers, and construction professionals interact with building models. VR enables immersive design reviews, construction simulations, and workforce training, while AR overlays digital information onto the physical world, providing on-site construction guidance and real-time data visualization (Qiao & Yin, 2024).

Digital twins, which are virtual replicas of physical assets, offer real-time synchronization with their physical counterparts. This technology enables continuous monitoring of building performance, early detection of potential issues, and optimization of maintenance schedules, thereby enhancing operational efficiency and lifespan of assets (Drobnyi et al., 2023).

Leveraging AI, generative design automates the creation of optimized design solutions based on specified criteria. This process fosters the development of more efficient, sustainable, and cost-effective designs, pushing the boundaries of traditional architectural and engineering practices (Gan, 2022; Pérez-Martínez et al., 2023).

The advent of 3D printing in the AECO industry facilitates the creation of prototypes, building components, and even entire structures from digital files. This technology accelerates the prototyping phase, reduces material waste, and opens new avenues for complex and custom designs in construction (Barjuei et al., 2024).

Internet of Things (IoT) sensors are instrumental in collecting real-time data from buildings and construction sites, such as temperature, humidity, and energy consumption. This data-driven approach enhances building performance, identifies safety hazards, and streamlines construction processes through predictive analytics and automated adjustments (Ioannides et al., 2024).

Robotics is increasingly being utilized for tasks such as demolition, welding, and painting on construction sites. These automated systems improve safety, precision, and productivity, reducing human exposure to hazardous environments and ensuring consistent quality in repetitive tasks (Oke et al., 2024; Siegele et al., 2024).

Drones offer a swift and efficient means of aerial photography, videography, surveying, and inspection. They provide an overview of construction sites and buildings, facilitating data collection, progress monitoring, and site safety assessments.

Blockchain technology brings transparency and accountability to the construction supply chain by tracking the provenance of materials and products. This distributed ledger technology ensures the integrity of transactions, reduces fraud, and enhances trust among stakeholders (Lou & Lu, 2022; Zhong et al., 2023).

BIM is a transformative process for creating and managing information throughout a construction project's lifecycle. By fostering improved collaboration, communication, and efficiency, BIM enhances the design, construction, and operational phases of buildings (Brückner et al., 2022; Elghaish et al., 2023).

These strategies resonate with recent studies emphasizing the role of digital platforms in bolstering urban resilience and disaster risk reduction (Hokmabadi et al., 2024; Rezvani et al., 2024; Rezvani et al., 2024a, 2024b, 2024c). By adopting technologies that enable real-time monitoring, predictive analytics, and enhanced collaboration among stakeholders, construction firms can mitigate risks associated with project complexity and scale.

The integration of these emerging technologies holds the potential to revolutionize the AECO industry by enhancing efficiency, productivity, safety, and sustainability. However, challenges such as implementation costs, the need for specialized training, and potential job displacement must be addressed to fully realize these benefits.

3 Methodology

The research methodology as shown on Fig. 5 for this study was designed to gather and analyse digitalization scenarios, solutions, and tools within the AECO industry, particularly focusing on the diverse sub-sectors of residential buildings, infrastructure projects, and fibre optic infrastructure.

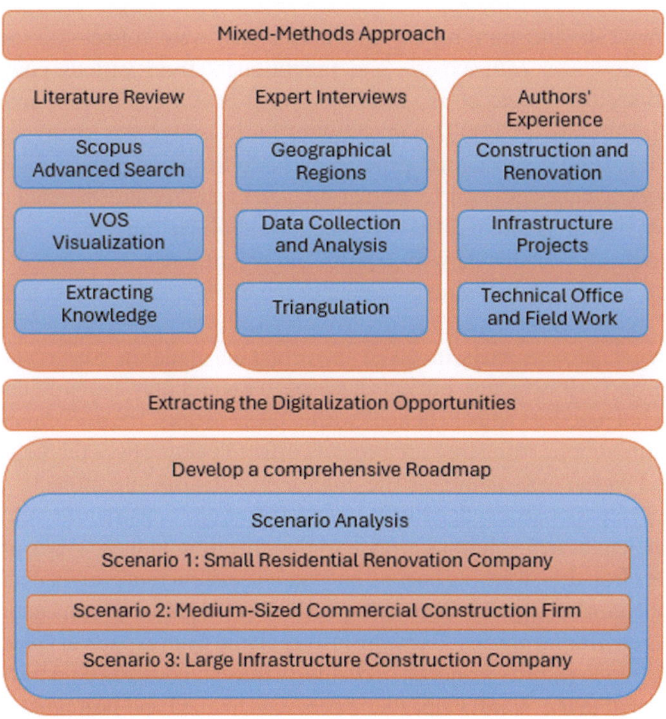

Fig. 5 Methodology diagram

The study employed a mixed-methods approach, integrating a thorough literature review with qualitative insights from expert and practitioner interviews across multiple geographical regions, including Europe, the Middle East, Southeast Asia, Oceania, and North America. This approach ensures a broad and deep understanding of the digitalization landscape, capturing both theoretical frameworks and practical experiences.

The literature review was an integral component of the research, focusing on peer-reviewed articles and industry reports related to the digitalization of the construction industry. The search criteria included keywords such as "construction," "digitalization," "technology adoption," and "productivity growth." Studies irrelevant to the focus of AECO digitalization, such as those related to digital storage, accident prevention, and unrelated academic fields, were excluded. The literature review aimed to identify current trends, challenges, and best practices in digital adoption within the AECO industry. The review also highlighted gaps in existing research, informing the subsequent interview design and ensuring that the study addressed underexplored areas.

3.1 Interview Selection and Procedure

To supplement the literature review, qualitative data were collected through semi-structured interviews with experts and practitioners from various countries and AECO sub-sectors (Begić et al., 2022; Elghaish et al., 2021; Marenco & Seidl, 2021; Nikmehr et al., 2021). The selection of interviewees was strategic, focusing on professionals with substantial experience in construction project digitalization. The interviews were designed to extract nuanced insights into the challenges and prospects of digitalization in different contexts and project types.

Interviews were conducted with experts and practitioners from various locations and projects to gain a broad understanding of the digitalization efforts in the AECO industry.

In Portugal, professionals involved in residential building construction, house renovation, and infrastructure projects such as roads and railways provided insights into the digital practices and challenges within these sectors. From Germany, experts working on fibreoptic infrastructure projects offered perspectives on the integration of advanced digital tools in large-scale, high-tech infrastructure projects.

In Iran, professionals engaged in highway and bridge construction discussed the specific challenges and solutions related to digitalization in these types of projects. Practitioners from Iraq working on road and tunnel construction provided information on the application of digital tools in complex and often politically and economically challenging environments. Insights were also gathered from experts in Qatar involved in highway and dry utility projects, particularly those who worked on infrastructure projects related to the World Cup, sharing lessons learned and best practices.

From Malaysia, interviews with professionals from the rail project sector contributed to understanding digitalization efforts in large-scale rail infrastructure.

Additionally, practitioners from Australia and Canada, particularly those involved in residential building construction and renovation, shared their experiences and the impact of digital tools on project efficiency and outcomes.

Interviews were conducted via video conferencing to facilitate participation from various geographical locations. Each interview lasted approximately 60–90 min, allowing for an in-depth discussion of the digitalization processes, tools, challenges, and future prospects. The interview guide included open-ended questions to encourage detailed responses and follow-up questions were used to delve deeper into specific topics.

The data collected from the literature review and interviews were systematically analyzed using qualitative content analysis. The process involved coding the interview transcripts to identify recurring themes and patterns related to digitalization in the AECO industry. Thematic analysis helped to categorize the findings into distinct areas such as technology adoption challenges, digital skills gaps, data management issues, and regulatory barriers. The insights from different regions and project types were compared to identify commonalities and regional-specific challenges.

To ensure the reliability and validity of the findings, a triangulation method was employed. The data from the literature review were cross verified with the interview responses to confirm consistency and credibility. Furthermore, the diversity of interviewees provided a broad view, mitigating the risk of bias and ensuring that the findings reflected a wide range of perspectives.

3.2 *Question Asked in Interviews*

During the interviews, the experts and practitioners were asked a series of targeted questions as shown on Fig. 6, to gather insights into various aspects of digitalization within the AECO industry (Hu et al., 2022; Kim et al., 2022; Liu et al., 2024). They were first prompted to describe their roles and extensive experience within the construction industry, particularly highlighting their involvement in digitalization projects. This initial inquiry aimed to establish a foundation of their expertise and direct involvement in leveraging digital tools and technologies.

Subsequently, the focus shifted to understanding the specific digital tools and technologies currently employed in their projects. Experts were asked to detail the technologies utilized, ranging from Building Information Modelling (BIM) and project management software to more specialized tools like drones, IoT devices, and digital twins. This line of questioning sought to uncover the practical applications of digital tools and their impact on project workflows and outcomes.

Another area explored during the interviews was the primary challenges encountered when implementing digital solutions in construction projects. Respondents discussed various obstacles such as the complexity of integrating different digital systems, data interoperability issues between stakeholders, and the overall resistance to change within their organizations. These insights provided a nuanced understanding of the barriers that hinder widespread digital adoption in the industry.

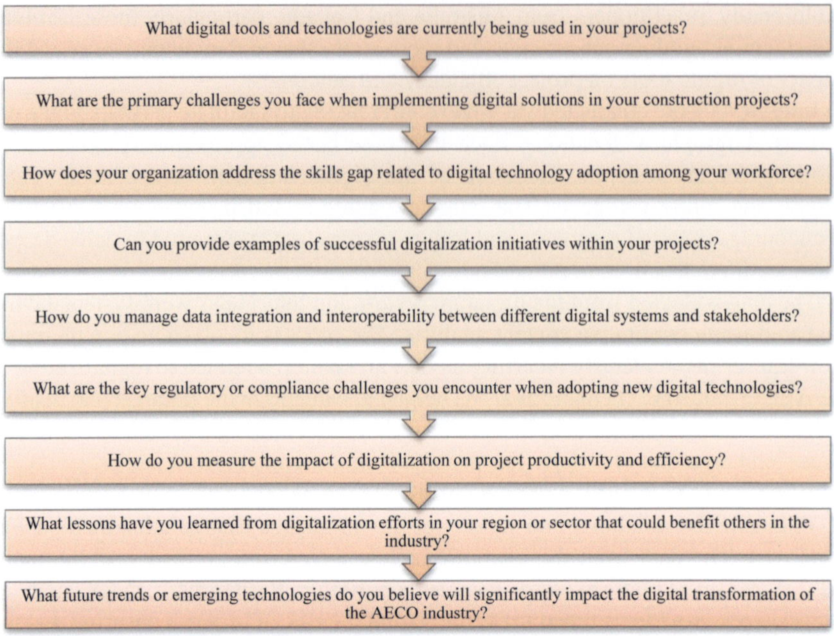

Fig. 6 Question asked on the survey about digitalization of construction industry

Addressing the skills gap related to digital technology adoption was also a key topic. Experts shared strategies and initiatives implemented within their organizations to bridge this gap, including training programs, upskilling initiatives, and the designation of digital champions to promote technology adoption among the workforce.

Furthermore, examples of successful digitalization initiatives within their projects were highlighted to illustrate tangible benefits and best practices. These examples ranged from enhancing project efficiency through real-time data analytics to improving collaboration and communication across project teams.

The management of data integration and interoperability between different digital systems and stakeholders was also explored. Experts elaborated on their approaches to streamline data flow, ensure data consistency, and facilitate seamless communication between project participants using integrated digital platforms.

In terms of regulatory and compliance challenges, respondents discussed the complexities of adhering to existing regulations while adopting new digital technologies. This included navigating data privacy laws, ensuring cybersecurity measures, and meeting industry-specific regulatory requirements without compromising innovation and efficiency.

Measuring the impact of digitalization on project productivity and efficiency was another critical aspect of the interviews. Experts shared methodologies and key performance indicators (KPIs) used to assess the effectiveness of digital tools in achieving project goals, improving timelines, and reducing costs.

Moreover, lessons learned from digitalization efforts within their respective regions or sectors were highlighted to provide valuable insights for industry peers. These lessons encompassed practical experiences, successes, failures, and pivotal moments that shaped their approach to digital transformation.

Finally, experts were asked about their perspectives on future trends and emerging technologies that could significantly impact the digital transformation of the AECO industry. They shared their outlook on advancements such as AI, machine learning, robotics, and sustainable construction practices, offering predictions and potential implications for the future of construction digitization.

Overall, these questions were designed to gather a holistic understanding of the current landscape of digitalization in the AECO industry, uncovering challenges, solutions, and future prospects directly from seasoned professionals and practitioners.

The authors' extensive experience in construction projects, spanning over a decade, also informed the research process. Their practical knowledge of the AECO industry provided a critical lens for interpreting the data and drawing relevant conclusions. This experience was contributory in understanding the practical implications of digitalization challenges and solutions identified in the study.

All participants were informed about the purpose of the study, and their consent was obtained prior to the interviews. Confidentiality was maintained by anonymizing the data to protect the identity of the participants and their organizations. Ethical guidelines were strictly followed throughout the research process to ensure the integrity of the study.

This methodological approach, combining a literature review with in-depth expert interviews and leveraging the authors' extensive industry experience, provides a robust foundation for understanding the digitalization challenges and prospects within the AECO industry. The findings from this study aim to contribute valuable insights into bridging the digitalization and productivity gap, offering practical strategies and tools for industry stakeholders globally.

3.3 Roadmap for Digitalization in the AECO Industry

The Architecture, Engineering, Construction, and Operations (AECO) industry is on a journey towards digital transformation. This roadmap outlines an approach to digitalization that can be adapted by both small renovation companies and large construction firms. The goal is to enhance efficiency, productivity, and competitiveness through the strategic adoption of digital technologies (Kim et al., 2024).

The digitalization process begins with a thorough assessment of the current state. Companies need to evaluate their existing digital tools and processes, identifying areas where technology can bring the most value. This involves analyzing pain points, studying competitors, and understanding industry best practices. With this information, firms can define clear, measurable goals that align with their overall business strategy (Barkokebas et al., 2023).

Developing a digital strategy is the next step. This strategy should outline the company's vision, priorities, and timelines for digital adoption. It's important to identify key performance indicators (KPIs) to measure progress and allocate an appropriate budget for digital initiatives, considering both initial investments and ongoing costs (Hartmann et al., 2023).

Once the strategy is in place, companies can move on to selecting and implementing appropriate technologies. For smaller firms, this might mean adopting cloud-based project management software and basic Building Information Modeling (BIM) tools. Larger companies might invest in more complete enterprise resource planning (ERP) systems and advanced BIM solutions. Regardless of size, it's wise to start with pilot projects to test new technologies before full-scale implementation.

Skills development and training are essential components of the digitalization roadmap. Companies should conduct a skills gap analysis to identify training needs and develop training programs. This might involve workshops, webinars, and hands-on sessions to ensure all employees can effectively use new digital tools. Fostering a culture of continuous learning is necessary for ongoing digital success.

As new technologies are adopted, companies need to focus on process optimization. This involves streamlining workflows to integrate digital tools seamlessly, automating repetitive tasks, and enhancing communication and collaboration through digital platforms. Improving data management is also key, with the implementation of centralized systems for secure data storage and analytics tools for informed decision-making.

The final phase of the roadmap focuses on continuous improvement and innovation. Companies should regularly monitor and evaluate the performance of their digital initiatives, tracking KPIs and gathering feedback from employees and clients. Staying updated with industry trends through conferences, webinars, and training sessions is important. This enables companies to continuously refine their digital strategies and explore new technologies to maintain competitiveness.

While the scale and pace of implementation may differ, both small and large companies in the AECO industry can benefit from following this roadmap. Smaller firms might progress more quickly through the steps but with less depth, focusing on cost-effective solutions that provide immediate value. Larger companies, with more resources, can invest in more sophisticated systems and potentially explore cutting-edge technologies like Internet of Things (IoT) or blockchain.

In conclusion, digitalizing an AECO company, regardless of its size, requires careful planning, strategic technology adoption, and a commitment to ongoing improvement. By following this roadmap and adapting it to their specific needs and resources, companies can enhance their operational efficiency, improve project outcomes, and position themselves for long-term success in an increasingly digital industry.

4 Digital Transformation Strategies of Construction Companies

This section presents three case studies that illustrate the practical application of the digital transformation roadmap outlined in Sect. 6. Each scenario showcases how companies of different sizes can tailor a digital transformation approach to their specific needs and resources, while aligning with the key phases of the roadmap.

4.1 Scenario 1: Small Residential Renovation Company

A small renovation company with 15 employees focuses on kitchen and bathroom remodels. Recognizing the need for improved efficiency and client satisfaction (aligned with the Assessment phase of the roadmap), they embark on a digital transformation journey. In line with the Strategy Development phase, they establish clear goals, such as reducing the average project completion time from 6 to 4 weeks and achieving a 90% client satisfaction rate.

To achieve these goals, the company adopts a cloud-based project management system and a simple 3D modeling tool (Technology Adoption phase). This integrated approach helps manage projects, schedules, and client communications more effectively. Furthermore, on-site workers use tablets for accessing project details and submitting daily reports, while a cloud-based document system ensures all team members have access to up-to-date information. The aim is to reduce the error rate and related rework, potentially leading to cost savings (Process Optimization phase).

For client communication, they develop a website showcasing their work and use a basic CRM system to manage interactions, adopting digital contracts and e-signatures for a more professional client experience. Skills development and training are prioritized with all employees receiving training and a designated "digital champion" encouraging broader technology adoption (Skills Development phase).

4.2 Scenario 2: Medium-Sized Commercial Construction Firm

A medium-sized commercial construction firm with 75 employees tackles projects like office and retail buildings. After assessing their current capabilities and recognizing the need to manage increasingly complex projects (Assessment phase), they develop a digital strategy (Strategy Development phase) focusing on improving project schedule adherence (aiming to complete 95% of tasks on time) and enhancing worker safety (targeting a reduced safety incident rate from 3 to 1 per 100,000 working hours).

To implement their strategy (Technology Adoption phase), they adopt a BIM system and enterprise-level project management software, enabling better design coordination, clash detection, and project visualization. Drone technology is introduced for site surveys and monitoring, and wearable technology enhances worker safety and productivity tracking. A Common Data Environment (CDE) platform facilitates collaboration among stakeholders, and virtual reality (VR) enhances client design reviews (Process Optimization phase). The firm also invests in training programs and establishes an innovation team to explore new technologies (Skills Development and Continuous Improvement phases).

4.3 Scenario 3: Large Infrastructure Construction Company

A large infrastructure company with over 500 employees works on major projects such as bridges and highways. Recognizing the need to become a leader in digital construction and efficiently manage large-scale, complex projects (Assessment phase), the company implements a comprehensive digital transformation strategy (Strategy Development phase). Their objectives include monitoring project cost performance, increasing construction productivity, reducing their environmental footprint, and enhancing asset performance through advanced technologies.

To achieve these ambitious goals (Technology Adoption phase), they implement an advanced integrated project delivery system, leveraging BIM, lean construction, and an ERP system. Robotics and automation are employed for repetitive tasks, enhancing safety and efficiency. IoT sensors monitor construction progress and structural health in real-time. Generative design and digital twins are used for design optimization and long-term asset performance analysis (Process Optimization phase).

A dedicated digital transformation team oversees technology implementation and drives cultural change within the organization. The company also actively partners with universities and tech firms to develop custom solutions (Skills Development and Continuous Improvement phases). They prioritize upskilling their workforce through extensive training programs, ensuring they are well-prepared for the future of construction.

These scenarios demonstrate the diverse applications of the digital transformation roadmap across different company sizes and project types. While the specific technologies and implementation strategies vary, the core principles of the roadmap, assessment, strategic planning, technology adoption, skills development, and continuous improvement, remain central to achieving successful digital transformation within the AECO industry. By tailoring their approach to their unique needs and resources, companies can leverage digital technologies to enhance their efficiency, productivity, sustainability, and competitiveness in a rapidly evolving construction landscape.

5 Discussion

The study reveals a complex landscape of digitalization in the AECO industry, highlighting both challenges and opportunities across different company sizes and project types. The findings underscore the industry's slow but steady progress towards digital transformation, with varying adoption rates and strategies based on company size and project complexity.

For small residential renovation companies, the focus is on implementing basic but effective digital tools that enhance project management, client communication, and on-site efficiency. The adoption of cloud-based project management software and simple 3D modeling tools represents a significant step forward for these smaller firms, potentially leading to improved client satisfaction and operational efficiency.

Medium-sized commercial construction firms are shown to be in a transitional phase, moving towards more advanced technologies like BIM systems and drone technology. This shift indicates a growing recognition of the need for more sophisticated digital solutions to manage complex projects and remain competitive in the market.

Large infrastructure construction companies are at the forefront of digital adoption, implementing cutting-edge technologies such as IoT sensors, digital twins, and advanced robotics. This high level of digitalization is driven by the need to manage large-scale, complex projects efficiently and to meet increasingly stringent requirements from government contracts.

Across all scenarios, the importance of employee training and cultural change emerges as a critical factor in successful digital transformation. The designation of "digital champions" and the establishment of dedicated innovation teams highlight the industry's recognition that technology alone is not sufficient; a workforce skilled in using these tools is equally important.

Moreover, the emphasis on workforce upskilling and cultural adaptation within the discussed scenarios parallels findings on the transformative impact of digital tools in urban resilience assessments (Garcia et al., 2023; Rezvani et al., 2023a, 2023b; Rezvani et al., 2023a, 2023b). These initiatives highlight a shift towards proactive risk management and sustainable infrastructure development, resonating with frameworks that advocate for integrated approaches to resilience enhancement through data-driven decision-making and stakeholder engagement (Rezvani et al., 2024a, 2024b, 2024c; Rezvani et al., 2024a, 2024b, 2024c; Rezvani et al., 2024a, 2024b, 2024c). As construction companies continue to navigate challenges posed by global urbanization and environmental uncertainties, the adoption of digital transformation strategies serves as a pivotal factor in fostering adaptive and resilient built environments.

The study also reveals a growing trend towards data-driven decision-making in construction, with companies of all sizes implementing various levels of data analytics. This shift towards data-centric operations has the potential to significantly improve project outcomes, risk management, and long-term asset performance.

6 Conclusion

The AECO industry is at a critical juncture in its digital transformation journey. While the sector has traditionally lagged behind others in digital adoption, this study demonstrates a growing momentum towards embracing digital technologies across all company sizes and project types.

The research highlights that successful digitalization in the AECO industry is not a one-size-fits-all approach. Small companies can achieve significant improvements with relatively simple digital tools, while larger firms are leveraging advanced technologies to transform their operations fundamentally. This varied approach suggests that digital transformation in construction is accessible to companies of all sizes, albeit at different scales and complexities.

The study concludes that the key to successful digital transformation lies not just in the adoption of technologies, but in a holistic approach that includes strategic planning, employee training, and a cultural shift towards innovation. Companies that can effectively integrate digital tools into their workflows, upskill their workforce, and foster a culture of continuous improvement are likely to gain a significant competitive advantage in the evolving construction landscape.

While this study provides valuable insights into the digitalization of the AECO industry, it has limitations. The geographic scope of the study primarily focused on specific regions, which may limit the generalizability of findings to other parts of the world with different technological infrastructures or regulatory environments. Given the fast-paced nature of technological advancements, some of the specific tools and technologies discussed may become outdated quickly. The sample size, although diverse, may not fully represent the entire spectrum of the AECO industry. Additionally, the study primarily focuses on the adoption of digital technologies and may not fully capture other aspects of digital transformation, such as organizational change management or long-term sustainability impacts.

To build upon this research, future studies could conduct longitudinal studies to track the long-term impacts of digital transformation on company performance and project outcomes. Exploring the environmental and sustainability impacts of increased digitalization in the construction industry would be valuable. Investigating the role of government policies and regulations in facilitating or hindering digital adoption in the AECO sector could provide important insights. Examining the potential of emerging technologies like artificial intelligence and machine learning in revolutionizing construction processes is another promising direction. Analyzing the economic implications of digital transformation in the AECO industry, including its effects on job markets and skill requirements, would be beneficial. Developing standardized metrics for measuring digital maturity in construction companies could facilitate industry-wide benchmarking and improvement. These future directions will enhance understanding of digital transformation in the AECO industry and its impact on society and the economy.

Acknowledgements This work is part of the research being carried out for the Civil Engineering Research and Innovation for Sustainability (CERIS) and was funded by Fundação para a Ciência e a Tecnologia (FCT) in the framework of project UIDB/04625/2020 and FCT grant number "2022.12886.BD" (carried out at the Instituto Superior Técnico (IST)).

References

Autodesk & Deloitte. (2024). *State of Digital Adoption in the Construction Industry 2024 Autodesk.*

Autodesk University. (2022). *Data, Reporting, and Analytics in Autodesk Construction Cloud | Autodesk University.* https://www.autodesk.com/autodesk-university/class/Data-Reporting-and-Analytics-Autodesk-Construction-Cloud-2022. Accessed 30 June 2024.

Autodesk University. (2024). *State of Digital Adoption in Construction 2024.* https://adskconstruction.autodesk.com/digital-journey-resources-apac/state-of-digital-adoption-in-construction-2024. Accessed 30 June 2024.

Bajpai, A., & Misra, S. C. (2022). Barriers to implementing digitalization in the Indian construction industry. *International Journal of Quality and Reliability Management, 39*(10), 2438–2464. https://doi.org/10.1108/IJQRM-09-2020-0318.

Barjuei, E.S., et al. (2024). Digital workflow for printability and prefabrication checking in robotic construction 3D printing based on Artificial Intelligence planning. *Engineering Applications of Artificial Intelligence, 133.* https://doi.org/10.1016/j.engappai.2024.108254.

Barkokebas, B. et al. (2023). Digitalization-based process improvement and decision-making in offsite construction. *Automation in Construction, 155.* https://doi.org/10.1016/j.autcon.2023.105052.

Begić, H., Galić, M., & Dolaček-Alduk, Z. (2022). Digitalization and automation in construction project's life-cycle: A review. *Journal of Information Technology in Construction, 27*, 441–460. https://doi.org/10.36680/j.itcon.2022.021.

Braun, K., Kropp, C., & Boeva, Y. (2022) From digital design to data-assets: competing visions, policy projects, and emerging arrangements of value creation in the digital transformation of construction. *Historical Social Research, 47*(3), 81–110. https://doi.org/10.12759/hsr.47.2022.27.

Brückner, I., Haverland, R., & Halbrügge, M. (2022). Interdisciplinary planning and building in a BIM-oriented manner. *Journal of Digital Landscape Architecture, 2022*(7), 249–257. https://doi.org/10.14627/537724024.

Drobnyi, V. et al. (2023). Construction and maintenance of building geometric digital twins: state of the art review. *Sensors, 23*(9). https://doi.org/10.3390/s23094382.

Elghaish, F. et al. (2021). Toward digitalization in the construction industry with immersive and drones technologies: a critical literature review. *Smart and Sustainable Built Environment, 10*(3), 345–363. https://doi.org/10.1108/SASBE-06-2020-0077.

Elghaish, F. et al. (2023). Digitalised circular construction supply chain: An integrated BIM-Blockchain solution. *Automation in Construction, 148.* https://doi.org/10.1016/j.autcon.2023.104746.

Gan, V. J. L. J. L. (2022). BIM-based building geometric modeling and automatic generative design for sustainable offsite construction. *Journal of Construction Engineering and Management, 148*(10). https://doi.org/10.1061/(ASCE)CO.1943-7862.0002369.

Garcia, J. et al. (2023). Resilience assessment of public treasury elementary school buildings in lisbon municipality. In Lecture Notes in Mechanical Engineering, pp. 636–644. https://doi.org/10.1007/978-3-031-25448-2_59.

Hartmann, S. et al. (2023). Optimizing interfaces of construction processes by digitalization using the example of hospital construction in Germany. *Buildings, 13*(6). https://doi.org/10.3390/buildings13061421.

Hokmabadi, H., Rezvani, S. M. H. S., & de Matos, C. A. (2024). Business resilience for small and medium enterprises and startups by digital transformation and the role of marketing capabilities—a systematic review. *Systems 2024, 12*(6), 220. https://doi.org/10.3390/SYSTEMS12060220.

Hu, W., Lim, K. Y. H., Cai, Y. (2022). Digital twin and ındustry 4.0 enablers in building and construction: A survey. *Buildings, 12*(11). https://doi.org/10.3390/buildings12112004.

Ioannides, M. G., et al. (2024). Internet of things-based control of ınduction machines: Specifics of electric drives and wind energy conversion systems. *Energies, 17*(3). https://doi.org/10.3390/en17030645.

Kim, C. -W. et al. (2024). A roadmap for applying digital technology to ımprove the efficiency of construction supervision in building projects: focusing on Korean cases. *Buildings, 14*(1). https://doi.org/10.3390/buildings14010075.

Kim, D., Bae, K. H., & Cho, J. (2022). Feasibility test with IoT-based DCPT system for digital compaction ınformation of smart construction. *Journal of the Korean Society of Surveying, Geodesy, Photogrammetry and Cartography, 40*(5), 421–428. https://doi.org/10.7848/ksgpc.2022.40.5.421.

Liu, G., Ma, Z., & Li, S. (2024). Survey on lean construction and digital technology ıntegration based on literature research | 基于文献研究的精益建造与数字技术集成综述. *Tongji Daxue Xuebao/Journal of Tongji University, 52*(1), 145–156. https://doi.org/10.11908/j.issn.0253-374x.22147.

Lou, J., & Lu, W. (2022). Construction information authentication and integrity using blockchain-oriented watermarking techniques. *Automation in Construction, 143*. https://doi.org/10.1016/j.autcon.2022.104570.

Marenco, M., & Seidl, T. (2021). The discursive construction of digitalization: A comparative analysis of national discourses on the digital future of work. *European Political Science Review, 13*(3), 391–409. https://doi.org/10.1017/S175577392100014X.

McKinsey. (2023). *From start-up to scale-up: Accelerating growth in construction technology*. https://www.mckinsey.com/industries/private-capital/our-insights/from-start-up-to-scale-up-accelerating-growth-in-construction-technology. Accessed 30 June 2024.

Musarat, M. A., et al. (2024). Digitalization in Malaysian construction industry: Awareness, challenges and opportunities. *Results in Engineering, 21*. https://doi.org/10.1016/j.rineng.2024.102013.

Nikmehr, B., et al. (2021). Digitalization as a strategic means of achieving sustainable efficiencies in construction management: A critical review. *Sustainability (Switzerland), 13*(9). https://doi.org/10.3390/su13095040.

Oke, A. E., et al. (2024). Robotics and automation for sustainable construction: microscoping the barriers to implementation. *Smart and Sustainable Built Environment, 13*(3), 625–643. https://doi.org/10.1108/SASBE-12-2022-0275.

Omari, R. A. et al. (2023). Barriers to the adoption of digitalization in the construction ındustry: Perspectives of owners, consultants, and contractors. *Construction Economics and Building, 23*(3–4), 87–106. https://doi.org/10.5130/AJCEB.v23i3/4.8636.

Pérez-Martínez, I., Martínez-Rojas, M., Soto-Hidalgo, J. M. (2023). A methodology for urban planning generation: A novel approach based on generative design. *Engineering Applications of Artificial Intelligence, 124*. https://doi.org/10.1016/j.engappai.2023.106609.

PlanRadar. (2023). *Digital Transformation in construction—PlanRadar*. PlanRadar. https://www.planradar.com/gb/digital-transformation-in-construction/. Accessed 30 June 2024.

Qiao, R., Yin, Z. (2024). Constructıon of life cycle predıctıon model for dıgıtal medıa based on vırtual realıty. *International Journal of Mechatronics and Applied Mechanics, 2024*(15), 28–34. https://doi.org/10.17683/ijomam/issue15.4.

Rezvani, S. M. et al. (2024). Smart hotspot detection using geospatial artificial intelligence: A machine learning approach to reduce flood risk. *Sustainable Cities and Society, 115*, 105873. https://doi.org/10.1016/J.SCS.2024.105873.

Rezvani, S. M., Falcão Silva, M. J., de Almeida, N. M. (2024). Urban resilience ındex for critical ınfrastructure: A scenario-based approach to disaster risk reduction in road networks. *Sustainability 2024 16*(10), 4143. https://doi.org/10.3390/SU16104143.

Rezvani, S. M. H. S. et al. (2023). *Resilience Exposure Assessment Using Multi-layer Mapping of Portuguese 308 Cities and Communities.* Lecture Notes in Mechanical Engineering. https://doi.org/10.1007/978-3-031-25448-2_57.

Rezvani, S. M. H. S. et al. (2024). Mapping geospatial AI flood risk in national road networks. *ISPRS International Journal of Geo-Information 2024, 13*(9), 323. https://doi.org/10.3390/IJGI13090323.

Rezvani, S. M. H. S., Almeida, N., Silva, M. J. F. (2023). *Multi-disciplinary and Dynamic Urban Resilience Assessment Through Stochastic Analysis of a Virtual City.* Lecture Notes in Mechanical Engineering. https://doi.org/10.1007/978-3-031-25448-2_62.

Rezvani, S. M. H. S., Falcao Silva, M. J., de Almeida, N. M. (2024). NETOBRA: Boosting urban resilience through a digital platform for the construction ecosystem. *Procedia Structural Integrity, 55*, 72–79. https://doi.org/10.1016/J.PROSTR.2024.02.010.

Rezvani, S. M. H. S., Falcão Silva, M. J., de Almeida, N. M. (2024). The risk-ınformed asset-centric (RIACT) urban resilience enhancement process: an outline and pilot-case demonstrator for earthquake risk mitigation in portuguese municipalities. *Applied Sciences 2024, 14*(2), 634. https://doi.org/10.3390/APP14020634.

Siegele, D., et al. (2024). *Advancing Construction Efficiency Through Collaborative Robotics: A Scalable Multi-agent-Based Logistics Solution.* Lecture Notes in Civil Engineering. https://doi.org/10.1007/978-3-031-44021-2_19.

Van Tam, N., Toan, N. Q., Van Phong, V. (2024). Investigating potential barriers to construction digitalization in emerging economies: A study in Vietnam. *International Journal of Information Management Data Insights, 4*(1). https://doi.org/10.1016/j.jjimei.2024.100226.

Yevu, S. K., Yu, A. T. W., Darko, A. (2021) Digitalization of construction supply chain and procurement in the built environment: Emerging technologies and opportunities for sustainable processes. *Journal of Cleaner Production, 322.* https://doi.org/10.1016/j.jclepro.2021.129093.

Yousif, O. S., et al. (2021). Review of big data ıntegration in construction ındustry digitalization. *Frontiers in Built Environment, 7.* https://doi.org/10.3389/fbuil.2021.770496.

Zhong, B., et al. (2023). 'Blockchain-driven integration technology for the AEC industry. *Automation in Construction, 150.* https://doi.org/10.1016/j.autcon.2023.104791.

Resilience and Life Cycle Management of Critical Urban Asset Systems in Face of Emerging Threats

Seyed Mohammad Hossein Seyedi Rezvani, Maria João Falcão Silva, and Nuno Marques de Almeida

Abstract With rapid urbanization comes an array of evolving risks. These risks, spanning environmental, socio-economic, and infrastructural realms, present a growing challenge to the stability of urban habitats. However, through strategic asset and risk management, cities have the potential to safeguard their futures. This study seeks to elucidate the nature of emerging urban risks and juxtapose them against the principles of asset life cycle management as well as critically examine the interplay between emerging risks in urban landscapes applied to critical infrastructure and the role other types of urban critical assets and asset and risk management in fortifying city resilience systems. By dissecting how cities can optimize their resources, both tangible and intangible, the research underscores how urban centers can not only shield themselves against immediate threats but also invest in long-term resilience. As we pivot towards a world where urban centers become even more central to global progress, this study aims to provide a robust framework for city administrators and policymakers, guiding them towards creating resilient and prosperous urban spaces.

Keywords Urban resilience · Asset life cycle management · Risk management · Emerging risks · City planning · Urban infrastructure

S. M. H. S. Rezvani (✉) · N. Marques de Almeida
Civil Engineering Research and Innovation for Sustainability (CERIS), Instituto Superior Técnico, Universidade de Lisboa, Lisboa, Portugal
e-mail: seyedi.rezvani@tecnico.ulisboa.pt

N. Marques de Almeida
e-mail: nunomarquesalmeida@tecnico.ulisboa.pt

M. J. F. Silva
Laboratório Nacional de Engenharia Civil, Lisboa, Portugal
e-mail: mjoaofalcao@lnec.pt

A. Crespo Márquez et al. (eds.), *Case Studies in Digital Transformation*, Engineering Asset Management Review 4, https://doi.org/10.1007/978-3-032-05592-7_3

1 Introduction

The rapid pace of urbanization presents a multitude of evolving risks that challenge the stability and sustainability of urban environments. These risks span across environmental, socio-economic, and infrastructural dimensions, necessitating robust strategies to manage and mitigate their impacts. This paper delves into the complexities of emerging urban risks and explores how life cycle management (LCM) principles can be effectively integrated to bolster the resilience of critical urban asset systems (Frangopol et al., 2012). By examining the interplay between emerging threats and urban resilience, the study aims to provide a comprehensive framework for improving the sustainability and adaptability of urban infrastructures (Chen et al., 2022; Shariatfar & Lee, 2020).

The urban resilience involves the capacity of urban as an asset systems to avoid, endure, recover, and adapt to various disruptions, ensuring the continuity of essential functions and services. Critical urban asset systems, such as transportation, water supply, energy, and communication networks, are vital for the functioning and well-being of cities (Meerow et al., 2016). This paper explores how life cycle management can optimize urban systems for immediate protection and long-term resilience. By managing urban assets from design to decommissioning, cities should prepare for and react to current and future challenges.

Emerging threats, including natural disasters, technological disruptions, and socio-economic changes, pose significant risks to urban infrastructure (Zawaideh et al., 2023). This paper aims to identify and assess these threats, providing insights into how urban centers can leverage asset and risk management strategies to build resilient and sustainable environments (ISO3, 1000, 2018; ISO55000, 2014). By integrating resilience thinking with life cycle management approaches, the study offers practical guidance for city administrators and policymakers, helping them to create robust and adaptive urban systems capable of thriving in the face of uncertainty and change (Wang et al., 2021).

This paper comprehensively analyzes urban resilience and risk assessment of critical urban asset systems. It begins with an introduction to the study's context and significance, followed by a Systematic Literature Review detailing the methodology, search strategy, and selection criteria. Subsequent sections discuss publication trends and subject area distribution, categorize research outputs, and present data visualizations to illustrate literature connections and trends. Definitions of key concepts like Resilience, Life Cycle Management, and Critical Urban Asset Systems are clarified. The paper addresses emerging threats and risk assessment methodologies, proposes a framework for enhancing urban resilience, and provides practical examples of its application. It concludes with a discussion and summary of key findings, suggesting directions for future research.

2 Bibliometric Analysis

The increasing impact of climate change, natural disasters, and urbanization has necessitated the development of resilient cities. For sustainable urban development, integrating Life Cycle Assessment (LCA) and Life Cycle Management (LCM) approaches is critical to enhance urban resilience. These methodologies evaluate the environmental impact of products and processes throughout their entire life-cycle, allowing cities to better absorb, recover, and prepare for future shocks while maintaining essential functions.

2.1 Scopus Search Publication Analysis

This systematic literature review explores the intersection of urban resilience and life cycle approaches by analyzing relevant scholarly articles. Using the Scopus database, the search query was: TITLE-ABS-KEY ((cities OR urban OR city) resilience AND (LCA OR LCM OR Life Cycle)) AND (LIMIT-TO (SUBJAREA, ENGI)). This query targeted engineering-related studies integrating urban resilience and life cycle methodologies. The search yielded 194 results, which were analyzed to identify key trends and insights. The selected terms ensured the inclusion of studies focused on urban areas, resilience, and life cycle assessment, with a specific emphasis on engineering to maintain a technical and methodological perspective.

Figure 1 illustrates the flow of the terms in the Scopus advanced search, resulting in 194 documents. The selected terms are pivotal in capturing the essence of urban resilience and life cycle methodologies within the engineering domain.

The distribution of documents over time (Fig. 2) shows a notable increase in publications in recent years. The number of documents has grown from a single publication in 2005 to 18 publications in 2024, reflecting the increasing recognition of the importance of integrating urban resilience with life cycle approaches.

Figure 2 presents the distribution of documents across various subject areas. Engineering dominates with 101 documents, followed by Environmental Science

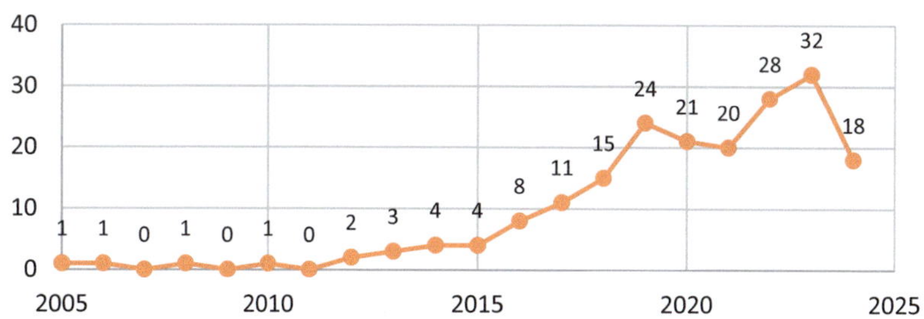

Fig. 1 The distribution of documents over time

Fig. 2 Subject area distribution

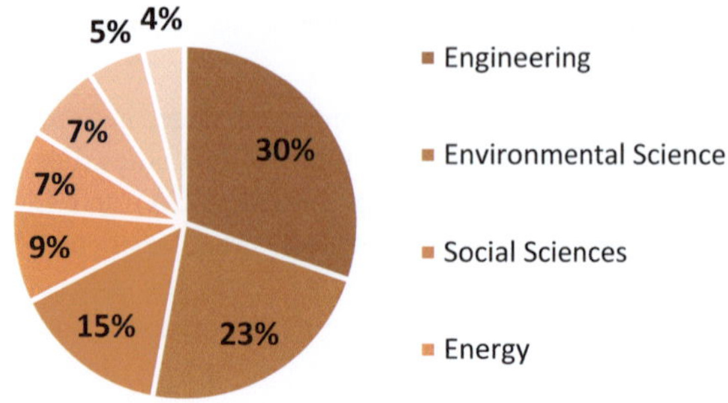

Fig. 3 Document types distribution

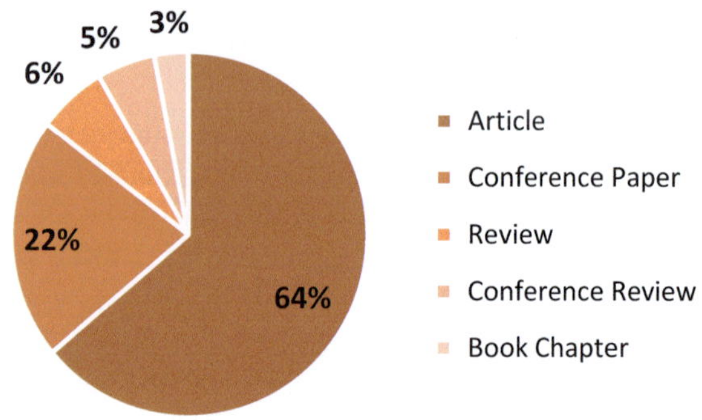

(76), Social Sciences (49), and Energy (29). This distribution highlights the multidisciplinary nature of research on urban resilience and life cycle approaches, with engineering providing the foundational methodologies and other fields contributing context and application perspectives.

The types of documents retrieved are shown in Fig. 3 Articles constitute the majority (122), followed by conference papers (41), reviews (12), and conference reviews (10). The predominance of articles indicates that the topic is well-established in peer-reviewed research, while the presence of conference papers suggests ongoing discussions and developments in the field.

2.2 *Key Themes and VOSviewer Network, Overlay, and Density Visualization*

To gain deeper insights into the key themes and their interrelationships, VOSviewer was used to create network visualizations based on co-occurrence of terms.

Figure 4 shows the VOS network visualization, where each node represents a keyword, and the links between them indicate co-occurrence in the same document.

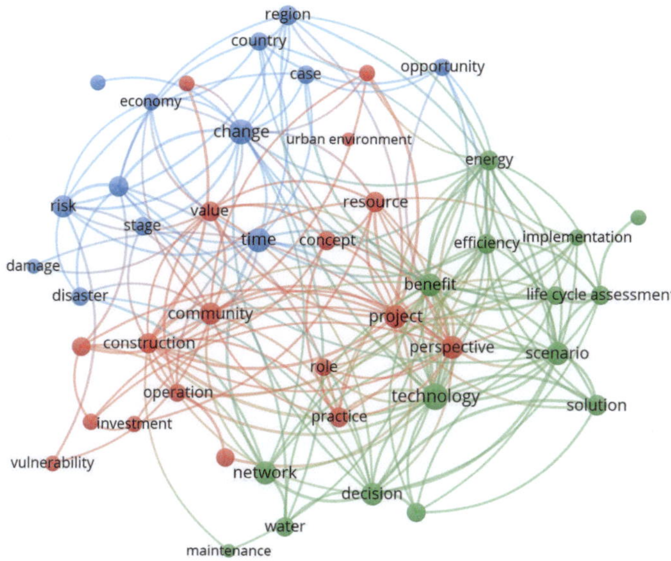

Fig. 4 VOSviewer network visualization

Larger nodes and thicker links represent more frequent occurrences and stronger connections, respectively.

The network visualization reveals several key clusters of terms:

Cluster 1 (Urban Resilience and Community): Includes terms like community, concept, construction, and practice, emphasizing the social and practical aspects of urban resilience.
Cluster 2 (Life Cycle Assessment and Efficiency): Includes terms like LCA, life cycle assessment, energy, efficiency, and environmental impact, focusing on the methodological and efficiency aspects of life cycle approaches.
Cluster 3 (Climate Change and Risk Management): Includes terms like climate change, risk, scenario, and response, highlighting the importance of addressing climate-related risks in urban resilience.

Figure 5 presents the VOS overlay visualization, which adds a temporal dimension to the network by showing the average publication year for each term. This visualization helps identify emerging trends and shifts in focus over time.

The overlay visualization indicates a recent focus on terms like environmental impact, maintenance, and scenario, suggesting a growing interest in the long-term sustainability and maintenance of urban resilience strategies.

Figure 6 illustrates the VOS density visualization, where the color intensity represents the frequency of term occurrences. This visualization highlights the most frequently discussed topics in literature.

The density visualization confirms that key terms such as technology, network, and decision are central to the discourse on urban resilience and life cycle approaches,

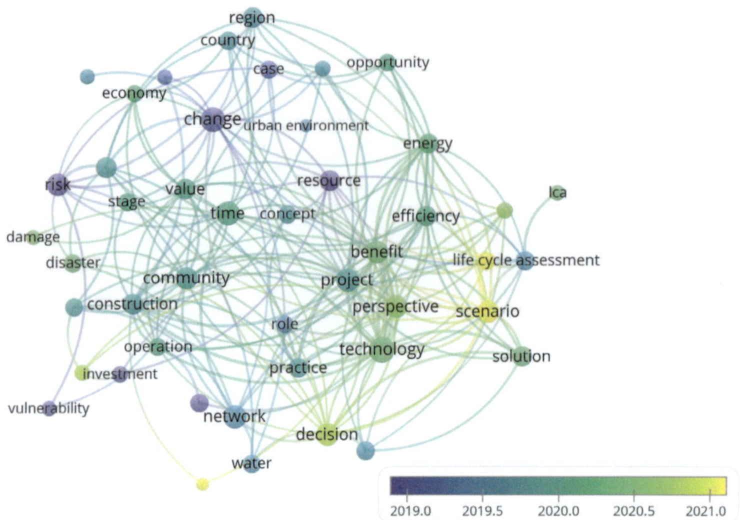

Fig. 5 VOSviewer overlay visualization

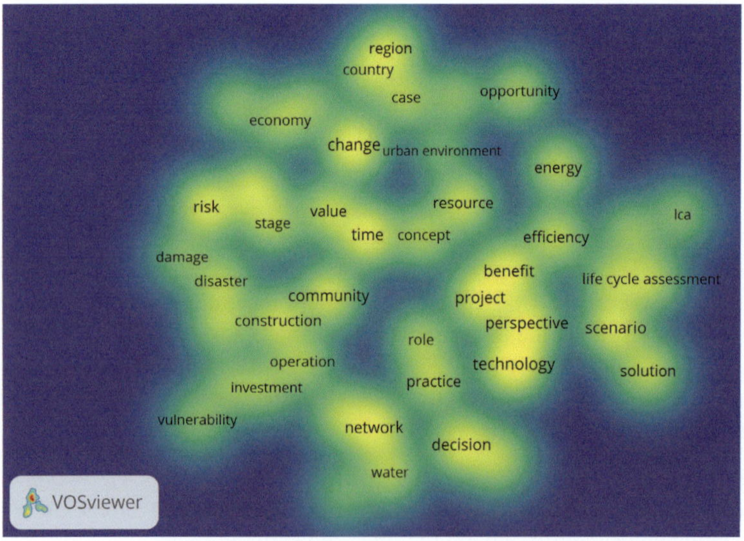

Fig. 6 VOSviewer density visualization

reflecting the critical role of technological innovation and decision-making processes in enhancing urban resilience.

3 Literature Review

In this section, we will define and explore several key concepts critical to understanding the intersection of urban resilience and life cycle approaches. These definitions will provide a foundational understanding of the terms used throughout the literature and clarify their significance in the context of enhancing the resilience of urban environments. Specifically, we will delve into the concepts of resilience, life cycle management (LCM), critical urban asset systems, and emerging threats. Each term will be discussed in detail to elucidate its relevance and application in the development and maintenance of resilient urban infrastructures.

Understanding these definitions is crucial for comprehending how urban resilience can be systematically enhanced through life cycle approaches. By defining resilience, we will explore its multifaceted nature and the various properties that characterize resilient systems. The definition of life cycle management will highlight the systematic approach to managing urban assets throughout their lifecycle, ensuring sustainability and reliability. Critical urban asset systems will be defined to understand the essential infrastructure that supports urban life, and emerging threats will be discussed to recognize the potential risks that these systems face. This understanding will set the stage for a deeper exploration of how these concepts intersect and inform strategies for resilient urban development.

3.1 Critical Urban Asset Systems

Critical urban asset systems refer to the essential infrastructure, facilities, and networks that underpin the functioning and well-being of cities and their populations (CISA, 2023; Rezvani et al., 2024a, 2024b, 2024c). These systems include but are not limited to: (i) Transportation systems: Roads, highways, bridges, railways, airports, and public transit networks that facilitate the movement of people and goods within and around urban areas. (ii) Water and wastewater systems: Water treatment and distribution networks, sewage collection and treatment facilities, and stormwater management systems that ensure access to clean water and proper waste management. (iii) Energy systems: Power generation plants, transmission and distribution networks, and natural gas pipelines that provide essential energy services to residential, commercial, and industrial sectors. (ix) Communication systems: Telecommunications networks, data centers, and information technology infrastructure that enable communication, data transfer, and digital services (Hokmabadi et al., 2024). (x) Emergency response systems: Fire stations, police stations, emergency operations centers, and healthcare facilities that are crucial for public safety and disaster response. (xi) public buildings and facilities: Government buildings, schools, libraries, community centers, and other public structures that support essential services and community functions.

These critical urban asset systems are interdependent and interconnected, forming a complex web of infrastructure that enables the functioning of modern cities. Their reliability, resilience, and effective management are vital for ensuring the continuity of essential services, economic activities, and the overall quality of life for urban residents.

3.2 Emerging Threats

Emerging threats refer to new or evolving risks, hazards, or challenges that have the potential to disrupt or adversely impact critical urban asset systems and the communities they serve (Duarte et al., 2022; Rezvani et al., 2023a, 2023b). These threats can arise from various sources, including: (i) Natural disasters: Extreme weather events, such as hurricanes, floods, or heatwaves, which are becoming more frequent and intense due to climate change, pose significant risks to urban infrastructure and populations. (ii) Technological disruptions: Cyber-attacks, data breaches, or failures in critical digital systems can compromise the operations and security of essential urban services and infrastructure. (iii) Terrorism and human-caused threats: Acts of terrorism, civil unrest, or intentional sabotage can target critical infrastructure and cause widespread disruptions or damage. (ix) public health emergencies: Pandemics, disease outbreaks, or other public health crises can strain healthcare systems, disrupt supply chains, and impact the functioning of urban economies and societies. (x) Aging infrastructure: The deterioration of aging infrastructure due to prolonged use, lack of maintenance, or outdated design standards can increase the vulnerability of critical urban asset systems to various threats and stresses. (xi) Resource scarcity: Diminishing natural resources, such as water or energy sources, can create supply challenges and limit the ability of urban systems to operate effectively. (xii) Socio-economic challenges: Rapid urbanization, population growth, income inequality, or economic downturns can exacerbate existing vulnerabilities and pose new challenges for the resilience and sustainability of urban environments. (xiii) Identifying, assessing, and addressing these emerging threats is crucial for enhancing the resilience and adaptive capacity of critical urban asset systems, ensuring the continuity of essential services, and safeguarding the well-being of urban populations.

By understanding the definitions and implications of resilience, life cycle management, critical urban asset systems, and emerging threats, stakeholders can develop comprehensive strategies and approaches to better prepare for, respond to, and recover from potential disruptions or adverse events. This knowledge serves as a foundation for effective decision-making, risk mitigation, and the implementation of resilience-enhancing measures in urban environments.

3.3 Life Cycle Management

Life cycle management (LCM) is a systematic approach to managing assets or systems throughout their entire life cycle, from conceptualization and design to operation, maintenance, and eventual decommissioning or disposal (Johansen & Rausand, 2014; Santos & Ferreira, 2013; Santos et al., 2015). This approach aims to optimize the performance, reliability, and cost-effectiveness of assets while minimizing their environmental impact and ensuring compliance with relevant regulations and standards.

LCM involves various stages and activities, including: (i) Planning and design: Defining requirements, conducting feasibility studies, and developing designs that consider long-term performance, maintainability, and sustainability. (ii) Procurement and construction: Acquiring or constructing assets based on specified requirements and quality standards. (iii) Operation and maintenance: Managing the day-to-day operation of assets, conducting preventive and corrective maintenance, and implementing strategies to extend their useful life. (ix) Monitoring and assessment: Continuously monitoring asset performance, condition, and risk, and conducting periodic assessments to identify potential issues or opportunities for improvement. (x) Renewal or replacement: Making informed decisions about asset renewal, refurbishment, or replacement based on performance data, risk analysis, and life cycle cost considerations. (xi) Decommissioning and disposal: Safely and responsibly decommissioning assets at the end of their useful life, while considering environmental and regulatory requirements.

Effective life cycle management involves integrating various disciplines, such as engineering, asset management, risk management, and sustainability practices, to ensure that assets or systems are managed in a holistic and cost-effective manner throughout their entire life cycle.

3.4 Risk Assessment

Risk and asset assessment and management are important processes in enhancing urban resilience, involving the identification, analysis, evaluation and prioritization of risks to critical urban asset systems. This process enables cities to develop strategies that mitigate potential disruptions and ensure the continued functionality of urban infrastructures. This section explores various facets of risk assessment, including vulnerability assessment, the analysis of interdependencies and cascading effects, and quantitative risk analysis.

Vulnerability assessment is a foundational component of risk assessment, focusing on identifying the weaknesses within urban infrastructure that make it susceptible to various hazards. According to Rezvani et al. (2023a, 2023b), a comprehensive approach to vulnerability assessment includes evaluating the physical, operational, and environmental susceptibilities of buildings and infrastructure. Their study on a virtual city modeled after Lisbon illustrates how different use-types of buildings exhibit varying levels of resilience based on intrinsic and contextual factors. By systematically assessing these vulnerabilities, cities can prioritize interventions that enhance the resilience of their most critical assets.

Urban systems are highly interconnected, and disruptions in one area can lead to cascading effects across multiple sectors. For example, a failure in the power grid can impact transportation, communication, and healthcare services. Understanding these interdependencies is crucial for accurate risk assessment. Garcia et al. (2023) highlight the importance of considering these interdependencies when assessing the resilience of public buildings in Lisbon. Their work emphasizes the need for a holistic approach that accounts for the complex interactions between different infrastructure systems and the potential for cascading failures.

Addressing the strategic needs of urban resilience requires sophisticated mapping and analysis tools. Rezvani et al. (2023a, 2023b) developed a multi-layer mapping system to evaluate the resilience of Portuguese cities against various disasters. This system aggregates and analyzes geo-data to produce heatmaps that highlight high-risk areas, providing valuable insights for the design and implementation of resilience and recovery plans. Such tools are essential for visualizing complex risk landscapes and making informed decisions about where to allocate resources and implement mitigation measures. Scenario-based approaches to risk reduction involve simulating various disaster scenarios to evaluate the effectiveness of different resilience strategies. In their study on the resilience of road networks to floods, another study demonstrated how different scenarios, such as proactive resilience planning and early warning systems, can significantly influence the outcomes of flood events (Rezvani et al., 2024a, 2024b, 2024c). By comparing these scenarios through cost-risk performance optimization, cities can identify the most effective and economically viable strategies for enhancing resilience.

The integration of data-driven decision support systems in the construction ecosystem can significantly enhance urban resilience. The NETOBRA platform (Rezvani et al., 2024a, 2024b, 2024c), exemplifies this approach by combining Multi-Criteria Decision Analysis (MCDA) as well as the Analytic Hierarchy Process (AHP) to facilitate comprehensive risk and asset management. This platform allows professionals to create interactive maps and assess various scenarios, thereby supporting strategic decision-making and improving urban resilience against both natural and man-made hazards. The practical applications of these risk assessment methodologies are evident in various case studies.

Effective risk assessment is essential for enhancing the resilience of critical urban asset systems. By incorporating vulnerability assessments, understanding interdependencies, and employing quantitative risk analysis, cities can develop robust strategies to mitigate potential disruptions and ensure the continued functionality of their infrastructure. The integration of advanced mapping systems and data-driven decision support tools further strengthens the capacity of urban areas to withstand, recover from, and adapt to various hazards, thereby fostering safer and more resilient communities.

3.5 Resilience of Constructed Assets

Resilience is a multifaceted concept that has gained significant attention in various disciplines, including urban planning, engineering, and disaster management. It refers to the ability of a system, community, or infrastructure to withstand, adapt to, and recover from disruptions or adverse events (Meerow & Newell, 2019; Meerow et al., 2016). In the context of urban environments, resilience encompasses the capacity of cities and their critical systems to maintain essential functions, minimize losses, and bounce back from shocks or stresses, whether natural or human induced.

Resilience is often characterized by four fundamental properties: robustness, redundancy, resourcefulness, and rapidity (Bruneau et al., 2003). Robustness refers to the inherent strength or resistance of a system to withstand external disturbances without significant degradation or failure. Redundancy involves the availability of backup systems, alternative pathways, or surplus capacity that can compensate for disruptions or losses. Resourcefulness is the ability to identify and mobilize resources, both internal and external, to respond effectively to adverse events. Lastly, rapidity refers to the speed at which a system can recover or restore its functionality to an acceptable level after a disruption.

Resilience is a multifaceted concept that has been widely discussed and applied across various disciplines, including engineering, psychology, ecology, and urban planning. In the context of critical urban asset systems, resilience refers to the ability of these systems to avoid, endure, recover, and adapt to disruptive events or emerging threats.

Figure 7 illustrates the four phases of resilience in the context of critical urban asset systems: avoid, endure, recover, and adapt. This framework highlights the importance of proactive planning, robust infrastructure, and adaptive capacity in ensuring the long-term sustainability and resilience of these vital systems. The "avoid" phase, for instance, emphasizes anticipating potential threats and taking steps to mitigate their impact, while the "endure" phase focuses on the system's ability to withstand disruptions and maintain functionality. The "recover" phase outlines the strategies for restoring operations following an event, and the "adapt" phase emphasizes continuous improvement and learning to build greater resilience in the face of evolving risks (Rezvani et al., 2024a, 2024b, 2024c).

Avoid is the first phase of resilience, and it involves anticipating potential threats and taking proactive measures to mitigate their impact. In the context of critical urban asset systems, avoid may involve conducting risk assessments, developing emergency response plans, implementing early warning systems, and ensuring adequate resources and personnel are available to respond effectively to disruptions.

The endure phase refers to the ability of critical urban asset systems to withstand and maintain their functionality during disruptive events or emerging threats. This phase emphasizes the robustness and redundancy of the systems, as well as their capacity to absorb shocks and continue operating, even if at a reduced level. Factors such as robust infrastructure design, redundant systems, and effective emergency

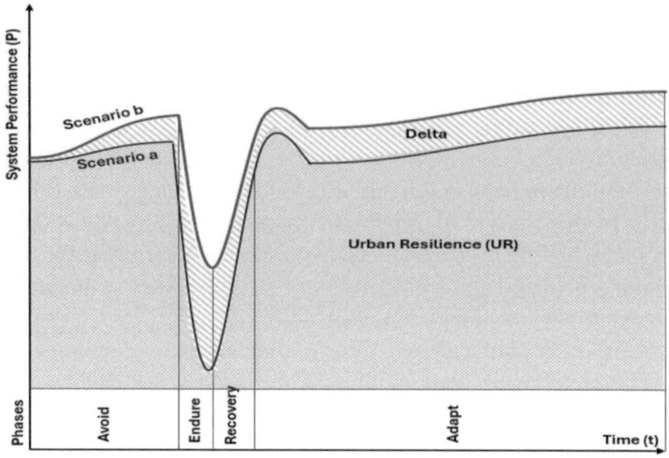

Fig. 7 Impact of the four urban resilience phases on system performance over time

response procedures contribute to the endurance capability of critical urban asset systems.

The recovery phase focuses on the ability of critical urban asset systems to restore their functionality and return to normal operations after a disruptive event or emerging threat has occurred. This phase involves implementing recovery strategies, repairing damaged infrastructure, and restoring essential services to ensure the system's operational continuity. Effective recovery planning, resource allocation, and coordination among various stakeholders are crucial for successful recovery efforts.

The adapt phase involves learning from past experiences and applying measures to improve the resilience of critical urban asset systems in the face of future threats. This phase encompasses the continuous improvement and modification of systems, processes, and policies to better prepare for and respond to evolving risks. Adaptation may involve incorporating new technologies, updating infrastructure designs, or revising emergency response plans based on lessons learned from previous disruptions.

The concept of resilience has evolved from an initial focus on response and recovery to a more proactive and holistic approach that encompasses preparedness, risk mitigation, and adaptation strategies (Cutter et al., 2013). This shift recognizes the importance of anticipating and mitigating potential threats, as well as enhancing the overall adaptability and transformative capacity of urban systems to cope with future challenges.

4 Methodology

Enhancing the resilience of critical urban asset systems in the face of emerging threats is a multifaceted endeavor that requires a comprehensive approach spanning the entire life cycle of these assets (Argyroudis et al., 2020). By integrating resilience strategies across the various stages of life cycle assessment as, planning, design, construction, operation, maintenance, and end-of-life, detailed in Table 1, cities can effectively avoid, endure, recover, and adapt to potential disruptions, ensuring the continuity of essential services and minimizing the impact on urban communities. This approach ensures that cities are prepared to face a wide range of challenges, from natural disasters to infrastructure failures, by embedding resilience at every stage of an asset's lifecycle (Salvado et al., 2020).

Avoiding potential disruptions begins with thorough planning and design (Houghton, 2011). During the planning phase, comprehensive risk assessments are conducted to identify potential hazards and develop strategic plans that incorporate disaster risk reduction measures (Guo, 1998). This might involve zoning laws that prevent construction in vulnerable areas or creating buffer zones with green spaces to absorb floodwater (Lai et al., 2016). In the design phase, resilient design principles are integrated to minimize vulnerabilities. Buildings might be designed with seismic-resistant features, and urban layouts could incorporate permeable pavements to manage stormwater effectively (Rezvani and Gomes, 2021). During construction, robust practices and resilient materials are employed to ensure the durability of the infrastructure. Regular maintenance further ensures that urban systems remain resilient, with proactive measures to address wear and tear before it becomes a significant issue. Finally, planning for the end-of-life phase involves sustainable disposal or repurposing strategies that prevent environmental contamination and promote recycling.

Practical examples of the "avoid" principle in action include applying zoning laws to avoid construction in flood-prone areas and designing buildings with seismic-resistant features in earthquake-prone regions (Bostenaru Dan, 2005; Wang et al., 2023). By creating green spaces and buffer zones, cities can mitigate the impact of natural disasters, while using resilient materials and construction techniques ensures

Table 1 Integrating Resilience Strategies across the Asset Lifecycle

UR stages LCA stages	Avoid	Endure	Recovery	Adapt
Planning	X	–	–	X
Design	X	–	-	X
Construction	X	–	X	X
Operation	–	X	X	–
Maintenance	X	–	X	X
End-of-Life	X	X	–	X

the longevity of infrastructure. Regular maintenance schedules and sustainable end-of-life planning further reinforce the city's ability to avoid major disruptions, thus preserving the functionality and safety of urban environments (Cecchin et al., 2019).

Enduring disruptions relies heavily on the efficient operation and maintenance of urban systems. Ensuring continued operation during adverse conditions involves implementing resilient operational practices (Datola et al., 2022). For instance, emergency protocols can keep public transportation running during disasters, and backup power systems can maintain critical infrastructure like hospitals and water treatment plants (Lu et al., 2019). Regular maintenance is also crucial; it includes proactive inspection and repair to prevent infrastructure from failing during stress events (Lenjani et al., 2020). By maintaining vegetation in green spaces, cities can also prevent erosion and improve water absorption, which helps in enduring natural disasters like floods and storms (Afriyanie et al., 2020).

Examples of enduring through effective operation and maintenance include ensuring critical facilities such as hospitals have reliable backup power systems like generators and solar panels. This ensures that these facilities can continue to function during power outages (Green et al., 2022). Advanced water management systems can provide a stable water supply during droughts and manage stormwater effectively during heavy rains. These strategies ensure that urban infrastructure remains functional and resilient, even when faced with severe challenges (Li & Zhang, 2022).

Recovering from disruptions requires rapid and efficient reconstruction, as well as the restoration of essential services. Post-disaster recovery begins with quickly rebuilding infrastructure using resilient designs and materials. Temporary housing for displaced populations can be rapidly constructed using modular designs, ensuring that people have safe shelter (Montalbano & Santi, 2023). Rebuilding bridges, roads, and other critical infrastructure with durable materials helps in restoring normalcy. Efficient recovery operations are vital; these include setting up temporary power and water supply systems in affected areas and re-establishing public transportation routes to support overall recovery efforts. Maintenance also plays a significant role in recovery, as it involves regular inspections and repairs to restore the resilience of damaged infrastructure.

Practical recovery strategies include the rapid construction of temporary housing for disaster victims using prefabricated materials (Afkhamiaghda et al., 2021). This approach ensures that displaced populations have immediate shelter. Prioritizing the repair and restoration of critical infrastructure, such as roads, bridges, and utilities, supports comprehensive recovery efforts (Liu et al., 2020). Post-disaster maintenance, such as inspecting and repairing buildings and infrastructure, addresses damage and enhances resilience, ensuring that the city can bounce back quickly and efficiently from disruptions.

Adapting to future risks and uncertainties involves developing urban plans and infrastructure that can be modified and improved over time. During the planning phase, adaptive strategies are incorporated to account for future risks, for instance sea-level rise as well as extreme weather events frequency increasing. Design principles that allow for future modifications and upgrades are integrated into the development of urban infrastructure. For example, buildings might be designed with modular components that can be easily replaced or upgraded (Hwang et al., 2023). During construction, infrastructure is built with adaptability in mind, allowing for spaces to be repurposed as needs change. Regular updates to maintenance practices are essential to address emerging risks and incorporate new technologies. End-of-life planning also supports adaptation by designing infrastructure components for disassembly and reuse, thus promoting sustainability and future resilience.

Examples of adaptive strategies include developing urban plans that incorporate green roofs, urban forests, and other features to respond to changing climate conditions (Almeida et al., 2023). Constructing multi-use buildings and adaptable public spaces allows for flexibility in meeting evolving community needs. Adopting new maintenance technologies, such as drones for infrastructure inspection, improves efficiency and resilience (Kocak, 2024). Planning for adaptive end-of-life strategies, like designing infrastructure for easy disassembly and reuse, supports long-term sustainability and adaptability.

In conclusion, integrating resilience strategies across the various life cycle stages of critical urban asset systems is crucial for enhancing their ability to withstand, recover from, and adapt to emerging threats. By adopting a comprehensive approach that considers risk assessment, resilient design, construction, operation, maintenance, and end-of-life strategies, cities can ensure the continuity of essential services and minimize the impact of disruptions on urban communities. This framework provides a roadmap for urban planners, asset managers, and stakeholders to prioritize resilience and proactively address the challenges posed by natural and human-induced threats, ultimately fostering more sustainable and resilient urban environments.

5 Practical Examples

Flood Risk for Transportation System on Avoid Stage at Design LCA Stage: To avoid flood risks in transportation systems during the design stage, incorporating resilient infrastructure features such as elevated roadways and flood-proof materials is crucial (Rezvani et al., 2024a, 2024b, 2024c). Elevated roadways prevent disruptions during flooding events, ensuring continued mobility for commuters. Additionally, utilizing smart traffic management systems equipped with real-time flood monitoring sensors allows for dynamic route adjustments, diverting traffic away from flooded areas and reducing congestion.

Cybersecurity Risk for Communication Network on Adapt Stage at Design LCA Stage: Adapting communication networks to cybersecurity risks during the design stage involves implementing blockchain technology for secure data transmission (Mantha and García de Soto, 2021). Blockchain ensures data integrity and confidentiality by creating a decentralized and tamper-proof network architecture. Furthermore, employing artificial intelligence (AI) algorithms for anomaly detection can proactively identify and mitigate potential cyber threats, safeguarding communication networks from malicious attacks and ensuring uninterrupted service delivery.

Fire Risk for Energy Distribution Network on Endure Stage at Operation LCA Stage: To endure fire risks in energy distribution networks during operation, advanced monitoring technologies such as drones equipped with thermal imaging cameras can be deployed (Li et al., 2019). These drones can detect hotspots and potential fire outbreaks in real-time, allowing for rapid response and preventive measures. Furthermore, implementing automated shutdown systems triggered by smoke or temperature sensors enhances safety by isolating affected sections of the grid, preventing the spread of fire and minimizing disruptions.

Drought Risk for Agricultural Irrigation Systems in the Recovery Stage of Construction LCA: At the recovery stage of constructing agricultural irrigation systems, integrating drought-resistant methods like drip irrigation and precision farming technologies is crucial (Freire et al., 2021). These systems enhance water efficiency by directing water precisely to plant roots, thereby reducing evaporation and runoff. Additionally, integrating soil moisture sensors and weather forecasting models enables adaptive irrigation scheduling, ensuring efficient water distribution and crop resilience during drought conditions.

Fire Risk for Emergency Response System on Endure Stage at Maintenance LCA Stage: Enduring fire risks in emergency response systems during maintenance involves implementing predictive maintenance techniques using Internet of Things (IoT) sensors and predictive analytics (Eslamzadeh et al., 2022). These sensors continuously monitor equipment health and performance metrics, detecting potential fire hazards such as overheating or electrical faults. Predictive analytics algorithms then analyze the sensor data to forecast equipment failures before they happen, allowing for proactive maintenance actions and reducing downtime.

Cybersecurity Risk for Power Generation Facility on Adapt Stage at Operation LCA Stage: Adapting power generation facilities to cybersecurity risks during operation involves implementing intrusion detection systems (IDS) and security information and event management (SIEM) solutions (Krause et al., 2021). IDS monitors network traffic for suspicious activities, while SIEM aggregates and analyzes security event logs to detect potential threats in real-time. Furthermore, leveraging blockchain-based smart contracts for access control enhances security by ensuring only authorized personnel can access critical infrastructure components, reducing the risk of cyber-attacks.

Fire Risk for Public Building on Endure Stage at Operation LCA Stage: Enduring fire risks in public buildings during operation involves implementing fire suppression systems equipped with advanced extinguishing agents such as environmentally friendly foam or mist (Eslamzadeh et al., 2023). These systems suppress fires quickly and effectively while minimizing water damage and environmental impact. Additionally, conducting regular fire drills and staff training sessions enhances preparedness and response capabilities, ensuring the safety of occupants and minimizing potential casualties.

6 Discussion of Results

The presented framework suggests a balanced approach to improving the resilience of essential urban asset systems against emerging threats. Integrating resilience strategies throughout the life cycle of these assets helps cities address a variety of challenges, from natural disasters to cybersecurity risks. Each phase of the asset's life cycle, from initial planning to its eventual end-of-life, contributes to developing and maintaining resilient infrastructure.

In the early planning and design phases, cities can take proactive steps to identify and lessen the impact of potential hazards. This involves performing risk assessments and incorporating resilient design features to reduce vulnerabilities. For example, building codes can limit construction in flood-prone areas, and buildings can be designed to withstand earthquakes. Furthermore, incorporating elements like green spaces and permeable pavements can help manage stormwater and mitigate flood risks.

During the construction phase, the focus shifts to using strong materials and methods that ensure the long-term viability of infrastructure. Advanced monitoring systems, such as drones with thermal imaging capabilities, can be deployed during the operational phase to promptly detect and address threats. Routine maintenance plays a significant role in ensuring that urban systems remain resilient by proactively managing wear and tear before it becomes a major issue.

The recovery phase is important for quickly restoring essential services after a disruption. Swift reconstruction using resilient designs and materials, along with effective recovery efforts like setting up temporary power and water systems, helps restore normalcy. Maintenance is also important during recovery, as it addresses damage and bolsters resilience, supporting a prompt and efficient return to normal functioning.

Adapting to future risks involves developing urban plans and infrastructure that can be changed and upgraded over time. This includes including adaptive strategies in the planning and design stages, such as designing buildings with modular parts that can be easily replaced or updated. Regular updates to maintenance practices and planning for adaptable end-of-life strategies further support long-term sustainability and resilience.

7 Conclusions and Future Works

Integrating resilience strategies into all phases of essential urban asset systems is important for improving their ability to withstand, recover from, and adapt to emerging threats. This approach promotes the continuity of essential services and limits disruptions in urban communities. By prioritizing resilience and proactively addressing natural and human-induced challenges, cities can contribute to more sustainable and resilient environments. The proposed framework can guide urban planners, asset managers, and stakeholders in developing and maintaining resilient infrastructure.

This framework also has some limitations. The complexity of urban systems can make it challenging to anticipate and mitigate all risks. Local contexts, including geographic, socio-economic, and political factors, can influence the effectiveness of resilience strategies. Additionally, implementing resilience measures often requires substantial financial investment and coordination among stakeholders, creating practical challenges.

Future research should consider these limitations by developing more thorough risk assessment methods to identify and prioritize emerging threats. Incorporating advanced modeling techniques and data analysis can improve understanding of natural and human-induced hazards. Innovative funding mechanisms and governance structures are needed to address barriers to implementing resilience strategies. Further empirical studies are needed to evaluate the effectiveness of resilience interventions in real-world settings, along with the development of relevant metrics to measure outcomes.

Furthermore, future work should explore the Risk informed asset centric approach and develop a unified, simplified Urban Resilience Index. This index can serve as a tool for decision-makers to compare different scenarios. An online platform could also be developed to facilitate the evaluation and practical implementation of these methodologies. Collaborative research across disciplines is necessary to develop holistic approaches to urban resilience that address the multifaceted nature of urban systems.

Acknowledgements This work is part of the research being carried out for the Civil Engineering Research and Innovation for Sustainability (CERIS) and was funded by Fundação para a Ciência e a Tecnologia (FCT) in the framework of project UIDB/04625/2020 and FCT grant number "2022.12886.BD" (carried out at the Instituto Superior Técnico (IST)).

List of Acronyms

LCA	Life Cycle Assessment
LCM	Life Cycle Management
MCDA	Multi-Criteria Decision Analysis
AHP	Analytic Hierarchy Process
IDS	Intrusion Detection Systems
SIEM	Security Information and Event Management
IoT	Internet of Things

References

Afkhamiaghda, M., Elwakil, E., & Kereshmeh, A. (2021). Creating a performance indicator for temporary housing. *Canadian Journal of Civil Engineering, 48*(9), 1093–1104. https://doi.org/10.1139/cjce-2020-0144.

Afriyanie, D. et al. (2020) Re-framing urban green spaces planning for flood protection through socio-ecological resilience in Bandung City, Indonesia. *Cities*, 102710. https://doi.org/10.1016/j.cities.2020.102710.

Almeida, A. P. et al. (2023). Combining green roofs and rainwater harvesting systems in university buildings under different climate conditions. *Science of the Total Environment, 887*. https://doi.org/10.1016/j.scitotenv.2023.163719.

Argyroudis, S. A. et al. (2020). Resilience assessment framework for critical infrastructure in a multi-hazard environment: Case study on transport assets. *Science of the Total Environment, 714*. https://doi.org/10.1016/j.scitotenv.2020.136854.

Bostenaru Dan, M. (2005). Multidisciplinary co-operation in building design according to urbanistic zoning and seismic microzonation. *Natural Hazards and Earth System Science, 5*(3), 397–411. Available at: https://doi.org/10.5194/nhess-5-397-2005.

Bruneau, M. et al. (2003). A framework to quantitatively assess and enhance the seismic resilience of communities. *Earthquake Spectra, 19*(4), 733–752. https://doi.org/10.1193/1.1623497.

Cecchin, A. et al. (2019). End-of-life product management as a resilience driver for developing countries: A policy experiment for used tires in Ecuador. *Journal of Industrial Ecology, 23*(5), 1292–1310. https://doi.org/10.1111/jiec.12861.

Chen, B., Sharifi, A., & Schlör, H. (2022) Integrated social-ecological-infrastructural management for urban resilience. *Resources, Conservation and Recycling, 181*. https://doi.org/10.1016/j.resconrec.2022.106268.

CISA. (2023). *Critical Infrastructure Systems*. CISA. https://www.cisa.gov/topics/critical-infrastructure-security-and-resilience/resilience-services/infrastructure-dependency-primer/learn/critical-infrastructure-systems. Accessed: 24 March 2024.

Cutter, S. L., et al. (2013). Disaster resilience: A national imperative. *Environment, 55*(2), 25–29. https://doi.org/10.1080/00139157.2013.768076

Datola, G., et al. (2022). Operationalising resilience: A methodological framework for assessing urban resilience through System Dynamics Model. *Ecological Modelling, 465*https://doi.org/10.1016/j.ecolmodel.2021.109851

Duarte, M., et al. (2022). Resilience rating system for buildings against natural hazards. *Lecture Notes in Mechanical Engineering*. https://doi.org/10.1007/978-3-030-96794-9_6

Eslamzadeh, M. K., Grilo, A., & Espadinha-Cruz, P. (2022). A framework for resource allocation in fire departments: a structured literature review. *Fire 2022, 5* (4), 109. https://doi.org/10.3390/FIRE5040109.

Eslamzadeh, M.K., Grilo, A. and Espadinha-Cruz, P. (2023) 'A Model for Fire Departments' Performance Assessment in Portugal', *Fire 2023, Vol. 6, Page 31*, 6(1), p. 31. Available at: https://doi.org/10.3390/FIRE6010031.

Frangopol, D. M., Saydam, D., & Kim, S. (2012). Maintenance, management, life-cycle design and performance of structures and infrastructures: A brief review. *Structure and Infrastructure Engineering, 8*(1), 1–25. https://doi.org/10.1080/15732479.2011.628962

Freire, P., et al. (2021). Flood and drought risk assessment for agricultural areas (Tagus Estuary, Portugal). *Natural Hazards and Earth System Sciences, 21*(8), 2503–2521. https://doi.org/10.5194/nhess-21-2503-2021

Garcia, J. et al. (2023) Resilience assessment of public treasury elementary school buildings in lisbon municipality, in *Lecture Notes in Mechanical Engineering*, pp. 636–644. https://doi.org/10.1007/978-3-031-25448-2_59.

Green, J., Newman, P., & Droege, P. (2022). *Transactive electricity: how decentralized renewable power can support security, resilience and decarbonization, Intelligent Environments: Advanced Systems for a Healthy Planet*, 2nd Edn. https://doi.org/10.1016/B978-0-12-820247-0.00006-0.

Guo, J. C. Y. (1998). Risk-cost approach to interim drainage structure design. *Journal of Water Resources Planning and Management, 124*(6), 330–333. https://doi.org/10.1061/(ASCE)0733-9496(1998)124:6(330)

Hokmabadi, H., Rezvani, S. M. H. S., & de Matos, C. A. (2024). Business resilience for small and medium enterprises and startups by digital transformation and the role of marketing capabilities—a systematic review. *Systems 2024, 12*(6), 220. https://doi.org/10.3390/SYSTEMS12060220.

Houghton, A. (2011). Health impact assessments a tool for designing climate change resilience into green building and planning projects. *Journal of Green Building, 6*(2), 66–87. https://doi.org/10.3992/jgb.6.2.66

Hwang, K.-E., et al. (2023). Client-engaged collaborative pre-design framework for modular housing. *Automation in Construction, 156*. https://doi.org/10.1016/j.autcon.2023.105123

ISO 31000. (2018). ISO 31000 Risk management—Principles and guidelines. *International Organization for Standardization*, p. 34.

ISO 55000 (2014) *ISO/CD: 2012. Asset management—Oveview principles and terminology*. International Organization for Standardization. www.iso.org. Accessed 26 June 2021.

Johansen, I. L., Rausand, M. (2014). Foundations and choice of risk metrics. *Safety Science, 62*, 386–399. https://doi.org/10.1016/j.ssci.2013.09.011.

Kocak, S. (2024). Cost-effective use of reclaimed asphalt mixtures with various rubber modification technologies for pavement maintenance applications. *Journal of Materials in Civil Engineering, 36*(4). https://doi.org/10.1061/JMCEE7.MTENG-17174.

Krause, T. et al. (2021). Cybersecurity in power grids: Challenges and opportunities. *Sensors 2021, 21*(18), 6225. https://doi.org/10.3390/S21186225.

Lai, C., et al. (2016). Flood risk zoning using a rule mining based on ant colony algorithm. *Journal of Hydrology, 542*, 268–280. https://doi.org/10.1016/j.jhydrol.2016.09.003

Lenjani, A., et al. (2020). A resilience-based method for prioritizing post-event building inspections. *Natural Hazards, 100*(2), 877–896. https://doi.org/10.1007/s11069-019-03849-0

Li, F., & Zhang, J. (2022). A review of the progress in Chinese Sponge City programme: Challenges and opportunities for urban stormwater management. *Water Supply, 22*(2), 1638–1651. https://doi.org/10.2166/ws.2021.327

Li, Y. et al. (2019). Reliability assessment model of water distribution networks against fire following earthquake (FFE). *Water (Switzerland), 11*(12). https://doi.org/10.3390/w11122536.

Liu, Y. et al. (2020). Prioritizing transportation network recovery using a resilience measure. *Sustainable and Resilient Infrastructure*. Informa UK Limited, pp. 1–12. https://doi.org/10.1080/23789689.2019.1708180.

Lu, X. et al. (2019). Real-time city-scale time-history analysis and its application in resilience-oriented earthquake emergency responses. *Applied Sciences (Switzerland*), 9(17). https://doi.org/10.3390/app9173497.

Mantha, B. R. K., & García de Soto, B. (2021). Assessment of the cybersecurity vulnerability of construction networks. *Engineering, Construction and Architectural Management, 28*(10), 3078–3105. https://doi.org/10.1108/ECAM-06-2020-0400

Meerow, S., et al. (2016). Defining urban resilience: A review. *Landscape and Urban Planning, 147*, 38–49. https://doi.org/10.1016/j.landurbplan.2015.11.011

Meerow, S., & Newell, J. P. J. P. (2019). Urban resilience for whom, what, when, where, and why? *Urban Geography, 40*(3), 309–329. https://doi.org/10.1080/02723638.2016.1206395

Montalbano, G., & Santi, G. (2023). Sustainability of temporary housing in post-disaster scenarios: A requirement-based design strategy. *Buildings, 13*(12). https://doi.org/10.3390/buildings13122952.

Rezvani, S., & Gomes, M. C. (2021). Assessment of pavement degradation through statistical analysis model A case study of the Department of Transportation (DOT) of Iowa, USA, in *Proceedings of the 11th IMA International Conference on Modelling in Industrial Maintenance and Reliability*. Essex UK (29 June–1 July 2021). Institute of Mathematics & its Applications. https://doi.org/10.19124/ima.2021.01.11.

Rezvani, S. M., Falcão Silva, M. J., & de Almeida, N. M. (2024). Urban resilience ındex for critical ınfrastructure: A scenario-based approach to disaster risk reduction in road networks. *Sustainability 2024, 16*(10), 4143. https://doi.org/10.3390/SU16104143.

Rezvani, S. M. H. S., et al. (2023a). Resilience exposure assessment using multi-layer mapping of Portuguese 308 cities and communities. *Lecture Notes in Mechanical Engineering*. https://doi.org/10.1007/978-3-031-25448-2_57

Rezvani, S. M. H. S., Almeida, N., & Silva, M. J. F. (2023b). Multi-disciplinary and dynamic urban resilience assessment through stochastic analysis of a virtual city. *Lecture Notes in Mechanical Engineering*. https://doi.org/10.1007/978-3-031-25448-2_62

Rezvani, S. M. H. S., Falcao Silva, M. J., & de Almeida, N. M. (2024b). NETOBRA: Boosting Urban Resilience through a digital platform for the construction ecosystem. *Procedia Structural Integrity, 55*, 72–79. https://doi.org/10.1016/J.PROSTR.2024.02.010

Rezvani, S. M. H. S., Falcão Silva, M. J., de Almeida, N. M. (2024). The risk-ınformed asset-centric (RIACT) urban resilience enhancement process: an outline and pilot-case demonstrator for earthquake risk mitigation in portuguese municipalities. *Applied Sciences 2024, 14*(2), 634. https://doi.org/10.3390/APP14020634.

Salvado, F., Marques de Almeida, N., & Vale e Azevedo, Á. (2020). Future-proofing and monitoring capital investments needs throughout the life cycle of building projects. *Sustainable Cities and Society, 59*, 102159. https://doi.org/10.1016/J.SCS.2020.102159.

Santos, J., Ferreira, A. (2013). Life-cycle cost analysis system for pavement management at project level. *International Journal of Pavement Engineering, 14*(1), 71–84. https://doi.org/10.1080/10298436.2011.618535.

Santos, J., Ferreira, A., & Flintsch, G. (2015). A life cycle assessment model for pavement management: Methodology and computational framework. *International Journal of Pavement Engineering, 16*(3), 268–286. https://doi.org/10.1080/10298436.2014.942861

Shariatfar, M., & Lee, Y. -C. (2020). Urban-level data ınteroperability of buildings and civil ınfrastructure systems for enhancing disaster resilience, in *Construction Research Congress 2020: Computer Applications—Selected Papers from the Construction Research Congress 2020*, pp. 1184–1193.

Wang, J.-H., et al. (2023). Application of hybrid machine learning model for flood hazard zoning assessments. *Stochastic Environmental Research and Risk Assessment, 37*(1), 395–412. https://doi.org/10.1007/s00477-022-02301-3

Wang, M. et al. (2021). Life-cycle cost analysis and resilience consideration for coupled grey infrastructure and low-impact development practices. *Sustainable Cities and Society, 75*. https://doi.org/10.1016/j.scs.2021.103358.

Zawaideh, F. H. et al. (2023). Blockchain solution For SMEs cybersecurity threats ın e-commerce, in *2023 International Conference on Computer Science and Emerging Technologies*. CSET 2023. https://doi.org/10.1109/CSET58993.2023.10346628.

The Impact of Blockchain Technology for Sustainable Asset Maintenance in Telecoms Domain in Emerging Markets

Charles Okeyia and Nuno Marques de Almeida

Abstract Blockchain technology (BCT) is a paradigm shift in the telecom domain, offering unparalleled benefits in asset maintenance adoption. It opens up new avenues for managing asset infrastructure, especially in the operation and maintenance activities and phases of asset life cycle management. This extended phase is pivotal for tackling intricate asset issues that involve energy supply concerns and intermittent outages caused by unstable, irregular and unreliable power supply and inefficient maintenance practices. Thus, customers face challenges related to unreliable network services, while telecom providers experience maintenance and operations challenges on their asset performance and operating expenditure. The primary aim of this study was to increase the understanding of sustainable asset maintenance management in emerging markets using blockchain technology. The study used a case study methodology to demonstrate its practical importance by drawing from a qualitative and quantitative data collection approach; this study also analysed the various features and characteristics of blockchain technology and identified some of the benefits of sustainable asset maintenance management. The quantitative data were analysed with SPSS AMOS by performing structural equation modelling to assist in supporting the theories and research and also understanding the variables to explore their relationships. The qualitative data were transcribed using the descriptive analysis of the semi-structured interview data. Our analysis of the procedures and adoption of each identified value of PdM and CBM from the BCT maintenance adoption, based on the extant studies and the generated quantitative data, reveals significant potential cost savings. The BCT application's effectiveness in asset performance not only significantly enhances network quality but also serves as a promising indicator of operations and maintenance benefits. The results present a robust data-driven model for BCT adoption, which not only enhances confidence in the thoroughness and validity of the research process but also instils a sense of encouragement in the

C. Okeyia (✉)
Engineering and Management, IST Lisboa, Lisboa, Portugal
e-mail: charles@snowviewssl.com

N. Marques de Almeida
Instituto Superior Técnico, Lisbon, Portugal

A. Crespo Márquez et al. (eds.), *Case Studies in Digital Transformation*, Engineering Asset Management Review 4, https://doi.org/10.1007/978-3-032-05592-7_4

research findings. The findings enable the BCT framework to predict asset infrastructure outages, ensuring an efficient integration of the asset maintenance activities in a BCT approach and adoption. This action includes addressing resource issues, outage visibility and monitoring, and asset infrastructure performance degradation, all of which contribute to reducing operating costs and enhancing financial sustainability. The potential for cost savings and improved network quality is a beacon of hope for the telecom industry's future.

Keywords Asset management · Condition-based maintenance · Blockchain technology · Infrastructure · Predictive maintenance

1 Overview

Telecom operations and maintenance in most emerging markets are confused by the persistent problems of power supply and asset malfunctionality caused by ineffective maintenance practices since reliable network services are dependent on the optimal performance and functionality of the assets, which in turn provides sustainable power and network availability. Therefore, telecom infrastructure providers using digital support and adoption in their asset management must continue to provide high-quality network availability and services by deploying infrastructure and efficient asset management maintenance practices.

Conversely, unreliable power supply caused by intermittent asset outages poses severe challenges to telecom providers and their customers, as reliable, efficient and cost-effective maintenance practices are a critical factor for sustainable asset maintenance management practices. This assertion is true based on the understanding that these telecom assets function continuously, making it important for proper maintenance practices. Thus, blockchain has appeared as a transformative force within asset maintenance management, as it facilitates real-time monitoring of activities, contributing to effective asset maintenance management practices (Wang et al., 2022). This assertion and perspective are particularly relevant for the telecom domain, where sustainable asset management is crucial for improved and optimal performance.

Additionally, the focus of blockchain technology application in the power supply segment, showing the BCT features capabilities to streamline processes and minimise inefficiencies in asset operations and maintenance (Rejeb et al., 2024) could make blockchain technology replace complex and manual workflow processes with real-time and efficient operations and maintenance practices, such as using technology to foster energy supply and load balancing, real-time visibility and functionality escalation, which can significantly impact sustainability efforts.

This discussion is pertinent to the telecoms domain as it aligns with the need for creativity and innovative resolutions to manage energy supply load balancing and consumption and foster sustainable asset practices with emerging markets. This background literature constructs an understanding of the multifaceted effect of the adoption of blockchain technology on sustainable asset maintenance management practices, as the collectively highlights the features and capabilities of blockchain technology that foster efficient asset maintenance practices through transparency, trust, security, traceability and immutability, thereby optimising performance and operating costs.

1.1 Background Context

The telecoms domain in emerging markets has become very demanding due to several factors, such as infrastructure management challenges, technology evolutions, strict managed service level agreements (SLA), maintenance of safety requirements, and the high cost of operation (Amadi-Echendu, 2021; Ayamolowo et al., 2019; Simon, 2021). Additionally, emerging markets are quite competitive in providing services to help customers maintain their social and economic activities. One of the critical services in high demand in this context is telecom services because of the support individuals and businesses use; thus, many customers are willing to pay for better telecom services. Asset maintenance is crucial for many companies, especially in the telecom sub-sector.

However, in this study context, customers experienced unstable network availability due to unreliable power supply from the assets caused by intermittent asset outages, diesel mismanagement, theft, community and landlord demand, double taxation and ineffective asset maintenance. Poor power supply to this telecom infrastructure asset severely impacts the performance of active components, potentially leading to poor quality of the network, traffic congestion dropped calls, and loss of value by businesses and organisations that depend on data from these assets.

Consequently, the main justification behind this exploration of using BCT in asset management is to develop enhanced, transparent, and immutable smart contracts that run on the distributed ledger technology platform blockchain and are responsible for maintaining telecoms' infrastructure assets. These smart contracts guarantee the integrity and validity of the maintenance data and provide a clear and transparent audit trail of the asset maintenance history. The success of this endeavour could lead to sustainable development in the telecoms asset maintenance domain generally, promoting the development of emerging markets.

1.2 Research Aims

The primary aim of this study is to have an in-depth understanding of blockchain technology adoption for sustainable asset maintenance from an efficient management perspective and practice. The study positioned the study focus on the connection between asset maintenance activities, blockchain technology features and asset management. The developed study scope intends to support the study aims to explore the effect of blockchain technology adoption in the telecoms domain to ensure efficient asset maintenance management practice using blockchain technology capabilities. Thus, the focus on efficient asset maintenance management using blockchain technology within the telecoms domain constitutes the key purpose of this study.

The research is divided into a series of closely interworking tasks to achieve these objectives. The first task aims to define the principles required for BCT in asset maintenance systems. This action involves determining the assets and related smart contracts on the blockchain, the representation of this information on the blockchain, the participants who write, read, and execute these blocks on the blockchain, and how these participants will interact with the blockchain. Thus, the objective is to understand the root causes of the inconsistent and intermittent asset outages, understand the effects of blockchain technology on asset maintenance management, and propose an efficient strategy that could impact effective asset maintenance management practices regarding the asset functionality, performance and operating costs.

Furthermore, the study intends to create an in-depth insight into the effect of sustainable asset maintenance management practices in emerging markets and seek practical maintenance strategies such as the predictive-based approach to address the identified problems of lack of visibility, real-time escalation, monitoring and tracking asset functionality and performance. Thus, the study will address these questions: what are the existing asset maintenance management practices? How can the existing asset maintenance management practices improved to optimise performance and reduce operating costs? Thus, the research aims to address the identified and existing gap in the literature and provide valuable insights into the problems facing the growing telecoms domain in emerging markets.

2 Theoretical Foundation

The theoretical foundation addresses the challenges of asset maintenance management practices of intermittent asset outages caused by ineffective asset maintenance in this study context, which also discloses a multifaceted interaction between monopolistic or conventional practices, systemic inefficiencies, manual processes and urgent requirements for sustainable asset management practices. However, this study is significant given the profound implications of intermittent outages, unreliable power supply and asset malfunction caused by ineffective maintenance, in which telecom assets functionality and performance rely heavily on consistent asset power supply and real-time visibility, monitoring and tracking for optimal performance and operational and maintenance efficiency.

In addition, the applied qualitative and quantitative methodology enables a comprehensive analysis of the existing asset maintenance management practices, as the structured questionnaire and semi-structured interview elucidate the ramifications of asset maintenance activities and their effect on performance and network sustainability. There are different policies and practices in asset maintenance; thus, the inquiry is divided into a series of tightly interworking tasks to achieve these objectives. The first task aims to define the principles required for BCT to be used in asset maintenance systems. This process involves determining the assets and associated smart contracts on the blockchain, the representation of this information on the blockchain, the participants who write, read, and execute these blocks on the blockchain, and how these participants will interact with the blockchain. It is crucial to note that the main challenge in the proposed research is defining how the different entities will be present in the blockchain network and how they will communicate their presence and actions through the features of blockchain operations.

2.1 Blockchain Technology Overview

The extant literature on blockchain technology in asset management has developed substantially, suggesting the developing attention and application of this modern and digitalised technology in the telecom domain. Afraz et al. (2023) suggested this discourse by emphasising the advantages of blockchain technology to optimise performance and reduce operating costs by improving the various activities and incidents, which has captured the attention of different stakeholders in the telecom domain. The authors highlight the significance of the diverse approach in exploring the effect of the adoption of blockchain technology on asset maintenance management, merging systematic literature review, industry knowledge and perceptions, and theoretical supports. This multifaceted analysis serves as a base for understanding how blockchain technology can remodel asset maintenance management practices, notwithstanding the constrained theoretical exploration from the operations and maintenance perspectives.

Given the understanding from Afraz et al. (2023), Zhang et al. (2023) and Hellenborn et al. (2024) explore transparency, trust, traceability and immutability features of blockchain technology, which are critical for the adoption and application in telecom asset maintenance management practices. Their systematic literature review identifies these blockchain technology features benefits as real-time monitoring and tracking, improved data integrity, decentralised validation and the visibility of asset maintenance activities. This assertion and insight mean that the adoption of blockchain technology in asset maintenance management has emerged as a transformative influence in improving sustainability practices within emerging markets, as blockchain technology highlights the capability to generate, store and record transactions or events and verify without reliance on interventions or intermediaries.

However, the basic idea of the blockchain is to use a decentralised network to eliminate the need for trusted third parties who would otherwise be the condition for trust in a transaction (Ahmed et al., 2022; Sadri et al., 2023). Therefore, the key part of the blockchain is verifying the validity of transactions through the consensus of participating entities known as nodes. A consensus is achieved through a technical and mathematical verification process called mining. This results in blocks, such as containers for time-stamped transactions, that are added to the hashed chain of previous blocks (Hellenborn et al., 2024). The set of transactions in all blocks forms the ledger accessible to everyone, ensuring transparency and immutability. This timestamp construct is important in telecom asset maintenance management practices, as it will assist with the actual root cause of failures and records of actually performed activities.

Additionally, it has been reported that public and private blockchains are two mechanisms that provide different approaches for blockchain implementation. A public blockchain is a permission-less distributed system (Azmi et al., 2022; Sadri et al., 2023). This assertion suggested that field team members can be connected to the network, submit and update transactions, and become validators. Once the transaction is made, consensus is reached through the mining process. The result is creating a new block that includes the transaction and places it at the end of the existing blockchain. This insight is consistent with the findings of Hellenborn et al. (2024) on asset information requirements for blockchain technology, as the data is transparent and visible to everyone on the network. If validators agree to a change and approve the transaction, the decision will be made, and a corresponding transaction will be approved.

In contrast, Sadri et al. (2023) and Hellenborn et al. (2024) highlight the dual nature of security features of blockchain technology adoption concerning the associated risk with centralised applications, such as single points of failure and unauthorised access, which is related to telecom operations and maintenance and reference approval on access to the site. From the decentralised perspective, blockchain technology does not eliminate security feature risks, but it introduces new challenges that must be resolved. For instance, in the telecom asset maintenance activities, improper records keeping and manipulation of generator run hours, diesel consumption quantity and load management. However, with immutability features, these concerns can be addressed, as it ensures that records stored in the blockchain cannot be altered or modified, thereby creating the integrity of the maintenance records.

Given this insight into blockchain technology security, the study underscores the necessity for ongoing study into the security of blockchain technology adoption and applications, suggesting that existing literature lacks a detailed understanding and overview of the likely risks. Thus, the gap in knowledge is particularly critical for telecom domains that are increasingly seeking blockchain technology to change their operations and maintenance processes, including asset maintenance management. This understanding offered by Sadri et al. (2023) and Hellenborn et al., (2024) could enable more informed decision-making and assessment in the adoption and implementation of blockchain technology within this context.

Accordingly, the study focuses on the applicability of blockchain technology's key features, such as transparency, trust, traceability, and immutability, which are critical in addressing asset maintenance management. Thus, this literature underlines an essential route for the theoretical overview surrounding blockchain technology in asset maintenance management, from the foundational concepts and concerns about transparency, trust, security, traceability, and immutability to practical applications and innovative resolutions.

2.2 Adoption of Blockchain in Telecom Infrastructure Asset Maintenance Management

The extant literature on the adoption of blockchain technology in asset maintenance management reveals a progressive insight into blockchain technology's features and capabilities and its transformative potential for data management, operations, and maintenance efficiency. The operational mechanisms of blockchain technology were explored by Wang et al. (2022) and Su et al. (2022), underlining the issues caused by heterogeneous data spawned from diverse maintenance activities. However, these authors argued that blockchain technology distributed storage, asymmetric encryption and peer-to-peer communication could efficiently address and manage these difficult data assets, thereby improving efficient maintenance practices.

Li et al. (2022) explore blockchain technology applicability and identify the potential to enhance adoption and integration, transparency and trust within digitalised asset maintenance management activities. The author's findings imply that blockchain provides considerable possibilities for improving operational performance and resilience. This assertion and insight highlight the significance of understanding blockchain technology enablers and barriers, which is critical for telecom providers as they contemplate the adoption and implementation of asset maintenance management. For instance, Li et al. (2022) suggested applying blockchain to protect digital asset management transactions for load use at mobile operators who conduct maintenance and network operations and transactions through mobile maintenance activities. According to previous studies, the purpose of the immutability integration process is to ensure maintenance activities' authenticity and exclude fraudulent activities with spare replacement and complete implementation of the services cycle.

Furthermore, Hamdan et al. (2022) and Afraz et al. (2023) provide another perspective on blockchain technology adoption in asset maintenance management by highlighting its role in improving transparency, traceability, and immutability. The authors noted that blockchain technology's decentralised features enable secure activities without the need for intervention, thereby streamlining maintenance activities and minimising operating costs. This perspective is in alignment with the research context and the needs of the telecom domain, where efficient asset maintenance management is important. In contrast, some of the studies believe that no existing digital maintenance activities or transaction solutions will provide irrefutability and full transparency for power management through reliable maintenance activities (Saravana et al., 2017; Afraz et al., 2023).

However, the blockchain solution is expected to offer independence and lower costs for power management and maintenance operations and maintenance. It will also ensure support and integration between the various distributed assets, such as the cooling systems, diesel management, consumption visibility and generator functionality. The blockchain protocol is expected to achieve the effectiveness and automation of system functions and maintain robust asset management practices, such as maintenance scheduling (Al-Emari et al., 2022), faults predictions and escalations, monitoring and tracking of asset functionality, and optimising performance and cost. With every activity recorded in the blockchain journal, valid activities are distinguished from incomplete and unauthorised activities and access to the base station. Accordingly, these studies illustrate and highlight the necessary features of blockchain technology that can address asset maintenance management practices based on their advantages to the research context.

2.2.1 Telecoms Infrastructure Asset Maintenance in Research Context

Nigeria has about 229,152,217 million population (NPC, 2024) with active mobile phone subscriptions of 222 million (NCC, 2023), supported by 45,288 base stations containing infrastructure assets such as towers, shelters, diesel generators, cooling systems, battery backup systems, hybrid and solar systems and diesel tanks. There are four mobile network operators (MNOs), MTN, Airtel, Globacom and 9Mobile, excluding the tower companies (IHS, ATC, Pan African, HTN) who are responsible for the management of these infrastructure assets. To compete, MNOs must provide quality services as the customer is now more knowledgeable and can research using the internet. To provide a better quality of services requires stable network availability, which is dependent on the infrastructure assets, thus the importance of having optimised performance from these assets.

Therefore, efficient asset management is important when base station—infrastructure asset maintenance is considered. Filed teams responsible for the provision of these maintenance activities should have complete visibility into all the relevant records and information on a particular asset and its life cycle. It is crucial to have an efficient asset management system in place that will streamline the operations related to asset functionality, spare parts management, and operational maintenance information. There is also the need to have a maintenance process that will enhance the effectiveness of the maintenance activities and reduce operating costs.

These types of maintenance strategies, such as preventive, condition-based, corrective or reactive and predictive maintenance strategies, should be designed to meet the needs of the tower companies and optimise functionality and performance (Crespo et al., 2020; Achouch et al., 2022). The study aims to create a model that focuses on effective asset maintenance management that enhances functionality, real-time visibility, monitoring and tracking, traceability, optimises performance and minimises operating cost and compliance assurance in the telecoms domain.

2.2.2 Asset Maintenance Management Practice

Asset maintenance management literature has evolved significantly, reflecting a shift from the conventional maintenance management practice to more predictive-based maintenance management (Botha, 2017; Hu & Chen, 2020; Li et al., 2021). These authors highlight the detrimental effects of the conventional reactive maintenance strategy, advocating for a digitalised and integrated maintenance strategy that aligns maintenance activities with wider operational objectives. This perspective underlines the significance of considering maintenance not as a separate function but as an essential element of complete asset performance. Three key components were identified (organisational, design and maintenance management) for efficient asset maintenance management, highlighting the necessity of optimising functionality and performance and minimising operating costs.

Emerging literature indicates the different policies and practices in asset maintenance management, as it has been reported that they are industry-specific. This study focuses on the telecoms industry, which uses BCT to preserve assets. BCT impacts the environment, economy, and society, leading to sustainable and effective asset functionality and performance (Hellenborn et al., 2024; Sadri et al., 2023). The study concentrates on theoretical research on how blockchain adds value in asset maintenance for sustainable asset management by some telecom operators in emerging markets. The telecom operators discussed in this study are based in Nigeria, Ghana and South Africa.

Previous literature on sustainable asset maintenance was explored, revealing that no prior studies have been done in the telecoms domain. This assertion indicates a literature gap that requires addressing. However, the potential application of BCT in asset management covers past the conventional activities and is also not limited to a specific field (Adelekan et al., 2024; Sadri et al., 2023) as it has been explored in the context of telecom asset management, combining permissioned and permissionless BCT for all-inclusive asset management practice. This assertion is because BCT in asset management practices can address problems related to data transparency, security, trust, traceability and immutability (Al-Dhlan et al., 2022; Sadri et al., 2023). This insight aligns with Su and Wang et al. (2022) proposition that the adoption of BCT in asset management has been tested to address digital asset management, providing characteristics such as distributed and peer-peer interface, which can alleviate data management and application.

Critiquing these literature perspectives, Huin et al. (2020) and Zonta et al. (2020) explore the optimisation approaches in asset maintenance management, focusing on processes that are based on the concepts of a predictive-based maintenance strategy that integrates blockchain technology in asset maintenance management. The insights from this perspective point toward the significance of data-driven decision-making in asset maintenance management practices, whereby the asset functionality could be evaluated to adopt and implement real-time maintenance actions. These authors also underscored the operating environment aspects of asset maintenance strategies, promoting a design philosophy that integrates hybrid and clean energy maintenance constructs to minimise environmental effects related to asset outages and repairs (Huin et al. 2020; Peters & Roecker, 2021).

Extant studies added to this discourse by exploring the strategic selection of asset maintenance strategy under varying operations and maintenance settings (Adelekan et al., 2024; Sadri et al., 2023; Hamasha et al., 2023). These authors underline the obligation and significance for asset practitioners to understand the relationship between maintenance results and resource contributions, which directly influences performance and cost efficiency. Thus, the importance of measurable performance indicators to validate and explain maintenance activities and the significant role of sustainable maintenance management practices across the telecom domain. Therefore, the paper can support the argument by these authors that efficient maintenance planning and implementation are critical factors for improving asset functionality and attaining optimal performance and cost reduction, thus reinforcing the predictive-strategic importance of maintenance management practices.

Collectively, the reviewed extant literature demonstrates a progressive understanding of asset maintenance management practices, highlighting the adoption and integration of maintenance strategies with general operations and maintenance objectives, the incorporation of digitalised and advanced technologies, and the necessity of sustainable maintenance management practices.

2.3 *Elements of Asset Maintenance Management Strategy*

The key significant components of efficient maintenance management are exceedingly problematic to adopt and implement in most telecom organisations. Nevertheless, these practices ensure operations and maintenance efficiency and operating cost savings, which is an important aspect of guaranteeing reliable maintenance critical activities; thus, the key elements of efficient maintenance strategies are preventive-based maintenance, predictive-based maintenance and condition-based maintenance strategies. Preventive-based maintenance is to prevent early asset outages and impairment, such as periodic checks, maintenance, the use of given service materials, and the use of field teams to evidence it.

2.3.1 Preventive-based Maintenance Strategy

The preventive-based maintenance strategy involves maintaining asset reliability and a safe working position, with activities that include regular spot checks, servicing and adjustments. This maintenance strategy is performed based on manufacturing recommendations, operating and usage based on time-based and broken-down preventive maintenance activities (Li et al., 2021). The time-based activities involve regular time intervals, while usage-based activities initiate activities based on asset functionality and use. Thus, the preventive-based maintenance strategy's key aim is to prevent asset outages before they happen, as its advantages include improved asset reliability and availability, lower-cost repairs associated with unscheduled outages and downtime incidents (Li et al., 2021; Wang et al., 2020) long asset functionality and lifecycle, and the ability to standardised routine maintenance practices.

Additionally, preventive-based maintenance has been commonly used in various aspects of asset maintenance management practices, including in this context. However, this paper focuses on a maintenance strategy that can be integrated with blockchain technology for sustainable asset maintenance management, which this paper believed that preventive-based maintenance cannot support because of the data-driven and analytical algorithms involved in digitalised technologies that predict unforeseen asset outages and real-time monitoring and tracking of asset functionality and maintenance activities, which is the focus of this paper.

2.3.2 Predictive-based Maintenance Strategy

Predictive-based maintenance strategies predict likely asset outages by using digitalised systems over IoT or machine learning technologies to monitor and track asset conditions and functionality. This kind of maintenance strategy focuses on repairing the asset issues prior to outages and downtime. Therefore, in a predictive-based maintenance strategy, the key principle is to monitor and track asset maintenance activities by automating maintenance scheduling for routine and planned maintenance activities.

The real-time data collection and analysis of asset behaviour and functionality under predictive-based maintenance is a critical function used in the predictive-based maintenance strategy. Thus, asset monitoring and tracking in predictive-based maintenance is conducted through condition-based maintenance monitoring and remote inspections (Zonta et al., 2020). By aiming for condition-based monitoring and tracking, minimal preventive-based maintenance is performed which in turn promotes efficient asset maintenance activities and maximising of uptime and optimal performance.

The application of digitalised sensors in real-time for visibility anticipates asset functionality and identifies abnormal or anomalous behaviour (Gupta et al., 2020; Jimenez et al., 2020). This insight involves predictive analytics, which includes a range of statistical and modelling techniques used to anticipate likely asset malfunctions. Teoh et al. (2021) and Hellenborn (2024) noted that predictive analytics is applied in conjunction with the condition-based monitoring process to help change maintenance practices because the data-driven capabilities emphasise asset behaviours and functionality. These insights align with the telecom domain based on data-driven operations and blockchain technology capability to ensure data integrity on asset maintenance records and transparency in allowing real-time visibility of asset maintenance activities.

Additionally, extant studies in condition-based maintenance practices advocate predictive-based maintenance strategy as the future of maintenance strategies (Hellenborn et al., 2024; Quatrini et al., 2020). This assertion is based on the capability of a predictive-based maintenance strategy to predict asset outages and function maintenance prior to the asset downtime or outage; thus, it is significant for practitioners and organisations to impart confidence in operating their assets at an optimal position based on their asset maintenance input and performance.

Furthermore, analysis from the reviewed theoretical models indicates a constructive impact and operational efficiency from the use of a predictive-based maintenance strategy based on its capabilities of automation, real-time monitoring, and the use of IoT for visibility and tracking of functionality. Thus, these features of predictive-based maintenance strategy align with this paper's focus on sustainable asset maintenance management practices that promote optimal functionality performance and minimise operating costs.

2.4 Maintenance Sustainability

Sustainability is one of the major themes in the literature on blockchain. The most obvious sustainability impact of this technology is provided by the need to reduce waste and resource consumption (Azmi et al., 2022). A blockchain data structure is an immutable linked record of entries blocks, and it is always stored in the same way (Grijalvo et al., 2020; Sadri et al., 2023). In theory, it is a simple but disruptive technology, both for what it can do and for what it does not require. It is also argued that nearly energy-neutral technology once has been established (Ahmed et al., 2022). As a result of these qualities, blockchains have been identified as potentially catalysing the sustainable transformation of sectors (Maletic et al., 2020; Sadri et al., 2023; Hellenborn et al., 2024), including identity, land registries, and supply chain management, thus, the sustainability capability of blockchain depend on upon the structure of its characteristic of a distributed ledger.

Additionally, BCT is both centralised and replicated (Azmi et al., 2022) as the decentralisation feature determines the trust between network nodes that helps data transparency and integrity whenever necessary. Thus, blockchain can provide certain assistance and advantages by eliminating deliberate manipulations of maintenance records and activities, which is mainly interesting to developing countries where operating costs are raised due to bureaucracy and mismanagement. Concerning cost-saving, blockchain asset maintenance adoption also brings long-term monetary advantages because of the BCT features and added values from traceability, traceable proprietorship, data validation, and lower regulatory costs. Accordingly, telecom organisations can benefit from these values that their telecom infrastructure assets are supposed to bring us in the era of a digitalised maintenance culture. As such, demand for digitalised predictive maintenance strategies that provide effective maintenance management practice.

3 Methodology Outline

This study used a design research methodology, where qualitative and quantitative techniques were used for data collection and interpretation to develop the results. The mixed method methodology, which consisted of a structured questionnaire—survey and semi-structured interviews—was developed and analysed using regression analysis and structural equation modelling to examine the theoretical framework. For this study, the design study process, which is explanatory sequential design, was selected for its support in testing theoretical knowledge and operational objects. The justification of the semi-structured interviews was to explain the concepts used in the identified problem, validate the accuracy of the raised problem, and measure the rationality and reliability of the methods used, where the questionnaire–survey methods were used to test this study through the dataset.

Conversely, it is essential to evaluate the significance of the several variables correctly, as the questionnaire survey for telecom asset maintenance management was crafted on a five-point Likert scale, where the general response structure was selected. The regression analysis and structural equation model were employed to develop a theoretical model for the adoption of blockchain technology, focusing on sustainable asset maintenance management reliability in the telecom domain in emerging markets, including the cause-and-effect relationship.

The results of this study assisted in identifying the key variables that facilitated the efficient adoption of blockchain technology for sustainable asset maintenance management in the telecom domain. The identified factors hold significant meaning for creating efficient maintenance strategies for the introduction of blockchain technology across other domains in emerging markets.

3.1 The Research Strategy

To address and attain this study's aims and objectives, the study performed a detailed systematic analysis of and review of blockchain technology by employing the case study research approach, which transcribed the interview responses and collected data from the survey concerning the issues in their real-world situation (Yin, 2009; Creswell et al., 2016). The study relied on the questionnaire-survey questions that featured the field teams' contribution and participation to express their opinions, experiences and attitudes relating to the research context and subject matter. The semi-structured interviews were designed to explain the results of quantitative, help make comparable data and enable flexibility that requires rich and detailed data from the supervisors and managers featured in the interview sessions.

These data collection techniques generated valuable and rich data that assisted in creating more constructs about the adoption of blockchain technology in asset maintenance management. The quantitative survey assisted in conducting the root-cause analysis of the identified problems based on the variables. The quantitative survey was used to analyse the correlation between the variables and the features of blockchain technology based on the respondent's perspective of the effects of blockchain technology in asset maintenance management practices. Thus, this process performed a descriptive analysis, using the survey to collect and analyse the data. For instance, the semi-structured interview was reviewed in a thematic format using Nvivo to explain the themes related to the subject matter. These themes were also aligned to the employed case during the synthesis stage with a comparative evaluation of the blockchain technology features.

3.1.1 The Case Study

IHS Towers focuses on enabling a connected world that strives to deliver infrastructure assets that support telecom services that bridge the gap between businesses and customers across its operating environment. IHS employs contemporary technology to improve its customers' experience and meet their service level agreement (SLA) and key performance indicators (KPI). Digitalised asset management process is a key area in maintaining these telecom infrastructure assets.

Therefore, this study focuses on using IHS operations in the south-south regions of Nigeria as a case study. This decision is based on the insight from Yin (2009) that a case study involves a details research of a specific phenomenon, event, individual, group or organisation in other to generate a detailed, in-depth, multifaceted understanding of complex problems in its real-life context. This study's case study will be guided by the tenets of qualitative and quantitative methodology using structured questionnaires and semi-structured interviews for collecting data from the selected participants, who are directly and indirectly involved in asset management in this context.

Additionally, the study ensures that efficient asset maintenance practices are the driving forces behind the study's use of BCT features of transparency, trust, security, and immutable factual evidence. These characteristics of BCT are the main motivation behind the BCT adoption planned in this study.

3.1.2 Research Method

The main justification behind the proposed method is based on the complexity of the explored phenomenon, with highlights on the dynamic operating context—infrastructure challenges, unstable, irregular and unreliability power supply, which is an appropriate method for understanding and examining the effects. Additionally, this research subject matter is novel, and many telecom operations in emerging markets could consider attempts at adopting or exploring blockchain technology in their asset maintenance management practices. Therefore, telecom service providers in emerging economies are under increasing pressure to maintain affordability while ensuring fast, reliable, and pervasive network availability. The pent-up demand for digital services and eroding unit prices of data characteristics this temporal shift. For telecom asset-managed providers, these paradigm shifts present dilemmatic adoptions of performance, ensuring continuous and high infrastructural and asset functionality, performance and cost management. Different asset maintenance approaches could be used to manage the delivery of persistent asset performance.

While most research has examined blockchain in industries like financial markets and monitoring and control of urban infrastructure, to the best of the study's knowledge to date, there is no evidence to demonstrate the use of BCT for sustainable infrastructure asset maintenance in the telecoms domain of emerging markets, predominantly in Nigeria. The study then provides a prerequisites-decision framework based on its decentralised distributed ledger functions by undertaking an empirical study to gather, analyse, and present more findings regarding these blockchain functions, performance and cost optimisation, asset functionalities and attributes, and the external organisational factors leveraging for sustainable infrastructure asset maintenance with the use-case in the telecoms domain (Grijalvo et al., 2020; Azmi et al., 2022; Joshi et al., 2023). Further, in alignment with scientific discourse, our study supports asset management researchers and practitioners in aligning the provided prerequisites-decision framework with areas requiring the development and integration of domain-specific functional analysis and maturity model frameworks to effectively guide the inheritance and operationalisation of the extensive intrinsic capabilities contained in blockchain technologies for the maintenance of telecom infrastructure assets.

3.2 Research Strategy—Mixed Method Approach

The research design or strategy is the master plan, framework, or roadmap that delineates, coordinates and enhances a study (Hirose & Creswell, 2023). Thus, this selected research design set the direction for the study to address research questions, data collection, analysis, and findings. The study adopts a mixed method to achieve this study's objectives, which comprises the integration of qualitative and quantitative data and techniques to develop theories about and explain the impact of blockchain on sustainable asset maintenance in the telecoms sector in emerging markets (Creswell, 2021).

This mixed method approach starts with data collection and analysis from quantitative techniques and continues with qualitative data collection and analysis. Given the quantitative data findings, insights and perspectives from the qualitative data can be used to explain the obtained results. Thus, the study aims to collect data from quantitative and qualitative to identify the reliability and feasibility of employing blockchain technology for sustainable asset maintenance management in emerging markets.

The first phase of the quantitative techniques involves a systematic exploration of the extant literature on blockchain technology on asset maintenance and asset management through a systematic literature review. The results demonstrated an absence of qualitative insight to endorse or refute the theoretical model. Thus, to address this identified gap, the study performed both positivist and interpretivist paradigms that are deductive and inductive (Creswell & Clark, 2017); therefore, the combination of these paradigms will assist the study with a complete understanding of the subject matter.

Thus, the deliberate and systematic usage of mixed methods, which constitutes the research foundation used in this study, merges the strengths and limitations of several techniques and mechanisms, resulting in an integrated or detailed framework and model.

3.3 Analysis of Collected Data

In striving for effective asset maintenance activities and other unethical practices, this study collects and evaluates the opinions and views of field technicians, supervisors, and managers with about 2 to 3 years of experience in their respective clusters, regions, and domains residing in emerging markets. The response incorporates subjective and objective measures suggesting that asset-managed telecom infrastructure organisations must integrate a robust, automated, self-governing feature embedding BCT to enhance the asset reliability and functionality and efficient asset management practice that must self-regulate and perform self-healing activities without human intervention.

This research article is reinforced by an extensive literature review, gaining valuable insights from digitalised technologies through the Internet of Things (IoT), telecoms, and Data Centers with the emerging markets stipulating the improvement of reliability and privacy requirements with the telecom infrastructure must self-regulate and form self-being activities with very minimal human interface and intervention.

The data is collected through structured questionnaires, surveys, and semi-structured interviews and presented concerning their perspectives and recommendations on aspects of implementation. It is assessed using SPSS AMOS and thematic analysis using NVivo. Additionally, these dimensions are rooted in resilience, human factors, operating cost, and operational difficulty. The systematic literature review was used to support the design of the framework from both theoretical and conceptual perspectives based on theory and practice.

Accordingly providing a more structure for implementing a digitalised asset management process, reducing and addressing asset maintenance challenges, such as monitoring and tracking asset activities effectively and in real-time. This concern involves tracking monitoring and tracking asset functionality and condition, maintenance records and optimising performance ensuring that these activities are properly and efficiently implemented and performed.

Data Collection Process: A deductive strategy assisted the study in developing and presenting blockchain's impact on sustainable asset maintenance. Firstly, a qualitative research method was used to understand the perspectives of the study population. In an ongoing quantitative study, qualitative data was used as either the primary or fundamental input (Azungah, 2018; Creswell, 2021), which formed the basis for developing the questionnaire deployed in the empirical stage of the study.

A non-probability sampling approach was used, and a purposive sample of 65 participants with detailed knowledge and experience in asset management in a telecoms environment (Acharya et al., 2013) was used. The sample configuration also assisted the study in understanding the function or depth dimension based on full self-actualisation, achieving a thorough analysis of the attributes, weaknesses, strengths, and individualities of the intercepts, experiences, and interests of each participant.

4 Findings and Discussion

The findings from the study and the analysis were arranged according to the research objectives for easy understanding, starting with addressing the research question, which is to determine the effectiveness of blockchain for asset maintenance management in the telecoms domain. The overwhelming answers obtained from the survey and the interviews reveal the importance of the efficacy of blockchain, based on their characteristics of transparent, secured and smart contracts using the technology for the telecoms domain. This outcome shows that the participants are correctly aware that blockchain is important for asset maintenance management and promoting sustainability in developing markets.

The explanations for the result are that it prevents deliberate manipulation of asset maintenance activities and records, real-time escalation of unforeseen failures, digitalised maintenance scheduling and remote resolutions of predicted faults. Therefore, the adoption of this technology will reduce unethical practices, unauthorised maintenance activities and other irregularities related to physical and logical assets maintenance management practices.

4.1 *The Quantitative Insights*

The result from the quantitative analysis indicates that blockchain technology shows significant considerations and differences with a p-value of < 0.01, which signifies the importance of blockchain technology's features of transparency, real-time, and immutability are denominators that enhance asset maintenance management through real-time monitoring and tracking of asset functionality and optimal performance.

From the results, blockchain, p-value < 0.01; transparency, p-value < 0.01; real-time, p-value < 0.01 and immutability, p-value < 0.01. These results imply that the asset maintenance activities used these blockchain technology features to address the identified problems that impact efficient asset maintenance management practices. Thus, this study recommends the adoption of blockchain technology since it provides visibility in monitoring and tracking asset maintenance activities and functionality.

4.1.1 Descriptive Analysis with SPPS

The data analysis predicts the various independent and dependent variable values and correlations based on the output from the regression analysis. Table 1 model summary presents the r-squared value of 0.914, representing a high ratio of the variance in the dependent variable that the independent variables jointly defined. This output means that the independent variables can describe the variance in the dependent variable.

Additionally, the F change value indicates a substantial relationship concerning the independent and dependent variables for the reason that the p-value of $< .0001$ is

Table 1 Model summary

Model summary									
Model	R	R square	Adjusted R square	Std. error of the estimate	Change statistics				
					R square change	F change	df1	df2	Sig. F Change
1	.956[a]	0.914	0.905	0.396740670328857	0.914	98.603	10	93	0.000

a. Predictors: (Constant), Immutability, PDM, Real-time, Traceability, Visibility, Trust, Security, SAMP, BCT, Transparency

within the accepted value of 0.05 and is considered statistically significantly based on Kline (2023) assertion on the common threshold of the accepted p-value, which signifies that 5% of the times, the model will falsely reject the null hypothesis.

Field (2018) noted that the value of the adjusted r-squared is usually lower than the r-squared. Therefore, the adjusted r-squared in this model is 0.905. In contrast, the standard error, which represents the average distance that the observed values fall within the regression line, is 0.3967 units from the regression line.

Table 2 presents the ANOVA, which indicates the degree of freedom (df), the sum of square and F statistics, the overall significance of the regression model, and the values that explain each parameter (Kline, 2023). The degree of freedom is the value equal to the sum of observations known as the data set or respondents—1. There are one hundred and four observations. Thus, the total degree of freedom is 104 – 1 = 103.

Similarly, the residual degrees of freedom are the sum equal to the total df – regression df, which is 103 – 93 = 10. These outputs and values mean the square is calculated by the regression number of a square divided by the regression of 155.204/ 10 = 15.520. At the same time, the residual means square is computed by the residual value of square divided by residual df, 14.638/0.157 = 93.235.

The F statistics are calculated as regression mean squared divided by residual means square. They indicate whether the regression model shows a suitable fit for the data compared to the model that consists of no independent variables; the F

Table 2 ANOVA

ANOVA[a]						
Model		Sum of squares	df	Mean square	F	Sig
1	Regression	155.204	10	15.520	98.603	<.001[b]
	Residual	14.638	93	0.157		
	Total	169.843	103			

a. Dependent Variable: IAMM

b. Predictors: (Constant), Immutability, PDM, Real-time, Traceability, Visibility, Trust, Security, SAMP, BCT, Transparency statistics for this model are 98.603/0.157 = 628.055. The importance of sig (p-value) indicates the significance of the regression model (Kline, 2023), as the model p-value is < 0.001, which shows the variables truly improve the goodness fit of the model (Field, 2018), and the model is statistically positive and significant.

From the independent variables from Table 3, the p-values show the average expected values for the infrastructure asset maintenance management (IAAM) variable when the variables are equal to zero (0). Thus, the coefficient for sustainable asset management practices is equal to −0.113, with a p-value of 0.01; blockchain variables coefficients are equal to 0.373 and a p-value of 0.00; transparency is 0.637 and a p-value of 0.001; real-time is 0.078 with a p-value of 0.01, and the immutability coefficient value is −0.067 with a p-value of 0.03.

These outputs and values mean that these independent variables improve infrastructure asset maintenance management, as the BCT coefficient value of 0.373 with a p-value of 0.00 indicates this variable as substantially significant and statistically different from zero (0).

In contrast, the predictive maintenance strategy has a coefficient value of 0.037 with a p-value of 0.41, trust 0.042 with a p-value of 0.182, security −0.009, with a p-value of 0.782; visibility −0.022 with a p-value of 0.486 and traceability −0.028 with a p-value of 0.367. These variables are not statistically significant, with the dependent variable infrastructure asset maintenance management based on the various p-values that are above the acceptable threshold.

Table 3 Coefficient

Coefficients[a]

Model		Unstandardised coefficients		Standardised coefficients	t	Sig	95.0% Confidence Interval for B	
		B	Std. error	Beta			Lower bound	Upper bound
1	(Constant)	−3.353	1.145		−2.930	0.004	−5.626	−1.080
	SAMP	−1.309	0.537	−0.113	−2.440	0.017	−2.375	−0.244
	PDM	0.293	0.359	0.037	0.816	0.417	−0.420	1.005
	BCT	0.613	0.106	0.373	5.767	0.000	0.402	0.824
	Transparency	6.467	0.855	0.637	7.560	0.000	4.769	8.166
	Trust	0.058	0.043	0.042	1.345	0.182	−0.028	0.143
	Security	−0.025	0.090	−0.009	−0.278	0.782	−0.204	0.154
	Real-time	0.066	0.027	0.078	2.437	0.017	0.012	0.120
	Visibility	−0.257	0.368	−0.022	−0.699	0.486	v0.987	0.473
	Traceability	−0.362	0.400	−0.028	−0.906	0.367	−1.157	0.432
	Immutability	−0.114	0.054	−0.067	−2.110	0.038	−0.222	−0.007

a. Dependent Variable: IAMM

From Table 3 coefficients, the t-stat for the BCT is 5.767/0.106 = 54.405, transparency 7.560/0.855 = 8.842 and real-time 2.437/0.027 = 90.259. The p-value related to the t-stat is statistically significant. However, the p-values for the other independent variables are not statistically significant because they are above the accepted value of 0.05. The insight from the independent variables that are not statistically significant signifies that the variables tend to decrease as the dependent variable increases.

Additionally, the 95% confidence interval for the statistically significant independent variables, such as BCT, is (0.402, 0.824), transparency (4.769, 8.166), and real-time (0.012, 0.120). The model observed that these independent variables' confidence intervals are lower, and upper sums do not include zero, which means that the model is quite confident that the actual and accurate values for the coefficient of the BCT are non-zero, implying a positive value.

However, the 95% confidence interval for the other non-statistically significant variables includes zero values, which means that the actual coefficients' numbers do not predict the dependent variable.

4.1.2 Structural Equation Modelling—AMOS

The standardised estimate of the relationship between the independent and dependent variables. The double-headed arrows between the boxes represent the corresponding values and correlation of each variable (see Appendix 1). For instance, BCT = (−.03) Immutability + (−.03) Realtime + (−.05) Security + (−.19) Traceability + (5.15) Transparency + (0.01) Trust + (−.26) Visibility + (1) d1; IAMM = (1.24) BCT + (1.37) PDM + (1.06) SAMP + (1) d4 PDM = (0.13) BCT + (1) d2; SAMP = (0.05) BCT + (1) d3 (see Appendix 1).

Additionally, the various variables outputs are; Immutability <> Transparency (0.01); Immutability <> Trust (0.11); Immutability <> ecurity (0.01); Immutability <> ealtime (0.02); Immutability <> isibility (−.01); Immutability <> raceability (−.01); Traceability <> ransparency (0.00); Traceability <> rust (−.01); Traceability <> Security (0.00); Traceability <> Realtime (0.00); Traceability <> Visibility (0.00); Visibility <> Transparency (0.00); Visibility <> Trust (−.01); Visibility <> Security (0.01); Visibility <> Realtime (0.00); Realtime <> Transparency (0.00); Realtime <> Trust (−.04); Realtime <> Security (−.16); Security <> Transparency (−.01); Security <> Trust (−.01); Trust <> Transparency (0.01).

4.1.3 Estimate Regression Weight

The level of significance for regression in Fig. 1 indicates that the probability of obtaining a critical ratio as large as 15.405 in absolute value is less than 0.001. In other words, the regression weight for the independent variable Transparency in the prediction of BCT is notably different from zero at the 0.001 level (two-tailed). These assertions are correct for large samples under suitable assumptions.

Estimates (Group number 1 - Default model)

Scalar Estimates (Group number 1 - Default model)

Maximum Likelihood Estimates

Regression Weights: (Group number 1 - Default model)

			Estimate	S.E.	C.R.	P	Label
BCT	<---	Immutability	-0.032	0.056	-0.566	0.571	par_22
BCT	<---	Traceability	-0.191	0.416	-0.461	0.645	par_23
BCT	<---	Visibility	-0.259	0.382	-0.679	0.497	par_24
BCT	<---	Real-time	-0.031	0.028	-1.127	0.26	par_25
BCT	<---	Security	-0.048	0.094	-0.511	0.61	par_26
BCT	<---	Trust	0.011	0.044	0.257	0.797	par_27
BCT	<---	Transparency	5.15	0.334	15.405	***	par_28
SAMP	<---	BCT	0.053	0.013	4.112	***	par_29
PDM	<---	BCT	0.133	0.015	8.611	***	par_30
IAMM	<---	SAMP	1.058	0.494	2.142	0.032	par_31
IAMM	<---	PDM	1.373	0.412	3.33	***	par_32
IAMM	<---	BCT	1.237	0.089	13.931	***	par_33

Fig. 1 Estimate regression weight

In addition, the likelihood of reaching a critical ratio as large as 4.112 in absolute value is less than 0.001, thus making the regression weight for BCT in the prediction of stainable asset management practices (SAMP) considerably different from zero at the 0.001 level (two-tailed). The possibility of finding a critical ratio as large as 8.611 in absolute value is less than 0.001, which means that the regression weight for BCT in the prediction of PDM is notably different from zero at the 0.001 level (two-tailed).

The likelihood of obtaining a critical ratio as large as 3.33 in absolute value is less than 0.001. In other words, the regression weight for PDM in the prediction of IAMM is notably different from zero at the 0.001 level (two-tailed).

The likelihood of reaching a critical ratio as large as 13.931 in absolute value is less than 0.001, which suggests that the regression weight for BCT in the prediction of IAMM is substantively different from zero at the 0.001 level (two-tailed). In contrast, the likelihood of finding a critical ratio as large as 2.142 in perfect value is.032, which signifies that the regression weight for SAMP in the prediction of IAMM is significantly separate from zero at the 0.05 level (two-tailed).

These assertions are almost true for large samples under appropriate assumptions based on the amount of change in the dependent variable IAAM attributed to these individual single standard deviations worth of modification in the independent variables (Hair et al., 2018; Kline, 2023). These regression weights influence the observation of the computed model parameters.

4.1.4 Covariance

Figure 2 indicates that the likelihood of obtaining a critical ratio as large as 2.26 in absolute value is.024. In other words, the covariance between security and real-time is substantially different from zero at the 0.05 level (two-tailed). These statements are almost true for large samples under suitable assumptions. Kline (2023) noted that covariance estimates and tests the relationships between the independent and dependent variables and the unseen structures.

The estimate of covariance between transparency and immutability is 0.008, which means that an increase in transparency is an increase in immutability; both independent variables are said to have a positive covariance. This output describes the changes between the two variables, such that a change in transparency is equal to a shift in immutability, as indicated in Fig. 2. In contrast, the covariance between Trust and Traceability is estimated to be −.009, which signifies a negative covariance with an inverse relationship between trust and traceability, that when trust increases, traceability tends to decrease.

Covariances: (Group number 1 - Default model)

			Estimate	S.E.	C.R.	P	Label
Transparency	<-->	Immutability	0.008	0.009	0.871	0.384	par_1
Immutability	<-->	Trust	0.107	0.07	1.532	0.125	par_2
Immutability	<-->	Security	0.008	0.034	0.243	0.808	par_3
Immutability	<-->	Real-time	0.023	0.11	0.207	0.836	par_4
Immutability	<-->	Visibility	-0.009	0.008	-1.136	0.256	par_5
Immutability	<-->	Traceability	-0.007	0.007	-0.928	0.354	par_6
Transparency	<-->	Traceability	-0.002	0.001	-1.267	0.205	par_7
Trust	<-->	Traceability	-0.009	0.009	-1.006	0.314	par_8
Security	<-->	Traceability	0.001	0.004	0.245	0.807	par_9
Real-time	<-->	Traceability	0	0.015	-0.028	0.978	par_10
Visibility	<-->	Traceability	-0.001	0.001	-0.918	0.358	par_11
Transparency	<-->	Visibility	-0.002	0.001	-1.135	0.256	par_12
Trust	<-->	Visibility	-0.011	0.01	-1.095	0.273	par_13
Security	<-->	Visibility	0.009	0.005	1.707	0.088	par_14
Real-time	<-->	Visibility	-0.004	0.016	-0.237	0.813	par_15
Transparency	<-->	Real-time	0	0.019	0.024	0.981	par_16
Trust	<-->	Real-time	-0.043	0.139	-0.309	0.757	par_17
Security	<-->	Real-time	-0.157	0.069	-2.26	0.024	par_18
Transparency	<-->	Security	-0.011	0.006	-1.824	0.068	par_19
Trust	<-->	Security	-0.008	0.042	-0.187	0.852	par_20
Transparency	<-->	Trust	0.015	0.012	1.275	0.202	par_21

Fig. 2 Covariances

4.1.5 Correlation

The estimate of the correlation between immutability and security is 0.024, immutability and real-time is 0.020, security and traceability are 0.024, and transparency and trust are 0.127 (see Fig. 3). For instance, blockchain's characteristics, such as trust, security, transparency, traceability, and immutability, make it an easier and better platform to use based on the multiple ledgers that cannot be manipulated easily.

The tamper-proof system needs to be more rigorous than the traditional centralised database. The transparency proposed by the participants as one of the key features of blockchain in real-time raises operators' confidence that things are in full compliance as they are connected with the assets of their industries (Hellenborn et al., 2024; Hemdan et al., 2023).

Additionally, the blockchain has validated permanent authenticity when used for transaction purposes (Joshi et al., 2023; Li et al., 2021, 2022). Blockchain and

Correlations: (Group number 1 - Default model)

			Estimate
Transparency	<-->	Immutability	0.086
Immutability	<-->	Trust	0.153
Immutability	<-->	Security	0.024
Immutability	<-->	Real-time	0.02
Immutability	<-->	Visibility	-0.113
Immutability	<-->	Traceability	-0.092
Transparency	<-->	Traceability	-0.126
Trust	<-->	Traceability	-0.1
Security	<-->	Traceability	0.024
Real-time	<-->	Traceability	-0.003
Visibility	<-->	Traceability	-0.091
Transparency	<-->	Visibility	-0.113
Trust	<-->	Visibility	-0.109
Security	<-->	Visibility	0.171
Real-time	<-->	Visibility	-0.023
Transparency	<-->	Real-time	0.002
Trust	<-->	Real-time	-0.03
Security	<-->	Real-time	-0.228
Transparency	<-->	Security	-0.183
Trust	<-->	Security	-0.018
Transparency	<-->	Trust	0.127

Fig. 3 Correlation

its smart contract are indeed the perfect combination for maintaining assets in the telecoms domain.

The technology is unstructured, unchanging, and intelligent, which can only provide a uniquely structured asset maintenance smart contract. In addition, blockchain is the closest solution to a well-performing, secure network, a part of the infrastructure that is essential to asset maintenance when compared to the centralised database, which has its ups and downs.

The decentralisation of the network reduces the amount of conflict in the middleware and infrastructure platform and enables the network to remain secure from different angles. Blockchain can also quickly inform maintenance field team members of approaching, scheduled or unprogrammed maintenance needs. Thus, Zheng et al. (2023) argued that the use of BCT can ensure that only the appropriate field team members perform maintenance at the suitable and scheduled period or cycle.

Efficiency Gains—as the BCT and network eliminates the need for an intermediary, it can reduce operating costs and substantially enhance the efficiency and security of maintenance data sharing. In contrast to conventional maintenance strategy, which may encounter issues such as manual detection of outages, scheduling and resolution with more human interface and interventions, when compared with digitalised predictive maintenance management that adopts blockchain-driven characteristics, it tends to be more efficient and reliable. Furthermore, immutability can be identified as an important factor in the blockchain's data access cost efficiency (Li et al., 2022; Sadri et al., 2023).

The cost-effectiveness of maintaining and keeping network data also plays an influential part in its sustainability, such as documentation, instead of just the risk or subjective honesty of the field member, resulting from team and peer interaction. Cross-organisational inconsistency in understanding and transparency is eradicated; as such, mistrust between the members is distributed, and the regulatory and implementation practices can be reduced. Such elevated transparency caused by fundamental transparency can be an advantage to the telecom industry.

For instance, the blockchain enables team members to have real-time insight and knowledge of asset maintenance management activities and processes. Additionally, BCT is a consensus-based technology; the data inside each new block relies on consensus capability to capture truly inclusive information about the infrastructure asset condition and physical health, operational functionality concerning the underpinning for developing an efficient, quicker, and effective predictive maintenance process. In the context of this study, the blockchain will deliver unequalled perceptive characteristics in the asset maintenance process that streamline asset operations and accessibility to such efficient maintenance practice.

4.2 *Qualitative Results*

The key theme obtained from the qualitative semi-structured interviews was the characteristics and understanding of the critical adoption of blockchain technology in the telecom domain of sustainable asset maintenance management, which is the aim of this study. The related sub-themes were the expectations and perspectives of key stakeholders from the context of sustainable asset maintenance management in the telecom domain, considered a very significant practice and foundation.

The stakeholders analysed and evaluated the expectations of adopting a predictive-based maintenance strategy over the conventional approach of preventive-based maintenance, whereby the effectiveness of predictive-based maintenance on asset functionality, optimal performance and operating cost reduction is statistically proven to have more benefits and effectiveness than the conventional preventive-based maintenance strategy in sustainable asset maintenance management practices. Thus, the vision of how to implement these maintenance strategies into blockchain technology for sustainable asset maintenance management practices was considered useful and applicable. Therefore, the qualitative results revealed a detailed perspective of the study, which improved the strength and usefulness of the study.

4.2.1 Operating Cost Reductions

BCT has been demonstrated in this study to assist with operating cost reductions related to routine and non-routine maintenance activities and the intermittent requirements to maintain the sustainable state condition of telecom assets. From the findings of the study, the following are the established approaches that BCT can assist with operating cost reductions: monitoring and tracking maintenance activities, which eradicate deliberate manipulation of services materials, and inputting wrong generator run hours, decentralised storage, authenticity verification or connecting quick telecoms asset maintenance with maintenance team members. Optimised routes of maintenance that include exploring the possibility of reducing human interface and interventions through remote access to resolution, reducing drive time and physical resolutions of outages.

It has been clarified that integrated Internet of Things (IoT) nodes have to be used in building blockchain solutions (Hellenborn et al., 2024; Sadri et al., 2023). With BCT and IoT, this study has shown how telecom asset maintenance practices have been affected. Instead of undergoing complex, lengthy mean-time-to-repair (MTTR), the decentralised features can be used to address this concern, by ensuring service quality and replacement of these spares are implemented accordingly..

5 Conclusion

This study has explored the perceived adoption of blockchain technology in improving sustainable asset maintenance management in the telecom domain in emerging markets. However, the study also mapped the primary areas of asset maintenance management that are potentially influenced by blockchain technology. The study draws on the asset maintenance strategy of predictive-based maintenance strategy as factors that could significantly affect the adoption of blockchain technology in the telecom domain. Thus, the reviewed extant literature and data findings on sustainable asset maintenance management in the telecom domain in emerging markets show significant insights into how blockchain technology features can change operations and maintenance practices. The studies by Sadri et al. (2023), and Hellenborn et al. (2024) establish this technology as a decentralised system that improves efficiency in transactions, incidents or events and activities based on transparency and trust, which are important for sustainable asset management practices.

This study highlights the multifaceted advantages of blockchain technology, including its enabling of smart systems and traceability, which are necessary for managing and maintaining intangible and tangible assets. This, in turn, promotes enhanced visibility in asset maintenance activities and minimises dependency on intermediaries and interventions. Additionally, Sadri et al. (2023), Joshi et al. (2023) and Zhang et al. (2023) added to this discourse by exploring blockchain technology's role in fostering sustainable asset management practices in various domains, where blockchain technology addresses immediate operations and maintenance challenges while aligning with wider sustainability objectives.

Accordingly, the study concludes that it provides a resolution to the growing request for managing infrastructure asset maintenance in developing markets. Blockchain, its inherent smart contract, and its services ultimately offer a workable and practical resolution to manage distributed telecom assets. The utilisation and adoption of BCT capture and document asset maintenance management practices through BCT features of traceable transactional activities related directly to individual asset functionality and performance conditions based on physical activities. This result is attained by implementing exceptional smart contracts programmed to ensure asset maintenance management sustainability while managing maintenance activities problems prone to non-automation of tasks and deliberate manipulation of records and activities.

The study develops a blockchain-based resolution, the sustainable asset maintenance resolution, for adoption in the telecom domain in the developing market. The resolution seeks to provide an immutable and secure structure using a digitalised predictive maintenance strategy in asset maintenance activities. This developed structure would enable field team access to real-time updates on asset maintenance activities, monitoring and tracking functionality and performance, as the developed framework would address these asset maintenance management needs and provide a significant number of improvements in the way these tower organisations manage their infrastructures. While a need for an all-inclusive resolution to maintain base station assets efficiently without high means-time-to-repair (MTTR) of downtime.

Adopting BCT-based solutions in telecom asset management is poised to revolutionise the telecom industry and drive significant advancement to sustainability and efficiency. This insight also means that the transformative approach of adopting BCT will use a new area of transparency, security, trust, immutability, accountability and cost efficiency, empowering tower organisations to optimise their operation and maintenance to minimise environmental impact. Thus, as BCT continues to evolve, the study expects more innovative and digitalised adoption and resolutions to emerge, shaping the future of sustainable asset maintenance practices in developing countries.

5.1 Theoretical Contribution

The theoretical contribution addresses the adoption of blockchain technology for the focused, sustainable asset maintenance management of the corpus of knowledge in the telecom domain in an emerging market in the field of passive infrastructure asset maintenance activities. The study is believed to the among the first articles to address issues of sustainable asset maintenance management in the context thus the important question of how the adoption of blockchain technology in asset maintenance management enhances asset maintenance efficiency, which contributes to asset functionality, optimal performance and costs reduction, as the study depends exclusively on an extensive extant literature review to support this work.

Additionally, the study provides specific instances and a detailed understanding of how, when, and what features of blockchain technology can be an enabler for efficient, sustainable asset maintenance management by offering empirical evidence based on the results. The study extends the literature by identifying some of the difficulties that telecom providers face in creating value in this telecom domain.

5.2 Future Direction of Study

The study provided more detailed insight into adopting BCT in telecoms asset maintenance management practice. Future research can expand the testing of these use cases in pilot projects. Based on our findings and critical analysis of existing research, the value of BCT was highlighted as a future research direction in academic and practical settings.

Blockchain is an evolving technology that is driving attention because value is derived directly from these attention shifts. However, even though this technology has been attracting attention, there has yet to be a generally accepted definition of what it actually is or does. Blockchain was designed to be a tool that only generates and ensures value. These moves in value are attained through the consensus-based process that is essential for the addition of a new block in the blockchain spaces.

Appendix 1: Structural Equation Modelling—Pathway Diagram

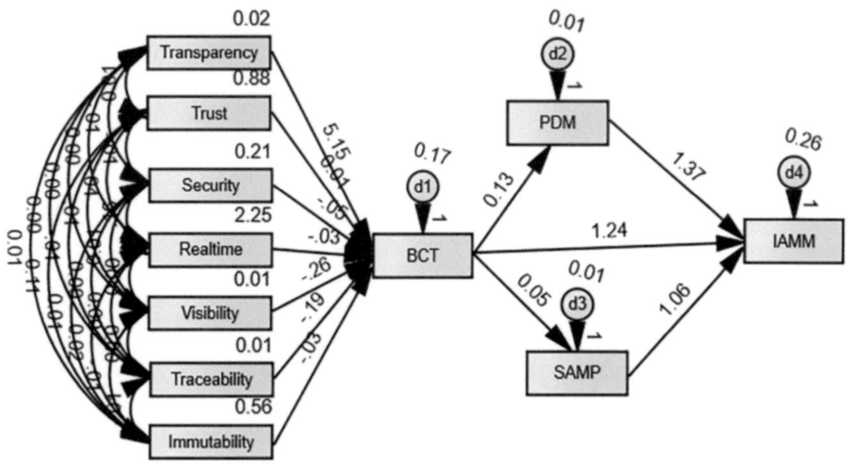

References

Acharya, A. S., Prakash, A., Saxena, P., & Nigam, A. (2013). Sampling: Why and how of it. *Indian Journal of Medical Specialties, 4*(2), 330–333.

Achouch, M., Dimitrova, M., Ziane, K., Sattarpanah Karganroudi, S., Dhouib, R., Ibrahim, H., & Adda, M. (2022). On predictive maintenance in industry 4.0: Overview, models, and challenges. *Applied Sciences, 12*(16), 8081.

Adelekan, O. A., Ilugbusi, B. S., Adisa, O., Franca, O., & Ndubuisi, L. (2024). Predictive maintenance in oil and gas facilities, leveraging ai for asset integrity management. *Engineering Science & Technology Journal*, *5*(2), 272–287.

Afraz, N., Wilhelmi, F., Ahmadi, H., & Ruffini, M. (2023). Blockchain and smart contracts for telecommunications: Requirements vs. cost analysis. *IEEE Access*.

Ahmed, A., Abdullah, S., Bukhsh, M., Ahmad, I., & Mushtaq, Z. (2022). An energy-efficient data aggregation mechanism for IoT secured by blockchain. *IEEE Access, 10*, 11404–11419.

Al-Dhlan, K. A., Alreshidi, H. A., Pervez, S., Paraveen, Z., Zeki, A. M., Sid Ahmed, N. M., Alshammari, E.J., & Lingamuthu, V. (2022). Customizable encryption algorithms to manage data assets based on blockchain technology in smart city. *Mathematical Problems in Engineering, 2022*(1), 8996629.

Al-Dhlan, K., Alreshidi, H., Pervez, S., Paraveen, Z., Zeki, A., Ahmed, N., & Lingamuthu, V. (2022). Customisable encryption algorithms to manage data assets based on blockchain technology in smart cities. Mathematical Problems in Engineering, 1–8. Retrieved July 20, 2024, from https://doi.org/10.1155/2022/8996629.

Al-Emari, S., Anbar, M., Sanjalawe, Y., Manickam, S., & Hasbullah, I. (2022). Intrusion detection systems using blockchain technology: a review, issues and challenges. *Computer Systems*

Science and Engineering, 40(1), 87–112. Retrieved July 20, 2024, from https://doi.org/10.32604/csse.2022.017941

Amadi-Echendu, J., (2021). *Managing engineered assets.* Springer International Publishing.

Amadi-Echendu, J., Botlholo, G., & Raman, K. (2021). Condition assessment of engineered assets in the era of Society 5.0. In *World Congress on Engineering Asset Management* (pp. 335–343). Cham: Springer International Publishing.

Amrani, H., Micucci, D., & Napoletano, P. (2021). Personalised models in human activity recognition using deep learning. In *2020 25th International Conference on Pattern Recognition (ICPR)* (pp. 9682–9688). IEEE.

Ayamolowo, O. J., Buraimoh, E., Salau, A. O., & Dada, J. O. (2019). Nigeria electricity power supply system: the past, present and the future. In *2019 IEEE PES/IAS PowerAfrica* (pp. 64–69). IEEE.

Azmi, N. A., Sweis, G., Sweis, R., & Sammour, F. (2022). Exploring implementation of blockchain for the supply chain resilience and replicate sustainability of the construction industry in Saudi Arabia. *Sustainability, 14*(11), 6427.

Azungah, T. (2018). Qualitative research: Deductive and inductive approaches to data analysis. *Qualitative Research Journal, 18*(4), 383–400.

Both, W. B. (2017). Three key elements of physical asset management. Retrieved August 25, 2024, from https://core.ac.uk/download/132283292.pdf

Campbell, J. D., Jardine, A. K., McGlynn, J., & Barry, D. M. eds. (2024). *Asset management excellence: optimising equipment lifecycle decisions.* CRC Press.

Chen, C., Zhu, Z. H., Shi, J., Lu, N., & Jiang, B. (2021). Dynamic predictive maintenance scheduling using deep learning ensemble for system health prognostics. *IEEE Sensors Journal, 21*(23), 26878–26891.

Creswell, J. W., & Poth, C. N. (2016). *Qualitative inquiry and research design: Choosing among five approaches.* Sage publications.

Creswell, J. W., & Clark, V. L. P. (2017). *Designing and conducting mixed methods research.* Sage publications.

Creswell, J. W. (2021). *A concise introduction to mixed methods research.* SAGE publications.

Crespo Marquez, A., Gomez Fernandez, J. F., Martínez-Galán Fernández, P., & Guillen Lopez, A. (2020). Maintenance management through intelligent asset management platforms (IAMP). Emerging factors, key impact areas and data models. *Energies, 13*(15), 3762.

De Jonge, B., & Scarf, P. A. (2020). A review on maintenance optimisation. *European Journal of Operational Research, 285*(3), 805–824.

Field, A. (2018). *Discovering statistics using IBM SPSS statistics* (5th ed.). SAGE Publications Ltd.

Florian, E., Sgarbossa, F., & Zennaro, I. (2021). Machine learning-based predictive maintenance: A cost-oriented model for implementation. *International Journal of Production Economics, 236*, Article 108114.

Frolov, V., Ma, L., Sun, Y., & Bandara, W. (2010). Identifying core functions of asset management. *Definitions, concepts and scope of engineering asset management*, pp.19–30.

Grijalvo Martín, M., Pacios Álvarez, A., Ordieres-Meré, J., Villalba-Díez, J., & Morales-Alonso, G. (2020). New business models from prescriptive maintenance strategies aligned with sustainable development goals. *Sustainability, 13*(1), 216.

Gupta, S., Drave, V. A., Dwivedi, Y. K., Baabdullah, A. M., & Ismagilova, E. (2020). Achieving superior organisational performance via big data predictive analytics: A dynamic capability view. *Industrial Marketing Management, 90*, 581–592.

Hair, J. F., Sarstedt, M., Ringle, C. M., & Gudergan, S. P. (2018). Advanced issues in partial least squares structural equation modeling (PLS-SEM). Thousand Oaks, CA: Sage. Available [online] from https://doi.org/10.3926/oss.37 (Accessed: 20th April 2025).

Hamasha, M., Bani-Irshid, A., Al Mashaqbeh, S., Shwaheen, G., Al Qadri, Shbool, M., Muathen, D., Ababneh, M., Harfoush, S., Albedoor, Q., & Al Bashir, A. (2023). Strategical selection of maintenance type under different conditions. Retrieved July 25, 2024, from https://ncb.nlm.nih.gov

Han, X., Wang, Z., Xie, M., He, Y., Li, Y., & Wang, W. (2021). Remaining useful life prediction and predictive maintenance strategies for multi-state manufacturing systems considering functional dependence. *Reliability Engineering and System Safety, 210*, Article 107560.

Hamdan, I. K., Sumarliah, E., & Fauziyah, F. (2022). A machine learning method to predict the technology adoption of blockchain in Palestinian firms. *International Journal of Emerging Markets, 17*(4), 1008–1029.

Hellenborn, B., Eliasson, O., Yitmen, I., & Sadri, H. (2024). Asset information requirements for blockchain-based digital twins: A data-driven predictive analytics perspective. *Smart and Sustainable Built Environment, 13*(1), 22–41.

Hemdan, E. E. D., El-Shafai, W., & Sayed, A. (2023). Integrating digital twins with IoT-based blockchain: Concept, architecture, challenges, and future scope. *Wireless Personal Communications, 131*(3), 2193–2216.

Hirose, M., & Creswell, J. W. (2023). Applying core quality criteria of mixed methods research to an empirical study. *Journal of Mixed Methods Research, 17*(1), 12–28.

Hu, J., & Chen, P. (2020). Predictive maintenance of systems subject to hard failure based on the proportional hazards model. *Reliability Engineering and System Safety, 196*, Article 106707.

Huang, J., You, J. X., Liu, H. C., & Song, M. S. (2020). Failure mode and effect analysis improvement: A systematic literature review and future research agenda. *Reliability Engineering and System Safety, 199*, Article 106885.

Huin Chin, H., Sabev Varbanov, P., Jaromir Klemes, J., Francis, D., Benjamin, M., & Tan, R. (2020). Asset maintenance optimisation approaches in the chemical and process industries–A review. Retrieved July 25, 2024, from https://ncbi.nlm.nih.gov.

Jimenez, J. J. M., Schwartz, S., Vingerhoeds, R., Grabot, B., & Salaün, M. (2020). Towards multi-model approaches to predictive maintenance: A systematic literature survey on diagnostics and prognostics. *Journal of Manufacturing Systems, 56*, 539–557.

Joshi, P., Tewari, V., Kumar, S., & Singh, A. (2023). Blockchain technology for sustainable development: A systematic literature review. *Journal of Global Operations and Strategic Sourcing, 16*(3), 683–717.

Kline, R. B. (2023). *Principles and practice of structural equation modelling*. Guilford publications.

Kuhn, T. S. (1997). *The structure of scientific revolutions* (Vol. 962). University of Chicago Press.

Li, L., Wang, Y., & Lin, K. Y. (2021). Preventive maintenance scheduling optimisation based on opportunistic production-maintenance synchronisation. *Journal of Intelligent Manufacturing, 32*(2), 545–558.

Li, H., Gao, P., Zhan, Y., & Tan, M. (2022). Blockchain technology empowers telecom network operations. *China Communications, 19*(1), 274–283.

Mangalathu, S., Hwang, S. H., & Jeon, J. S. (2020). Failure mode and effects analysis of R.C. members based on machine-learning-based SHapley Additive explanations (SHAP) approach. *Engineering Structures, 219*, 110927.

Martínez-Galán, P., Crespo, A., de la Fuente, A., & Guillén, A. (2020). A new model to compare intelligent asset management platforms (IAMP). *IFAC-StudysOnLine, 53*(3), 13–18.

Maletič, D., Maletič, M., Al-Najjar, B., & Gomišček, B. (2020). An analysis of physical asset management core practices and their influence on operational performance. *Sustainability, 12*(21), 9097.

Marquez, A. C., Fernandez, J. F. G., Fernández, P. M. G., Lopez, A. G. (2020). Maintenance management through intelligent asset management platforms (IAMP). Emerging factors, key impact areas and data models. *Energies, 13*(15), 3762.

National Population Commission (2024). 2024 Nigeria Demographic and Health Survey (NDHS) Report. https://nationalpopulation.gov.ng/publications.

NCC. (2019). Nigerian Communication Commission official page. Retrieved July 10, 2024, from https://www.ncc.gov.ng/.

NCC. (2023) Nigerian Communications Commission Annual Report. Available [online] from: https://www.ncc.gov.ng/(Accessed: 10th April 2025).

Parra, C., González-Prida, V., Candón, E., De la Fuente, A., Martínez-Galán, P., & Crespo, A. (2021). Integration of asset management standard ISO55000 with a maintenance management model. In *14th WCEAM proceedings* (pp. 189–200). Springer International Publishing.

Peters, E. L., & Roecker, J. A. (2021). Hybrid tracking of low snr targets. In *2021 IEEE Aerospace Conference (50100)* (pp. 1–6). IEEE.

Quatrini, E., Costantino, F., Di Gravio, G., & Patriarca, R. (2020). Condition-based maintenance—an extensive literature review. *Machines, 8*(2), 31.

Qin, J., Xi, Y., & Pedrycz, W. (2020). Failure mode and effects analysis (FMEA) for risk assessment based on interval type-2 fuzzy evidential reasoning method. *Applied Soft Computing, 89*, Article 106134.

Raj, A. S., Oliver, D. H., & Srinivas, Y. (2017). Geoelectrical data processing using neuro-fuzzy pattern recognition scheme for unambiguous subsurface modelling. *International Journal of Hydrology Science and Technology, 7*(4), 364–389.

Rejeb, A., Rejeb, K., Zrelli, I., Sule, E., & Iranmanesh, M. (2024). Blockchain technology in the renewable energy sector: A co-word analysis of academic discourse. Retrieved August 25, 2024, from https://ncbi.nlm.nih.gov.

Sanchez-Londono, D., Barbieri, G., & Fumagalli, L. (2023). Smart retrofitting in maintenance: A systematic literature review. *Journal of Intelligent Manufacturing, 34*(1), 1–19.

Sadeghi, M., Mahmoudi, A., & Deng, X. (2022). Adopting distributed ledger technology for the sustainable construction industry: evaluating the barriers using Ordinal Priority Approach. Retrieved August 25, 2024, from https://ncbi.nlm.nih.gov.

Sadri, H., Yitmen, I., Tagliabue, L. C., Westphal, F., Tezel, A., Taheri, A., & Sibenik, G., (2023). Integration of blockchain and digital twins in the smart built environment adopting disruptive technologies—a systematic review. *Sustainability 15*, 3713.

Saravanan, M., Behera, S., & Iyer, V. (2017). Smart contracts in mobile telecom networks. In *2017 23RD Annual International Conference in Advanced Computing and Communications (ADCOM)* (pp. 27–33). IEEE.

Simon, E. (2021). The effect of internal control on organisational performance in the telecommunications industry in South-South and Southeast Nigeria. *International Journal of Social Sciences, 4*(1), 78–97.

Su, X., & Wang, S. (2022). Research on model design and operation mechanism of enterprise blockchain digital system. *Scientific Reports, 12*(1). Retrieved July 20, 2024, from https://doi.org/10.1038/s41598-022-24796-0.

Sun, H., Yang, M., & Wang, H. (2022). Resilience-based approach to maintenance asset and operational cost planning. *Process Safety and Environmental Protection, 162*, 987–997.

Teoh, Y. K., Gill, S. S., & Parlikad, A. K. (2021). IoT and fog-computing-based predictive maintenance model for effective asset management in Industry 4.0 using machine learning. *IEEE Internet of Things Journal, 10*(3), 2087–2094.

Wang, Z., Li, M., Lu, J., & Cheng, X. (2022). Business Innovation based on artificial intelligence and Blockchain technology. *Information Processing & Management, 59*(1), 102759.

Wang, N., Ren, S., Liu, Y., Yang, M., Wang, J., & Huisingh, D. (2020). An active preventive maintenance approach of complex equipment based on a novel product-service system operation mode. *Journal of Cleaner Production, 277*, Article 123365.

Xu, M., Chen, X., & Kou, G. (2019). A systematic review of blockchain. *Financial Innovation, 5*(1). Retrieved July 20, 2024, from https://doi.org/10.1186/s40854-019-0147-z.

Yin, R. K. (2009). *Case study research: Design and methods* (Vol. 5). Sage.

Yin, S., Liu, L., & Hou, J. (2016). A multivariate statistical combination forecasting method for product quality evaluation. *Information Sciences, 355*, 229–236.

Zhang, X., Sheng, Y., & Liu, Z. (2023). Using expertise as an intermediary: Unleashing the power of blockchain technology to drive future sustainable management using hidden champions. Retrieved August 25, 2024, from https://ncbi.nlm.nih.gov.

Zheng, C., Huang, X., & Xu, Y. (2023). The impact of blockchain on enterprises sharing real data based on dynamic evolutionary game analysis. *Sustainability*, *15*(12), 9439. Retrieved June 29, 2024, from https://doi.org/10.3390/su15129439.

Zhou, W., Zhou, Y., Grace, M., Jiang, X., & Zou, S. (2013). Fast, scalable detection of" piggybacked" mobile applications. In *Proceedings of the third ACM conference on Data and application security and privacy* (pp. 185–196).

Zonta, T., Da Costa, C. A., da Rosa Righi, R., de Lima, M. J., da Trindade, E. S., & Li, G. P. (2020). Predictive maintenance in the Industry 4.0: A systematic literature review. *Computers and Industrial Engineering*, *150*, 106889.

Data-Driven Asset Management and IoT Applications

From Data to Decisions: Empowering Pipeline Operators with Actionable Insights

Ana Silva, Luís Evangelista, Cláudia Ferreira, Jónatas Valença, and Maria Paula Mendes

Abstract Understanding the mechanisms behind pipeline failures is critical for identifying vulnerabilities in gas transmission pipelines and developing strategies to enhance energy supply chain reliability. Pipelines are recognised as the most cost-effective and reliable solution for energy transportation, playing a vital role in modern societies among increasing global demand for natural gas resources. Despite their reliability, pipelines are susceptible to various deterioration mechanisms, making them prone to catastrophic incidents. While fatalities due to pipeline leaks are relatively low in absolute numbers, the consequences pose significant threats to human safety, the environment, and economic stability. Pipeline failures result from cumulative aging processes influenced by physical, operational, and environmental factors. Time-dependent hazards such as corrosion evolve progressively, while time-independent hazards like natural disasters and third-party activities pose immediate risks. The interplay among these factors requires a comprehensive understanding to prioritize maintenance and implement effective risk control measures. This study proposes an innovative approach to analyse historical pipeline failure data, based on incident records from 1970 to 2023 provided by the Pipeline & Hazardous Materials Safety Administration (PHMSA) of the United States. With the United States housing 65% of the world's pipeline length, a dataset of 12,182 incidents from 1970

A. Silva (✉)
CERIS/CENTEC, IST-ID, University of Lisbon, Lisbon, Portugal
e-mail: ana.ferreira.silva@tecnico.ulisboa.pt

L. Evangelista
CERIS, ISEL–Polytechnic Institute of Lisbon, Lisbon, Portugal
e-mail: evangelista@dec.isel.pt

C. Ferreira · J. Valença
IST-ID, CERIS, University of Lisbon, Lisbon, Portugal
e-mail: claudiaarferreira@tecnico.ulisboa.pt

J. Valença
e-mail: jonatas.valenca@tecnico.ulisboa.pt

M. P. Mendes
IST-ID, CERENA, University of Lisbon, Lisbon, Portugal
e-mail: mpaulamendes@tecnico.ulisboa.pt

A. Crespo Márquez et al. (eds.), *Case Studies in Digital Transformation*, Engineering Asset Management Review 4, https://doi.org/10.1007/978-3-032-05592-7_5

to 2023 provides a unique opportunity for analysis. However, the lack of comprehensive historical failure data analysis underscores the need for predictive models capable of identifying multi-cause-and-effect relationships. To address this gap, by offering a data-driven and precise prediction of incident years, this study enhances understanding of underlying causes and circumstances, enabling interventions to mitigate future incidents. By adopting a "lessons learned" perspective, this study provides strategic insights for operators to proactively address potential vulnerabilities, promoting sustained operational integrity and minimizing unexpected events throughout pipeline service life. This study converts data from self-contained case reports into a user-friendly knowledge framework. The results are expected to assist pipeline operators in evaluating and predicting the condition of existing gas pipelines, enabling them to prioritize inspections and maintenance activities effectively. By using the heat maps created in this study, potential failure points can be identified proactively, assisting the implementation of timely maintenance procedures tailored to the estimated service life of each pipeline. By leveraging this knowledge for proactive maintenance, organizations can mitigate risks, enhance operational efficiency, and gain a competitive advantage in their industries.

Keywords Gas pipelines · Historical failures · Service life · Pipelines' management · Maintenance

1 Introduction

Pipelines are considered cost-effective and reliable means for energy transportation, particularly crucial for gas conveyance in modern societies among rising global demand for natural gas resources (Zhou et al., 2022). Despite their relatively low probability of operational failures compared to alternative methods, pipelines, as complex systems carrying hazardous materials, are susceptible to catastrophic incidents (Seghier et al., 2022). Although fatalities from pipeline leaks are relatively rare, such incidents pose significant threats to human safety, the environment, and economic stability.

The degradation of pipelines over their operational lifespan results from a multitude of physical, operational, and environmental factors (Pourazizi et al., 2020). These factors include material type, pipeline section, welding failures, operational parameters like pressure and flow velocity, and environmental conditions such as temperature, humidity, and natural hazards (El-Abbasy et al., 2014). The main hazards associated with incidents in gas transmission pipelines can be categorised into time-dependent (i.e. internal and external corrosion, which progressively evolve over time), stable (i.e. construction defects or equipment failure) or time-independent (i.e. natural disasters and damage caused by third parties) (Woldesellasse & Tesfamariam, 2023). While prior research has extensively explored the influence of physical factors—particularly pipe diameter, thickness, and age—on gas pipeline failures (Wang et al., 2014; Lam & Zhou, 2016), there has been less focus on the operational and environmental factors (Xiao et al., 2023).

The cumulative aging process and the exposure to a multitude of degradation mechanisms compromise the structural integrity of pipelines, reducing their durability and service life. A comprehensive understanding of the interactions among the various degradation agents is essential for assessing the probability of pipeline failures (Xiao et al., 2023). Moreover, beyond risk analysis, implementing effective risk control measures is equally vital (Arya et al., 2022; Chen et al., 2021).

Since pipelines currently deliver the majority of the global natural gas supply and operate extensively worldwide, prioritizing the maintenance and effective risk management of gas transportation infrastructures is paramount (Xiao et al., 2023). The United States, housing a significant portion of the world's pipeline length and facilitating a quarter of its energy consumption through gas pipelines, provides a unique dataset for comprehensive analysis (Dey, 2001).

Since the introduction of pipeline incident regulations in 1970, the U.S. Pipeline & Hazardous Materials Safety Administration (PHMSA) has recorded 12,182 incidents up until 2023, providing a robust foundation for investigation (PHMSA, 2023). This study aims to conduct a comprehensive analysis of gas transmission pipeline failures across all U.S. states, focusing on the interaction between various contributing factors, underlying causes, and the resulting consequences, using the PHMSA incident database. By analysing the relationship of physical, operational, and environmental factors, the research intends to enhance understanding and develop predictive risk models to improve future pipeline safety. Enhanced pipeline safety is crucial not only for minimising service disruptions and strengthening infrastructure resilience but also for reducing environmental impact and ensuring public safety. These efforts are essential to addressing the energy crisis, contributing to reliable, sustainable, and secure energy supplies for communities, industries, and economies.

2 Methodology

In the last 60 years, the failure of gas pipelines has been extensively analysed (Khan et al., 2021) but are focused on specific degradation mechanisms tested in laboratory environments, which do not resemble in situ conditions. The existing condition assessment models are either subjective (without any information on historical data) or address each degradation mechanism individually (Bersani et al., 2010). Despite the attempts made, the relevant interdependency between different degradation mechanisms was not considered. The creation of any risk assessment model should consider the frequency and consequences of past events (Elshaboury et al., 2014).

This study employs incident data from gas transmission pipelines, provided by the U.S. Pipeline and Hazardous Materials Safety Administration (PHMSA), which has been systematically collected from pipeline operators since 1970. The methodology involves a thorough examination of incident reports, which document critical details such as failure causes, pipeline characteristics (e.g., material, diameter, age), environmental conditions (e.g., temperature, soil type), and operational factors (e.g., pressure, flow velocity). By analysing this historical dataset, the study intends to identify patterns and interactions between these variables that may influence the likelihood and severity of pipeline failures.

This study applies a bivariate statistical analysis to describe the relationship between the different variables that affect the service life of gas transmission pipelines, by employing historical data of past incidents from 1970 to 2023. The bivariate analysis will allow detecting potential correlations between these variables, providing deeper insight into how certain combinations of physical, operational, and environmental factors affect pipeline performance and failure rates.

Moreover, the analysis of failure data from PHMSA allows for a thorough investigation of the different degradation mechanisms that affect gas pipelines and offers valuable insights into the service life of pipeline infrastructures. By integrating this data with advanced analytical techniques, the study aims to provide a more holistic view of pipeline deterioration, considering both mechanical and operational factors. This approach not only enhances the accuracy of service life estimations but also helps in identifying key areas for improvement in pipeline management and maintenance strategies.

In this context, the service life of gas transmission pipelines refers to the period of time during which the pipelines can operate safely and reliably without significant failures or repairs. In this study, the estimated service life of gas pipelines is obtained by the difference between the year of the incident and the installation year. In other words, it represents the period from installation until the occurrence of the failure or incident that disrupted the pipeline's operation, reflecting the age of the pipeline at the time of the incident. The service life of pipelines is influenced by various factors, including design and manufacturing conditions, inspection and maintenance practices, as well as environmental and operational conditions they are subjected to.

2.1 Analysis of the Main Causes of Incidents

Figure 1 presents the frequency distribution of various incident causes in gas pipelines across the United States from 1970 to 2023. These causes are classified into nine categories: construction defects or material failure; corrosion; damage by external forces; equipment failure; excavation damage; incorrect operation; natural forces; pipe, weld, or joint failures; and other causes, which encompass instances where the detailed cause is either unknown or unreported. The results reveal that incidents caused by external forces are predominant in the sample studied, accounting for approximately 67%. These incidents are primarily attributed to motorized vehicles or equipment not involved in excavations, nearby industrial or man-made fires/explosions, electrical arcing from other equipment or facilities, boats and fishery anchors, or vandalism (Vishnuvardhan et al., 2023). Such events are highly complex and nearly impossible to predict in terms of timing, location, and impact on pipeline

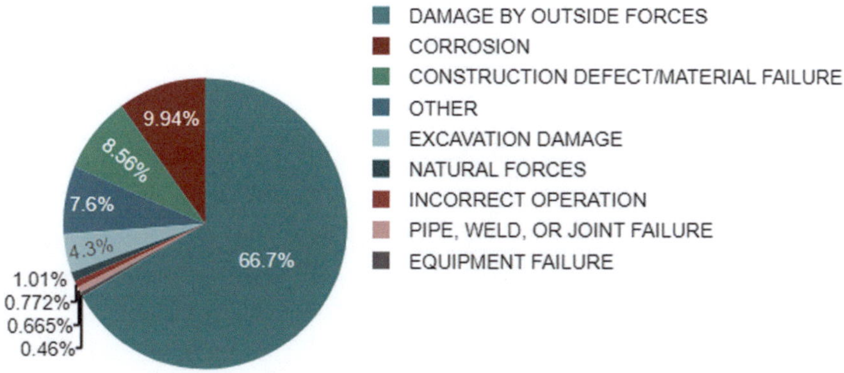

Fig. 1 Frequency of main causes of incidents between 1970 and 2023

integrity, as they depend on various uncontrollable factors beyond the scope of pipeline operators. Corrosion ranks as the second most common cause of incidents, followed by construction defects or material failures. These occurrences often stem from inadequate design or material deficiencies, such as incorrect material specifications or construction errors.

Gas transmission pipelines tend to experience a noticeable reduction in service life when the incident is caused by third-party actions, as shown in Table 1 and Fig. 2, with an average service life of 19 years for damage caused by outside forces. Time-independent failure mechanisms can occur unexpectedly and without warning. By analysing the frequency of past incidents, this study provides some information about the probability of failure according to the pipelines' location and materials, providing a risk profile, which enables pipeline operators to implement proactive measures and effective emergency response plans.

The results highlight a causal relationship between the incident cause and the service life of gas pipelines. Incidents stemming from natural degradation processes or stable hazards, such as pipe, weld, or joint failure, corrosion, equipment failure, or construction defects, as well as those due to natural hazards, generally exhibit longer estimated service lives, i.e. average estimated service lives of 40, 33, 30, 28 and 38, respectively. On the contrary, the service life of gas pipelines is compromised when incidents result from third-party actions, such as damage by outside forces, other causes, or vandalism. While incidents arising from corrosion are often predictable and can be modelled by degradation curves within the assumed service life designated by industry standards, those caused by third-party activities introduce an element of unpredictability. It is challenging to proactively mitigate the impact of these actions.

Table 1 Average estimated service life of gas transmission pipelines according to the cause of the incident

	Damage by outside forces	Corrosion	Construction defect/ Material failure	Other	Natural forces	Excavation damage	Incorrect operation	Equipment failure	Pipe, weld, or joint failure
Average estimated service life (years)	19	33	28	23	38	31	31	30	40

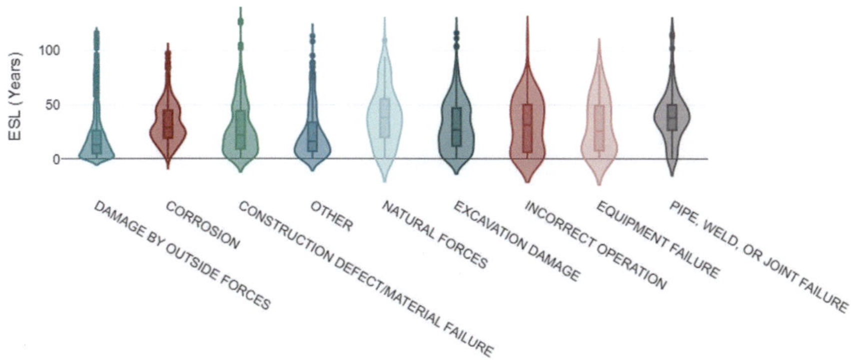

Fig. 2 Violin diagrams of the estimated service life of gas pipelines according to the cause of the incident

2.2 Analysis of the Influence of Pipelines' Design

The distribution system encompasses various types of lines, as outlined by PHMSA (2023). Table 2 and Fig. 4 present the estimated service life (ESL) of gas pipelines according to the leak part (i.e. part in which occur the incident). The distribution system consists of several types of pipelines, each serving distinct functions within the network (PHMSA, 2023). The supply main operates between the connection point with the transmission system and the feeder mains, typically functioning at pressures between 150 and 400 psi. The feeder main links the supply main to the distribution main, with pressure reduced at a regulator station to levels ranging from 26 to 60 psi. The distribution main extends through service areas, delivering gas to regions of high consumption, usually at pressures between 1 and 25 psi. Finally, the service line connects individual homes or businesses to the distribution main, which often runs beneath city streets, and typically operates at pressures between ¼ and 1 psi, though higher pressures may be used for larger customers.

The analysis reveals that service risers exhibit the highest estimated service life, attributed to the application of prefabricated risers equipped with buoyancy systems,

Table 2 Average estimated service life of gas transmission pipelines according to the leak part

	District regulator/metering station	Main	Meter set	No data	Other	Pressure limiting and regulating facility	Regulator set	Service line	Service riser	Service valve
Average estimated service life (years)	27	27	19	16	16	24	22	31	32	0

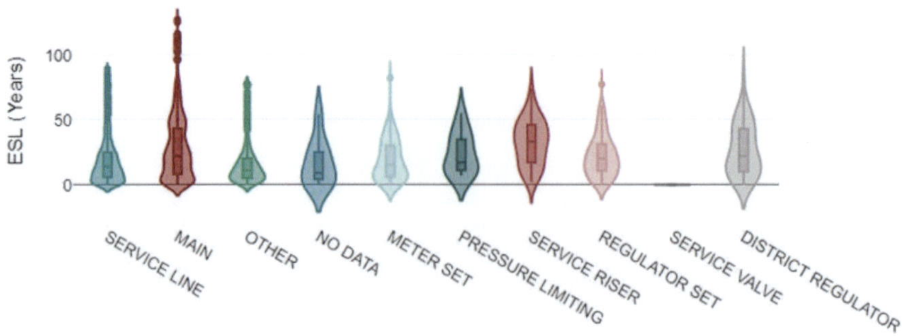

Fig. 3 Violin diagrams of the estimated service life of gas pipelines according to the leak part

enhancing pipeline installation safety. Main lines and district regulators also demonstrate high estimated service lives, with maximum values reaching 95 and 87, respectively. These pipeline segments are typically designed and constructed according to stringent industry standards and regulations, given the potential catastrophic consequences of incidents involving large-diameter and high-pressure pipelines for both society and the environment (Speight, 2014). Additionally, these segments are often located in less populated or remote areas and buried at greater depths, thereby reducing exposure to external threats or third-party activities—the primary causes of incidents—thus minimizing the likelihood of events that could compromise their service life. Many corporations and design standards recognize the crucial role of maintaining adequate depth of cover in mitigating susceptibility to external interference (Fig. 3).

A correlation is observed between the year of an incident and the year of pipeline installation (Fig. 4). A higher frequency of incidents can be observed between 1950 and 1980. The reduction in pipeline incidents over time can be attributed to significant advancements in the design, assessment, and maintenance of pipelines. Improvements in steel production and line-pipe manufacturing, along with the development of more resilient materials, have played a key role in enhancing the structural integrity of pipelines. Additionally, the implementation of advanced corrosion protection measures (coatings and cathodic protection) has further contributed to minimizing failures (Lawson et al., 2024). As a result, these innovations collectively improve pipeline reliability, thereby reducing the occurrence of incidents and ensuring safer, more efficient operations.

An analysis of European onshore gas pipeline data from 2010 to 2019, covering approximately 140,000 cumulative kilometres—the second-largest natural gas pipeline incident dataset after PHMSA's also reveals a reduction in failure frequencies over time, largely due to technological developments, such as advances in welding techniques, enhanced inspection technologies, the implementation of in-line inspections for continuous condition monitoring, and improved strategies for damage prevention and detection (EGIG, 2020).

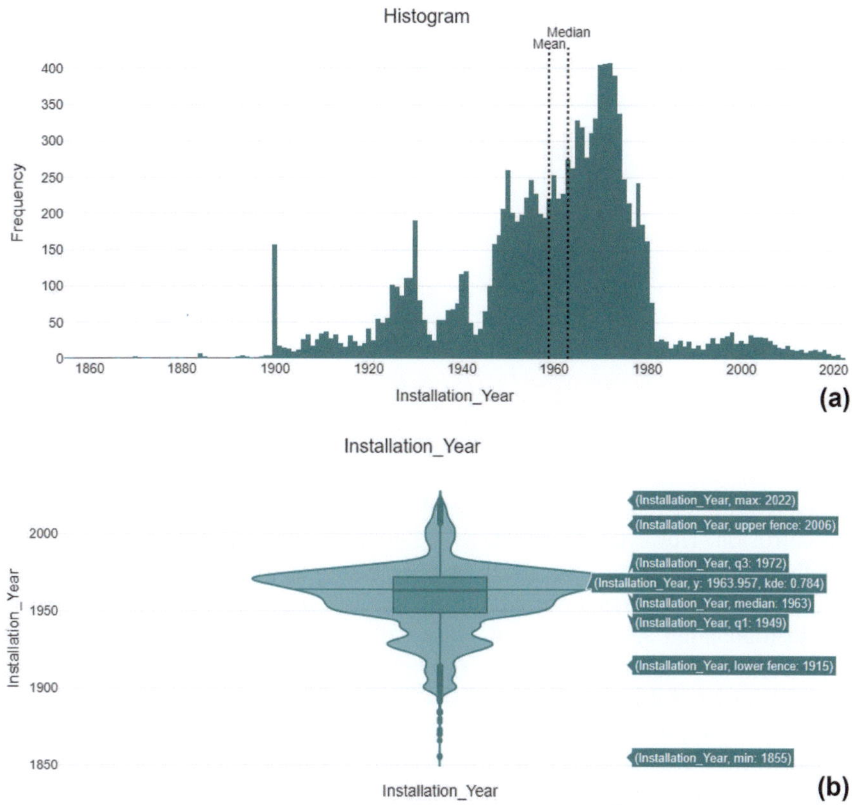

Fig. 4 Histogram of the frequency of incidents according to the year of installation of the pipelines (**a**) and the respective violin plot (**b**)

PHMSA data also reveal a gradual increase in incidents caused by excavation activities, operational errors, and natural forces (Fig. 5). This trend can be predominantly correlated to the expansion of pipeline infrastructure, growing urban development, higher population density near pipelines, and the rising occurrence of extreme weather events due to climate change (Dong et al., 2022).

Since the 1990s, there has been a substantial reduction in the use of cast iron and unprotected steel pipelines (Fig. 6). These have been systematically replaced by protected steel and plastic, which offer greater durability and resistance to environmental factors (Lamb et al., 2015; Vetter et al., 2019).

Figure 7 and Table 3 present the average estimated service life of gas transmission pipelines according to the type of material used. The results reveal lower estimated service lives for plastic materials. Plastic and polyethylene (PE) pipes have become the predominant choice for new gas distribution pipelines in Europe and the United States, mainly due to the advantages PE offers over traditional steel pipelines,

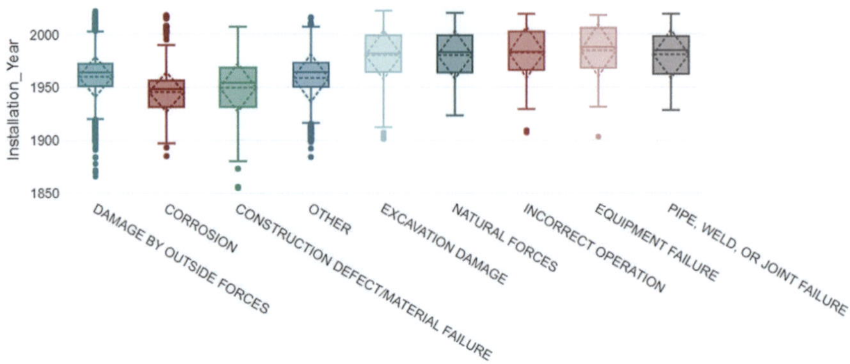

Fig. 5 Histogram of the frequency of incidents according to the year of installation of the pipelines and the cause of the incident

including its lightweight nature, greater flexibility, and higher resistance to chemical corrosion. However, despite these material benefits, PE pipes are still prone to failures arising from factors such as poor fusion at joints, third-party damage, and foundation settlement (Wang et al., 2024). Over-urbanization, in particular, can lead to foundation settlements that cause deflections in the pipeline, which may result in leaks or even burst failures (Wang & Far, 2015). These issues highlight the need for careful installation practices and monitoring to ensure the long-term reliability of PE pipelines. Additionally, plastic materials possess lower mechanical strength, making them more vulnerable to physical damage, such as deformation or puncturing under high pressure, heavy loads, or during excavation activities (Zhou et al., 2019). The sensitivity of plastics to temperature variations further reduces their durability, as elevated temperatures can weaken the material, while low temperatures may cause brittleness. Although plastics are resistant to corrosion from water and certain chemicals, they can degrade when exposed to specific solvents, oils, or gases. Furthermore, plastics exhibit time-dependent deformation, known as creep, where prolonged exposure to stress results in gradual material distortion, compromising pipeline integrity (Nasiri & Khosravani, 2023). In some soil environments, microbial activity can also contribute to the deterioration of plastic materials. These factors collectively contribute to the shorter service life of plastic pipelines, particularly in demanding environmental and operational conditions.

Table 4 presents a two-dimensional analysis of the number of incidents in gas transmission pipelines, correlating the type of material used and the leak part. The results reveal that the main and service lines are the elements of pipeline infrastructure more prone to incidents, in particular when made by steel and plastic.

The data presented in Table 5 and Fig. 8 provide a comprehensive analysis of the estimated service life of pipelines based on their location. Critical points have been identified for pressure limiting and regulating facilities underground. Pipelines installed in open ditches and subjected to incorrect operation present an average estimated service life of 8 years, while pipelines above ground with construction defects

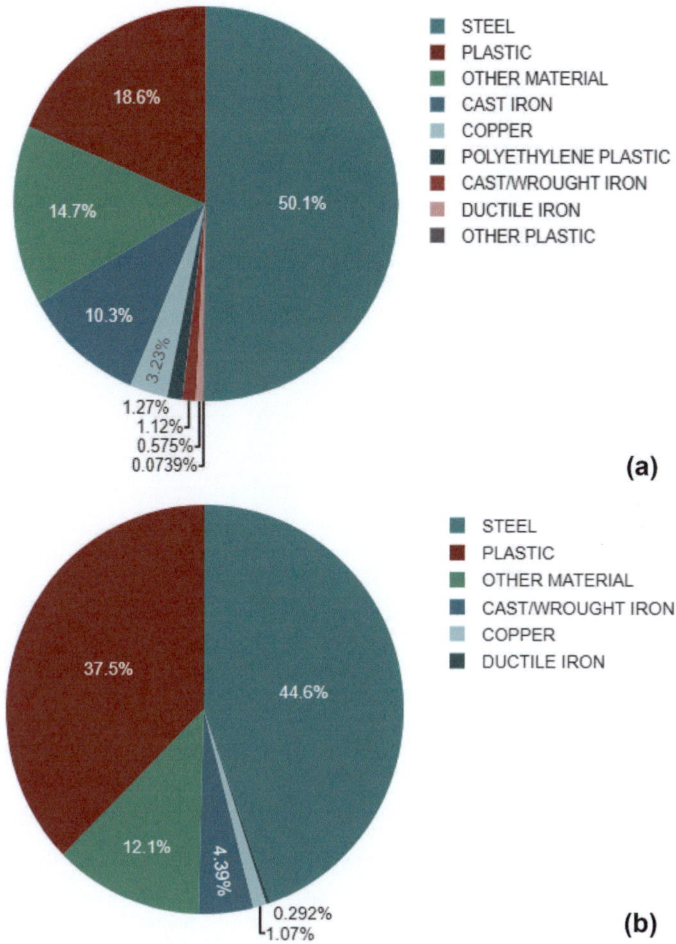

Fig. 6 Frequency of materials used in gas transmission pipelines since 1970 until 2023 (**a**) and in the last 13 years (**b**)

have a service life of 10 years, which is evidently insufficient. These results highlight the need for rigorous construction and operational standards to mitigate such defects and extend the service life of pipelines under these specific conditions. Moreover, proactive measures must be taken to implement robust maintenance protocols, ensuring proper installation practices, and employing protective measures that can significantly improve the durability and functionality of these pipelines.

In the analysed sample, pipelines above ground, inside buildings, and beneath unpaved roads demonstrate lower estimated service lives and higher number of incidents (Table 6), making them particularly vulnerable to construction defects and

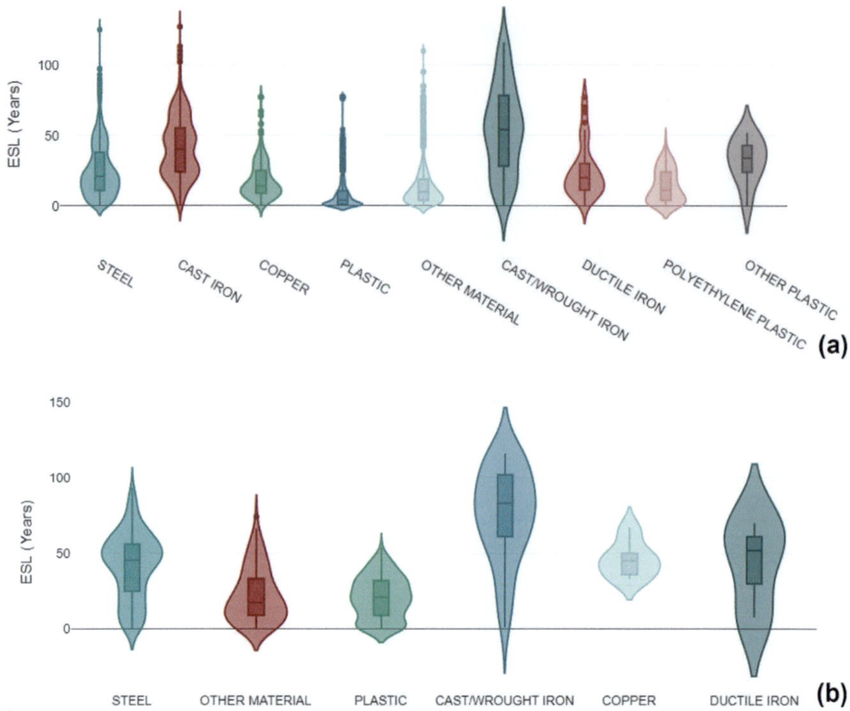

Fig. 7 Violin diagrams of the estimated service life of gas pipelines according to the material used since 1970 until 2023 (**a**) and in the last 13 years (**b**)

Table 3 Average estimated service life of gas transmission pipelines according to the material used

	Wrought iron	Cast iron	Ductile iron	Steel	Copper	Plastic	Polyethylene plastic	Other plastic	Other material
Average Estimated service life (years), considering the incidents occurred since 1970 until 2023	54	41	25	25	18	8	14	32	15

damage caused by outside forces. The vulnerability of pipelines in these environments requires enhanced protective measures and regular maintenance to prevent premature failure and ensure operational efficiency.

Table 4 Bivariate analysis of the number of incidents according to the leak part and the material used in the gas transmission pipelines

Leak part	Material								Overall
	Cast iron	Wrought iron	Copper	Ductile iron	Other material	Plastic	Polyethylene plastic	Steel	
District regulator	0	1	0	0	21	0	0	40	62
Main	1094	83	57	18	157	1169	80	2755	5413
Meter station	0	1	0	0	61	0	14	53	129
No data	2	0	0	0	1	2	0	4	9
Other	53	7	17	13	842	34	2	486	1454
Pressure limiting	0	0	0	0	3	0	0	13	16
Regulator set	0	4	1	0	75	18	0	81	179
Service line	103	40	319	39	643	1044	59	2673	4920

3 Results and Discussion

In the United States, pipeline design complies with standards set by the American Society of Mechanical Engineers (ASME, 2020), which assume a service life of 50 years with a conservative safety factor. Similarly, European onshore gas pipelines support the idea that pipelines built in the past 50 years show no significant correlation between the frequency of corrosion-related failures and their age or construction year class (EGIG, 2020). Properly maintained gas pipelines are generally expected to last several decades; however, in certain cases, pipelines may require replacement after only a few years of operation. In the U.S., federal regulations consider pipelines older than 25 years to be potentially at risk, depending on factors such as coating and corrosion conditions, steel quality, toughness, and welding integrity.

The average estimated service life observed in this study, based on the analysed sample, is 23 years, aligning with values reported in the literature. However, when considering factors such as construction defects, material failures, equipment malfunctions, corrosion, and pipe/weld/joint failures, the estimated service life increases to 33 years. This estimation shows a higher standard deviation and can vary significantly based on the range of variables considered in this study. Given the complexity of pipeline conditions and their substantial influence on degradation rates, a more detailed analysis is required to understand the causal relationships between these variables. Such analysis is crucial for developing more accurate predictive models and implementing strategies to improve the resilience and durability of gas pipelines under diverse conditions.

The failure of gas pipelines represents a highly adverse event with severe consequences, including economic losses, environmental impacts, and, in the most severe cases, human injuries or casualties. Even minor leakages can lead to catastrophic outcomes and affect a significant number of people.

Table 5 Average estimated service life of gas transmission pipelines according to their location

	Above ground	Below road (paved)	Below road (unpaved)	Below walkway	No data	Open ditch	Other	Transition area	Under ground	Under pavement	Under water	Within building
Average estimated service life (years)	16	31	18	29	24	25	27	36	22	26	27	17

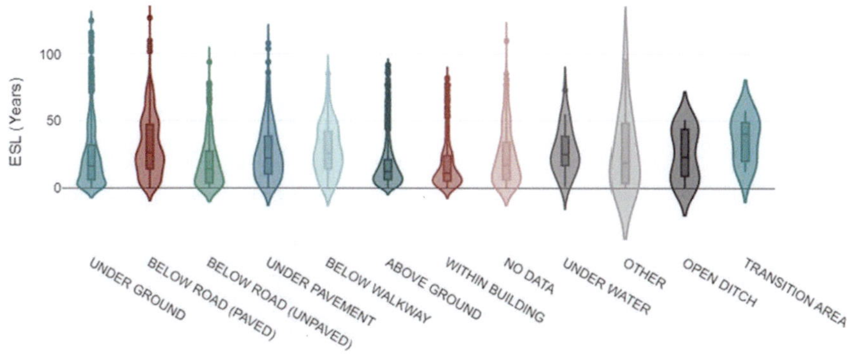

Fig. 8 Violin diagrams of the estimated service life of gas pipelines according to their location

Table 6 Bivariate analysis of the number of incidents according to the leak part and the location of the gas transmission pipelines

Location	Leak part								Overall
	District regulator	Main	Meter station	No data	Other	Pressure limiting	Regulator set	Service line	
Above ground	53	148	110	4	778	12	178	1137	2069
Below road	0	1961	0	1	62	0	0	750	2774
Below walkway	0	109	0	0	7	0	0	76	192
No data	0	154	5	2	68	1	0	119	349
Open ditch	0	19	0	0	0	0	0	10	29
Other	0	6	2	0	0	0	0	4	12
Transition area	0	3	0	0	0	0	2	5	10
Under ground	9	2808	1	2	158	2	0	2216	5196
Under pavement	0	170	0	0	25	0	0	145	340
Under water	0	26	0	0	0	0	0	6	32
Within build	0	9	11	0	356	1	0	452	829

Figure 9 shows the frequency of injuries and fatalities according to the cause of the incident. In the 12,182 failure incidents analysed, 6,506 ignitions (53.4%) and 1,807 explosions (15% of reported incidents) were documented, yielding an odds ratio of 28% for ignition resulting in explosion. The occurrence of an explosion increases the prevalence of fatalities, i.e. 74% of fatalities occur when the incident triggered an explosion.

Over time, the incidence of failures in pipelines has undergone significant changes (Fig. 10). In particular, these changes are more noticeable in the last 13 years (Fig. 11),

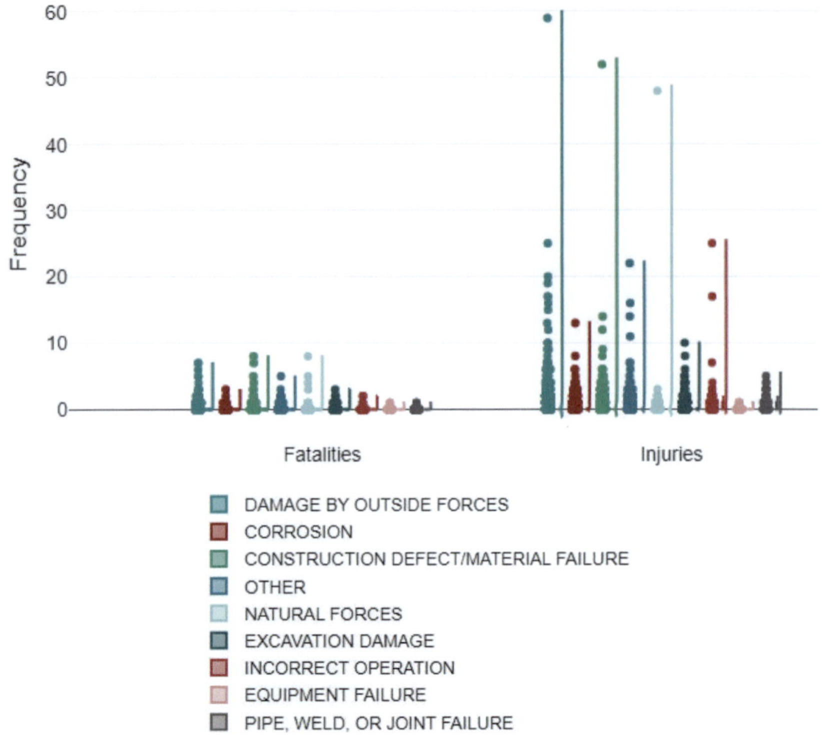

Fig. 9 Raincloud plot of the frequency of fatalities and injuries according to the cause of the incident

revealing a noticeable decrease in the of incidents involving gas transmission pipelines, and consequently, in the number of explosions and fatalities.

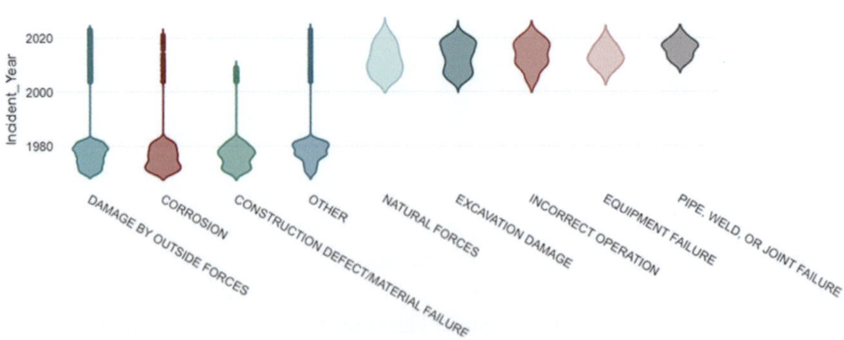

Fig. 10 Violin diagrams of the incident year according to the cause of the incident occurred between 1970 and 2023

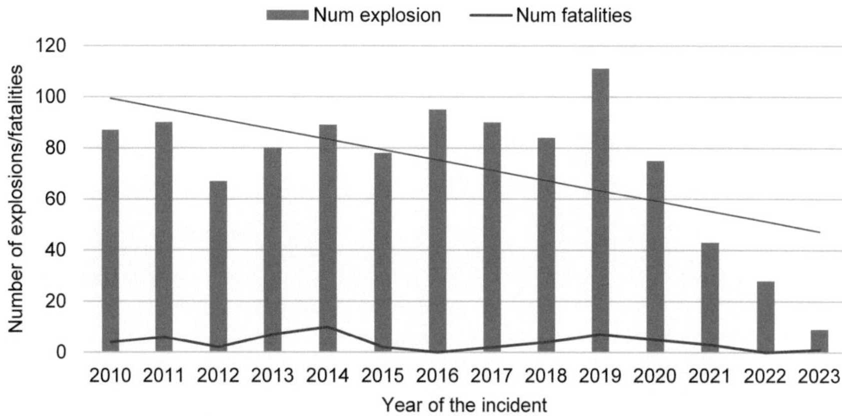

Fig. 11 Number of explosions and fatalities over the last 13 years

These changes are mainly influenced by the materials used in their construction and regulatory initiatives aimed at enhancing safety (Bubbico et al., 2018). Enhanced regulatory frameworks and stricter safety standards have been implemented and initiatives such as the Pipeline Safety, Regulatory Certainty, and Job Creation Act of 2011 have been instrumental in promoting the removal and replacement of cast and wrought iron pipes as well as unprotected steel pipelines, which are seen as high-risk pipelines. In 2022, around 98% of natural gas distribution pipelines in the U.S. were made of plastic or protected steel, with only 1% consisting of iron (PHMSA, 2023). This substantial shift towards using different materials (Fig. 6) has had a direct impact on the incidence of failures.

One of the most notable changes is the reduction in time-dependent failures, such as corrosion, which has historically been a major cause of pipeline failures (Table 7). This decrease is largely due to the replacement of older iron and unprotected steel pipelines with plastic pipelines. Plastic pipelines have long been regarded as a safe and cost-effective alternative to traditional steel or other materials. However, the National Transportation Safety Board (NTSB) has highlighted several cases of brittle-like cracking in plastic pipes that have led to pipeline accidents. According to a special investigation by the NTSB, the strength rating procedure for plastic pipelines in the United States may have overestimated their resilience and resistance to brittle-like cracking. This problem is notably prevalent in pipes manufactured and used for gas services from the 1960s through the early 1980s. Consequently, a considerable portion of these pipelines may be vulnerable to premature brittle-like failures under stress, posing a significant public safety risk (National Transportation Safety Board, 1998). Analysis of past incidents revealed a notable frequency of explosions in plastic pipelines, mainly attributable to pipe, weld, or joint failures, as well as damage from excavation activities.

The results (Table 7) show that while the incidence of time-dependent failures has decreased, the frequency of time-independent failures has increased. These include

Table 7 Probability of explosion according to the cause of the incident, in the last 13 years

Likelihood of explosion per year	Cause								
	Time-dependent	Stable cause			Time-independent				
Incident year	Corrosion	Construction defect/ material	Equipment failure	Pipe, weld, or joint failure	Damage by outside forces	Excavation damage	Incorrect operation	Natural forces	Other
2010	5.0%	0.0%	0.0%	10.0%	15.0%	35.0%	10.0%	10.0%	15.0%
2011	0.0%	0.0%	4.2%	16.7%	20.8%	25.0%	8.3%	20.8%	4.2%
2012	5.9%	0.0%	0.0%	0.0%	23.5%	29.4%	5.9%	23.5%	11.8%
2013	0.0%	0.0%	0.0%	7.1%	7.1%	57.1%	0.0%	21.4%	7.1%
2014	0.0%	0.0%	0.0%	20.8%	37.5%	16.7%	0.0%	12.5%	12.5%
2015	0.0%	0.0%	4.5%	9.1%	27.3%	22.7%	0.0%	22.7%	13.6%
2016	8.3%	0.0%	0.0%	25.0%	29.2%	29.2%	0.0%	8.3%	0.0%
2017	6.3%	0.0%	0.0%	31.3%	6.3%	31.3%	12.5%	6.3%	6.3%
2018	8.3%	0.0%	0.0%	25.0%	8.3%	37.5%	8.3%	8.3%	4.2%
2019	0.0%	0.0%	0.0%	25.0%	45.0%	25.0%	0.0%	0.0%	5.0%
2020	0.0%	0.0%	0.0%	16.7%	33.3%	41.7%	0.0%	0.0%	8.3%
2021	7.1%	0.0%	7.1%	7.1%	28.6%	35.7%	7.1%	0.0%	7.1%
2022	0.0%	0.0%	0.0%	33.3%	11.1%	33.3%	0.0%	11.1%	11.1%
2023	0.0%	0.0%	0.0%	0.0%	0.0%	33.3%	0.0%	33.3%	33.3%

failures due to natural disasters, equipment malfunction, and failures due to outside forces or third-party actions. This trend underscores the importance of analysing past incidents to understand the patterns and causes of time-independent failures. Learning from historical data enables pipeline operators to develop better predictive models and preventive measures, addressing the unique challenges posed by these types of failures.

Over the past 60 years, steel has been the predominant material used in gas transmission pipelines, and they have historically presented a higher incidence of explosions and casualties (Fig. 11). This trend can be attributed to several factors, including the extensive use of steel pipelines during the early and mid-twentieth century, combined with the limitations in technology and safety standards at that time. However, advancements in materials science and engineering practices have led to significant improvements in the safety and reliability of steel pipelines.

However, in the last 13 years, plastic pipelines seem to pose higher risks of explosions compared to steel pipelines (Table 8). This shift can be attributed to the increasing adoption of plastic materials, such as polyethylene (PE), for gas transmission. While plastic pipelines offer several advantages, including flexibility, corrosion resistance, and ease of installation, they also present unique challenges that can lead to severe consequences in the event of a failure (Fig. 12).

The inherent properties of plastic materials contribute to the increased risk of explosions and extensive damage when failures occur. Unlike steel, which can withstand higher pressures and temperatures, plastic materials are more susceptible to degradation over time due to environmental factors such as UV radiation, temperature fluctuations, and chemical exposure. This degradation can compromise the structural integrity of plastic pipelines, increasing the likelihood of leaks and ruptures.

The nature of plastic materials means that when failures do occur, they can result in more severe consequences, including explosions and extensive damage. The potential for severe outcomes requires a thorough risk assessment and stringent safety measures to mitigate the risks associated with plastic pipelines. Operators must

Table 8 Sum of fatalities if an explosion occurs according to the pipelines' material, in the last 13 years

Sum of fatalities if an explosion occurs	Material									
	CAST IRON	WROUGHT IRON	COPPER	DUCTILE IRON	OTHER MATERIAL	OTHER PLASTIC	PLASTIC	POLYETHYLENE PLASTIC	STEEL	Overall
2010	0	0	0	0	1	0	1	0	3	5
NO	0	0	0	0	0	0	1	0	0	1
YES	0	0	0	0	1	0	0	0	3	4
2011	0	5	0	0	2	0	2	0	0	9
NO	0	0	0	0	1	0	2	0	0	3
YES	0	5	0	0	1	0	0	0	0	6
2012	0	1	0	0	0	0	0	0	8	9
NO	0	0	0	0	0	0	0	0	7	7
YES	0	1	0	0	0	0	0	0	1	2
2013	0	1	0	0	1	0	4	0	1	7
NO	0	0	0	0	0	0	0	0	0	0
YES	0	1	0	0	1	0	4	0	1	7
2014	0	0	0	0	0	0	11	0	3	14
NO	0	0	0	0	0	0	1	0	3	4
YES	0	0	0	0	0	0	10	0	0	10
2015	0	2	0	0	0	0	0	0	0	2
NO	0	0	0	0	0	0	0	0	0	0
YES	0	2	0	0	0	0	0	0	0	2
2016	0	1	0	0	0	0	0	0	0	1
NO	0	1	0	0	0	0	0	0	0	1
YES	0	0	0	0	0	0	0	0	0	0
2017	0	0	0	0	0	0	0	0	2	2
NO	0	0	0	0	0	0	0	0	0	0
YES	0	0	0	0	0	0	0	0	2	2
2018	0	0	0	0	1	0	1	0	3	5
NO	0	0	0	0	0	0	0	0	1	1
YES	0	0	0	0	1	0	1	0	2	4
2019	0	2	0	0	2	0	4	0	0	8
NO	0	0	0	0	1	0	0	0	0	1
YES	0	2	0	0	1	0	4	0	0	7
2020	0	0	0	0	1	0	2	0	4	7
NO	0	0	0	0	1	0	0	0	1	2
YES	0	0	0	0	0	0	2	0	3	5
2021	0	0	0	0	0	0	2	0	2	4
NO	0	0	0	0	0	0	0	0	1	1
YES	0	0	0	0	0	0	2	0	1	3
2022	0	0	0	0	0	0	1	0	0	1
NO	0	0	0	0	0	0	1	0	0	1
YES	0	0	0	0	0	0	0	0	0	0
2023	0	0	0	0	1	0	0	0	1	2
NO	0	0	0	0	1	0	0	0	0	1
YES	0	0	0	0	0	0	0	0	1	1
Overall	0	24	0	0	18	0	56	0	54	152

be vigilant in monitoring and maintaining these pipelines to prevent catastrophic incidents.

While controlling operating pressure is a critical safety measure for preventing incidents in gas transmission pipelines, the data analysed in this study, reveal a surprising trend. Data indicates that 98% of explosions occur without pressure overload, suggesting that incidents often emerge at operating pressures below the

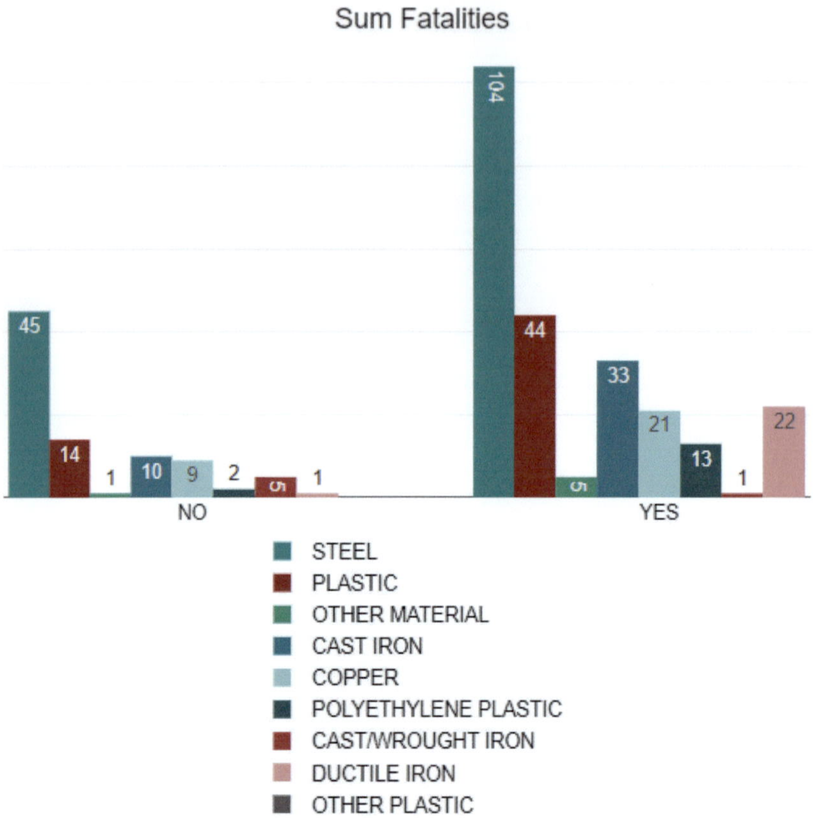

Fig. 12 Frequency of fatalities due to explosion and according to the pipeline' material

maximum allowable limit. This finding challenges the conventional focus on pressure control as the primary preventive measure and highlights the need for a more comprehensive approach to pipeline safety.

Over time, pipeline materials can degrade due to environmental exposure, chemical reactions, and mechanical stress. This degradation can weaken the pipeline structure, making it susceptible to failures even at normal operating pressures. Given the potential for severe outcomes, it is crucial to conduct thorough risk assessments and implement stringent safety measures to mitigate the risks associated with pipelines' failures.

Operators must consider multiple factors beyond pressure control to effectively mitigate risks. Key strategies include: (i) implementing advanced monitoring technologies, such as smart sensors and real-time data analytics, which can help to detect early signs of material degradation, corrosion, and other potential risks; (ii) defining a robust inspection and maintenance strategy to identify and address potential issues before they lead to catastrophic failures; (iii) developing and regularly updating emergency response plans to ensure that operators are prepared to respond quickly and effectively in the event of a pipeline failure; (iv) sharing information and best practices within the industry can help operators learn from each other's experiences and adopt effective safety measures. Organizations like the Pipeline and Hazardous Materials Safety Administration (PHMSA) and the European Gas pipeline incident database (EGIG) play a vital role in facilitating this collaboration.

4 Conclusions

This study highlights the importance of situational awareness in the pipelines industry for anticipating hazards and ensuring safety. Near-miss incident reporting is crucial for learning and prevention, while addressing human factors is key for effective accident mitigation. Improving human performance involves strengthening management, crew, and company-wide proficiency, alongside adherence to established policies and procedures. Current models for predicting pipeline service life and risk assessment mainly focus on specific degradation mechanisms, with corrosion being extensively studied. However, conventional corrosion assessment codes often lead to unnecessary repairs and premature pipeline replacements, resulting in high costs. Moreover, in the last 13 years, there has been a notable transition from using steel gas pipelines and other materials susceptible to corrosion to using plastic pipelines. This shift is primarily driven by the desire to mitigate corrosion-related issues and extend the service life of the infrastructure. However, this change introduces new challenges. Plastic pipelines, while resistant to corrosion, face different types of vulnerabilities. For instance, they can be more prone to damage from outside forces.

The evolution of pipeline failure mechanisms over the past 13 years highlights the dual nature of progress in pipeline safety. While advancements in material technology have successfully reduced time-dependent failures like corrosion, time-independent failures have become more prominent, requiring a focus on analysing historical data and learning from past incidents. Additionally, the inherent risks associated with plastic pipelines, particularly their higher explosion potential, require ongoing attention and proactive safety measures. The combined efforts of regulatory frameworks and continuous infrastructure investments are crucial for maintaining and improving the safety and reliability of natural gas pipelines.

In this sense, there is a need for comprehensive risk assessment strategies and maintenance protocols aligned with industry standards and organizational culture to enhance pipeline resilience, particularly against third-party activities. This study transforms data from self-contained case reports into an accessible knowledge framework. The results obtained are expected to assist pipeline operators in assessing and predicting the condition of existing gas pipelines, enabling them to prioritize inspections and maintenance needs effectively. The knowledge related to the service life of pipelines according to their characteristics, allowing for the implementation of proactive maintenance procedures at the opportune time. By leveraging this knowledge to implement proactive maintenance procedures, organizations can minimize risks, optimize operations, and maintain a competitive edge in their respective industries.

Acknowledgements The authors acknowledge the Portuguese Foundation for Science and Technology (FCT) the funding of the project UIDB/04625/2020 from the research unit CERIS (DOI: https://doi.org/10.54499/UIDB/04625/2020) and the project UID/ECI/04028/2019 from the research unit CERENA, from Instituto Superior Técnico, University of Lisbon. J. Valença and A. Silva acknowledge the support of FCT through the individual projects CEECIND/04463/2017 and CEECIND/01337/2017, respectively.

References

Arya, A. K., Jain, R., Yadav, S., Bisht, S., & Gautam, S. (2022). Recent trends in gas pipeline optimization. *Materials Today: Proceedings, 57*(Part4), 1455–1461. https://doi.org/10.1016/j.matpr.2021.11.232

ASME B31.8–2010. (2022). *Gas transmission and distribution piping systems.* The American Society of Mechanical Engineers, USA. ISBN: 9780791875421

Bersani, C., Citro, L., Gagliardi, R. V., Sacile, R., & Tomasoni, A. M. (2010) Accident occurence evaluation in the pipeline transport dangerous goods. *4th International Conference on Safety & Environment in Process Industry, 19*, 249–254. https://doi.org/10.3303/CET1019041

National Transportation Safety Board (NTSB). (1998). Brittle-like cracking in plastic pipe for gas service. Special investigation report, Washington, D.C. 20594

Bubbico, R., Casal, J., Pastor, E., & Santone, F. (2018). Transportation of hazardous materials via pipeline: A his-torical overview. *Chemical Engineering Transactions, 67*, 751–756. https://doi.org/10.3303/CET1867126

Chen, Q., Wu, C., Zuo, L., Mehrtash, M., Wang, Y., Bu, Y., Sadiq, R., & Cao, Y. (2021). Multi-objective transient peak shaving optimization of a gas pipeline system under demand uncertainty. *Computers & Chemical Engineering, 147*, Article 107260. https://doi.org/10.1016/j.compchemeng.2021.107260

Dey, P. K. (2001). A risk-based model for inspection and maintenance of cross country petroleum pipelines. *Journal of Quality in Maintenance Engineering, 7*(1), 25–43. https://doi.org/10.1108/13552510110386874

Dong, J., Asif, Z., Shi, Y., Zhu, Y., & Chen, Z. (2022). Climate change impacts on coastal and offshore petroleum infrastructure and the associated oil spill risk: A review. *Journal of Marine Science and Engineering, 10*, 849. https://doi.org/10.3390/jmse10070849

EGIG. (2020). 11th Report of the European Gas Pipeline Incident Data Group (period 1970–2019), European Gas Pipeline Incident Data Group (EGIG).

El-Abbasy, M. S., Senouci, A., Zayed, T., Mirahadi, F., & Parvizsedghy, L. (2014). Artificial neural network models for predicting condition of offshore oil and gas pipelines. *Automation in Construction, 45*, 50–65. https://doi.org/10.1016/j.autcon.2014.05.003

Elshaboury, N., Al-Sakkaf, A., Alfalah, G., & Abdelkader, E. M. (2022). Data-driven models for forecasting failure modes in oil and gas pipes. *Processes, 10*, 400. https://doi.org/10.3390/pr10020400

Khan, F., Yarveisy, R., & Abbassi, R. (2021). Risk-based pipeline integrity management: A road map for the resilient pipelines. *Journal of Pipeline Science and Engineering, 1*(1), 74–87. https://doi.org/10.1016/j.jpse.2021.02.001

Lam, C., & Zhou, W. (2016). Statistical analyses of incidents on onshore gas transmission pipelines based on PHMSA database. *International Journal of Pressure Vessels and Piping, 145*, 29–40. https://doi.org/10.1016/j.ijpvp.2016.06.003

Lamb, B. K., Edburg, S. L., Ferrara, T. W., Howard, T., Harrison, M. R., Kolb, C. E., Townsend-Small, A., Dyck, W., Possolo, A., & Whetstone, J. R. (2015). Direct measurements show decreasing methane emissions from natural gas local distribution systems in the United States. *Environmental Science & Technology, 49*(8), 5161–5169. https://doi.org/10.1021/es505116p

Lawson, K., Land, J. C., & Kowalski, A. R. (2024). Vintage pipeline enhanced corrosion management analysis. AMPP Annual Conference + Expo, New Orleans, Louisiana, USA

Nasiri, S., & Khosravani, M. R. (2023). Failure and fracture in polyethylene pipes: Overview, prediction methods, and challenges. *Engineering Failure Analysis, 152*, Article 107496. https://doi.org/10.1016/j.engfailanal.2023.107496

PHMSA, Annual Report Mileage Summary Statistics. (2023). https://www.phmsa.dot.gov/data-and-statistics/pipeline/annual-report-mileage-summary-statistics

Pourazizi, R., Mohtadi-Bonab, M. A., & Szpunar, J. A. (2020). Investigation of different failure modes in oil and natural gas pipeline steels. *Engineering Failure Analysis, 109*, Article 104400. https://doi.org/10.1016/j.engfailanal.2020.104400

Seghier, M. E. A. B., Höche, D., & Zheludkevich, M. (2022). Prediction of the internal corrosion rate for oil and gas pipeline: Implementation of ensemble learning techniques. *Journal of Natural Gas Science and Engineering, 99*, Article 104425. https://doi.org/10.1016/j.jngse.2022.104425

Speight, J. G. (2014). *Oil and gas corrosion prevention. Chapter 6-Corrosion monitoring and control.* Boston, USA: Gulf Professional Publishing. https://doi.org/10.1016/B978-0-12-800346-6.00006-5

Vetter, C. P., Kuebel, L. A., Natarajan, D., & Mentzer, R. A. (2019). Review of failure trends in the US natural gas pipeline industry: An in-depth analysis of transmission and distribution system incidents. *Journal of Loss Prevention in the Process Industries, 60*, 317–333. https://doi.org/10.1016/j.jlp.2019.04.014

Vishnuvardhan, S., Murthy, A. R., & Choudhary, A. (2023). A review on pipeline failures, defects in pipelines and their assessment and fatigue life prediction methods. *International Journal of Pressure Vessels and Piping, 201*, Article 104853. https://doi.org/10.1016/j.ijpvp.2022.104853

Wang, H., & Duncan, I. J. (2014). Understanding the nature of risks associated with onshore natural gas gathering pipelines. *Journal of Loss Prevention in the Process Industries, 29*, 49–55. https://doi.org/10.1016/j.jlp.2014.01.007

Wang, Y., & Far, M. S. (2015). Discussion of "numerical simulation of strength failure of buried polyethylene pipe under foundation settlement." *Engineering Failure Analysis, 70*(2016), 44–47. https://doi.org/10.1016/j.engfailanal.2016.07.009

Wang, H., Shah, J., Hawwat, S.-E., Huang, Q., & Khatami, A. (2024). A comprehensive review of polyethylene pipes: Failure mechanisms, performance models, inspection methods, and repair solutions. *Journal of Pipeline Science and Engineering, 4*(2), Article 100174. https://doi.org/10.1016/j.jpse.2024.100174

Woldesellasse, H., Tesfamariam, S. (2023). Risk analysis of onshore oil and gas pipelines: Literature review and bibliometric analysis. *Journal of Infrastructure Intelligence and Resilience, 2*, 100052. https://doi.org/10.1016/j.iintel.2023.100052

Xiao, R., Zayed, T., Meguid, M. A., & Sushama, L. (2023). Understanding the factors and consequences of pipeline incidents: An analysis of gas transmission pipelines in the US. *Engineering Failure Analysis, 152*, Article 107498. https://doi.org/10.1016/j.engfailanal.2023.107498

Zhou, M., Wang, F., Du, Y. J., & Liu, M. D. (2019). Laboratory evaluation of buried high-density polyethylene pipes subjected to localized ground subsidence. *Acta Geotechnica, 14*(4), 1081–1099. https://doi.org/10.1007/s11440-018-0698-6

Zhou, D., Jia, X., Ma, S., Shao, T., Huang, D., Hao, J., & Li, T. (2022). Dynamic simulation of natural gas pipeline network based on interpretable machine learning model. *Energy, 253*, Article 124068. https://doi.org/10.1016/j.energy.2022.124068

Industrial IoT and 3D Digital Twin for Real Time-Evergreening of Engineering Assets Subjected to Corrosion Under Insulation

Alvaro Rodríguez-Prieto, Alberto Mura, Eduardo Nuevo, Manuel Callejas, Ernesto Primera, and Franco Gambato

Abstract Corrosion under insulation (CUI) is a big problem that can affect any industrial process plant and could generate plant unavailability with often high production losses. CUI is a phenomenon that normally affects carbon steel pipes and pressure equipment, as a result of the entry or condensation of water under the thermal insulation. The recent development of technologies 4.0 opens the door to real-time monitoring of relevant degradation mechanisms like CUI. The advancement of non-destructive testing techniques and their practical applications provide data with more quality. During the last decade, several disruptive technologies has been consolidated, such as the Internet of Things (IoT) and big data, as well as the popularization of data science, Digital Twins and artificial intelligence-based techniques. Recently, the worldwide industry has required a mindset change, switching from corrective maintenance to predictive maintenance and recently focusing on approaches related to prescriptive maintenance and prognosis. Therefore, the aim of this work is to present a new methodology for dynamic risk analysis and evaluation of engineering-assets performance. This type of tools that are based on the use of collected data (by using IoT sensors) of process parameters and materials condition can provide a real time (updated) evergreening of engineering assets like

A. Rodríguez-Prieto (✉)
National Distance Education University, Madrid, Spain
e-mail: alvaro.rodriguez@ind.uned.es

A. Mura · F. Gambato
Department of Asset Integrity Software and Digital Twin, ANTEA, Padova, Italy
e-mail: mura.alberto@anteash.com

F. Gambato
e-mail: franco.gambato@antea.tech

E. Nuevo · M. Callejas
Department of Industrial Inspection and Technical Assistance, SGS Tecnos, Madrid, Spain
e-mail: eduardo.nuevocalle@sgs.com

E. Primera
Department of Applied Statistics, University of Delaware, Newark, DE, USA
e-mail: eprimera@udel.edu

A. Crespo Márquez et al. (eds.), *Case Studies in Digital Transformation*, Engineering Asset Management Review 4, https://doi.org/10.1007/978-3-032-05592-7_6

thermal-insulated piping and equipment based on a robustly built Dynamic Digital Twin.

Keywords Mechanical integrity · Materials performance · Industry 4.0 · Advanced risk-based Inspection

1 Introduction

Corrosion under insulation (CUI) is a phenomenon that normally affects carbon steel pipes and pressure equipment, as a result of the entry or condensation of water under the thermal insulation. This category of corrosion can also include corrosion generated—for the same reason—under the heat insulation (CUF, corrosion under fireproofing) of pipes and pressure vessels. Similarly, stress corrosion that occurs under insulation in austenitic and duplex steels, caused by water containing chlorides (ECSCC), is usually included in this general classification (CUI/CUF) related to corrosion under insulation (Table 1).

Reliability estimation plays a critical role according to the design and development of any type of engineering system (Song et al., 2017). Customary material investigation typically relies on a big amount of experiments, that supposes a great time-consuming and big costs (Deng et al., 2020; Xu & Hua, 2017).

Traditionally, a maintenance strategy must be balanced to maximize equipment operability and production unit performance while requiring the least resources and costs (Oropallo et al., 2024), specifically these aspects are important to consider:

- In the short term, the maintenance strategy should be selected appropriately to improve the competitiveness of the production (Velmurugan & Dhingra, 2015). Three leading maintenance strategies are failure maintenance, preventive maintenance, and predictive maintenance.
- To reduce maintenance costs and improve maintenance approaches, various techniques are used to assess equipment risks. The reliability of equipment and systems is currently one of the main business strategies to improve an organization's position in the market to get a competitive advantage (Mohammed, 2023).

Table 1 Type of corrosion under insulation depending on the material type used according to API RP 583 (2021)

Types of steels most susceptible to CUI/CUF/ECSCC	CUI	CUF	ECSCC
Carbon and alloy steel	x	x	
Low carbon steel	x	x	
Austenitic stainless steels			x
Duplex steels			x

- On the other hand, failure of equipment and systems can be highly costly for companies. Failure maintenance is the most straightforward maintenance strategy to implement, where the equipment can operate until it fails and, consequently, is repaired or replaced. Preventive maintenance is widely used in manufacturing operations, where equipment is inspected, repaired, and overhauled regularly to avoid shutdown periods.
- Predictive maintenance uses sensors to monitor the assets condition. Sensor data is analysed to monitor equipment behaviour, notice approaching item failures, and identify the failures root cause (Ramotsoela et al., 2018; Tamilselvan & Wang, 2013). Such data is often used to establish an alarm system to indicate abnormal behaviour ensuring continuous operation (Joung et al., 2020).

The recent development of technologies 4.0 opens the door to real-time monitoring of relevant degradation mechanisms like CUI. The advancement of non-destructive testing techniques and their practical applications provide data with more quality. During the last decade, several disruptive technologies has been consolidated, such as the Internet of Things (IoT) and big data, as well as the popularization of data science, Digital Twins and artificial intelligence-based techniques.

Recently, the worldwide industry has required a mindset change, switching from corrective maintenance to predictive maintenance and recently focusing on approaches related to prescriptive maintenance and prognosis. Therefore, the aim of this work is to present a new methodology for dynamic risk analysis and evaluation of engineering-assets performance. This type of tools that are based on the use of collected data (by using IoT sensors) of process parameters and materials condition can provide a real time (updated) evergreening of engineering assets like thermal-insulated piping and equipment based on a robustly built Dynamic Digital Twin.

Recently, the worldwide industry has required a change of approach, moving from corrective maintenance through predictive maintenance and recently addressing prescriptive and prognosis approaches. Therefore, the aim of this work is to present a new methodology for dynamic risk analysis and evaluation of engineering-assets performance.

This type of tools that are based on the use of collected data (by using IoT sensors) of process parameters and materials condition can provide a real time (updated) evergreening of engineering assets like thermal-insulated piping and equipment based on a robustly built Dynamic Digital Twin.

The application of this type of methodologies can be extended for the use in other demanding applications such as the power generation, the manufacturing, or the infrastructure management. The combination of Technologies 4.0 and data analytics is crucial to obtain a smart asset management.

2 Methodology and Materials

Reliability pretends to give an estimation of the failure probability of a system (Das Neves & António, 2019). To obtain the model, considerable quantities of very high-quality information (usually from experimental sources) are needed to build precise probability distributions. However, in many applications, the data from physic models (experimental data) are scarce (Shi & Lu, 2019).

The reliability of an engineering system may be evaluated at two scales: the engineering asset and the system level (Cao et al., 2022; Jiang et al., 2017). In this research, reliability is focused at the engineering asset level (Rodríguez-Prieto et al., 2020).

The optimization of industrial plants heavily depends on the reliability improvement of their components and equipment as reliability improvement results in failure reduction. And, failure reduction would inevitably improve industrial plants' sustainability and would contribute to compliance with the SDGs, in particular, SDG 7 ("Affordable and non-polluting energy") and SDG 9 ("Industry, Innovation and Infrastructure").

2.1 Critical Factors for CUI

Corrosion under insulation is favored by the entry of moisture between the pipe and the insulation. This phenomenon is aggravated by the presence of chlorides or sulfides. At a general level, the reaction kinetics depends mainly on temperature (Fig. 1).

In any screening study, the following factors should be considered for their influence on the probability of producing CUI/CUF:

- The duration of exposure to humidity.
- The design of the insulation system, type of insulation, temperature, and the environment to which it is subjected.
- The presence of insulation materials that retain moisture (hygroscopic characteristics).
- Cyclic thermal operation/intermittent service can accelerate corrosion mechanisms.
- Equipment operating below the water dew point provokes water condensation on the metal surface increasing corrosion risk.
- Corrosive character of the aqueous solution. The damage is aggravated by the presence of contaminants such as chlorides or sulfides.
- Corrosion rate: the kinetics of the reaction increase with the temperature of the metal up to temperatures from which the rate of water evaporation is very fast. Likewise, different corrosion mechanisms can be activated in the presence of chlorides or sulfides.

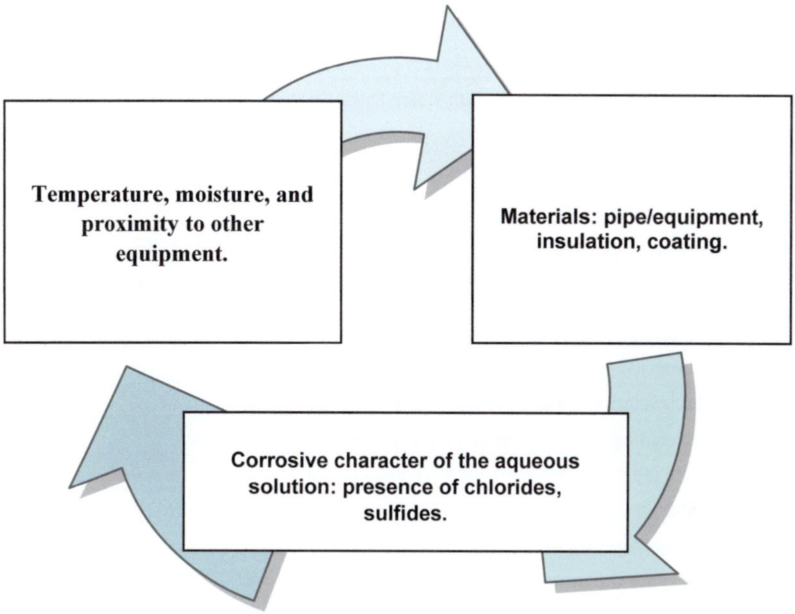

Fig. 1 Main influencing factors on corrosion under insulation

- Below are the temperature ranges that, according to the usual corrosion kinetics, favor this CUI and/or ECSCC phenomenon (Table 2).

During the external inspection, according to API RP 583, the following areas (Table 3) of the systems that are potentially most susceptible to CUI should be considered.

In pressure equipment (vessels, columns, heat exchangers, etc.…) the following areas (Table 4) are characterized by being more prone to presenting CUI/CUF.

Likewise, in pipes the following areas (Table 5) are characterized by being more prone to presenting CUI/CUF.

Table 2 Type of steel and temperature range that increases the kinetics of the corrosion reaction

Steel type	Corrosion mechanism	Critical temperatures
Carbon	CUI	Between −12 and 175 °C. Greater kinetics of the reaction in the range 77 and 110 °C
Austenitic stainless steels	ECSCC	Between 60 and 175 °C (highest corrosion rate), and it can occur up to 205 °C
Duplex	ECSCC	At temperatures above 140 °C in the presence of high concentrations of chloride. The phenomenon can occur up to a temperature of 205 °C

Table 3 Areas of the systems that are potentially most susceptible to CUI

Critical areas
Areas closed to steam vents and areas with steam leaks
Areas near cooling towers
Areas exposed to fire sprinklers
Areas subject to process spills that can facilitate the entry of humidity or vapors of certain acids
Carbon steel piping systems operating above 120ºC and in intermittent service
Operation below or around the atmospheric dew point
Areas with penetrations (vents, drains, supports, nozzles, instrument connections) through insulation in equipment/piping. Special attention to services that operate at room temperature or maintain a cold service
Areas where the insulation coating is damaged or has disappeared
Areas where the coating system is bulging or shows signs of deterioration
Areas where there are no access areas for thickness control
Damage in insulation coating caused by vibrations
Areas prone to rainwater entering
Isolated areas only for the protection of personnel
Areas under insulation with deteriorated coatings or wrappers
Ice/air interfaces in isolated systems that undergo constant freezing and thawing processes
Dead legs (areas with very low or no flow) that protrude from insulated pipes and operate at a temperature different from the temperature of the active line
Vibration of piping systems that have a tendency to cause damage to the insulation, causing areas that facilitate the entry of water
Piping systems showing deteriorated insulation, coatings and/or wraps; bulges or stains on the insulation system, deteriorated seals
Pipes susceptible to physical damage to the coating or insulation
Valves and accessories such as tubes and flanges in pressure safety valves

Table 4 Zones more prone to presenting CUI/CUF (pressure equipment)

Zones prone to CUI
– Fastening rings under damaged or improperly installed insulation
– Reinforcement rings in insulated containers or in columns in vacuum service
– Insulation in welded areas
– Isolated supports in small containers
– Ladder and platform accessories
– Termination of insulation on nozzles and other accessories
– Fireproof coatings (CUF)
– Anchor screws (CUF)
– Bottom in horizontal containers (from the lower third to the middle of the container)
– Irregular shapes resulting in complex insulation configurations

Table 5 Zones more prone to presenting CUI/CUF (piping)

Zones prone to CUI
– Vents and drains
– Supports and supports for pipes
– Valves and accessories
– Screwed into pipe supports
– Steam lines / electric tubing
– Termination of insulation on pipe fittings
– Carbon or low-alloy steel components on alloy steel pipes
– Seams in the lining (top of the horizontal pipe)
– Finishing/termination of insulation in vertical pipes
– Areas where smaller line connections intersect with larger diameter lines
– Low points of the pipe with gaps in the insulation
– Immediacy to water and/or land
– Wet due to flooding or even because it is submerged in water
– Damage due to the passage of people
– Additionally, in pipes that operate below the dew point, special vigilance must be taken at the following points:
• Pipe supports • Pipe-flange joints • Studded flanges where insulation is installed but not sealed • Pipes below flood level with water penetrating in the insulation coating, causing the cladding (external insulation coating) to warp and degrade • Areas with a high flow of people, where the insulation is degraded for this reason • Areas where the insulation jacket or cladding shows signs of continuous surface condensation • Holes or cuts in the insulation jacket or cladding, especially at ice-air interfaces or vapor systems

According to API 583, the following information (Table 6) is required to estimate the failure probability regarding to corrosion under insulation.

With the starting information and carrying out a study using various non-destructive testing techniques–such as neutron backscattering (NB), infrared thermography (IR), pulsed induced currents (PEC) or digital radiography and guided waves between others-, a series of data is obtained that allows calculating the probability of failure.

To evaluate the risk, it is necessary to evaluate, first of all, the criticality of the degradation mechanisms that can generate permanent damage to structures and equipment. Secondly, it is necessary to analyze the maintenance plan for each of the equipment and the existing inspection plans.

To reduce or mitigate the risk of failure, the International Atomic Energy Agency (IAEA) proposes (IAEA-TECDOC-, 1209, 2001) a series of actions that, in the methodology presented in this work, are organized according to Fig. 2.

Table 6 Information required to estimate the probability of failure due to corrosion under insulation

Required information
– Environmental conditions
– Construction materials of the system/equipment
– Age of the component/equipment/system
– Service temperature
– Cyclic or intermittent operation
– Areas with loss of insulation
– Type of insulation and/or heat insulation
– Type of external insulation and/or heat insulation coating
– Exposure to vapor flows

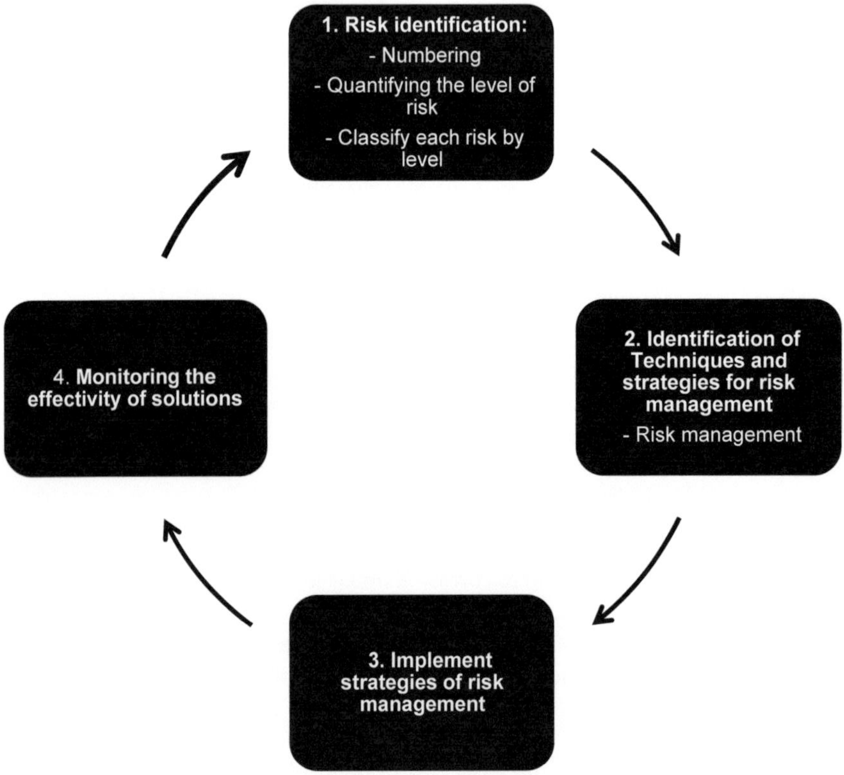

Fig. 2 Framework of risk assessment

In this way, once the risks have been quantified, the methodology involves the development of risk reduction strategies, such as increasing the precision and frequency of inspections, to finally validate the effectiveness of the safety solutions. risk mitigation implemented.

2.2 Parameters Controlled by IoT Sensors for Monitoring CUI

The digitalization of their existing processes should be achieved through the use of asset management software, EAM (enterprise asset management), mobile technologies, devices, and sensors, as well as cloud computing and big data technologies. In addition, it is necessary to identify and evaluate the risks to create inspection plans. This would result in the optimization of the plant maintenance strategy by feeding the mechanical integrity evaluation software with data and valuable information (Rodríguez-Prieto et al., 2024).

The management of physical assets in Industry 4.0 environments requires new control models and methods that optimize the reliability, availability, safety, and feasibility of modern sensors and digital tools. In addition, this problem is expected to be further exacerbated in plants with complex operational processes or in organizations with inadequate operative experience for such applications.

Considering modern Internet of Things (IoT) sensors for CUI, the following parameters can be taken into account:

- External corrosion rate.
- Moisture level in the sub coating area.
- Current thickness. This value is obtained indirectly by considering an initial thickness and the actual corrosion rate over the specified time period.
- Condition of the coating.

2.3 Monitoring System

To enhance the monitoring level of the damage mechanism of the CUI (Corrosion Under Insulation), the following tools are used:

- An IDMS (Integrity Data Management System) to store and manage the inspection data
- Online sensors for monitoring the condition of insulated equipment
- A quantitative risk-based inspection (RBI) calculation machine following API RP 581 (2016)
- An alert and alarm application for monitoring key parameters based on Integrity Operating Window (IOW) according to API RP 584 (2021)

2.4 Integration Platform

Most companies in the petrochemical sector that intend to implement asset management software are looking for a solution that allows them to add new functionalities to the existing systems in their plants. This software selection criterion is usually not the most appropriate. In reality, it is recommended to review the various approaches in the market to find an optimized solution that meets real needs of the plants, which would help prevent implementing solutions with an unnecessarily excessive number of functionalities and characteristics.

As indicated above, it is necessary to define a general asset management strategy with a systems (bird's eye) point of view that would include many aspects along with specific measures and objectives that allow the success rate to be quantified. This systems view should include an understanding of the optimization of various plant processes, operations, maintenance, engineering as well as the environment, incorporating all functional departments in the plant. All company objectives must be aligned with adequate asset management that is compliant with the security requirements of the company (EAM asset management software) as well as the company's continuous improvement (ISO55000, 2014) goals (Rodríguez-Prieto et al., 2024).

A key difference in terms of the software implementation strategy, and the methodologies discussed in the previous sections, is defining how they are integrated with plant management systems and third-party software, such as databases, BIM (building information) models, modeling) or enterprise resource planning devices. It is important that data collection in the plant is accurate using analysis tools for a correct evaluation of the data.

The quality of the data is a differential factor that will allow us to define a fluid and automated process to obtain the greatest possible benefit. To do this, the software must use production data collection systems, sophisticated algorithms to detect the ingestion of errors and tracking of approvals and codes linked to assets.

This integration will allow us to finish defining the digitalization process of plant assets. After defining the integration of the different management systems, asset management software and methodologies, the processes will be digitized, allowing bidirectional data to be obtained between the various platforms that will be used to implement new operations and maintenance strategies, both preventive and predictive. This allows improvements to be reflected in operations, optimizing the useful life of assets and, therefore, increasing safety in the plants (Rodríguez-Prieto et al., 2024).

With the appropriate connections it is potentially possible to create a system for controlling and updating risk data deriving from under-insulation corrosion. The complete integration schema is reported in Fig. 3.

The part of the schema on the left (IDMS) includes historical data storage. Certainly, to use such data in a quantitative Risk-Based Inspection process, it is necessary to set up the input of inspection activities in a standardized manner and with the inclusion of specific data.

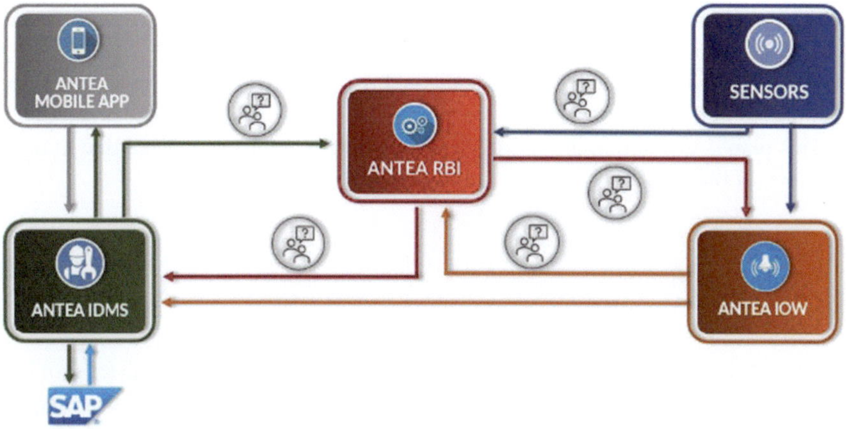

Fig. 3 Integration schema

In case of component in carbon or alloy steel or low carbon steel, if an automatic procedure is required, for each record of inspection activity it will be requested:

- the effectiveness of such inspection for detecting Corrosion Under Insulation.
- the insulation condition revealed during the inspection.

Other data to be used, but already available in uploading of inspection activity is the date of inspection, the thickness of the component and the corrosion rate. Also, a rule of determination of the most appropriate value of thickness and corrosion rate using medium or minimum values (conservative approaches).

In case of component built in austenitic stainless steel or duplex the important information are.

- the effectiveness of such inspection for detecting external chloride stress corrosion cracking under insulation.
- the insulation condition revealed during the inspection.
- If a crack has been found during the inspection.

For sure the date of inspection is interesting also in this case, but not the thickness data and corrosion rate.

Therefore, the heart of the workflow is composed of the RBI module, which serves as the engine that, by analyzing technical and inspection data, provides a risk and an appropriate inspection plan based on damage mechanisms, particularly in the case of corrosion under insulation. The tool allows to perform qualitative, semi-quantitative and quantitative analysis, but the most reproducible methodology is the quantitative one according to API RP 581 (2016), whose adherence to the software is certified.

Reading the technical and inspection data coming from the IDMS, the tool, certainly operated by expert personnel, can define the probability and consequence of each equipment with the possibility to visualize it in a risk matrix or in an iso-risk graph. In this way it will be possible to calculate the risk (probability x consequence) and define its criticality.

The next step provided by the software is the definition of an adequate inspection plan based on the level of risk and the damage mechanisms to which it is subject.

This plan is inserted in the IDMS module where it can be optimized due to other activities of the plant.

3 Results

The use of the digital twin certainly allows a better understanding of the level of risk on the plant. The usage of mobile apps to consult technical data and to insert inspection data directly in the field and the connection with a computerized maintenance management system (CMMS) provide further added value.

3.1 Connectivity and Real Time Updating in an Advanced Modeling Tool Environment

Real-time data from online sensors can be used to conduct more reliable Risk-Based Inspection (RBI) analyses that are aligned with the actual conditions. Both the RBI tool and the sensors themselves can feed into the Integrity Operating Windows (IOW) module. The goal is to alert operators if more critical conditions than those identified are occurring, which could lead to an increased risk. The RBI tool provides guidance for setting rules for warnings and alarms, while the sensors are continuously monitored based on the established rules.

It would be possible to simulate the effects that a variable can have in the total risk. For example, evaluating the increasing of risk due to modification of corrosion rate, insulation condition or the presence of a crack can be the input of setting up some limits linked to data from the field (from inspection or from sensors).

Other data that indirectly can affect the ones mentioned are the moisture level, external environmental conditions and others.

In this case IOWs can be used to intervene on the operating conditions to prevent the onset of unwanted damage mechanisms but they can also be useful to inform users when data have changed, and the RBI analysis performed is no longer current. Figure 4 shows the process monitoring connected with RBI software to help modelling IOW.

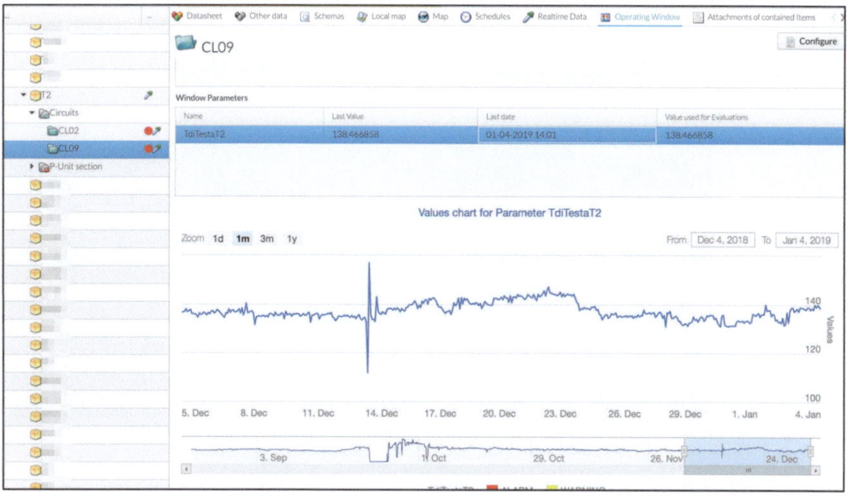

Fig. 4 Process monitoring connected with RBI software

3.2 *3D Visualization for Plant Integrity Management. Use of 3D Models and IoT Data to Build a Digital Twin*

The platform managed by senior materials engineers is a software designed to manage the integrity of all equipment within a facility. Developed to allow direct web access, it can integrate the management of inspection and maintenance activities according to the Risk-Based Inspection (RBI) methodology/procedure.

It includes interactive 2D navigation graphics for plant documentation and 3D visualization for the digital twin of the plant, using 3D models and laser scanning acquisitions. The software structure, as depicted in Figs. 3, 4, 5 and 6 consists of a central Asset Management section and detailed modules that enable the specific management of certain types of engineering assets or equipment (pressure equipment, pipelines, electrical and instrumental equipment, pipelines, structures, and more). This structure ensures centralized and integrated management of data from various sources, as well as detailed management of functionalities specific to certain equipment categories. For this purpose, specific calculation modules have been integrated to assist analysts in making technical assessments based on real and up-to-date data.

Navigate in 2D schemas allow to reduce time of searching information for specific item, avoiding the need for knowing the tag. All types of documents can be attached but the interactive functionality of reaching a specific item in the drawing automatically is useful for the schemas like P&IDs, PFDs, electrical diagrams, site plans and others.

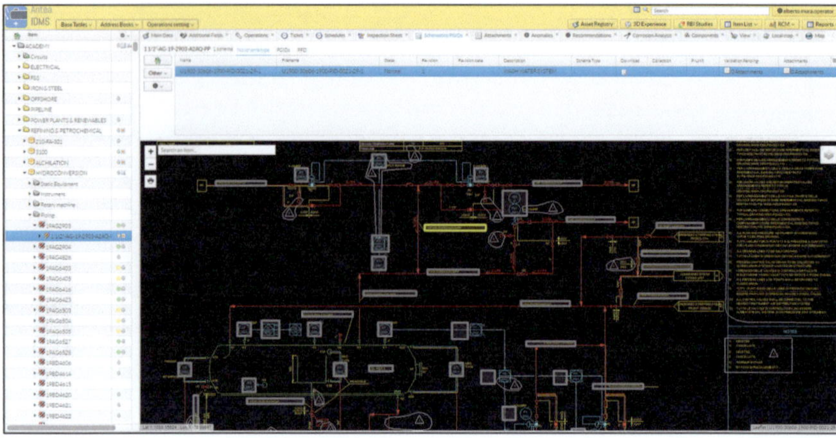

Fig. 5 Localizing a piping in its P&ID's location–Software platform

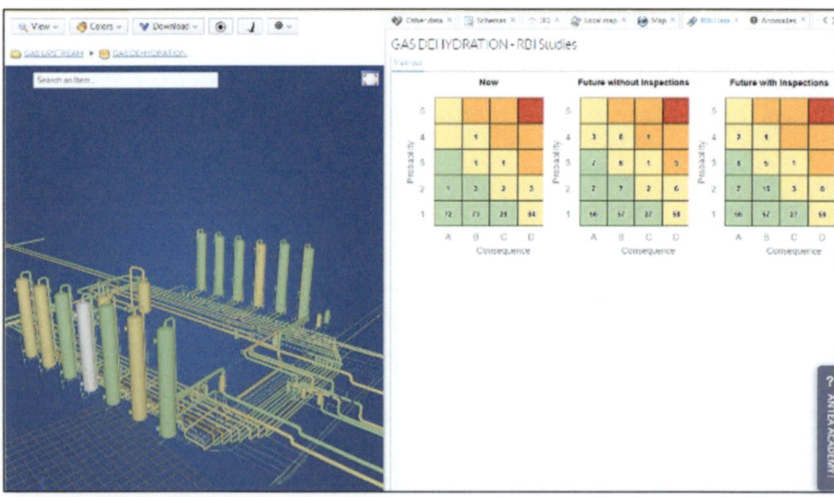

Fig. 6 Managing the risk and integrity of the plant–Software platform

It is possible to consult the process directly from the schema and localizing each interesting items clicking on the tag. In this way all the data and information can be retrieved and consulted.

The purpose of the usage of this 3D model is specifically adapted for Asset Integrity and Maintenance and not for traditional engineering usage. In fact, to simplify the usage, only the active part of the process is represented as active, and all support structures can be seen as a background 3D visualization.

The way of reaching the 3D visualization can be multiple and depends on the case. Below the different possibilities:

- Importing of engineering model. If an "intelligent" engineering model is available, it can be imported. The word "intelligent" indicate that each component has a reference to a specific item in the asset register and contains geometrical and technical information. For sure a model derived from the AS BUILT will be preferable to one created for construction purposes, because it already contains the changes inserted during assembly. The model can be updated at the AS BUILT through the usage of the editor.
- Built the 3D model starting from documentation. If at least general arrangements of the equipment and isometric drawings for the piping are available and in an acceptable level of updating it would be possible to recreate the 3D overview of the plant.
- Using laser scanning acquisition. When the documentation is not available or not updated it would be possible to organize a campaign of acquisition of 3D point cloud from laser scanning. The output of the laser scanning can already be used as a 3D model, after importing it into the platform and proceeding with a labelling activity on the equipment. Alternatively, the intelligent 3D model can be recreated using the editor (reverse engineering activity).

It would be optimal to establish updating procedures to follow the actual changes to the plants. Having the 3D model allows to optimize the analysis and the management of the plants with a graphical perception of the information. In fact, in the 3D model, it would be possible to visualize all the equipment with different colors depending on the criticality coming from RBI studies (high red, medium–high orange, medium yellow and low green). In addition, other data can be seen directly in 3D like:

- Type of fluid in each equipment/pipe.
- Specific color depending on the results of inspections.
- Specific color of thickness measurement location depending on the status of corrosion.
- Specific color depending on dates of inspection plan.
- Results of sensors specific color.
- Others.

3.3 Mobile Apps and CMMS Connection

To improve the monitoring, management, and repair activities of the corrosion under insulation, further improvements in terms of integration and optimization are given using mobile apps and the connection with CMMS systems (such as SAP® and/or Maximo®).

Mobile Apps (Fig. 7) are useful for consulting data or inserting inspection results directly from the field.

Consulting the data: Having the information in the field is of fundamental importance, but it is difficult to carry bulky documentation, without considering the need to have all the documentation that may be useful, even that which becomes important

Fig. 7 Mobile Apps usage of the Software platform

following observations that emerged during the inspection activity. Having a proper ATEX device connected with the main Asset Integrity and RBI platform is the solution. For each item it is possible to view technical data, attachments and schedules, to view position in P&ID or another schema, localize it in a map, view 3D models and point clouds, consult inspection maintenance history and anomalies status and visualize RBI results and sensors data.

Inserting inspection and maintenance data: through mobile apps it is also possible to retrieve specific item in the field (also through QR code if an activity of census has been done) and perform specific activities like inserting inspection and maintenance activity or report anomalies.

A proper workflow is available assigning activities to different operators from the main platform and executing them through mobile apps.

An operator can retrieve in his/her device all the planned activities he has to do like thickness measurement inspection with all the list of TMLs with the indication of their position (using both 2D and 3D graphics), or sequential activities managed with specific checklist with the possibility to insert results, notes, pictures and audio. If some findings are retrieved, they can insert specific anomalies to be managed in the main platform.

4 Discussion

Also, the connection between the IDMS/RBI platform with the CMMS can also bring certain benefits in terms of centralization and speed, while also avoiding information losses. Below it is suggested a typical structure of integration:

A. The first level of integration consists in the alignment of asset register. This alignment must be done at the beginning of the project, and it is necessary to keep it aligned ensuring a unique line of creation or deletion of items.
B. The second level concerns an alignment at level of Predictive maintenance. In this case it is suggested the IDMS will be the master and CMMS will receipt the plan. The process of execution of the activities will be connected between the two platforms, sharing the status and the work Order reference.
C. The third level concerns an alignment at level of Corrective maintenance. All the findings reported as "Anomalies" in the IDMS platform will be analyzed by expert personnel and appropriate recommendations will be provided, including the assignment of the deadline, the responsible and the priority. These recommendations will be automatically converted in specific work order in the CMMS. The process of execution of the activities will be connected between the two platforms, sharing the status and the work Order reference.
D. The last level regards the events of failure. In this case the starting point will be the CMMS, from where the IDMS will be receiving the request of activity and will manage the execution. When the activity will be executed both platforms will be updated and aligned.

Figure 8 represents the workflow just described.

While the integration of Technologies 4.0 can be an important challenge to integrate in the Asset Management operations in critical industrial sectors, several limitations arise moreover for Small and Medium Enterprises (SMEs) that need to do

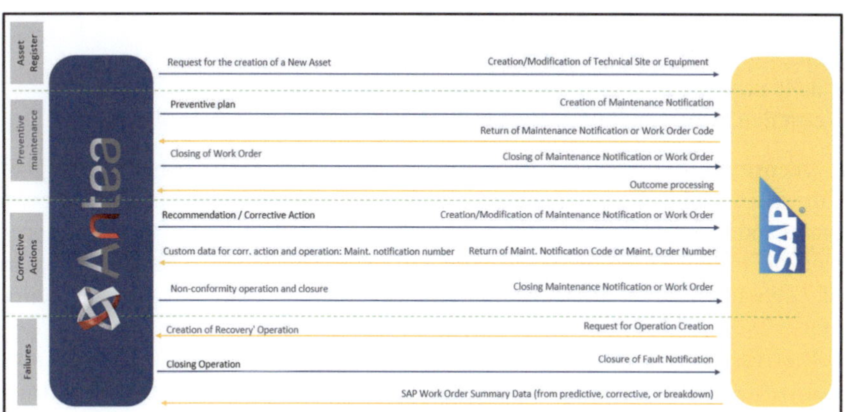

Fig. 8 Integration between AIM/RBI and CMMS platforms

a great financial effort to costs the acquisition of sensors, software licenses, among others. Nevertheless, some SMEs can be eligible to obtain funding for government and/or state.

4.1 Economic Benefits Obtained with the Application of This Methodology. Analysis Centered in the CUI Problem in the Petrochemical Industry

This methodology has demonstrated several improvements in the Asset Management of critical equipment affected by CUI. External corrosion rates for calculating the external corrosion and corrosion under insulation damage factors in ferritic steels were obtained from Tables 15.2 M and 16.2 M in API RP 581 (2016) or marine environments. Values of 0.025 mm/year and 0.127 mm/year were applied for these parameters, respectively. Based on the designed external and internal corrosion rates, the estimated total corrosion rate is 0.132 mm/year. Some inspections were performed on the equipment in the past. However, these inspections were considered ineffective for the calculation because they involved a reduced scope. To analyze the advantages of the application of this methodology, a comparison between a Risk-based Inspection methodology (supported by the application of Technologies 4.0—IoT sensors and Digital Twin—and data analytics using IOW) and a basic Time-based Inspection (TBI) has been performed.

As for the adjustment factors for the calculation of the thinning damage factor, all of them were set to 1. The detection system was evaluated as consisting of instrumentation specifically designed to detect material loss due to changes in operating conditions in the system. The isolation system consists of isolation devices activated by operators in the control room. The mitigation system consists of inventory purging. The costs for the calculation of the financial consequence were applied as follows, considering the plant assessments:

- cost of replacing equipment in the affected area: €4,000/m^2
- daily production in the unit: €40,000/m^2
- cost due to relevant injuries/fatalities: €10,000/person

A density of 0.1 persons/m^2 was estimated. The TBI strategy that had been applied to the asset until this assessment was carried out was an external inspection every 3 years and an internal inspection every 9 years. The RBI study has been developed using the imbalance risk matrix according to API RP 581 (2016) as a reference. The risk target has been set at the medium risk level. For the analysis a planning period from 2023 to 2056 has been considered.

The resulting cumulative costs versus time for the TBI strategy with non-intrusive inspection are compared to those of the best RBI strategy with non-intrusive inspection using Technologies 4.0, as shown in Fig. 9.

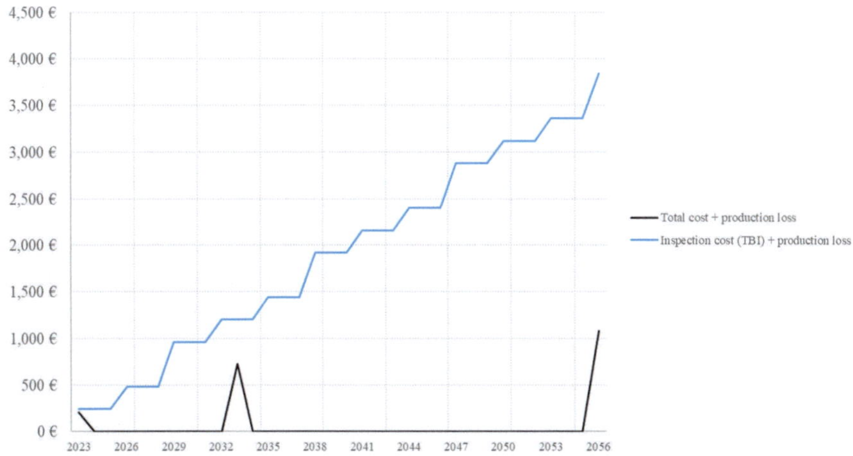

Fig. 9 Evolution of total accumulated costs vs time for the TBI strategy with non-intrusive inspection (blue line) and for the RBI 1 strategy with non-intrusive inspection (black line)

It can be observed that the RBI strategy supported by Technologies 4.0 is relatively more profitable than the basic TBI strategy and this difference increases over time.

5 Conclusions

Having real data and advanced modeling tools to analyze them, the effectiveness and reliability of RBI analyses can be strongly improved. Thus, all controlled parameters can be used to estimate the damage factor that impact on the probability of failure. This information can also be used to define the rules and the limits for Integrity Operating Windows. Specifically, it is possible to set a limit on the value of the damage factor "Corrosion Under Insulation" connected with the humidity level, coating condition, and corrosion rate.

Real-time data from online sensors can be used to conduct more reliable Risk-Based Inspection (RBI) analyses that are aligned with the actual conditions. Both the RBI tool and the sensors themselves can feed into the Integrity Operating Windows (IOW) module. The goal is to alert operators if more critical conditions than those identified are occurring, which could lead to an increased risk. The RBI tool provides guidance for setting rules for warnings and alarms, while the sensors are continuously monitored based on the established rules. It would be possible to simulate the effects that a variable can have in the total risk.

Having the 3D model allows to optimize the analysis and the management of the plants with a graphical perception of the information. In fact, in the 3D model, it would be possible to visualize all the equipment with different colors depending on the criticality coming from RBI studies.

The use of the digital twin certainly allows a better understanding of the level of risk on the plant, as can be seen in the image. The usage of mobile apps to consult technical data and to insert inspection data directly in the field and the connection with a computerized maintenance management system (CMMS) provide further added value. To improve the monitoring, management, and repair activities of the corrosion under insulation, further improvements in terms of integration and optimization are given using mobile apps and the connection with CMMS systems.

The platform managed by senior materials engineers is a software designed to manage the integrity of all equipment within a facility. Developed to allow direct web access, it can integrate the management of inspection and maintenance activities according to the Risk-Based Inspection (RBI) methodology/procedure. It generates a dynamic risk evaluation system that allows to obtain a real-time evergreening of assets.

When the combination of these values reaches the warning or alert limits of the damage factor, the user can be instantly notified, or if the limit is exceeded for certain defined periods of time. Simpler limits on individual parameters can certainly be defined.

Finally, using the available information, the Inspection Program is defined in which certain points will be periodically covered that, according to the study, are more susceptible to corrosion under insulation. In this way, in a reasonable period, 100% of the isolated systems could be covered, greatly reducing the expense that would be involved in inspecting 100% of the isolated systems in each intervention (the entire installation with insulation). This plan is part of a plant integrity plan that allows predicting and mitigating the consequences of material degradation mechanisms like corrosion under insulation.

References

API RP 581. (2016). *Risk-based inspection technology*. Washington D.C.–USA: American Petroleum Institute (API).

API RP 583. (2021). *Corrosion under insulation and fireproofing*. Washington D.C.–USA: American Petroleum Institute (API).

API RP 584. (2021). *Integrity operating windows*. Washington D.C.–USA: American Petroleum Institute (API).

Cao, Q., Pojtanabuntoeng, T., Esmaily, M., Thomas, S., Brameld, M., Amer, A., & Birbilis, N. (2022). A review of corrosion under insulation: A critical issue in the oil and gas industry. *Metals, 12*, 561.

Chris, K. M., & Wang, Z. (2001). Using fuzzy linguistics to select optimum & condition based strategies. *International Journal of Mechanical Systems & Signal Processing, 15*(6), 1129–1140.

Das Neves, G., & António, C. C. (2019). Robustness and reliability of composite structures: Effects of different sources of uncertainty. *International Journal of Mechanics and Materials in Design, 15*, 93–107.

Deng, Y., Qiao, L., Zhu, J., & Yang, B. (2020). Mechanical performance and microstructure prediction of hypereutectoid rail steels based on BP neural networks. *IEEE Access, 8*, 41905–41912.

IAEA-TECDOC-1209. (2001). *Risk management: A tool for improving nuclear power plant performance*. Vienna: International Atomic Energy Agency.
ISO 14224. (2016). *Petroleum, petrochemical and natural gas industries—collection and exchange of reliability and maintenance data for equipment*. Geneva: International Standardization Organization.
ISO 55000. (2014). *Asset management. Overview, principles and terminology*. Geneva: International Organization for Standardization.
Jiang, C., Huang, X. P., Wei, X. P., & Liu, N. Y. (2017). A time-variant reliability analysis method for structural systems based on stochastic process discretization. *International Journal of Mechanics and Materials in Design, 13*, 173–193.
Joung, B. G., Lee, W. J., Huang, A., & Sutherland, J. W. (2020). Development and application of a method for real time motor fault detection. In Y. R. Gao R. X. (Ed.), *Procedia Manufacturing* 49, 4–98.
Lees, F. P. (2012). *Loss prevention in the process industries* (4th ed.). Butterworth-Heinemann.
Mohammed, A. (2023). Data driven-based model for predicting pump failures in the oil and gas industry. *Engineering Failure Analysis, 145*, Article 107019.
Oropallo, E., Piscopo, P., Centobelli, P., Cerchione, R., Nuevo, E., & Rodríguez-Prieto, A. (2024). A decision support system to assess the operational safety and economic benefits of risk-based inspection implementation strategies. *Safety Science, 177*, Article 106570.
Ramotsoela, D., Abu-Mahfouz, A., & Hancke, G. (2018). A survey of anomaly detection in industrial wireless sensor networks with critical water system infrastructure as a case study. *Sensors, 18*(8), 2491.
Rodríguez-Prieto, A., Camacho, A. M., Callejas, M., & Sebastián, M. A. (2020). Fitness for service and reliability of materials for manufacturing components intended for demanding service conditions in the petrochemical industry. *IEEE Access, 8*, 92275–92286.
Rodríguez-Prieto, A., Sireli, Y., Primera, E. (2024). *Digitalization strategy for Engineering Asset Management in the context of Industry's net-zero transition*. 1st Ibero-American Congress on Engineering Asset Management (congrEGA'24), July 3–5, Lisbon.
Shi, Y., & Lu, Z. (2019). Dynamic reliability analysis model for structure with both random and interval uncertainties. *International Journal of Mechanics and Materials in Design, 15*, 521–537.
Song, X., Zhai, Z., Zhu, P., & Han, J. (2017). A stochastic computational approach for the analysis of fuzzy systems. *IEEE Access, 5*, 13465–13477.
Tamilselvan, P., & Wang, P. (2013). Failure diagnosis using deep belief learning based health state classification. *Reliability Engineering and System Safety, 115*, 124–135.
Velmurugan, R. S., & Dhingra, T. (2015). Maintenance strategy selection and its impact in maintenance function: A conceptual framework. *International Journal of Operations and Production Management, 35*(12), 1622–1661.
Xu, X., & Hua, Q. (2017). Industrial big data analysis in smart factory: Current status and research strategies. *IEEE Access, 5*, 17543–17551

Optimization of Maintenance Management Through Digital Integration: AMORMS Audit and SAP Implementation in a Cosmetics Manufacturing Company

Pablo Andrés Duque Ramírez, Carlos Parra, Félix Pizarro, Vicente Gonzalez-Prida, Carlos Baldi, and Emanuel Vega

Abstract This study aims to enhance the maintenance management of a Chilean cosmetics manufacturing company through the application of the AMORMS audit (Asset Management, Operational Reliability & Maintenance Survey). The audit follows the 8-phase Maintenance Management Model (MGM) proposed by INGEMAN, which identified several areas for improvement in the company's maintenance processes. The audit results revealed that six out of eight maintenance processes were classified as "below average." Based on these findings, specific improvement actions were proposed for each phase of the model, categorized into four key areas: Effectiveness, Efficiency, Optimization, and Continuous Improvement. The proposed actions include defining maintenance objectives and policies, developing a ranking

---

The original version of the chapter has been revised. A correction to this chapter can be found at https://doi.org/10.1007/978-3-032-05592-7_17

P. Andrés Duque Ramírez (✉) · C. Parra
Departamento de Mecánica, Universidad Técnica Federico Santa María, Viña del Mar, Chile
e-mail: pablo.duque@usm.cl

C. Parra
e-mail: carlos.parram@usm.cl

F. Pizarro · C. Baldi
Mecánica, Universidad Técnica Federico Santa María, Viña del Mar, Chile
e-mail: felix.pizarro@usm.cl

C. Baldi
e-mail: carlos.baldi@usm.cl

V. Gonzalez-Prida
Industrial Management I, University of Seville, Seville, Spain
e-mail: vgonzalezprida@us.es

E. Vega
School of Computer Engineering, Pontifical Catholic University of Valparaíso, Valparaíso, Chile
e-mail: emanuel.vega@pucv.cl

A. Crespo Márquez et al. (eds.), *Case Studies in Digital Transformation*, Engineering Asset Management Review 4, https://doi.org/10.1007/978-3-032-05592-7_7

method and criticality analysis of assets, identifying and analysing failures, designing efficient maintenance plans, and implementing continuous improvement processes. The implementation of these improvements will be guided by agile methodologies, specifically Scrum, to organize the work in iterative cycles and allow for continuous adjustments. This approach enables the company to remain flexible, making data-driven decisions based on feedback and real-time insights. The integration of SAP as a management and data collection tool is central to this process, serving as the core system for tracking performance, analysing maintenance needs, and ensuring that improvements are aligned with operational goals. SAP's capabilities for integrating maintenance schedules, asset data, and real-time reporting provide the company with a comprehensive view of asset performance, facilitating strategic decision-making. External consulting will play a key role in optimizing the use of SAP and guiding the development of strategic asset management plans, ensuring that the improvements are effectively implemented and sustained over time. Additionally, consultants will provide staff training on the use of SAP to maximize the value of data integration and process automation in the maintenance management framework. A technical–economic analysis indicates that a 2% increase in equipment availability in the selected pilot area could generate savings equivalent to 20% of the maintenance budget, resulting in a benefit–cost ratio (BCR) of 4. These results suggest that the financial benefits would significantly exceed the costs within the first year of implementation, greatly improving the economic viability of the project.

Keywords Maintenance · Management · Assets · Audit · Agile methodology · Scrum

1 Introduction

In recent years, the development of new technologies, methods, and tools has significantly enhanced the optimized use of resources, yielding greater benefits for stakeholders, management, and decision-makers. The integration of digital technologies, such as enterprise resource planning (ERP) systems, predictive maintenance tools, and real-time data analytics platforms, has transformed the way organizations manage their assets, leading to improved operational efficiency and decision-making capabilities. These digital tools allow for a more proactive approach to maintenance and asset management by facilitating data-driven insights and automating key processes (Tsang & Jardine, 2022; Lee et al., 2014).

The case study presented in this work corresponds to an intervention conducted in a Chilean company dedicated to the manufacture of cosmetic products. Significant opportunities for improvement in Maintenance Management have been identified, primarily due to the absence of a structured maintenance management model and clearly defined policies. The lack of performance indicators has made it difficult to assess the effectiveness of maintenance and production operations. Furthermore, the absence of inventory management models has complicated the administration of spare parts and materials necessary for equipment maintenance. This lack of digital integration and control has resulted in the company's inability to evaluate plant availability, calculate real maintenance costs, measure overall equipment effectiveness (OEE), and assess the criticality of equipment and spare parts. Additionally, it is estimated that the current maintenance plan consists of 80% corrective tasks and only 20% preventive tasks, with no data on its actual effectiveness.

These deficiencies in maintenance management, combined with the lack of digital tools for data collection and analysis, negatively impact the company's productivity and profitability. To address these issues, it is essential to adopt digital technologies such as SAP, which integrates asset management functions within a unified platform. ERP systems like SAP facilitate the collection of real-time data, enabling companies to track asset performance, schedule maintenance efficiently, and ensure that decisions are based on accurate and timely information (Van Horenbeek et al., 2018). Additionally, the implementation of predictive maintenance systems, based on Internet of Things (IoT) technologies, can significantly enhance the company's ability to transition from reactive to proactive maintenance strategies (Lee et al., 2014).

With the objective of identifying opportunities for improvement and establishing a work plan for their implementation, this study proposes conducting a maintenance audit aimed at improving the profitability of the production system and reducing uncertainty in decision-making. The AMORMS audit will be applied, based on the INGEMAN Maintenance Management Model (MGM). This model has been successfully used in various industries, including pulp manufacturing (Aránguiz et al., 2023), desalination plants (Duque et al., 2023), and electrical transmission (Parra Márquez et al., 2022), with positive outcomes in optimizing asset management processes (González-Prida et al., 2022).

The audit will assess the use of digital tools to support the management process in the eight phases of the MGM. Critical areas for improvement will be identified, and concrete actions will be proposed to optimize the asset management process. The implementation of these improvements will adopt an agile approach, utilizing methodologies such as Scrum to organize work in iterative cycles and enable continuous adjustments. Agile methodologies like Scrum allow organizations to remain flexible and responsive to changing operational conditions, ensuring continuous improvement in asset management processes (Rigby et al., 2016).

2 General Background

A maintenance audit is a systematic review process whose objective is to determine the current state of the maintenance department, identifying points of improvement and the actions necessary to achieve them. The objective is to improve the profitability of the production system and reduce uncertainty in decision-making in the maintenance management process (Parra & Crespo, 2024).

In the literature, maintenance audits have been proposed to evaluate different processes and areas that make up maintenance management. The evaluation focuses on identifying gaps and generating recommendations to reduce or eliminate deviations (Parra Márquez et al., 2021). According to the Maintenance Management Model, audits are part of Phase 8: Implementation of the continuous improvement process and adoption of new technologies as shown in Fig. 1.

The methodologies for auditing maintenance management processes are varied, but they share the use of questionnaires applied to the organization's personnel, both operations and maintenance, in order to achieve a comprehensive evaluation. In this case study, the AMORMS audit will be used. This decision is based on the fact that the company does not have its own maintenance management model. Therefore, opportunities for improvement will be developed following the 8-phase Management Model proposed by Parra and Crespo. Once improvement opportunities are identified, action plans will be generated. Improvements will be implemented with an agile approach, using methodologies such as Scrum to organize work in iterative cycles and allow for continuous adjustments.

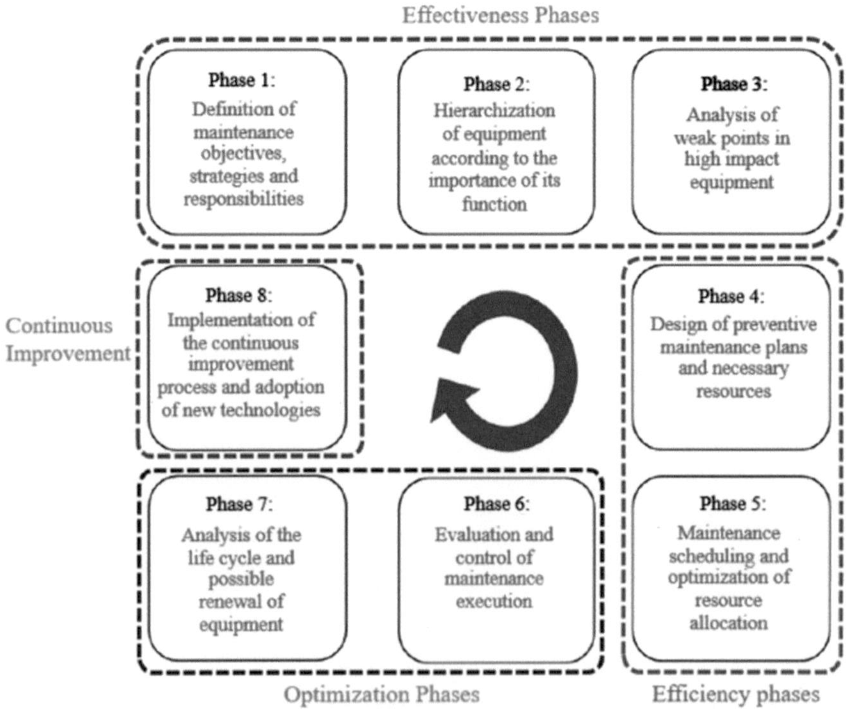

Fig. 1 Phases of the maintenance management model

2.1 AMORMS Audit

The different maintenance audit models are distinguished by their objectives and focus areas. According to Woodhouse (Woodhouse, 1996), common objectives include ensuring acceptable operational risk values, improving maintainability, and optimizing operational continuity. The AMORMS audit (Asset Management, Operational Reliability & Maintenance Survey) focuses on the 8 phases of the Maintenance Management Model (MGM) developed by Parra and Crespo, integrating requirements of the management model of the ISO 55001 standard (Duque et al., 2023). Its main objective is to measure the use of the tools to support the management process proposed by the MGM, distributed in 4 stages and 8 phases (Parra & Crespo, 2024).

The stages of the MGM are as follows, see Fig. 1:

- Effectiveness: Define objectives, indicators, prioritize teams and perform analysis of weak points (phases 1–3).
- Efficiency: Define, schedule and optimize maintenance plans (phases 4–5).
- Evaluation: Evaluate and analyze actions proposed in the previous stages (phases 6–7).
- Improvement: Implement continuous improvement processes based on the previous evaluation (phase 8)

The audit must involve staff, from supervisors to managers, with a minimum of eight people answering a 150-question questionnaire. Each participant will provide answers evaluating from 1 to 5 according to the description of each process (Parra & Crespo, 2020). The result of each phase will be evaluated using the scale shown in Table 1. This table is a modification of the original and allows the processes to be classified in the best way (Duque et al., 2023). The questionnaire consists of closed-ended questions designed to provide a quantitative assessment of key areas such as maintenance planning, resource optimization, failure analysis, and continuous improvement. Responses are collected using a 5-point Likert scale, where 1 represents an inefficient process and 5 represents a world-class process. In addition to the quantitative evaluation, qualitative information is also collected through interviews with the participants, providing further insights into the perceptions of staff regarding the audited areas. This qualitative information is analysed separately to complement the quantitative results and offer a more comprehensive view of the current state of maintenance management. See Table 1.

Table 1 AMORMS audit scores

Initial score	Process description	Final score
1	Very poor process	1.0–1.5
2	Below average process	1.6–2.5
3	Average standard process	2.6–3.5
4	Process with very good practices	3.6–4.5
5	World class process	4.6–5.0

The AMORMS audit allows you to audit the following areas, processes and use of tools (Parra & Crespo, 2020), see Table 2 and 3.

Some of the areas and tools audited include (Aránguiz et al., 2023):

- Asset management, business objectives and support organization.
- Risk-based ranking models.
- Programming and planning processes.
- Resource allocation processes, IT and logistical support.
- Control processes and analysis of RAM technical indicators.
- Life cycle cost analysis processes.
- Review and continuous improvement processes.

The AMORMS audit has proven to be a robust tool for evaluating processes both quantitatively, through a 5-point Likert scale, and qualitatively, based on interviews conducted with the evaluated personnel. These complementary methodologies allow for a comprehensive assessment of critical areas such as maintenance planning, resource optimization, failure analysis, and continuous improvement. In various studies, this methodology has been successfully applied in pulp mills (Aránguiz et al., 2023), desalination plants (Duque et al., 2023), and in the electricity transmission sector (Parra Márquez et al., 2022), validating its applicability and effectiveness in asset management across different industrial environments.

Table 2 AMORMS audit questionnaire summary

Phase		Processes, areas and tools	
1	Asset management, business objectives (KPIS) and support organization	1.1	Overview and leadership
		1.2	Comprehensive asset management plan
		1.3	Comprehensive maintenance policies (Management)
		1.4	Organizational structure
		1.5	Financial control (KPIS)
2	Hierarchy models based on risk (equipment criticality)	2.1	Risk management
		2.2	Equipment prioritization
		23	Management of safety, health and environment processes
3	Problem analysis (fault handling, root cause analysis)	3.1	Failure management
		3.2	Multidisciplinary optimization teams
		3.3	Failure analysis methods
4	Programming, planning and optimization processes for maintenance, inspection and operations plans	4.1	Programming and planning
		4.2	Procedures and work instructions
		4.3	Maintenance plans by condition (predictive techniques)
		4.4	Optimization techniques in the areas of reliability, maintenance and operations

Table 3 AMORMS audit questionnaire summary (continuation)

Phase		Processes, areas and tools	
5	Resource allocation processes, computer and logistical support for maintenance and reliability processes	5.1	Computer Maintenance Support System (Maintenance Software)
		5.2	Document control system
		5.3	Management of spare parts and materials (logistics)
		5.4	Inventory warehouse management process
6	Control processes and analysis of RAM technical indicators	6.1	Technical performance indicators
		6.2	Maintenance plan review programs
		6.3	Operations control processes
		6.4	Contractor control
		6.5	Workshop management
7	Life cycle cost analysis process	7.1	Asset life cycle
		7.2	Information management in the asset life cycle
		7.3	Special maintenance (plant shutdowns, overhauls, etc.)
8	Review and continuous improvement processes	8.1	QA
		8.2	Continuous improvement programs
		8.3	Personal development programs

2.2 *Maintenance Management Model*

The 8-phase Maintenance Management Model integrates various models and tools present in the literature (Parra & Crespo, 2024), See Fig. 2. These phases are divided into four groups: Effectiveness, Efficiency, Optimization and Continuous Improvement. The tools that can be used in each phase are described below.

2.3 *Audited Unit*

According to SAE JA 1011, operational context is defined as "The circumstances under which the physical asset or system is expected to operate (Society of Automotive Engineers, 1999)." The SAE JA 1012 standard indicates the specific aspects that must be documented in the definition of the operational context include: Description of manufacturing processes, quality standards, environmental standards, safety standards, place of operations, intensity of operations, redundancy, work during operation, market demand and raw material supply (Society of Automotive Engineers, 2002).

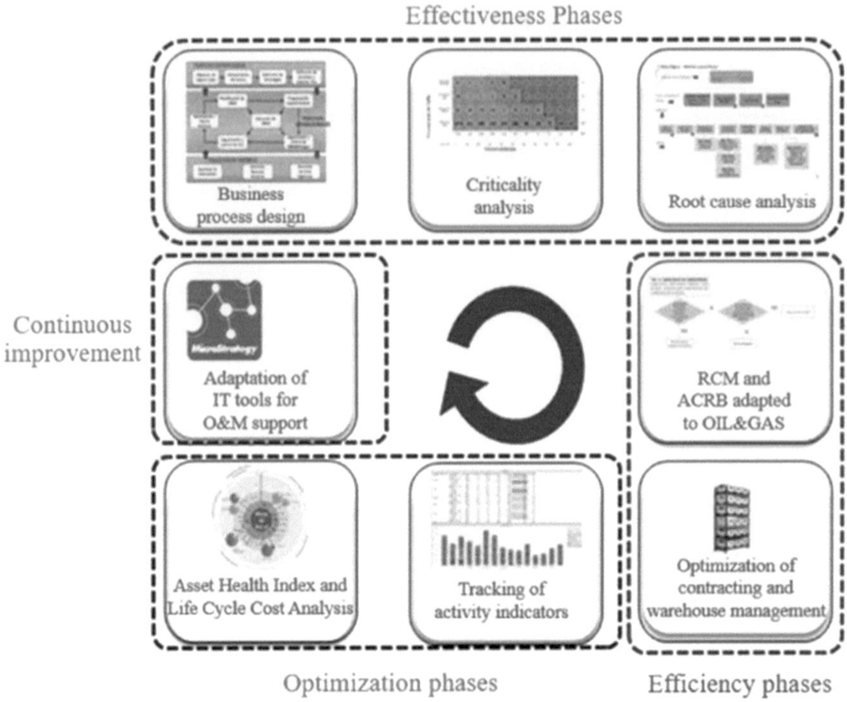

Fig. 2 Support structure for the maintenance management model

- Phase 1, Balanced Scorecard. Scorecard (BSC) and developing key business indicators (KPIs).
- Phase 2, Equipment Hierarchy: A method of hierarchization and asset criticality analysis must be developed and applied, considering risk factors aligned with the organization's objectives. Tools such as qualitative and quantitative criticality analysis can be useful in this phase.
- Phase 3, Weak Point Analysis: Identify and analyse repetitive and high-impact failures in critical assets, using cause analysis procedures such as Root Cause Failure Analysis. Analysis—RCFA).
- Phase 4, Design of Maintenance Plans: Define efficient maintenance functions and tasks based on the impact of failures on safety, the environment and production, using tools such as Reliability Centered Maintenance. Centered Maintenance—RCM) and Total Productive Maintenance (Total Productive Maintenance—TPM).
- Phase 5, Maintenance Scheduling and Resource Optimization: Apply optimization models to improve the effectiveness and efficiency of maintenance policies, reviewing cost-risk–benefit models and using reliability engineering computer tools.
- Phase 6, Maintenance Evaluation and Control: Monitor maintenance activities by evaluating deviations and business objectives based on maintenance and reliability

KPIs. Tools such as the analysis of performance indicators (MTBF, MTTR, etc.) are essential in this phase.
- Phase 7, Life Cycle Cost Analysis and Asset Renewal: Analyze costs throughout the life cycle of assets, including acquisition, research, design, testing, production and construction, using cycle cost analysis tools of life (Life Cycle Costing—LCC).
- Phase 8, Continuous Improvement and Introduction of New Maintenance and Reliability Techniques: Implement continuous improvement processes, reviewing emerging techniques and technologies (such as Maintenance 4.0 and Digitalization) and analysing alternatives to correct errors and maximize the profitability of the asset throughout its life cycle.

The company, with a batch production process, makes format changes in its lines according to the weekly plan delivered to Administrators and Operators. Production follows the Decree "Regulation of the National Cosmetics Control System" (Biblioteca del Congreso Nacional, 2023) and the ISO 22716 standard (International Organization for Standardization, 2023), called "Guide to good practices for the manufacture of cosmetic products". Both documents refer, the first with the force of law and the second as a recommendation, to: Manufacturing, packaging, testing, storage and transportation of cosmetic products.

The company's organizational structure is headed by the Chief Operating Officer, who supervises and manages all operational activities of the company, including production, supply chain, logistics, quality, manufacturing, engineering and maintenance, as shown in Fig. 3. Production Management includes a Production Manager, two Production Coordinators, a Production Planner and an Administrative Officer. The production unit works with thirty-four operators during the day shift and eight during the night shift. On the other hand, the Engineering and Maintenance Management is responsible for the maintenance of assets and the development of engineering projects. This management is made up of a Productive Maintenance Coordinator, who has four mechanics, and a Facilities and Services Maintenance Coordinator, who works together with a general services maintainer and an industrial services operator.

The audit was conducted with the participation of 5 people. Table 4 indicates the position in which each of them works and their level of education.

3 Results

According to Table 5 and Fig. 4, the audited unit has an average of 2.2 in the 8 phases, being classified as "Below Average Processes", as are six of the eight phases. Only the first two phases are classified as "Average Standard Processes."

The results of the maintenance audit, as can be seen in Table 6, reveal that the majority of evaluators consider that the maintenance unit operates below average. In particular, the Maintenance and Engineering Manager gives the lowest rating,

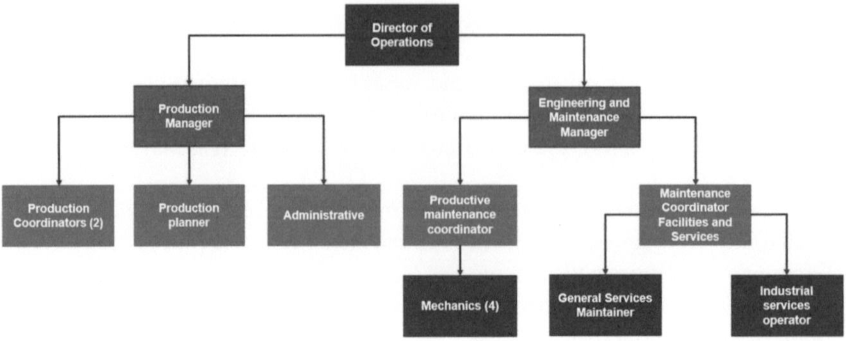

Fig. 3 Cosmetics company organization chart

Table 4 Characterization of audited personnel

Post	Qualification
Production manager	Chemical engineer
Maintenance and engineering manager	Mechanical engineer
Productive maintenance coordinator	Industrial technician
Facilities and services maintenance coordinator	Industrial engineer
Production planner	Industrial engineer

Table 5 AMORMS audit result

Phase	Average	Process description
1. Asset management, business objectives (KPIS) and supporting organization	2.7	Average standard process
2. Hierarchy models based on risk (criticality of equipment)	2.6	Average standard process
3. Problem analysis (fault handling)	2.2	Below average process
4. Programming and planning processes	2.2	Below average process
5. Resource allocation processes, IT and logistical support	23	Below average process
6. Control processes and analysis of RAM technical indicators	2.1	Below average process
7. Life cycle cost analysis process	1.7	Below average process
8. Review and continuous improvement processes	2.1	Below average process
Average of the eight phases	2.2	Below average process

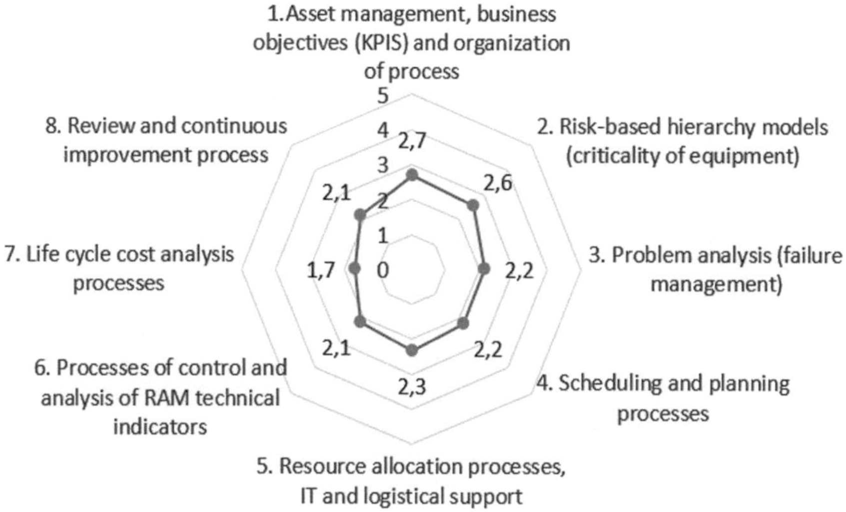

Fig. 4 AMORMS audit results

with an average of 1.8, indicating a clear perception of deficiencies in the process. Additionally, the following can be observed:

- The Maintenance Coordinators agree with this evaluation, also classifying the maintenance unit as "Below Average Process" and obtaining an overall average of 2.2.

Table 6 Individual and area results

Positions	Result by position	Process description by position	Average per area	Process description by area
Production manager	2.4	Below average process	2.6	Average standard process
Production planner	2.9	Average standard process		
Maintenance and engineering manager	1.8	Below average process	2.0	Below average process
Productive maintenance coordinator	2.2	Below average process		
Facilities and services maintenance coordinator	2.2	Below average process		

- The Maintenance unit as a whole gives an average rating of 2.0, placing it in the "Below Average Process" category.
- The Production Manager and the Production Planner are the ones who evaluate the maintenance unit most favourably, with ratings of 2.4 and 2.9, respectively. This results in different classifications, rating the maintenance unit as "Below Average Process" and "Average Standard Process," respectively.
- As a whole, the Production unit rates the maintenance process with an average of 2.6, placing it in the "Average Standard Process" category.

Based on the previous results, it can be stated that maintenance users or clients, such as the Production Manager and the Production Planner, have a more positive perception of the performance of the maintenance unit compared to the collaborators of this unit. This discrepancy in the evaluations could indicate that, from the Production perspective, the maintenance unit is meeting its expectations. However, it is important to note that the perceptions of the maintenance unit's own employees are critical. This can point to specific areas that require improvement. Lower internal evaluations could reflect underlying problems in processes, resources or strategies that are not as evident to external users. Addressing these critical perceptions is essential to improving the overall performance of the maintenance unit and ensuring that internal and external expectations are aligned.

3.1 Analysis of Results

To identify areas with the greatest opportunities for improvement, a detailed analysis of the AMORMS audit results is conducted for each phase in three dimensions:

- Identification of Critical Subcategories: The subcategories that have been evaluated as "Process below average" are identified, that is, those with a score equal to or less than 2.5. Subsequently, improvements are proposed aimed at reducing the gaps with the objective that, in a second audit, a classification of "Average Standard Process" is obtained for each of the phases. See Table 7.
- Standard Deviation (SD) Analysis: The standard deviation is used as a measure of dispersion of the audit responses. Questions with a standard deviation greater than 1 are identified, indicating variability in the answers, which suggests subjective or controversial aspects that require special attention. See Tables 8, 9 and 10.
- Analysis of Staff Interviews: The interviews conducted with audited staff are analysed, highlighting information relevant to each audited phase to provide a comprehensive and contextual view of perceptions and areas for improvement.

The proposed approach allows:

- Highlight Critical Questions: Based on the score obtained or the information provided by the audited personnel, critical areas that need a deeper analysis can

Table 7 Results by processes, areas and tools

Phase	Processes, areas and tools	Score
1. Asset management KPI business objectives and support organization	1.2 Comprehensive asset management plan	2.0
	1.3 Comprehensive maintenance policies	2.4
2. Risk management	2.1 Risk management	2.5
	2.2 equipment prioritization	2.4
3. problem analysis process (Root Cause Analysis)	3.1 Failure management	1.9
	3.3 Failure analysis method	2.0
4. Maintenance, inspection and operations programming, planning and optimization process	4.1 Programming and planning	2.4
	4.3 Maintenance plans by condition (Predictive techniques)	1.8
	4.4 Optimization techniques in the area of reliability, maintenance and operations	1.7
5. Resource allocation processes, IT support and logistical support for maintenance and reliability processes	5.1 Maintenance computer support system (Maintenance Software)	2.2
	5.3 Management of spare parts, materials (logistics)	2.1
	5.4 Warehouse and inventory management processes	2.4
6. Control processes and analysis of technical business indicators (RAM)	6.1 Technical performance indicators	1.5
	6.2 Maintenance plan review programs	1.8
	6.5 Workshop management	2.1
7. Life cycle cost analysis process	7.1 Life cycle cost management of assets	1.4
	7.2 Information management in asset life cycle management	1.8
	7.3 Special maintenance (plant shutdowns, overhaul, etc	1.9
8. Review and continuous improvement processes	8.1 Quality control	2.0
	8.2 Continuous improvement programs	1.9
	8.3 Personnel improvement programs	2.5

Table 8 Standard deviation analysis

Processes, areas and tools	Ask	Average maintenance	Average production	Average question	SD
1.1 Overview and leadership	1	2.3	3.0	2.6	1.2
	2	2.3	3.0	2.6	1.0
	3	2.3	3.5	2.8	1.0
	5	2.0	4.0	2.8	1.0
1.2 Comprehensive asset management plan	6	2.0	3.5	2.6	1.0
	7	1.7	2.0	1.8	1.0
	8	1.7	3.0	2.2	1.0
1.3 Comprehensive maintenance policies	14	2.0	4.0	2.8	1.2
	15	1.7	3.0	2.2	1.0
2.1 Risk management	29	2.7	2.5	2.6	1.0
	31	23	3.0	2.6	1.2
	32	23	3.0	2.6	1.2
	33	1.7	3.0	2.2	1.0
3.2 Multidisciplinary action teams	46	2.0	3.0	2.4	1.2
	54	1.7	3.5	2.4	1.2
4.1 Programming and planning	59	2.0	3.5	2.6	1.0

Table 9 Standard deviation analysis (continuation)

Processes, areas and tools	Ask	Average maintenance	Average production	Average question	SD
5.2 Document control system	81	23	3.0	2.6	1.2
5.3 Management of spare parts, materials (logistics)	90	1.0	3.0	1.8	1.2
5.4 Warehouse and inventory management processes	92	2.7	3.5	3.0	1.1
6.2 Maintenance plan review programs	102	1.0	3.0	1.8	1.0
6.3 Operations control process	110	1.0	3.0	1.8	1.0
8.3 Personnel improvement programs	148	23	2.0	2.2	1.0

Table 10 Questions with standard deviation greater than 1[-]

No	Ask
1	Are there corporate guidelines on the asset management process?
2	Is there awareness of asset management and its administration? (Roles/Scopes/ Responsibilities)
3	Is there detailed control over the business objectives from corporate management?
5	Do Corporate Management, middle management, and technical and execution levels efficiently share business leadership? (Empowerment)
6	Does the organization have a comprehensive asset management model included in its vision and mission?
7	Is there a comprehensive plan designed to implement the various processes proposed by the asset management model?
8	Is there a long-term asset management plan and is it integrated with the business objectives and goals?
14	Are operation and maintenance policies linked and integrated with business objectives and goals?
15	Are the maintenance and reliability policies integrated with the vision and mission of the business?
29	Are the risks in maintenance and reliability processes analyzed, reviewed and updated on a regular basis?
31	The organization has developed a risk-based equipment criticality model?
32	The risk prioritization model of teams is aligned with business objectives?
33	The information used to estimate the frequency and frequency of failures is taken from a reliable and truthful source?
46	Are workers well organized and motivated to achieve business objectives?
54	Are the recommendations generated from the failure analyzes selected based on a Cost Risk Benefit Analysis procedure?
59	Are maintenance planning and scheduling strategies aligned with the organization's business plan?
81	There is a general management system for technical maintenance documents (drawings, P&D, process flowcharts, operations manual, etc.)
90	Does the Materials Supply and Planning process have optimization indicators integrated at the level of business objectives that are evaluated, analyzed, used and audited on a continuous basis?
92	Is inventory management conducted and controlled by a computer support tool?
102	Are actions taken on the analyzes conducted on the different types of maintenance carried out?
110	Are operation and production strategies integrated with maintenance scheduling and planning processes?
148	Is there a specific training plan tailored to the entire life cycle of the worker?

be identified, since the answers may indicate problems or potential areas for improvement.

- Identify Areas of High Variability: Questions with high standard deviation indicate that responses differ significantly between participants, which may suggest subjective or controversial aspects that require special attention.

Identifying the phases with the greatest opportunities for improvement and the questions with the highest standard deviation provides valuable information for decision making, planning and prioritizing improvement actions. This helps direct efforts toward critical areas. However, it is essential to analyse these results in context and consider other variables that may affect the variability of the responses.

During the field audit, deficiencies in the company's maintenance management were identified, highlighting.

- Phase 1, Definition of Maintenance Objectives, Strategies and Responsibilities: There is no Asset Management model or defined maintenance policies. The company lacks specific positions for maintenance engineering and continuous improvement processes, using only financial indicators.
- Phase 2, Team Hierarchy: The lack of a comprehensive Risk Management policy and a team prioritization model was observed. There are no failure frequency records and the list of critical equipment lacks a reliable source.
- Phase 3, Weak Point Analysis: There is no standard process for managing failures or a failure analysis method. Workers do not have the necessary skills to form multidisciplinary teams and there is no cost-risk–benefit analysis procedure.
- Phase 4, Design of Maintenance Plans: The absence of a management strategy for maintenance optimization and personnel dedicated to planning and programming was found. There is a preventive maintenance plan of unknown origin and not aligned with the business plan. Furthermore, the use of SAP is insufficient and staff have not been trained in its use.
- Phase 5, Maintenance Scheduling and Resource Optimization: Maintenance scheduling and resource optimization present deficiencies. SAP is not used properly, work order design is poor and there is no document control system. Spare parts planning is not integrated with the maintenance plan and there are no optimization indicators.
- Phase 6, Evaluation and Maintenance Control: There is a lack of an efficient record of historical information on the equipment and performance indicators such as MTBF and MTTR. No benchmarking is conducted with other factories of the international group and there is no evaluation process for contractors or internal services.
- Phase 7, Life Cycle Analysis: No specific model is followed to evaluate costs throughout the life cycle of the assets. Economic and technical information is considered, but a structured analysis is not conducted following a specific model.
- Phase 8, Continuous Improvement Processes: There is no quality management model within the maintenance area nor adequate continuous improvement programs. Human Resources is in charge of training, but there is no plan adequate to the needs of the maintenance area.

Table 11 Budget and production year 2021 to 2023

Period	Budget [CLP]	Budget variation (%)	Production [uni.]	Production variation (%)
2021–2022	208,502,044	–	16,390,371	
2022–2023	295,051,241	42	12,302,184	−24.9
2023–2024	382,124,222	30	12,257,987	−0.4

The budgets requested for the last three years and the variations in production levels for the same period are also analysed, see Table 11. A sustained increase in the maintenance budget is evident over time, contrasted with a reduction of almost 25% in production levels between 2022 and 2023. The cost centers were analysed seeking to identify the origin of the increase in costs of maintenance, it is observed that the budget structure has undergone modifications year after year, reflected in changes in the number and name of the cost centers.

4 Improvement Proposals

The company currently lacks a structured maintenance management model, so it seeks to improve through the adoption of the 8-Phase Maintenance Management Model (MGM). The improvement proposals are divided into four time horizons: immediate, short-term, medium-term, and long-term. The implementation plan includes the hiring of external consultants who will focus on developing asset management strategies, integrating these strategies with the MGM, and optimizing the use of SAP for efficient information collection and asset management. The role of the consultants is critical to ensuring the effectiveness and consistency of the implementation, providing expertise on both asset management and the integration of digital tools like SAP (Parra Márquez et al., 2021).

The implementation approach adopts principles from the agile methodology, which is recognized for its flexibility, adaptability, and collaborative nature. These qualities make it particularly suitable for pilot programs and gradual improvements (Metso & Thenent, 2023). Scrum stands out as a key agile framework, promoting continuous learning, self-organized teams, and regular reflection on processes. Scrum organizes the work into Sprints, which are iterative cycles typically lasting one month, during which prioritized tasks are completed and product increments are delivered (Rigby et al., 2016). This structure ensures that tasks of highest relevance are prioritized, offering the flexibility to adjust to changing operational conditions and needs.

In alignment with this approach, the concept of Quick Wins is introduced—small, fast improvements that deliver immediate positive results and build team motivation. These early successes help maintain momentum for more significant, long-term improvements. The Scrum methodology supports the implementation of the MGM, as it fosters collaboration between the internal team and external consultants, ensuring that improvements are effectively applied, and progress is consistently tracked (Hobbs & Petit, 2017).

A core element of the implementation strategy is the use of SAP as the primary tool for managing asset data and tracking maintenance activities. SAP allows for the centralization of maintenance information, facilitating the monitoring of asset performance, planning of preventive maintenance, and ensuring that resources are efficiently allocated. By integrating SAP into the maintenance process, the company can better manage spare parts inventory, track maintenance costs, and optimize asset availability, aligning maintenance tasks with operational goals (Van Horenbeek et al., 2018).

The external consultants will also provide training on the effective use of SAP, ensuring that the maintenance team is fully equipped to utilize the system's capabilities for asset management and decision-making. The agile methodology will support continuous adjustments and refinements to the maintenance strategies, with feedback loops built into the Scrum cycles, allowing for regular evaluation of progress and the effectiveness of the improvements (Parra Márquez et al., 2021).

In summary, the implementation of the improvement plan is grounded in the agile methodology and emphasizes the effective use of SAP as a central tool for asset management. This combination will ensure the success and sustainability of the proposed improvements, leading to better maintenance management, resource optimization, and enhanced asset reliability (Metso & Thenent, 2023).

An implementation plan is presented, visualizing milestones and dependencies, see Fig. 5.

Immediate Actions (0–3 months): Immediate actions focus on the effectiveness phases of the 8-Phase Management Model. These actions are designed to be implemented in an agile and efficient manner, laying the foundation for continuous

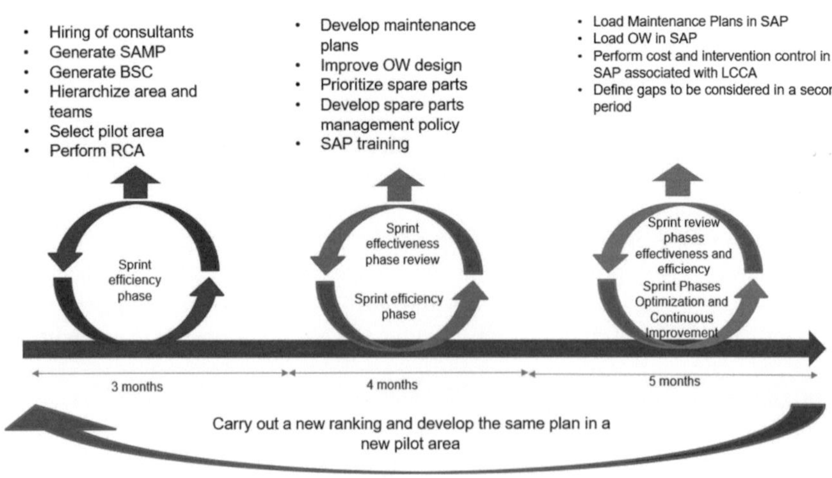

Fig. 5 Implementation of improvements

improvements in asset management. A pilot area will be selected according to the criticality analysis developed.

- **Phase 1: Definition of Maintenance Objectives, Strategies and Responsibilities**

    Implement the 8 Phase Management Model.
    Develop a Strategic Asset Management Plan (SAMP) aligned with business objectives.
    Establish specific maintenance policies and strategies.
    Balanced Scorecard and develop key performance indicators (KPIs).

- **Phase 2: Team Hierarchy**

    Identify critical equipment using qualitative techniques.
    Review and adjust existing maintenance strategies.
    Collect technical indicators for quantitative criticality analysis.

- **Phase 3: Analysis of Weak Points**

    Establish a standard process for failure analysis and evaluate repetitive failures in critical assets.

Short-Term Actions (3–7 months): During this period, the improvements made will be reviewed and improvements related to the efficiency phases will be proposed.

- **Phase 4: Design of Maintenance Plans**

    Define functions and propose efficient maintenance tasks.
    Review the current maintenance plan and establish scheduling and planning processes.
    Evaluate the relationship between logistics and maintenance and define a list of critical spare parts.
    Train staff in the use of SAP.

- **Phase 5: Maintenance Scheduling and Resource Optimization**

    Collaborate with the supply unit to establish spare parts management policies.
    Review and modify maintenance plans in SAP and improve the design of work orders (WO).
    Work in accordance with the UNE 13,460 standard for maintenance.

Medium-Term Actions (7–12 months): Focused on the optimization and continuous improvement phases of the 8-Phase Management Model.

- **Phase 6: Evaluation and Maintenance Control**

    Use SAP as a historical record and source of technical–economic indicators.
    Integrate operation and production strategies with maintenance programming and planning.
    Establish procedures for the effective control of contractors and internal workshops.

- **Phase 7: Life Cycle Cost Analysis and Asset Renewal**

  Establish a procedure for the life cycle cost analysis of assets.

- **Phase 8: Continuous Improvement and Introduction of New Maintenance and Reliability Techniques**

  Define a structured model of continuous improvement for the maintenance area.
  Identify gaps and propose corrective actions in the short, medium and long term.

4.1 Implementation Proposal

To implement the proposed improvements, the hiring of external consultants specialized in asset management and SAP integration is deemed essential. These consultants will focus on developing strategic asset management plans, aligning the improvements with the company's Maintenance Management Model (MGM), and ensuring the effective use of SAP as a comprehensive system for management and data collection. This external guidance will provide critical expertise and strategic direction, guaranteeing the effectiveness, consistency, and sustainability of the proposed improvements.

The specific tasks to be addressed by the external consultants include:

- Development of strategic asset management plans: Including asset criticality assessments, risk management strategies, and lifecycle cost analysis.
- Design and implementation of maintenance optimization strategies: Tailored maintenance plans will be designed to minimize downtime and improve equipment availability.
- Integration of SAP: Consultants will train maintenance staff in the effective use of SAP, ensuring that it serves as a tool for real-time monitoring and data-driven decision-making.
- Staff training and development: Comprehensive workshops and training programs will be implemented to enhance the team's understanding of modern maintenance strategies, such as reliability-centered maintenance (RCM) and total productive maintenance (TPM).

The proposed improvements are expected to incur an additional annual cost equivalent to 5% of the maintenance budget, covering consulting and training expenses. The primary objective is not merely to reduce costs but to increase the overall value of maintenance by addressing key aspects such as:

- Identifying acceptable levels of maintenance and operational risk.
- Improving equipment reliability and reducing time to recover from failures.
- Maximizing equipment availability and ensuring effective integration between the Maintenance, Production, and Inventory departments.

- Generating both qualitative and quantitative data to enhance decision-making processes, particularly regarding human reliability factors such as motivation, communication, and training.

However, due to the lack of detailed data on current maintenance unit costs, a full quantitative analysis of the proposed plan is not feasible at this time. Additionally, the absence of comprehensive data on process performance and the impact of current maintenance policies further limits the precision of the evaluation.

To address this, a qualitative ranking analysis was performed, which identified a pilot area within the company with an availability rate of 90%. This area experienced a loss of 233,205 units due to machine unavailability, as measured by the Overall Equipment Effectiveness (OEE) indicator. Penalty costs were calculated based on the number of lost units and the actual cost of production.

Based on these calculations, it is estimated that a 2% increase in equipment availability would result in a monthly saving of $13,405,672 CLP, representing approximately 20% of the annual maintenance budget. This would yield a benefit–cost ratio (BCR) of 4, indicating that the financial benefits would significantly exceed the costs in the first year of implementation.

The anticipated return on investment (ROI) would be achieved in less than a year, even under conservative projections. Any additional savings derived from increased availability, reduced unplanned downtime, and more efficient process execution would further enhance the economic viability and long-term sustainability of the project.

Furthermore, the implementation of continuous improvement processes, supported by agile methodologies such as Scrum, will ensure that initial gains are sustained, and further optimization opportunities are identified over time. This iterative approach will allow for real-time adjustments and ongoing evaluation based on the data generated by SAP, leading to a continuous reduction in operational costs while improving equipment reliability and Overall Equipment Effectiveness (OEE).

5 Conclusions

The maintenance audit conducted has successfully identified significant deficiencies and gaps within the maintenance unit, providing a clear basis for identifying areas that require improvement and establishing a comprehensive action plan. The results from the eight phases of the audit revealed that six of the phases were classified as "Below Average Processes," with only the first two phases reaching the classification of "Average Standard Processes." These results highlight the critical need for structural improvements in the company's maintenance management practices.

In response to these findings, specific improvement proposals have been formulated to address the identified gaps. These proposals have been designed with a practical and strategic approach, emphasizing the importance of hiring external consultants to develop a Strategic Asset Management Plan and to implement maintenance engineering practices. The goal is to establish the necessary infrastructure for the execution of the Strategic Asset Management Plan model. Additionally, a pilot area was selected based on the results of the criticality analysis, and it is proposed to train the maintenance team in the effective use of SAP as a comprehensive tool for data management and decision-making. These proposals represent an investment equivalent to 5% of the annual maintenance budget.

A technical–economic analysis was conducted to evaluate the feasibility and effectiveness of the proposed improvements. This analysis demonstrated that the investment required for the implementation of these improvements is justified by the potential savings and efficiency gains. It is estimated that a 2% increase in the availability of the selected pilot area would generate savings equivalent to 20% of the annual maintenance budget. This provides strong support for the economic viability of the proposals, as the projected return on investment is expected to be realized within the first year of implementation.

The maintenance audit has provided a clear roadmap for improving maintenance management within the company. The proposed actions are not only expected to optimize maintenance processes but also to enhance the overall effectiveness and efficiency of operations. By implementing these improvements, the company will benefit from better resource allocation, reduced downtime, and enhanced equipment reliability. This structured approach also has the potential to drive continuous improvements within the cosmetics industry, offering a model that can be replicated by other companies seeking to strengthen their maintenance management practices.

References

Aránguiz, A., et al. (2023). Audit model for asset management, maintenance and reliability processes: a case study applied to pulp mill sector. In: 16th *WCEAM Proceeding*, Vol. 1, pp. 323–330.

Biblioteca del Congreso Nacional. (2023). *Decreto 239. Reglamento del sistema nacional de control de cosméticos.* [En línea]. Available at: https://www.bcn.cl/leychile/navegar?idNorma=211455

Duque, P., et al. (2023). Audit models for asset management, maintenance and reliability processes: A case study applied to the desalination plant. In *16th WCEAM Proceedings,* pp. 375–384.

González-Prida, V., Parra Márquez, C. & Crespo Márquez, A. (2022). En: *Cases on Optimizing the Asset Management Process.* s.l.:IGI Global, p. 457.

Hobbs, B., & Petit, Y. (2017). Agile methods on large projects in large organizations. *Project Management Journal, 48*(3), 3–19.

International Organization for Standardization. (2023). *ISO 22716:2007 Cosmetics—Good Manufacturing Practices (GMP)—Guidelines on Good Manufacturing Practices.* [En línea] Available at: https://www.iso.org/standard/36437.html

Lee, J., Kao, H., & Yang, S. (2014). Service innovation and smart analytics for industry 4.0 and big data environment. *Procedia CIRP, 16*, 3–8.

Metso, L., & Thenent, N.E. (2023). Agile Methods in Industrial Maintenance. In *16th WCEAM Proceedings,* 1(1), pp. 716–723.

Parra Márquez, C., Crespo Márquez, A. & González-Prida Díaz, V., 2021. *Técnica de Auditoría para los procesos de Mantenimiento, Fiabilidad Operacional y Gestión de Activos (AMORS & AMS-ISO 55001),* s.l.: s.n.

Parra Márquez, C., et al. (2022). *Audit Models for Asset Management, Maintenance and Reliability Processes. Case study: Electricity Transmission sector.*, s.l.: s.n.

Parra, C., & Crespo, A. (2020). *Técnicas de Auditorías aplicadas en los procesos de Gestión del Mantenimiento y de la Confiabilidad.* Sevilla: INGEMAN.

Parra, C., & Crespo, A. (2024). *Ingeniería de Mantenimiento y Fiabilidad Aplicada en la Gestión de Activos* (Tercera). Universidad Técnica Federico Santa María.

Rigby, D., Sutherland, J., & Takeuchi, H. (2016). Embracing agile. *Harvard Business Review, 94*(5), 40–50.

Society of Automotive Engineers. (1999). *SAE JA 1011: Evaluation Criteria for Reliability-Centered Maintenance (RCM) Processes.* s.l.:s.n.

Society of Automotive Engineers. (2002). *SAE JA1012: A Guide to the Reliability-Centered Maintenance (RCM) Standard.* s.l.:s.n.

Tsang, A. H. C. & Jardine, A. K. S. (2022). *Maintenance, Replacement, and Reliability: Theory and Applications*, 3rd ed. s.l.:CRC Press.

Van Horenbeek, A., Pintelon, L., & Muchiri, P. (2018). Maintenance optimization models and criteria. *International Journal of Production Economics, 112*(1), 667–669.

Woodhouse, J. (1996). *Managing industrial risk: getting value for money in your business.* Chapman Hill Inc.

Case Studies and Implementation Frameworks

Implementation of an Asset Management Plan According to ISO 55001 at the Colmito Power Generation Plant—Chile

Carlos Parra, Carlos Baldi, Cristian Cuadra, Pablo Duque, José Núñez, Juan Araya, Vicente González-Prida, and Jorge Parra

Abstract The proposed article describes the key factors of a Maintenance Management Model (MMM) aligned with an Asset Management implementation plan following the NCh-ISO 55001 standard for the Colmito Power Generation Plant in Chile. The aim is to improve service quality by reducing downtime caused by faults, optimizing operations, and extending asset lifespan. This implementation aligns with current legislation and fulfills the objectives and goals defined in asset management, in compliance with Supreme Decree 109 of 2017 from the Ministry of Energy. This decree regulates the safety of electrical installations involved in production, transportation, provision of complementary services, energy storage systems, and the

The original version of the chapter has been revised. A correction to this chapter can be found at https://doi.org/10.1007/978-3-032-05592-7_17

C. Parra (✉) · C. Baldi · C. Cuadra · P. Duque
Universidad Técnica Federico Santa María, Valparaíso, Chile
e-mail: carlos.parram@usm.cl

C. Baldi
e-mail: carlos.baldi@usm.cl

C. Cuadra
e-mail: cristian.cuadra@usm.cl

P. Duque
e-mail: pablo.duque@usm.cl

J. Núñez · J. Araya
INKIA ENERGY, Santiago, Chile
e-mail: jose.nunez@inkiaenergy.cl

J. Araya
e-mail: juan.araya@inkiaenergy.com

J. Parra
Universidad Tecnológica de Panamá, Panama City, Panamá

V. González-Prida
Universidad de Sevilla, Sevilla, Spain

A. Crespo Márquez et al. (eds.), *Case Studies in Digital Transformation*, Engineering Asset Management Review 4, https://doi.org/10.1007/978-3-032-05592-7_8

distribution of electrical energy. It specifically refers to Normative Technical Specification RPTD No. 17, which establishes the requirements for the SGIIE (Integrity Management System for Electrical Installations) in Chile. The first part describes the most important aspects of the MMM: Maintenance Management Model developed by INGEMAN. It discusses the eight phases of the MMM and explains the key fundamentals that organizations must implement to apply the MMM and optimize the technical and economic performance of assets throughout their life cycle. Additionally, it analyzes the relationship between the MMM and the requirements of the Asset Management Standard ISO 55001. The second part provides details on the AMS-ISO 55001 diagnostic tool (Asset Management Survey—ISO 55001), used to assess the requirements stipulated by the Asset Management standard NCh-ISO 55001 at the Colmito Power Generation Plant, referencing a tool developed by the IAM (Institute of Asset Management). The article also includes the results of the maturity level assessment of the Colmito Power Generation Plant in relation to the requirements of the NCh-ISO 55001 standard. Additionally, the operational context of the Colmito Power Generation Plant and the regulatory framework of the electrical market are presented to provide an understanding of the organization and its interactions with various market entities. Finally, the article describes the guidelines for the development and implementation of the Asset Management System for the Colmito Power Generation Plant. It outlines the planning, support, operation, performance evaluation, and improvement processes proposed to consolidate the Asset Management Strategic Plan (PGEA). The goal is to comply with items 4 to 10 of the NCh-ISO 55001 standard in order to minimize operational risks and maximize the profitability of the assets of the Colmito Power Generation Plant throughout their entire lifecycle.

Keywords Asset · Management · Risk · Maintenance

1 Introduction to the Maintenance Management Process

The modern maintenance process involves a comprehensive set of management activities aimed at establishing maintenance objectives or priorities—these are the goals defined and approved by the leadership of the maintenance department. It also includes determining the strategies and methods to achieve these objectives, as well as outlining specific management responsibilities. Maintenance management plays a critical role in ensuring the functionality and health of assets, thereby supporting the broader goal of asset management: maximizing asset value throughout its entire life cycle (Crespo, 2007). Both maintenance management and asset management are vital for organizations, as they empower maintenance managers to make more informed and effective decisions in daily operations. For optimal results, maintenance management should align maintenance activities with the organization's overarching business strategy, ideally as part of a holistic asset management framework (Parra & Crespo, 2015).

To effectively and efficiently manage the maintenance management process, an organization must consider the following aspects (Crespo, 2007; Woodhouse, 1996):

- The maintenance management process: This consists of a defined course of action, comprising a series of steps to follow.
- The general reference model for management: This serves as the foundational support structure, made up of various tools that form a basic system essential for advanced reliability and maintenance management (Woodhouse, 1996).

The maintenance management process can be divided into two key components (Crespo Márquez et al., 2009):

- Defining the maintenance strategy
- Implementing the maintenance strategy

The first component, defining the maintenance strategy, begins with establishing maintenance objectives as the initial input. These objectives must align with the organization's overarching business plan. Crafting maintenance strategies that are congruent with business goals is critical, as this alignment significantly impacts the success of achieving the defined maintenance objectives.

The second component, implementing the strategy, is equally important. It involves several critical activities, such as ensuring adequate staff training, preparing for tasks, selecting appropriate tools for each job, and designing and executing maintenance programs promptly and efficiently (Campbell & Jardine, 2001).

The process of defining a maintenance strategy can be structured using well-established standard strategic planning methods, typically encompassing the following steps (Crespo, 2007) (see Fig. 1):

- Deriving Maintenance Objectives and Policies: Starting from the organization's overarching corporate objectives, at the highest level, maintenance goals and guidelines are created. For factors like equipment availability, dependability, safety, risk, and maintenance budget, these could include projected and achievable goals. All employees engaged in maintenance tasks, including external stakeholders and third-party service providers, must be made fully aware of these goals.
- Assessing Current Facility Performance: Evaluating the current performance of production facilities to establish a baseline for future improvements.
- Identifying Key Performance Indicators (KPIs): Determining the critical metrics to evaluate facility performance. These KPIs, agreed upon by Operations and Maintenance Management, will serve as the basis for identifying and pursuing improvements.
- Establishing Guiding Principles for Strategy Implementation: Defining a set of principles to guide the implementation of the strategy. These principles will shape subsequent activities, including planning, execution, evaluation, control, and the continuous improvement of maintenance processes.

Fig. 1 Model for defining the maintenance strategy. *Source* Crespo (2007)

2 Proposed Maintenance Management Model (MMM)

A proposal for a Generic Maintenance Management Model (MMM) (2007) (Crespo, 2007; Parra & Crespo, 2015) is presented, integrating various models documented in the literature and applied by companies renowned for their excellence in maintenance management (Campbell & Jardine, 2001; Pintelon & Gelders, 1992). The proposed MMM comprises eight interconnected blocks (Fig. 2), each defining specific actions for different stages of maintenance management. This dynamic, sequential, closed-loop model is designed to ensure efficiency, effectiveness, and continuous improvement. As illustrated in the MMM reference figure:

- Blocks 1–3 focus on management effectiveness.
- Blocks 4–5 address planning and scheduling actions, including the department's planning capacity.
- Blocks 6–7 emphasize evaluation and control of maintenance and asset costs throughout their life cycles.
- Block 8 ensures continuous improvement in management practices.

This support structure incorporates essential techniques, organized into several foundational pillars (Crespo, 2007; Parra & Crespo, 2015):

1. The Information Technologies (IT) Pillar. This includes tools such as CMMS (e.g., SAP PM, MAXIMO) and advanced technologies like Maintenance 4.0, Internet of Things (IoT), Neural Networks (NN), Artificial Intelligence (AI), Digitalization (D), and Machine Learning (ML). These technologies enhance

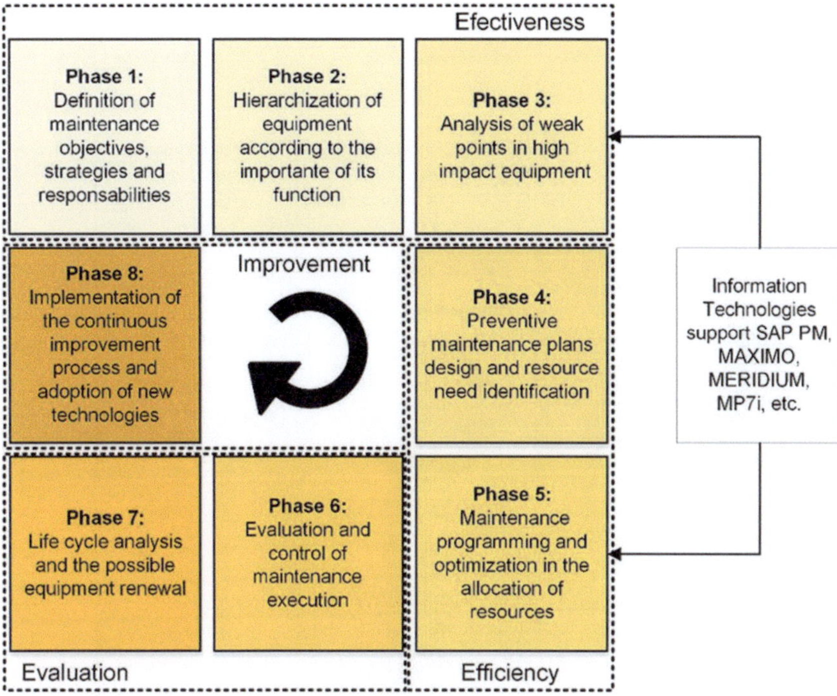

Fig. 2 Maintenance Management Model (MMM). *Source* Parra and Crespo (2015)

the effectiveness and efficiency of maintenance management by continuously aligning operational and tactical decisions with business objectives.

2. The Maintenance Engineering Techniques Pillar. This pillar incorporates techniques such as: Root Cause Analysis (RCA), Reliability-Centered Maintenance (RCM), Total Productive Maintenance (TPM), Stochastic models for failure analysis, Quantitative optimization techniques and other operations research methods designed to optimize resource allocation in maintenance activities.
3. The Organizational Improvement Techniques Pillar. Equally critical as the previous pillars, this area focuses on techniques that promote improved management of internal and external organizational relationships across all activity levels, enhancing overall organizational competitiveness.

By leveraging these pillars, the MMM ensures a structured and systematic approach to achieving excellence in maintenance management.

Figure 3 illustrates a practical model that integrates various commercial tools related to maintenance and reliability engineering, each mapped to one of the eight blocks (or stages) of the Maintenance Management Model (MMM) (Crespo, 2007; Parra & Crespo, 2015). Below is an overview of Phase 1, including a key technique and its impact on decision- making within the MMM:

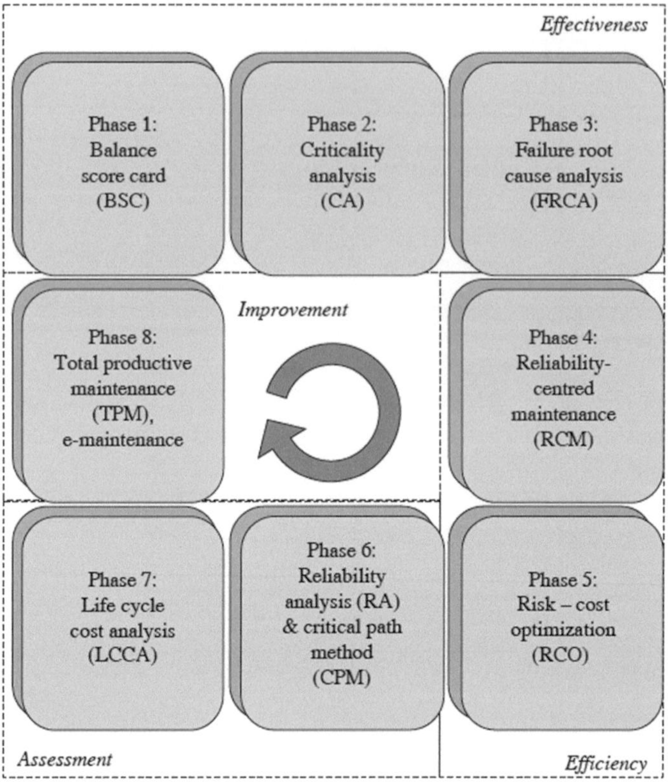

Fig. 3 Example of optimization techniques for making decisions and support systems for the MMM. *Source* Crespo (2007)

- Phase 1: Defining the Maintenance Strategy. To ensure that maintenance objectives and strategies align with the organization's broader business objectives, tools like the Balanced Scorecard (BSC) can be introduced and implemented in maintenance management (Kaplan & Nortonm, 1992). The Balanced Scorecard is tailored to the organization in which it is implemented and facilitates the development of KPIs, or key performance indicators, which assess how well maintenance management is performing. The strategic goals of the firm are directly correlated with these KPIs. Unlike traditional control-oriented measures, the BSC emphasizes the global strategy and business vision, guiding efforts toward achieving the organization's overarching goals. The process of defining BSC goals involves collaboration across various stakeholders:
  - Internal stakeholders: company leadership, maintenance managers, and key personnel in operational units.
  - External stakeholders: Key users of maintenance services. This participatory approach fosters alignment and ensures that maintenance goals contribute to the organization's overall success.

Benefits of the BSC in Maintenance Strategy Management:

- Aligns operational maintenance objectives with broader business goals
- Ensures maintenance KPIs reflect strategic priorities, fostering clarity and focus.
- Encourages a holistic approach by involving key stakeholders from various levels of the organization.
- Promotes a shared vision, motivating individuals and teams to contribute toward achieving unified objectives.

By linking maintenance performance measures to the organization's success, the BSC bridges the gap between strategic planning and operational execution. This alignment not only enhances decision-making within Phase 1 but also sets the foundation for the subsequent stages of the MMM (Roda & Macchi, 2018a). In conclusion, the incorporation of tools like the BSC in Phase 1 of the MMM ensures that the maintenance function is fully integrated into the organization's strategic framework, driving both operational efficiency and strategic alignment.

- Phase 2: Production asset ranking techniques. A range of qualitative and quantitative methods offer a methodical basis for deciding how to classify productive assets according to their significance in accomplishing corporate goals once the goals and maintenance plans have been established (Phase 2). Numerous quantitative methods make use of variants of probabilistic risk assessment (PRA), a crucial idea in this stage that determines the probability/rate of risk for every asset (Parra & Crespo, 2015). Analysis of assets with a higher index will be given priority. In many cases, the maintenance organization may still need a fundamental assessment to inform initial decision-making even while data records are not accessible to produce these indices. More qualitative methods can be used in these situations to guarantee a sufficient degree of initial efficacy in maintenance procedures. Following the establishment of asset priorities, each asset category needs to have a clear maintenance plan, with the knowledge that these plans will be improved over time.
- Phase 3. Instruments to eradicate deficiencies in high-impact equipment/systems. Prior to formulating activities for our maintenance plans, it is essential to examine potential recurring chronic failures, particularly those with excessive frequency (phase 3). Identifying and eliminating, if feasible, we will be able to give a significant early return on investment in our maintenance management program by identifying the reasons behind these failures. Subsequently, it becomes considerably more manageable to execute consecutive stages of research and design for maintenance plans, which necessitate substantial commitment of time and money. Various methodologies exist for conducting an examination of vulnerabilities in critical assets, among which the most recognized is Failure Root-Cause Analysis (FRCA). This method entails a sequence of procedures aimed at identifying the cause of a specific failure mode and determining corrective measures. The causes of these failures might be categorized as physical, human, or latent. The physical cause refers to the underlying reason for the asset's failure, providing a technical explanation for the issue encountered. Human errors (either actions

or inactions) that eventually result in physical causes of failure are included in the human element. In the end, latent causes include all managerial and organizational shortcomings that allow human errors to occur and prevent them from being corrected over time (failures in systems and procedures). At this stage of the maintenance management process, we will primarily concentrate on the root causes of failure.

- Phase 4: Supporting the proper definition of a Preventive Maintenance Plan. Designing an effective preventive maintenance plan for a given system (Phase 4) involves identifying the system's key functions and analyzing how these functions might fail. This process also entails developing a series of efficient and effective maintenance tasks that emphasize safety and cost-efficiency. A systematic and formal approach to achieving this objective is through Reliability Centered Maintenance (RCM) (Moubray, 1997).
- Phase 5. Optimization strategies for enhancing maintenance programs. To improve the effectiveness and efficiency of maintenance policies obtained from the original design of the plan and the scheduled chores, optimization methods and maintenance protocols (phase 5) can be devised. The temporal horizon chosen for the analysis determines which models will be used. Long-term models concentrate on maintainability capacity, spare parts warehouse layout, and the best times or intervals to carry out maintenance tasks. Medium-term optimization models can address the sequencing of activities during a significant plant shutdown, whereas short-term maintenance models can concentrate on enhancing resource allocation and management. Modeling methodologies, both analytical and empirical, exhibit significant diversity. The problem's complexity is frequently substantial, necessitating specific assumptions to facilitate the analytical resolution of models or to diminish processing requirements.
- Phase 6: Maintenance operations supervision and management. The execution of maintenance operations, once conceived, planned, and scheduled as described in the preceding sections, must be assessed to make sure that the company's business objectives and the target values of the maintenance KPIs chosen by the organization are regularly satisfied. (ORA: Operational Reliability Analysis). Deviations should be managed. This is implemented during Phase 6. A significant number of key performance indicators (KPIs) are derived from other technical and economic indicators that are more simplistic. Therefore, it is imperative that the organization obtains precise data and that this data is accurately aggregated or disaggregated to the appropriate level for maintenance analysis.
- Phase 7: Instruments for analyzing and controlling asset life-cycle costs. Phase 7 of a life-cycle cost analysis assesses an asset's overall cost over the course of its life. The expenses of planning, R&D, production, operation, maintenance, and equipment removal are all included in the study of a typical asset. Equipment acquisition costs, including research, design, testing, production, and building, are usually transparent. However, figures derived from dependability assessments have a considerable impact on life-cycle cost analysis. For instance, regarding the analysis of failure rates, costs of replacement parts, service times, and component

costs. A life-cycle cost analysis is essential for determining the acquisition of new equipment or to determine the optimal replacement time.

- Phase 8. Strategies for the ongoing enhancement of maintenance practices. The ongoing enhancement of maintenance management (phase 8) will be achievable through the application of techniques and developing technology in high-impact areas identified in prior phases of our management process. The application of new maintenance technologies introduces the "e- maintenance" idea, which is a facet of "e-manufacturing." This idea promotes the benefits of new information and communication technologies for creating remote and multi-user corporate settings. "E-Maintenance" is the term used to describe the maintenance assistance that includes the tools, services, and administration required to carry out a proactive maintenance decision- making process (Crespo Márquez, 2022). This support includes "e-maintenance" activities (operations and processes) like "e-monitoring," "e-diagnosis," and "e-prognosis," among others, in addition to Internet technologies (e.g., ICT, web-based applications, Internet of Things/IoT, Wi-Fi, wireless technologies, informatics, machine learning, neural networks, Maintenance 4.0, etc.). A key factor in determining success will be the new maintenance technology and the maintenance staff's participation in the improvement process. They will surely require the highest degrees of education, training, and experience; however, the fundamental techniques enabling operator engagement in maintenance tasks will be crucial for attaining superior maintenance quality and overall equipment efficiency.

3 The Asset Management Process

The asset management optimization model, termed "Asset Management," is a discipline that originated in the late 1990s that concentrates on decision-making throughout the whole life cycle of a physical asset, encompassing its production or purchase, utilization, maintenance, and eventual renewal or disposal. This contrasts with the typical management approach to maintenance, which focuses solely on equipment during its operational lifespan. Consequently, the administration of asset link concepts and methodologies from other domains, including finance, engineering, technology, and operations, is essential. Clearly, companies' endeavors to enhance asset performance extend beyond the establishment of maintenance and reliability management systems; they also involve maximizing several facets related to the asset life cycle. Nevertheless, the view that integrates the asset management process throughout its life cycle is highly advantageous for optimizing asset maintenance. The prevention and repair of failures to enhance equipment operational security is significantly impacted by management associated with the equipment's design, manufacture, installation, use, maintenance, and replacement (The Institute of Asset Management 2015; Woodhouse 1996). Since the middle of the 1990s, enterprise asset management has been recognized as a field. It incorporates ideas and methods from various disciplines, including finance, engineering, technology, and operations, emphasizing decision- making across the entire life cycle of physical assets while optimizing diverse aspects consistently with a holistic perspective. The Institute of Asset Management (IAM), an independent and non-profit organization, has been a principal advocate of this initiative. IAM characterizes asset management as "the art and science of making appropriate decisions and optimizing the processes of selection, maintenance, inspection, and renewal of assets" (The Institute of Asset Management 2015). It also states that a primary purpose is to reduce the entire lifecycle cost of the asset, while potentially facilitating other essential considerations such as risk and business continuity, which must be evaluated objectively for informed decision-making. A public specification called the standard PAS 55 proposal was created to improve infrastructure and physical asset management. The process of creating it began in 1995 when a Committee of Managers, which included members of the Institute of Management of Assets as well as other participants from business, government, and British regulatory organizations, met for the first time to outline the direction of this standard. The British Standards Institute (BSI) spent nine years on their work, which included publishing and modification (The Institute of Asset Management 2015). It was first published in April 2004 and continues to serve as the major basis for the ISO 55000 standard. The planned PAS 55 standard has gained approval since 2006 and proliferated within the industry following a strong recommendation from the UK Office of Gas and Electric Markets, the Regulatory Bureau of Gas and Electric Power in the United Kingdom, for public businesses to implement inside their operational network (PAS55–1, 2004). By 2008, the vast majority of UK public gas and electricity companies complied with the planned standard PAS 55. This tendency subsequently extended to the sectors of transportation, public enterprise management, food, pharmaceuticals, and chemicals, among others. Furthermore, other companies outside the United Kingdom have increasingly referenced the planned standard PAS 55. Regarding its significance and applicability, the following analogy may be drawn: PAS 55 pertains to asset management. ISO 9001 pertains to quality management, while ISO 14000 relates to environmental management (The Institute of Asset Management 2015).The PAS 55 standard defines asset management as "controlled and systematic practices and activities through which an organization optimally manages its assets, associated performance, risks, and expenses throughout their life cycle to fulfill the organization's strategic plan" (The Institute of Asset Management, 2015). PAS 55 is applicable to every business sector that oversees physical infrastructure, regardless of the function or type of asset involved. Successful applications have been observed in enterprises involved in roadways, airports, railways, and petrochemical facilities. This standard, grounded in self-evaluations, benchmarking, planned improvements, independent audits, certification, contractor selection, and competency demonstration are just a few of the goals that can be achieved by applying Deming's cycle of planning, doing, checking, and acting. Significant improvements in cost and performance/service indicators were reported by organizations that adopted the PAS 55 standard. For consumers, investors, regulators, and other stakeholders, PAS 55 provides unquestionable proof of efficient asset management (The Institute of Asset Management, 2015). The proposed standard PAS 55 served as the first basis for the ISO Organization's recommendation in late 2009 to create an asset management standard. The 2014 adoption of ISO 55000, 55,001, and 55,002 is one of the asset management standards that are now in use., with ISO 55001 being the certifiable standard. These standards have established themselves as the international benchmark in asset management. The design and implementation of an asset management system, aligned with the 24 standards of ISO 55001, (2014), is a comprehensive topic of debate. This paper outlines the model established by ISO 55001 and suggests a process for integrating the Maintenance Management Model (MMM, Fig. 2) with the asset management framework proposed by ISO 55000.

3.1 Description of Standard of Management of Assets ISO 55000

This international standard offers a comprehensive overview of asset management systems. It encompasses the standards ISO 55000, 55,001, (2014; 2014), and 55,002, (2014). The intended audience for this standard is defined as those specified in ISO 55000, (2014):

- Who is contemplating the enhancement of their businesses' value chain, beginning with their asset foundations?
- Who is involved in the establishment, implementation, maintenance, and enhancement of an asset management system?
- Who participates in the planning, design, implementation, and evaluation of asset management activities with service providers?

An organization can achieve its goals by managing its assets effectively and efficiently by using these international standards. Implementing an asset management system ensures that goals will be consistently and sustainably met over time.

The ISO 55000 standard defines an asset as "an element, thing, or entity that possesses real or potential value to an organization." The value will differ among various firms and their stakeholders, and may be either tangible or intangible, as well as financial or non-financial. The duration from the inception of an asset to the conclusion of its utility is referred to as the asset's useful life. The useful life of an asset does not necessarily align with the duration an organization is accountable for it; instead, throughout its useful life, an asset may yield actual or potential value to one or more organizations, and the asset's value to the organization may fluctuate during its useful life. Asset management enables an organization to identify the necessity for and evaluate the performance of assets and asset systems across several levels. Similarly, it facilitates the implementation of analytical methodologies for asset management across various phases of its lifecycle, commencing from the identification of the asset's necessity to its disposal, encompassing the management of potential liabilities post-disposal (ISO 55000).

The following are major elements that influence an organization's attainment of its objectives according to standard ISO 55000:

- The organization's nature and aim.
- The operational environment.
- Financial constraints and regulatory obligations.
- The requirements and anticipations of the Organization and relevant stakeholders.

Organizations must maintain effective control and efficient asset management strategies to create value by managing risks and opportunities, achieving desired cost balance, reducing risks, and enhancing performance. The management of assets converts the organization's objectives into activities, strategies, and choices about the asset, employing a risk-based approach (ISO 55000). ISO 55000 establishes a methodology for asset management grounded in certifiable criteria. There are 24 requirements in the full version of the standard ISO 55000 proposal, which maintain a logical elemental sequence in line with the common framework for quality processes: Plan, do, check, and act ISO55001, (2014).

4 Aligning the Maintenance Management Model (MMM) with ISO 55000 Asset Management Standard

Although there are no straightforward formulas for executing a comprehensive asset management model, nor are there fixed or universal rules applicable to all production assets, the 24 requirements delineated by the ISO 55000 standard proposal can be addressed through the integrated Maintenance Management Model (MMM) illustrated in Fig. 4. The MMM has eight phases that delineate particular actions to be undertaken at various stages of the maintenance management process, which are directly incorporated into an asset management process (Parra et al., 2021). The MMM offers a dynamic, sequential, closed-loop process designed to precisely delineate the actions necessary for achieving efficiency, effectiveness, and ongoing enhancement in asset management by integrating engineering, maintenance management, and reliability methodologies.

The eight phases of the suggested model (Fig. 4) and the essential elements of the ISO 55000 standard are fundamentally related, as shown in Tables 1 and 2. This makes it possible to examine how the generic model's gradual implementation relates to ISO 55000 requirements. Referencing the UNE 16,646 standard on maintenance within physical asset management (see Fig. 5), Table 2.1 shows that the tasks described in the 8 stages of the MMM can help firms meet the 24 requirements put out by the ISO 55000 standard. The relationship between the MMM phases and ISO 55000 standards is explained in detail in this publication.

Tables 1 and 2 indicate that the Maintenance Management Model (MMM) can facilitate compliance with the 24 standards established by the ISO 55000 standard.

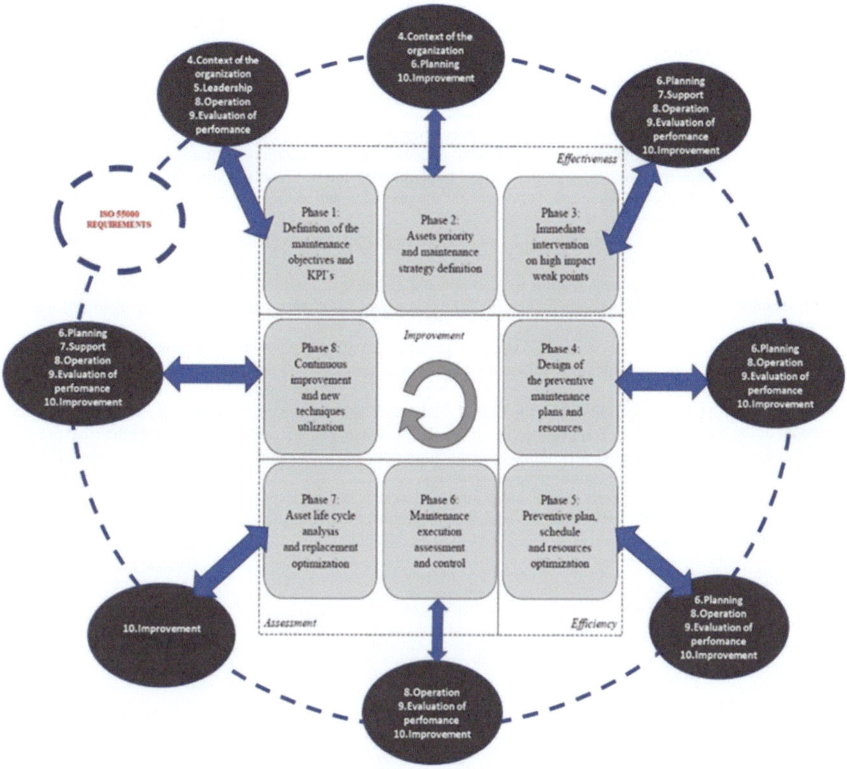

Fig. 4 Relationship between ISO 55000 criteria and the stages of the maintenance management model (MMM). *Source* Parra et al. (2021)

5 Implementation of Audit Techniques in the Asset Management Area (ISO 55000 Standard Approach)

ISO 55000-compliant asset management businesses must implement audit techniques (UNE, 16646, 2013). Value creation, risk management, and cost-efficiency are the focus of this standard for lifetime management of physical assets. This type of audit checks that asset management rules and procedures fulfill goals and regulations. Parts of this process include:

- Gap Analysis identifies differences between current processes and ISO 55000 standards.
- Regular internal audits oversee asset management operations to guarantee compliance.
- Risk Assessment—Assesses asset management risks and institutes mitigating strategies.

Table 1 Connection between the suggested maintenance management model (MMM) stages and ISO 55000 standards

ISO 55000 requirements	Integration of the phases of the mmm proposed with standard ISO 55000
4 Context of the Organization 4.1 Understanding the Organization and its context 4.2 Understanding the needs and expectations of interested parties 4.3 Determining the extent of the asset management system 4.4 System of management of assets 5 Leadership 5.1 Leadership and commitment 5.2 Policies 5.3 Roles, organizational responsibilities and authorities	Phase 1: Advocates for the implementation of the Balanced Scorecard (BSC), conceived by Kaplan and Norton, which converts a business unit's mission into a strategy via a series of objectives and measurable metrics. Implementing the BSC enables firms to: – Develop policies and strategies for the operation and maintenance of assets throughout their lifecycle – Execute maintenance and operating strategies as short-term, medium-term, and long-term objectives – Formulate action plans to accomplish the objectives established by management – Implement leadership across diverse processes to enhance performance in all organizational sectors – Periodically review and audit the performance of adopted methods, examining causal linkages between indicators, validating them at predetermined intervals, and formulating contingency plans Furthermore, Phase 1 of the MMM model advocates for the establishment of a unified organizational framework that facilitates asset management and promotes comprehensive process optimization via dependability and maintenance methodologies, delineating roles, responsibilities, and leadership for all lifecycle activities Phase 2: Suggests employing prioritizing models that correspond with stakeholder expectations and comply with the legal requirements pertinent to the asset's operational context
6 Planning 6.1 Actions to address the risks and the opportunities in the system of management of assets 6.2 Objectives for the management of assets and planning to achieve them 7 Support 7.1 Resources 7.2 Competencies 7.3 Awareness 7.4 Communication 7.5 Requirements of information 7.6 Documented information	Phase 2: Commences the enhancement process by formulating and implementing fundamental asset prioritization models grounded in risk factor analysis (e.g., qualitative risk matrices, Analytical Hierarchy Process [AHP], etc.) Phase 3: Employs Root Cause Analysis (RCA) to evaluate failures of significant occurrences, utilizing the risk level associated with each failure event to formulate solutions Phase 4: Advocates for the implementation of Reliability-Centered Maintenance (RCM) methodology to enhance maintenance and operational strategies, customized according to the risk levels linked to failures in certain operating environments Phase 5: Proposes optimization techniques for scheduling and resource allocation in maintenance and operations. Chosen methodologies encompass risk analysis techniques, including queue theory, Monte Carlo simulation, and probabilistic inventory reorder points Furthermore, Phase 5 promotes ongoing enhancement strategies in maintenance and operations programming, planning, and resource distribution grounded in risk management principles Phase 8: Advocates for the utilization of information support systems (ERP, EAM, reliability software, etc.) to oversee and distribute documentation and information produced during the operation and maintenance of assets. Asset management information systems are essential instruments that facilitate and optimize management by providing rapid data transmission and processing that surpasses organizational limits and promotes inter-sectoral integration. The successful execution of information management systems is essential for creating programs that improve reliability, maintenance, and operations

Source Own elaboration

Table 2 Connection between the suggested maintenance management model (MMM) stages and ISO 55000 standards

ISO 55000 requirements	Integration of the phases of the mmm with the standard ISO 55000
8 Operation 8.1 Operational planning and control 8.2 Change management 8.3 Outsourcing 9 Evaluation of performance 9.1 Monitoring, measurement, analysis and Evaluation 9.2 Internal audit 9.3 Revision of the management	Phase 1: Proposes utilizing the Balanced Scorecard (BSC) to assess and evaluate the organization's economic performance indicators, while integrating these with the technical indicators related to operations and maintenance (developed in Phase 6). This phase also incorporates control and continuous improvement audits, such as the Maintenance Effectiveness Survey (MES) and the Qualitative Matrix of Excellence in Maintenance (QMEM), among others Phases 3 and 4: It is advisable to implement reliability techniques, including Root Cause Analysis (RCA) and Reliability-Centered Maintenance (RCM), to evaluate failure modes and identify their underlying causes. These methods facilitate the identification of incidents and non-conformities, assess the potential safety, environmental, and operational impacts of failures, and recommend procedures for establishing corrective, preventive, redesign, and condition-based improvement actions Phase 5: Promotes the application of maintenance optimization and reliability engineering techniques, which aid in delineating the planning, scheduling, outsourcing, and training processes essential for improving asset management across its lifecycle Phase 6: Establishes a systematic approach for measuring, analyzing, and evaluating performance and improvement indicators, encompassing probabilistic assessments of reliability, maintainability, availability, cost, and risk Phase 8 proposes the establishment of a continuous improvement process that can adapt to ongoing changes in high-impact techniques and emerging technologies, as identified through studies conducted in the preceding eight phases of the proposed Maintenance Management Model
10 Improvement 10.1 Non-conformity and corrective action 10.2 Preventive action 10.3 Continuous improvement	Phase 2: Commences the enhancement process through the formulation and implementation of fundamental asset prioritization models grounded in risk factor analysis (e.g., qualitative and technical risk matrices, AHP: Analytical Hierarchy Process, etc.) Phase 3: Advocates for the Root Cause Analysis (RCA) technique to evaluate significant failure events, utilizing the associated risk levels as a foundation for formulating solutions, managing non-conformance processes, and executing corrective measures Phase 4: Proposes the implementation of Reliability-Centered Maintenance (RCM) methodology to enhance maintenance and operational strategies based on failure modes and their corresponding risks within the operational framework, emphasizing preventive measures Phase 5: Suggests optimization techniques for resource scheduling and allocation in maintenance and operations. Chosen methodologies encompass risk analysis approaches like queuing theory, Monte Carlo simulation, and probabilistic inventory reorder point analysis Phase 6: Proposes a comprehensive probabilistic assessment methodology for critical performance metrics, encompassing reliability, maintainability, availability, cost, and risk. This phase outlines a method to associate reliability and maintainability metrics with optimization choices in maintenance and operations, employing cost-risk–benefit analysis approaches for continuous improvement Phase 7: Describes a lifespan cost analysis procedure that enhances decision-making for the design, selection, development, and replacement of assets within a production system. The lifecycle process commences with the delineation of production tasks in the preliminary design phase, succeeded by activities such as production planning, facility layout, equipment selection, and manufacturing process specification, among others. Logistical factors are incorporated prior to the design phase, encompassing design support, production stages, user assistance, asset maintenance strategies, and asset disposal procedures (continuous enhancement) Phase 8: Implements a continuous improvement approach for the perpetual assessment and evaluation of the organization's technical and economic performance

Source Own elaboration

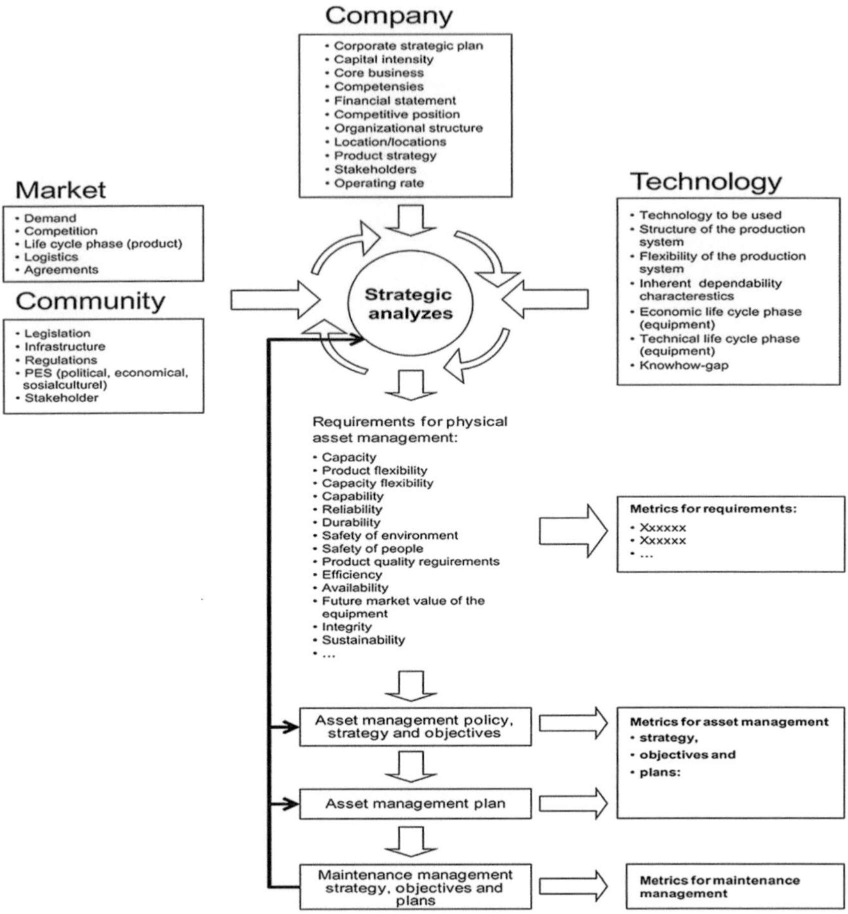

Fig. 5 Relationships among asset management, maintenance management, and organizational context. *Source* Standard UNE-16646 (2013)

- Effective asset management is measured using Key Performance Indicators (KPIs).
- Implemented corrective actions based on audit findings to enhance asset performance and compliance.

Audits require logically sequenced steps. Figure 6 shows a basic audit implementation (Crespo, 2007; Parra & Crespo, 2015). Choose a production system first. Definition of process goals follows. The audit goals define the most crucial components of the asset management audit, making this stage crucial to its success. Key maintenance and reliability goals are listed below (Parra & Crespo, 2015; Crespo Márquez et al., 2009):

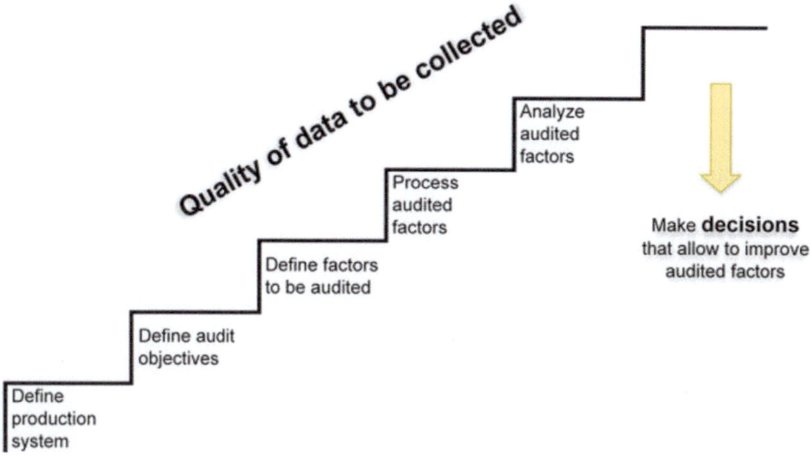

Fig. 6 General procedure for the implementation of an audit. *Source* Parra and Crespo, (2015)

- Ensure acceptable operational risk for production assets, decreasing failures and minimizing adverse effects on operations, safety, and the environment.
- Ensure efficient system recovery after interruptions (enhancing maintenance).
- Improve operational continuity and availability to enhance asset economic performance and reduce costs.
- Improve communication channels between clients, manufacturers, and company departments to provide high-quality services.

Upon establishing the audit objectives, it is essential to identify the area that has the most significant potential for evaluation. The criteria to be assessed in the maintenance audit are identified, processed, and analyzed based on this selection. The criteria to consider are as follows (González-Prida et al., 2021):

- Managerial Resources
- Information Management Systems (CMMS)
- Technologies Utilized for Preventive and Predictive Maintenance
- Planning and Estimation Processes • Quality Control in Maintenance
- Support Processes (Logistics, Inventories)
- Plant Shutdown Planning • Integration of Maintenance and Production
- Reliability Engineering Methodologies
- Motivation and Communication Aspects
- Post-purchase support, etc.

Numerous audit models exist within the sector, each employing distinct methodologies. Audits have been effectively utilized in the literature to assess various attributes, elements, and activities pertinent to asset management (Pintelon & Gelders, 1992). The audit process is a systematic, independent, and recorded procedure for acquiring audit data and assessing it objectively to ascertain the degree to which audit criteria are fulfilled.

Phase 1 of the 8-phase Maintenance Management Model (MMM) illustrated in Fig. 2 emphasizes the establishment of maintenance objectives, strategies, and responsibilities, directly correlating with the implementation of AMS-ISO 55001 (ASSET MANAGEMENT SURVEY-ISO 55001), as the organization must assess its maturity level. In this manner, it can discern deficiencies and formulate a plan for enhancement. The repercussions of inadequate maintenance are widely recognized, leading to process failures and threats to asset integrity, among other issues (Parra et al., 2021; Parra-Márquez et al., 2020).

The efficacy of a maintenance management process can be assessed by examining many parameters related to essential maintenance elements, reliability, and their influence on the whole asset management process (Roda & Macchi, 2018b).

In conclusion, the fundamental characteristics that influence the choice of the AMS-ISO 55001 audit for this application article are as follows (Parra et al., 2021):

- They must facilitate decision-making using qualitative and/or quantitative data.
- They must assess the aspects that contribute the most value to the business.
- They must integrate economic terminology (financial) with technical terminology (engineering).
- Their application must be swift and straightforward to execute.
- Mathematical complexities must be managed by computers.
- The outcomes of the factor analysis must produce actions that facilitate the attainment of the business's strategic objectives and optimize the profitability of production assets.

5.1 Audit Technique: AMS-ISO 55001 (ASSET MANAGEMENT SURVEY-ISO 55001)

The AMS-ISO 55001 diagnostic approach (Parra et al., 2021; Parra-Márquez et al., 2020) proficiently assesses the compliance with ISO 55001 and identifies the discrepancies (gaps) present inside the company regarding the standard's stipulations. ISO 55000-based audit methodologies assist firms in establishing a systematic and uniform framework for asset management that optimizes value, mitigates risks, and aligns with strategic goals. The following are the verifiable criteria of ISO 55001, (2014):

1. Organizational Context
2. Leadership
3. Strategic Planning
4. Support
5. Operation
6. Assessment of performance
7. Improvement

This article employs the maturity level derived from the "Asset Management Maturity Scale and Guidance" by IAM (The Institute of Asset Management, 2015)

(June 2016). This scale categorizes the prerequisites of NCh-ISO 55001, which establishes the IAM maturity scale outlined in Table 3.

Next, a group of people (minimum of 6) from different areas of the organization is selected to objectively evaluate the AMS-ISO 55001 audit questions. The evaluation is carried out at two levels:

Table 3 Asset management maturity scale (IAM Methodology: Institute of Asset Management)

	Description	Definition	Maturity characteristics
0	Innocent	The organization has not recognized the need for this requirement and/or there is no evidence of commitment to implementing it	
1	Aware	The organization has identified the need for this requirement and there is evidence of attempts to progress	Proposals are in development and some requirements may be implemented. Processes are weakly controlled, reactive, and their performance is unpredictable
2	Developing	The organization has identified means to systematically and consistently meet the requirements and can demonstrate progress with credible plans and established resources	Processes are planned, documented (when necessary), applied, and controlled locally or within functional departments; often reactive but could achieve expected results repetitively. Processes are insufficiently integrated with limited consistency or coordination within the organization
3	Competent	The organization can systematically and consistently meet the established requirements of NCh-ISO 55001	This level involves a formally documented asset management system incorporated into the organization. The performance of asset management system elements is measured, reviewed, and continuously improved to achieve asset management objectives
4	Optimized	The organization can systematically and consistently optimize its asset management practice aligned with corporate objectives and operational context	Characteristics of this level include performance monitoring and evaluation, balancing competitive goals in an agile decision-making structure, innovation as a lifestyle, widespread demonstration of continuous improvement with evidence of results, benchmarking to identify additional improvement opportunities, and a more integrated and effective management system
5	Excellent	The organization can demonstrate it employs cutting-edge practices and achieves maximum value with its asset management aligned with corporate objectives and operational context	This is a dynamic state sensitive to context, so evidence must include demonstrating awareness of benchmark positions against the best similar organizations and that both asset management practices and results (value generation) have no known improvements yet to be implemented

Existence scale of the requirement

1 Very poor process
2 Below average process
3 Standard average process
4 Very good practices process
5 World-Class process

Application scale of the requirement

20% Very poor process.
40% Below average process.
60% Standard average process.
80% Very good practices process.
100% World-Class process.

6 Case Study: Inkia Energy Central Colmito

The DS109/2017 decree (Ministry of Energy of Chile, 2018) from the Ministry of Energy "Safety regulations for electrical installations for production, transportation, provision of complementary services, energy storage systems, and distribution of electrical energy" establishes the obligation for generation companies to have an Electrical Installations Integrity Management System (SGIIE). The Technical Normative Specification RPTD N° 17 (Superintendency of Electricity and Fuels, Ministry of Energy of Chile, 2020) establishes the SGIIE requirements based on ISO 55001:2014 "Asset Management".

The SGIIE requirements aim to maximize the safety, continuity, and quality of electrical supply conditions by preventing the occurrence of accidents and incidents and, if they occur, minimizing their consequences.

If the Central Colmito does not comply with the RPTD N°17 technical specifications within the indicated deadlines for each process, it is subject to sanctions as indicated in Supreme Decree N° 119 (Ministry of Economy, Development and Reconstruction, 1989) Regulations on Sanctions in Electricity and Fuel Matters.

The methodology used included an initial workshop introducing the NCh-ISO 55001 requirements, reviewing existing management system documentation in generation, transmission, and distribution processes, and holding meetings with the Inkia Energy team.

According to Article 4°, sanctions that may apply under this regulation, without prejudice to others specifically established in Law 20.936 (Ministry of Energy of Chile, 2016) or other legal or regulatory bodies, are as follows:

- Censure: A formal reprimand directed in writing to the offender, notifying them that they are in an illegal or non-regulatory situation and warning them of a greater sanction if the infraction persists.

- Fine: A pecuniary sanction applied to the offender according to amounts established by law, ranging from one to five hundred monthly tax units. For repeated infractions of the same nature, a fine up to three times the maximum indicated amount may be applied. For these purposes, repetition is understood as committing two or more infractions within a period not exceeding twelve months.
- Temporary or permanent suspension of authorizations or licenses: Temporarily or permanently deprives the offender of the rights granted or encompassed by them.
- Seizure: Involves the loss of the species object of the infraction.
- Closure: Involves the temporary or permanent closure of the factory, commercial establishment, or warehouse where the infraction is found. Temporary closure may be for a specified period or the time necessary to correct the violation.
- Revocation of provisional concession: Deprives the holder of all inherent rights.
- Disconnection of installations: Separates the installation from the electrical, gas, or fuel supply system to which it is connected.

The audit application used as a reference was the NCh-ISO 55001–2014 Asset Management and the IAM evaluation scale. Inkia Energy contracted the service of Task Energy at the Central Colmito. The diagnosis was carried out from October to November 2020 to determine the asset management system's maturity level. Eleven members of the organization participated in the audit process (Table 4).

The evaluation result indicates that Central Colmito has a maturity level of 1,26 for the SGIIE, which translates to an "Aware" system according to the IAM evaluation scale (Fig. 7).

6.1 Improvement Plan—Weak Points

Among the weakest requirements identified by the audit process are Monitoring, Measurement, Analysis, and Evaluation (9.1), Management Review (9.3), and Continual Improvement (10.3). These are at an Innocent maturity level, indicating that the organization has no evidence of commitment to implementing them.

After the audit process, the organization determined the following improvement action plans (this article will only present the improvement plans for requirements at the Innocent level):

- **Requirement 9.1:** The organization will develop a monthly tracking log of the SGIIE objectives and goals, assigning a responsible person. Using the Inkia Goals platform, health, safety, and environmental indicators will be reported. Preventive maintenance compliance objectives will be managed and recorded in the InforEAM platform.

Table 4 Summary of results inkia energy—central colmito

Number	Requirement name	Maturity level
4.1	Understanding the organization and its context	1
4.2	Understanding the needs and expectations of interested parties	1
4.3	Determination of the scope of the asset management system	1
4.4	Management system	1
5.1	Leadership and commitment	1
5.2	Policy	2
5.3	Organizational roles, responsibilities, and authority	1
6.1	Actions to address risks and opportunities for the asset management system	2
6.2.1	Asset management objectives	1
6.2.2	Planning to achieve asset management objectives	1
7.1	Resources	1
7.2	Competence	2
7.3	Awareness	1
7.4	Comunication	2
7.5	Information requirements	1
7.6.1	Documented information—general	2
7.6.2	Documented information—creation and update	2
7.6.3	Documented information—control of documented information	2
8.1	Operational planning and control	1
8.2	Change management	2
8.3	Outsourcing	1
9.1	Monitoring, measurement, analysis, and evaluation	0
9.2	Internal audit	2
9.3	Management review	0
10.1	Non-conformity and corrective action	2
10.2	Preventive action	1
10.3	Continual improvement	0
Company maturity level		1,26

- **Requirement 9.3:** To ensure the execution of the asset management system, resource use, process effectiveness, and continuous improvement execution at Central Colmito, an annual review by management will be conducted. Participants in this review will include:

  Operations Manager
  Operations and Maintenance Engineer
  Operations Manager
  Maintenance Manager

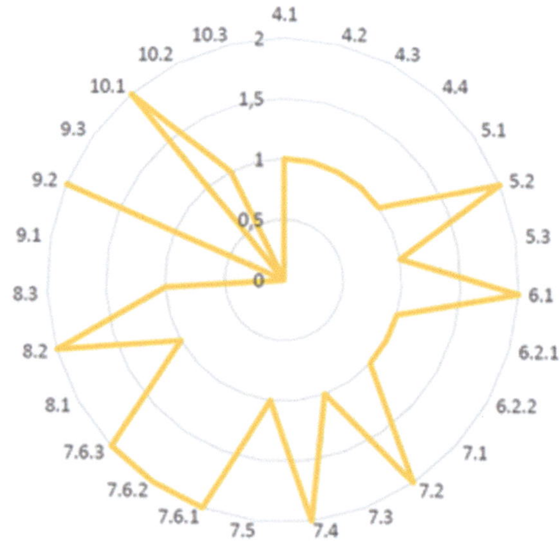

Fig. 7 Radar chart with maturity level

EHS Supervisor.

For each management review, the following points will be reviewed:

Ensure compliance with SGIIE objectives.
Ensure compliance with PGA objectives established at Inkia Energy Chile.
Conduct risk analysis of the asset portfolio defined within the SGIIE scope.
Update the PGA if necessary.
Review the progress of the latest modifications made to the PGA.
Establish and coordinate meetings to set the annual maintenance plan.
Channel information about inspection update proposals to Maintenance and Operations Managers.
Manage preventive maintenance work orders for thermal plants.
Analyze the results of inspections performed on electrical assets.
Validate inspection updates.
Conduct stock inventory control in the warehouse.
Manage spare parts acquisition as needed.

All agreements, actions, changes, and/or topics discussed during the Management Review will be recorded in the Change Control document associated with all SGIIE forms and procedures.

- **Requirement 10.3:** The organization will develop combined efforts (currently underway) to comply with the asset management system. Some of these efforts include:

  Monthly KPI review: The Operations and Maintenance Engineer collects the necessary information from all SGIIE-established KPIs and sends an email to

share the analysis results with the Operations Manager, Operations Manager, Maintenance Manager, and EHS Supervisor.
Root Cause Analysis (RCA): The goal is to establish the root cause of the event studied under this method. It can be used as a method to investigate failures, incidents, accidents, and near-misses.
Near Miss: Establishes a guide to provide a safe and healthy environment for Central Colmito employees and contractors.

The most crucial factors to take into account when aligning a maintenance management model (MMM) with a comprehensive asset management process are outlined in the paragraphs that follow. (Carnero, 2015; Parra-Márquez et al., 2020; Roda & Macchi, 2018b):

- Maintenance must be acknowledged as a critical priority and a strategic business opportunity within the organization. It should be regarded not merely as a necessary expense but as a fundamental component of business operations that can directly improve profitability. Organizations can enhance their bottom line by implementing a strategy focused on profit, customer satisfaction, and ongoing improvements in maintenance practices.
- Promote leadership and technical proficiency. Effective maintenance leaders require a thorough understanding of maintenance challenges and the capability to manage maintenance as an internal business function. Leaders must consistently develop the skills, competencies, and progressive mindsets necessary to advance maintenance excellence in the future.
- Encourage pride in maintenance-related tasks. Work ethic, attitude, values, job performance, and customer service will all significantly improve in maintenance operations, fostering a true sense of pride in maintenance excellence. Ongoing maintenance enhancements will yield measurable savings and performance improvements.
- It is essential to acknowledge the significance of the maintenance profession. Maintenance will be recognized as a vital profession crucial to the success of various organizations, leading to the establishment of the Chief Maintenance Officer (CMO) role. Maintenance leaders are recognized as essential contributors to the overall success of operations.
- Maintenance and Operations. A Collaborative Approach to Profit Generation. Through better scheduling, planning, and cooperative improvement projects, maintenance and operations will work together as a single team. Operations will be recognized as an important internal client, with enhanced coordination in planning and scheduling maintenance activities resulting in improved support and service for manufacturing operations. Collaboration between maintenance and operations is essential for minimizing unplanned breakdowns, enhancing equipment effectiveness, and reducing overall maintenance costs.
- Improve Equipment Efficiency. To thoroughly evaluate and improve all aspects influencing equipment efficacy, a team-based, leadership-driven strategy will be used in maintenance and production processes. Ensuring the asset's optimal availability for carrying out its primary function is the goal.

- Ongoing enhancement Reliability and Maintainability. Reliability and maintenance efficiency will be prioritized in the specification, design, retrofitting, and installation of machines and systems. The design of the equipment will prioritize dependability and maintainability, rather than solely focusing on performance metrics. The design for maintainability will gain widespread acceptance, recognizing the significant influence of maintenance costs on an asset's life-cycle expenses. Implementing effective principles of maintainability and reliability in the design phase will reduce the root causes of elevated life-cycle costs. Optimizing the use of enterprise asset management and computerized maintenance management systems is crucial. By integrating with the organization's overall business processes, technologies that enable comprehensive maintenance operations will enhance the quality of physical asset management and maintenance. By addressing every aspect of maintenance operations, computerized maintenance management systems (CMMS) help to optimize maintenance procedures and raise the standard of maintenance management. Software for enterprise asset management (EAM) offers a thorough, integrated platform for controlling inventories of parts, human resources, and physical assets. It includes functionalities for maintenance management, procurement, inventory control, work management, asset performance, and process monitoring.
- Ensure robust adherence to environmental, health, and safety regulations. Maintenance should assume a proactive leadership position in facilitating regulatory compliance. Maintenance leaders must consistently enhance their technical knowledge and expertise to ensure compliance with all local, state, and federal regulations. Maintaining indoor air quality necessitates continuous attention to avert possible problems. Maintenance teams should collaborate with other departments, including quality and safety, to ensure a cohesive and supportive strategy for regulatory compliance.
- Oversee life-cycle costs and obsolescence. To reduce overall expenses, the life-cycle costs of systems and physical assets will be tracked, evaluated, and controlled. Significant life-cycle cost reductions will result from a profit-and customer-centered strategy. by implementing a well-structured design phase prior to purchase and installation. In the operational phase, systems will be implemented to monitor equipment costs continuously, offering insights into cost trends and identifying equipment with elevated maintenance expenses.

7 Conclusions and Further Works

The diagnosis carried out at the Colmito Power Generation Plant based on the ISO 55001 standard requirements involved all areas of the organization for a common objective: to develop an Electrical Installations Integrity Management System (SGIIE) covering the factors required in the Normative Technical Specification—RPTD N° 17. The diagnosis results placed the organization at an "aware" maturity level, position 1,26—scale of 0 to 5 (maturity evaluation scale based on the document developed by the Institute of Asset Management (IAM) titled: Asset Management Maturity Scale and Guidance 2016).

Specifically, regarding the audit process results at the Colmito Power Generation Plant concerning the ISO 55001 standard, the organization has an asset management system with many improvement opportunities. Referring to the characteristics of the "aware" maturity level, the Colmito Power Generation Plant's management processes are weakly controlled, reactive, and their performance is unpredictable (see Table 3).

Below are some strengths, weaknesses, opportunities, and threats detected from the diagnosis:

Strengths:

- Internal audit, document generation and control, contractor management, training procedure, and maintenance procedures are some of the topics that can be discussed in relation to certain advancements or components. It is feasible to make reference to these topics.
- Senior management has demonstrated leadership and dedication to the implementation of an asset management system, as well as the formation of a specialist team that is familiar with the applicable procedures and apparatus.
- The organizational structure is consistent, which provides a clear benefit in the process of adopting, running, and maintaining the SGIIE.
- The generating technology is mature, which makes operation and maintenance effective and known, changing the system into a reliable energy production system.

Weaknesses:

- The modification of existing papers is a difficult task because of the structure of the organization. Other management systems cannot be integrated with the one that has already been implemented because there is no opportunity to do so.
- The management system that has been implemented needs to be certified.
- It is possible for there to be inconsistencies in the broadcast of information from the central office to each generation plant in Chile.
- If administrative concerns are dependent on the headquarters, it may take some time to resolve them.

Opportunities:

- In light of the growing demand for energy, this alternative solution for the production of energy that is both continuous and dependable may be relied upon.
- New investment requirements arise as a result of the increased demand for energy and, as a consequence, the capacity that has been constructed across the nation.
- The availability of new technologies that can improve the efficiency of processes and the maintenance of essential pieces of equipment
- The incorporation of various generation technologies that are based on non-conventional renewable energy (NCRE).

- Improvements in asset performance and value addition of generation technologies based on NCRE, such as solar, are brought about by national regulatory requirements, such as the introduction of SGIIE.

Threats:

- Demonstrations and conflicts with adjacent communities for environmental preservation. Although the likelihood of it happening is low, it is nevertheless regarded a threat despite the fact that it is uncommon.
- The implementation of new regulations prohibiting emissions of greenhouse gases, which contribute to climate change and its repercussions. It is possible that these limits will become more harsh in accordance with the global context in order to counteract global warming.
- In accordance with the regulations that are now in place, there will be restrictions placed on the emission of PM, SOx, and NOx. The failure to comply with these rules may result in legal complications.
- As a result of the current geopolitical situation, the prices of fossil fuels are on the rise, which may lead to an increase in operational costs.

On the basis of the aforementioned elements, the Maintenance Management Model (MMM) provides enterprises with assistance in aligning themselves with the requirements of ISO 55000. Importantly, despite the fact that the MMM's major objective is to offer a structured strategy for organizing and optimizing basic maintenance management activities, it should not be misunderstood as a straight pathway for the implementation of ISO 55001 (Parra et al., 2021). In addition, the article provides an overview of the most important findings from the evaluation that was carried out at the Colmito Power Generation Plant of INKIA ENERGY (Chile) in relation to the requirements of ISO 55001, as well as specific action plans that are intended to clarify the roles and responsibilities of team members who were involved in the establishment of the Electrical Installations Integrity Management System (SGIIE). This will contribute to the Colmito Plant's ability to manage its assets over their entire lifecycle in an effective and efficient manner.

References

Campbell, J. D., & Jardine, A. K. S. (2001). *Maintenance excellence*. Marcel Dekker.

Carnero, M. C. (2015). Auditing model for the introduction of computerized maintenance management systems. *International Journal of Data Science, 1*, 17–41.

Crespo, A. (2007). *The maintenance management framework*. London, Springer Verlag. https://doi.org/10.13140/RG.2.2.16765.38884

Crespo Márquez, A., Moreu de León, P., Gómez Fernández, J. F., Parra Márquez, C., & López Campos, M. (2009). The maintenance management framework: A practical view to maintenance management. *Journal of Quality in Maintenance Engineering, 15*(2), 167–178. https://doi.org/10.1108/13552510910961110

Crespo Márquez, A. (2022). Asset health indexing and life cycle costing. In *Digital Maintenance Management*. Cham: Springer Series in Reliability Engineering. https://doi.org/10.1007/978-3-030-97660-6_12

Duffuaa, S. O. (2000). Mathematical models in maintenance planning and scheduling. In M. Ben-Daya, S. O. Duffuaa, A. Raouf (Eds.), *Maintenance, Modelling and Optimization.* Boston: Kluwer Academic Publishers.

González-Prida, V., Parra, C., Gómez J.F., & Crespo A. (2021). Audit of a specific study scenario according to a reference framework for improving warranty management. In: Grall, G. Soares (Eds.), *Advances in Safety, Reliability and Risk Management-Berenguer*. https://doi.org/10.1201/b11433.

ISO 55000. (2014). *Asset management—Overview, principles and terminology*

ISO 55001.(2014). *Asset management-Management Systems-Requirements*

ISO 55002.(2014). *Asset management-Management Systems-Guidelines on the application of ISO 55001*

Kaplan, R. S., & Nortonm, D. P. (1992). The balanced scorecard—measures that drive performance. *Harvard Business Review, 70*(1), 71–79.

Kings-Picknell, J. (2007). *An introduction to PAS 55 optimal management of physical assets.* Works Management Tutorial.

Ministry of Economy, Development and Reconstruction. (1989). Regulations on sanctions in electricity and fuel matters N° 119 of 17 April 1989. Ministry of Economy, Development and Reconstruction. https://www.bcn.cl/leychile/navegar?idNorma=9554

Ministry of Energy of Chile. (2016). New Electrical Transmission System Law and creates an independent coordinating body of the National Electrical System N° 20.936 of 20 July 2016. Ministry of Energy of Chile. https://www.bcn.cl/leychile/navegar?idNorma=1092695&idParte=9716002

Ministry of Energy of Chile. (2018). Safety regulations for electrical installations for production, transportation, provision of complementary services, energy storage systems, and distribution of electrical energy N° 109 of 12 June 2018. Ministry of Energy of Chile. https://www.bcn.cl/leychile/navegar?i=1119451&f=2022-04-25

Moubray, J. (1997). *Reliability-centered maintenance* (2nd ed.). Butterworth-Heinemann.

Parra, C., & Crespo, A. (2015). *Ingeniería de Mantenimiento y Fiabilidad aplicada en la Gestión de Activos.* Segunda Edición., Sevilla, España: INGEMAN. https://doi.org/10.13140/RG.2.2.29363.66083

Parra, C., González-Prida, V., Candón, E., De la Fuente, A., Martínez-Galán, P., & Crespo, A. (2021). Integration of asset management standard ISO 55000 with a maintenance management model. In: A. Crespo Márquez, D. Komljenovic, J. Amadi-Echendu (Eds.), *14th WCEAM Proceedings. WCEAM 2019.* Lecture Notes in Mechanical Engineering. Cham: Springer. https://doi.org/10.1007/978-3-030-64228-0_17

Parra-Márquez, C., Viveros-Gunckel, P., Kristjanpoller-Rodríguez, F., Crespo-Márquez, A., & González- Prida- Diaz, V. (2020). Audit models for asset management, maintenance and reliability processes case study: Electricity transmission sector. *DYNA Management, 8*(1), 14. https://doi.org/10.6036/MN9826.

PAS 55–1. (2004). Asset Management. Specification for the optimized management of physical infrastructure assets. United Kingdom: BSI.

Pintelon, L. M., & Gelders, L. F. (1992). Maintenance management decision making. *European Journal of Operational Re-Search, 58*, 301–317.

Roda, I., & Macchi, M. (2018). A framework to embed Asset Management in production companies. *Proceedings of the Institution of Mechanical Engineers Part O: Journal of Risk and Reliability,232*(4, SI), 368–378.

Roda, I., & Macchi, M. (2018). A framework to embed Asset Management in production companies. *Proceedings of the Institution of Mechanical Engineers Part O: Journal of Risk and Reliability, 232*(4, SI), p. 368–378. https://doi.org/10.1177/1748006X17753501.

Superintendency of Electricity and Fuels, Ministry of Energy of Chile. (2020). Exempt Resolution 31876 Technical Annex of RPTD N° 17 "Electrical Installations Integrity Management System" of 14 May 2020. Superintendency of Electricity and Fuels, Ministry of Energy of Chile. https://www.bcn.cl/leychile/consulta/listaresultadosimple?cadena=RPTD%20N%C2%B0%2017&itemsporpagina=10&npagina=1
The Institute of Asset Management. (2015). *Gestión de activos: una anatomía.* 3a ed., p. 84.
UNE 16646. (2013). *Maintenance within physical asset management*
Woodhouse, J. (1996). Managing Industrial Risk. Londres: Chapman & Hall Inc.

BIM-Powered Asset Management Solutions—Digitalizing Building Maintenance

Jónatas Valença, Cláudia Ferreira, Maria Paula Mendes, and Ana Silva

Abstract Building maintenance is often seen as a low-priority financial burden, which is a paradox, since given that the built environment corresponds to approximately 50% of the wealth of most European countries. Buildings are one of the most valuable assets of any individual or collective entity, public or private. Reactive maintenance, based on subjective criteria, is still current practice. In a Society with scarce resources facing the challenges of economic and environmental sustainability, typified measures for the maintenance of buildings can no longer be applied. Currently, paper-based records and digital spreadsheets are still the best approach used in buildings' management, resulting in inefficient operations and maintenance. Building information modelling (BIM) is a practical approach to store, visualize and exchange building information in design and construction, but it is still at its beginning concerning the operation and maintenance phases, which comprise around 80% of whole life-cycle costs. To overcome the current limitations, image-based methods for the inspection of buildings' facades can be very effective, particularly when combined with advanced technologies such as computer vision and machine learning. The image-based methods allow a promptly capture of large amounts of data in a relatively short amount of time. This can lead to more efficient inspections, especially for a large set of buildings. The computer vision and machine learning algorithms can automate the analysis of images, making it easier to detect defects, anomalies, or critical areas. These algorithms can be trained on large datasets to improve accuracy and reliability over time. Factors such as lighting conditions, weather, and the presence of obstructions can affect the quality of images, and the effectiveness of

J. Valença · C. Ferreira · A. Silva (✉)
CERIS, IST-ID, University of Lisbon, Lisbon, Portugal
e-mail: ana.ferreira.silva@tecnico.ulisboa.pt

J. Valença
e-mail: jonatas.valenca@tecnico.ulisboa.pt

C. Ferreira
e-mail: claudiaarferreira@tecnico.ulisboa.pt

M. P. Mendes
CERENA, IST-ID, University of Lisbon, Lisbon, Portugal
e-mail: mpaulamendes@tecnico.ulisboa.pt

A. Crespo Márquez et al. (eds.), *Case Studies in Digital Transformation*, Engineering Asset Management Review 4, https://doi.org/10.1007/978-3-032-05592-7_9

analysis algorithms, being essential to take it into account. This paper presents a methodology to build a digital model of buildings to support management maintenance, by merging the damage maps by computer vision and a degradation index, both automatically obtained. The automatic mapping of facades is performed by a supervised classification, followed by the calculation of the degradation index, based on the maps obtained. The results are introduced in a digital model of the buildings (such as BIM) for a comprehensive analysis of the actual state of conservation on the building as well as its evolution during service life. The methodology is showcased with a real building, evaluating the impact of different maintenance strategies in the performance of the case study under analysis. The results demonstrate the applicability of the proposed approach to support decision making in terms of maintenance. The final digital model enables the integration of all data, being a valuable and useful tool for different stakeholders', such as asset managers.

Keywords Buildings · Computer vision · Degradation index · Asset management · Decision-making

1 Introduction

Building maintenance must be a priority since the built environment corresponds to approximately 50% of the wealth of most European countries. Traditionally, maintenance practices have been reactive, and the repair of anomalies tend to occur when the building already reveals a high degradation condition. This approach is often costly and can lead to further deterioration of assets over time. Proactive maintenance, on the other hand, involves identifying and addressing potential anomalies and defects before they escalate, thereby preventing costly repairs and extending the service life of buildings and infrastructure (Pourebrahimi et al., 2020).

The current economic and environmental sustainability challenges reinforce the need for change in building maintenance practices. Additionally, integrating maintenance plans into Building Information Modelling (BIM) is crucial. This integration allows for the consolidation of all relevant information, enabling visualization and holistic analysis of data. Due to their exposure, facades are more susceptible to damage, and 20% of defects in buildings are related to facades, to cladding (Watt, 1999). Analysis of facade claddings' durability is essential for most decisions associated with the built environment (Silva et al., 2022). Data considering their durability allows evaluating total cost, incorporating initial construction cost and the maintenance costs over their service life (Silva et al., 2016). This approach enables us to define the most cost-effective proposal.

Visual inspections are widely used and still the most common method for inspection (Lee & Kalos, 2014; Chen et al., 2021). Advantages of using automatic classification of damages based on computer vision have been presented, showing that these technologies consistently deliver results (Pantoja-Rosero et al., 2023). To overcome the limitations of visual inspection performed by paper-based records and digital spreadsheets, image-based methods has been applied (Valença et al., 2013; Santos et al., 2019; Zhang et al., 2023). These methods enable the acquisition of larger amounts of data in a relatively short amount of time, resulting in an efficient inspection tool. The application of computer vision and machine learning algorithms enables automatic classification and segmentation of images, rendering it an effective approach for detecting damages and anomalies. These capabilities can be further enhanced when integrated with systematic and planned image acquisition processes. The current state of the art of technologies such as Unmanned aerial vehicle (UAV), high-resolution cameras, and computer vision algorithms, enable detailed inspections without the need for physical scaffolding or direct human access. By capturing and analysing visual data, image-based methods detect surface cracks, discolorations, and other signs of wear or damage, making it easier to monitor building health, plan maintenance, and ensure safety (Yiğit & Uysal, 2025). These approaches not only improve the precision of inspections but also significantly reduce inspection time and costs.

Asset management involves maintaining and optimizing assets, such as buildings, over their entire lifespan, including maintenance, repairs, and monitoring. Effective asset management ensures optimal performance, cost efficiency, and compliance with regulations and codes. Linking BIM and asset management databases allows improving information management and, for example, creates a "digital twin" of the building (Tuhaise et al., 2023). This provides accurate real-time information across asset categories, benefiting facility managers and involving all stakeholders. BIM are transforming traditional Facilities Management (FM) practices, revolutionizing methodologies and procedures in FM, where managers can visually manage the inspection data (Tan et al., 2024; Yilmaz et al., 2023). This enhancing the efficiency, accuracy, and effectiveness of managing building operations and maintenance. By integrating comprehensive building data, including information from the inspection and state of conservation, BIM enables better decision-making, optimized resource allocation, and improved lifecycle management (Kulinan et al., 2024; Valença et al., 2024). For example, BIM can generate walk-through visualizations of a building or provide a 360-degree view of a large asset and evaluate its state of conservation at different years, in a simple, complete and effective way. The proper use of these tools supports the longevity of assets due to regular maintenance based on anticipated scenarios. This ensures that building systems and components operate efficiently, extending their lifespan. Furthermore, proper maintenance can improve energy efficiency and reduce the building's environmental impact, i.e., promotes sustainability.

This paper introduces a methodology for developing a digital model of buildings to support asset management regarding their maintenance needs. The methodology integrates damage mapping through computer vision and a degradation index, both obtained automatically. All pertinent information is then incorporated into Building Information Modelling (BIM) for comprehensive analysis and visualization purposes.

2 Methodology

The methodology proposed follows the flowchart of Fig. 1, and can be divided into two initial stages, "Image-based assessment of the buildings' facades" and "Maintenance analysis". These stages operate sequentially, with the output of the first stage acting as the input for the second. The third stage consists in merge the information generated from the previously stages in a digital model to reach a "BIM-Powered Asset Management Solutions".

2.1 Image-Based Assessment of Facades

The first stage deals with image acquisition and image classification to map the anomalies observed in buildings' facades and can follows several image-based approaches such as the ones proposed in Valença et al. (2024) or Torres-González et al. (2023). Independently of the algorithms used, the image-based classification consists in the following main steps:

2.1.1 Systematic and Planned Image Acquisition.

The goal of this step is to ensure that the images are well-aligned, distortion-free, and have enough overlap to allow for accurate stitching and alignment, enabling to build ortho-mosaics of the building's facades. The key elements to consider are the following:

a. Survey Planning. Define the exact boundaries of the area you need to cover. The more precise the definition of these boundaries, the less data processing required and the more efficient the survey will be. Fronto-parallel acquisition is standard for ortho-mosaics, as they minimize distortion. Some specialized surveys may benefit from oblique angles, but fronto-parallel images are typically required for accurate ortho-mosaic creation.
b. Images Overlap. At least 60–80% is typically recommended. This overlap ensures that each feature on the surface is captured in multiple images for better alignment and mosaic stitching.
c. Camera Settings and Calibration. Regular calibration ensures the camera is capturing consistent and undistorted images. Use manual focus, ISO, and exposure settings to avoid inconsistencies due to automatic adjustments, which may introduce artifacts in the orthoimages.
d. Environmental Conditions. Ideal weather conditions for image acquisition include clear skies with minimal wind. Clouds and strong shadows can create inconsistencies in images and make stitching difficult. Optimal lighting is typically around midday to reduce shadows. For some projects, diffused light on overcast days can provide even lighting and reduce brightness. In relation to wind

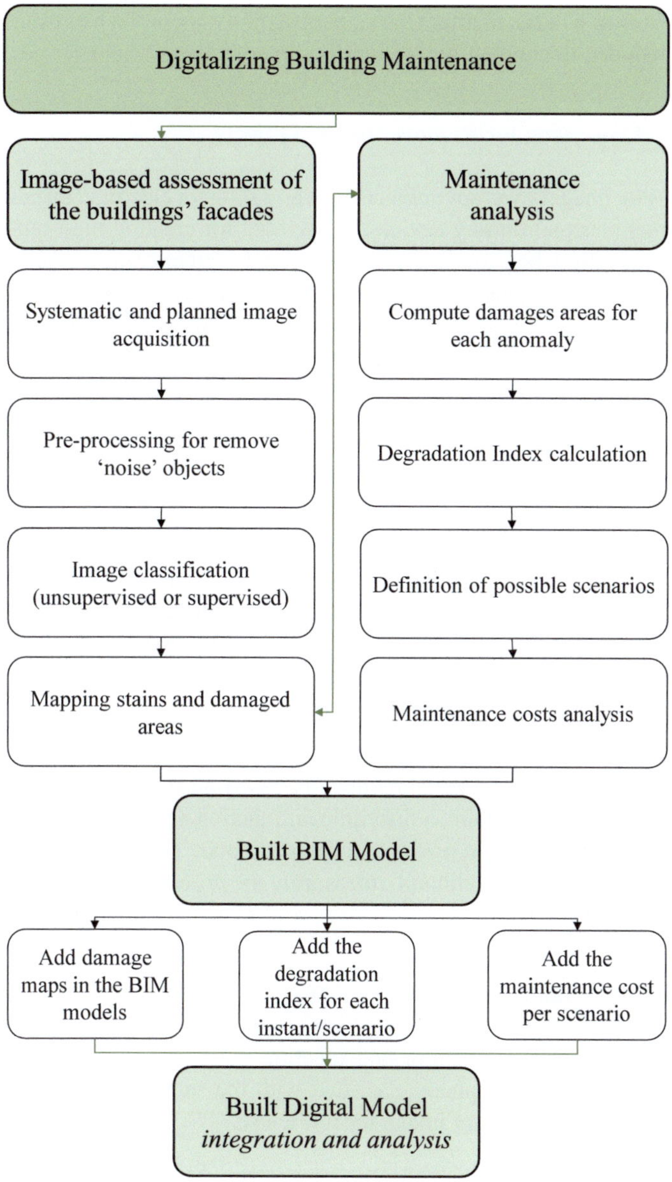

Fig. 1 Flowchart of the methodology proposed

speed, strong winds can affect the camera stability, mainly when using UAV. It's recommended to conduct flights under calm conditions whenever possible.

2.1.2 Pre-Processing for Remove 'Noise' Objects

Pre-processing images to remove objects such as wiring for electrical installations and fixed external air conditioning devices, is essential for creating high-quality ortho-mosaics, especially when image classification and segmentation is then performed Further, non-cladding areas of the facade must be defined as background, improving the efficiency and quality of processing applied. The latter can be done using color-based segmentation as in Torres-Gonzáles et al. (2023).

2.1.3 Image Classification

The image classification can be computed using an unsupervised or supervised approach and applying an automatic pixel-wise identification of the damage in the ortho-mosaic of the facade cladding. The supervised classification can be performed as in Valença et al. (2024), by applying the maximum likelihood algorithm using using MultiSpec (Landgrebe & Biehl, 2005). After definition of the image classes to be classified, a supervised classification based on the selection on a training area for each class is performed. The key path is the following:

a. Definition of image classes to be classified and selection of the training areas.
b. Application of a supervised classification based on the selected training areas for each class. At this point, a discriminant function assigns each pixel to one of the classes defined, based on the highest likelihood. This last parameter is evaluated by the 'average likelihood', measuring the probability of the classification conducted are correct.

2.1.4 Mapping Stains and Damaged Areas

The final outputs imply labelling and creating maps for each damage. This is performed by selecting all pixels classified with the same class (in this case, it's damage) and saved in a binary image for future use.

2.2 Maintenance Analysis

The second stage focuses on computing a degradation index using the mapped damages and estimating maintenance costs across various scenarios. Its main steps are:

1. Compute damages areas for each anomaly. Computing all relevant parameters from the map of damages computed, such as the area of each damage for each time instant.
2. Degradation Index calculation. The degradation index, called as severity of degradation (S_w), is determined by a ratio calculated using the weighted degraded area (considering the severity of the defects observed) and a reference area equivalent to the total cladding area with the highest possible level of degradation, as shown in Eq. (1). A_n represents the area of the cladding affected by a defect *n*, in m^2, k_n the defects' "*n*" multiplying factor, as a function of its condition (between 1 and 4) and $k_{a,n}$ the weighting coefficient corresponding to the relative importance of each defect obtained through cost of repair or risk ($k_{a,n} \in R^+$) (Silva et al., 2016).

$$S_w = \frac{\Sigma(A_n \times k_n \times k_{a,n})}{A \times \Sigma(k_{máx.})} \tag{1}$$

   Based on the degradation index, a condition scale of five levels is considered. Level A corresponds to a well-maintained facade with no visible signs of degradation. Level B to a rendered façade with slight discoloration and the occasional presence of microorganisms. Level C to a rendered noticeable degradation, with some areas showing dark patches of damp and dirt, often with microorganisms and algae. Level D to a rendered with significant degradation, with widespread detachment and the presence of very dark patches with probable presence of algae. Level E to a rendered with severe degradation, with large areas of detachment and extensive wide cracks.
3. Definition of possible scenarios for a building maintenance plan. This step is crucial for a proactive problem identification, based on early detection and correction, for anticipating potential anomalies and preventing minor problems from becoming major, resulting in costly repairs. Scenarios also help identifying risks and vulnerabilities, enabling the development of strategies to mitigate risks before they cause significant damage that may compromise the buildings' performance and durability.
4. Maintenance costs analysis. By predicting various scenarios, the asset managers can allocate resources more efficiently and avoid unexpected expenses, which leads to better financial planning and control. Preventive maintenance based on scenario planning can also reduce the need for expensive emergency repairs.

2.3 BIM-Powered Asset Management Solutions

In the third stage, the information generated from both Stage 1 and Stage 2 is integrated into a digital model such as Building Information Modelling (BIM), as shown

Fig. 2 Example of a BIM with map of stains from an in situ inspection

in Fig. 2. The model can support inspection over time and compute the major differences between service life instants. This consolidated dataset supports decision-making processes related to maintenance strategies and resource allocation. This stage has the following main steps.

1. Add damage maps in the BIM models. Built a reference BIM of the buildings with all materials and geometry of the facades. This can be done from paper or CAD plans and modelling in BIM software. The maps of damages of the facades are added in the BIM, allowing to visualize the results of the inspections.
2. Add the degradation index for each instant/scenario. The degradation index is linking to the correspondent map, instant and scenario and added to the model in text format. In addition, the variation of the S_w per year for the different scenarios defined are visualized next to the model.
3. Add the maintenance cost per scenario. A cost variation for each scenario is also plotted per year in €/m^2.

The BIM-based methodology outlined here, while focused on a specific building type, is adaptable to various structures by modifying certain parameters, such as types of facade materials, environmental conditions, and degradation factors. The flexibility of this method could be valuable in different climates or regions by enabling specified adjustments, making it broadly applicable and insightful for both regional and international asset management practices.

3 The Case Study of Bairro De Alvalade, in Lisbon, Portugal

The methodology proposed was validated in Bairro de Alvalade, in Lisbon, Portugal. Alvalade is a neighbourhood located in the northern part of Lisbon, with a population of approximately 30,000 people and an area of 5.34 square kilometres. Lisbon is situated at a latitude of 38°43′ N and is positioned on hilly terrain along the northern bank of the Tagus estuary, approximately 30 km east of the Atlantic Ocean. The city experiences a Mediterranean climate characterized by dry summers and rainfall primarily during the colder months (Salvador et al., 2021). The methodology was applied in three identical buildings of João Lúcio St., which were built in 1958 (Fig. 3). The facades have red glazed brick, half meter-high cement mortar plinth and presents different states of conservation. The east–west orientation of the street promotes vegetation growth and supports various biological organisms, as indicated by the high soil moisture and indirect sunlight in the front gardens (Barberousse et al., 2006). Additionally, the front facades of two of the buildings analysed, case study #7 and case study #7, which face north, never receive direct sunlight (Fig. 4). The most significant anomaly of the facades, reported in previous studies and during the inspection, was stains (Fig. 5), namely lighter and darker areas. This results mainly from the moisture and relative humidity conditions common in this neighbourhood.

In this study, different scenarios are analysed considering only maintenance plans to correct stains, as shown in Table 1. Maintenance actions aimed at correcting stains are crucial for preserving the aesthetic appearance and structural integrity of buildings. Stains on building facades not only weaken the visual value of the asset but can indicate underlying problems such as moisture infiltration, mould growth, or surface deterioration. The selection of six maintenance plans offers a balanced framework for testing different strategies with enough variety to cover common approaches without overcomplicating the analysis. Each plan represents a unique combination of maintenance interventions, from minimal to intensive approaches, enabling a comparison of effectiveness and costs. This range captures both preventive and reactive approaches, which provides insights into how varying frequencies and types of interventions impact building longevity and maintenance budgets. More than six plans could dilute the focus, while fewer would not capture the range of strategies that stakeholders might consider.

4 Results and Discussion

4.1 *Image-Based Assessment of the Facades*

The mosaic of image built from the systematic acquisition was classified based on a supervised classification, using an approach previously proposed and presented (Valença et al., 2024). It is also important to mention that, at this stage, it can be

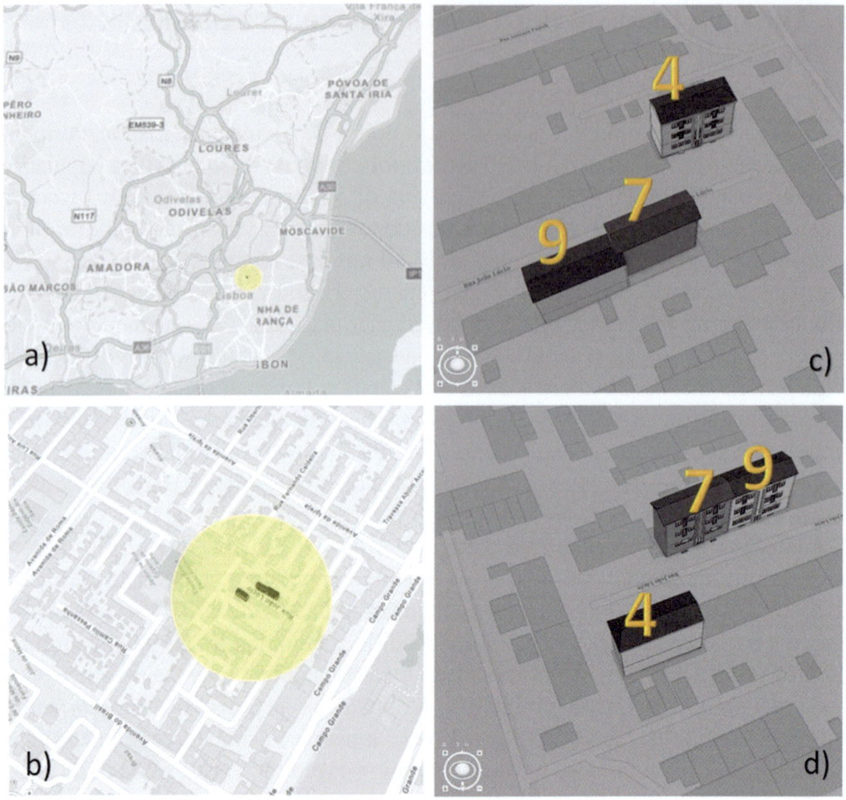

Fig. 3 Buildings used as case study, located in Lisbon, Portugal: **a** location in the city; **b** neighbourhood location; **c** street location, south view; **d** street location, north view

applied different algorithms and methods, since the output is the mapping of damages. The methodology developed can therefore always be up to date with the state of the art. Figure 5, 6, 7 and 8 shows the maps obtained from the supervised image-based classification using the algorithms mentioned in 2.1 Image-based assessment of facades'. The method used was previously validated by comparing with a traditional visual inspection and consequent mapping on CAD software, as in Torres-Gonzáles et al. (2023). The anomalies selected for mapping in the cladding area were -Dark stains- and 'Light stains'.

4.2 Maintenance Analysis

Figures 9, 10, 11, 12, 13 and 14 present the impact of the different maintenance plans on the degradation condition of the buildings and on the maintenance costs

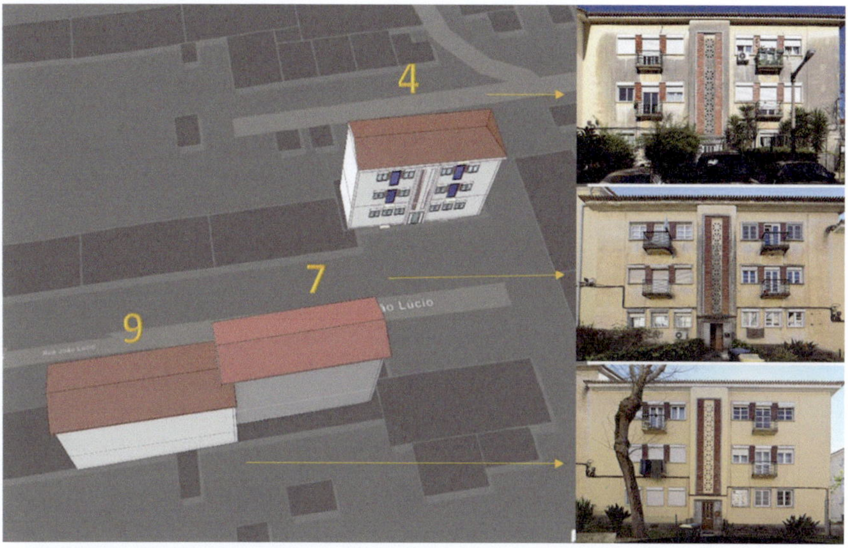

Fig. 4 Facades of the buildings used as case study

Fig. 5 Example of facades' stains

Table 1 Different scenarios tested to correct the presence of stains in the case study analysed

Plan 1	– Medium cleaning in condition B (applied at most 3 times before the next level of intervention) – Replacement in condition D or E
Plan 2	– Medium cleaning in condition C (applied at most 3 times before the next level of intervention) – Replacement in condition D or E
Plan 3	– Minimum cleaning in condition B (applied at most 2 times before the next level of intervention) – Maximum cleaning in condition C (applied at most 2 times before the next level of intervention) – Replacement in condition D or E
Plan 4	– Minimum cleaning in condition B (applied at most 2 times before the next level of intervention) – Painting in condition C (applied at most 2 times before the next level of intervention) – Replacement in condition D or E
Plan 5	– Painting in condition C (applied at most 2 times before the next level of intervention) – Replacement in condition D or E
Plan 6	– Painting in condition D or E

Fig. 6 Map of stains of the case study #4 (adapted from Valença et al., 2024)

over the buildings' life cycle. For each of the three case studies, two graphics with were plotted: (i) the variation of the degradation index (S_w) over time, in a 30-year projection; (ii) the variation of intervention costs (€/m^2) over time, also for a 30-year projection. In both cases, six maintenance plans were considered. The plans aim to simulate the most common situations in this type of cases. To understand these impacts comprehensively, it is essential to examine each maintenance plan in detail, which were as follows:

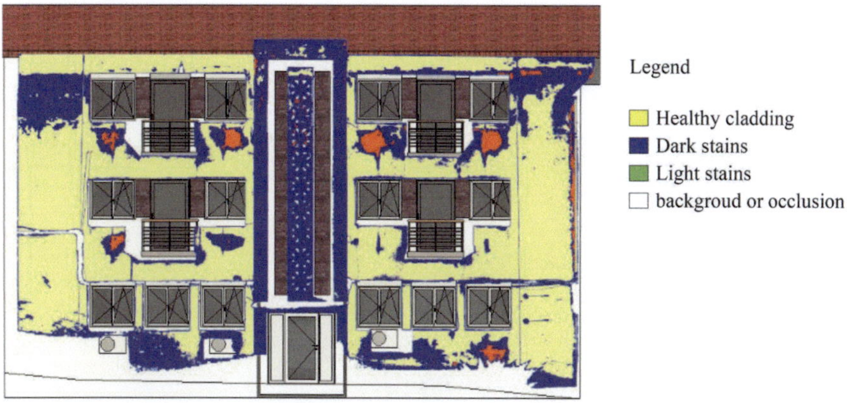

Fig. 7 Map of stains of the case study #7 (adapted from Valença et al., 2024)

Fig. 8 Map of stains of the case study #9 (adapted from Valença et al, 2024)

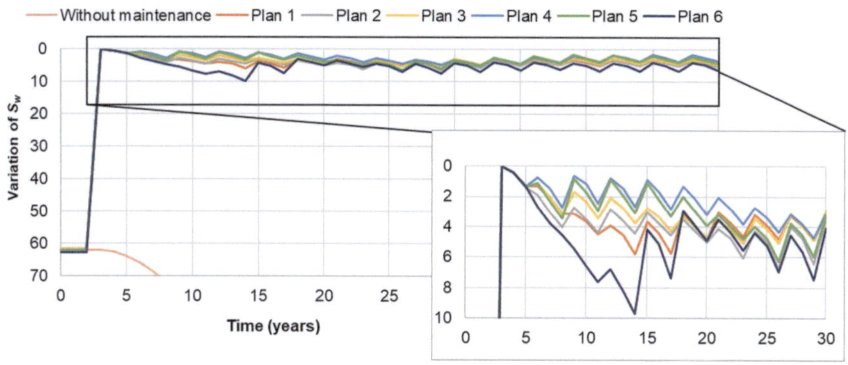

Fig. 9 Degradation Index (S_w) variation for the case study #4

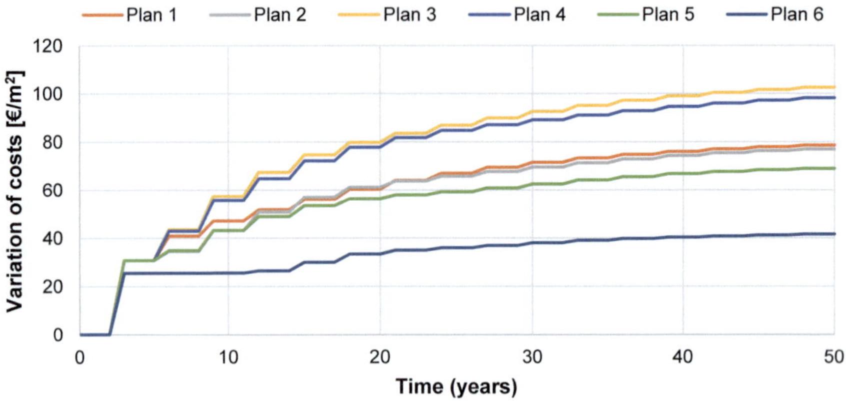

Fig. 10 Cost variation for the case study #4 [€/m^2]

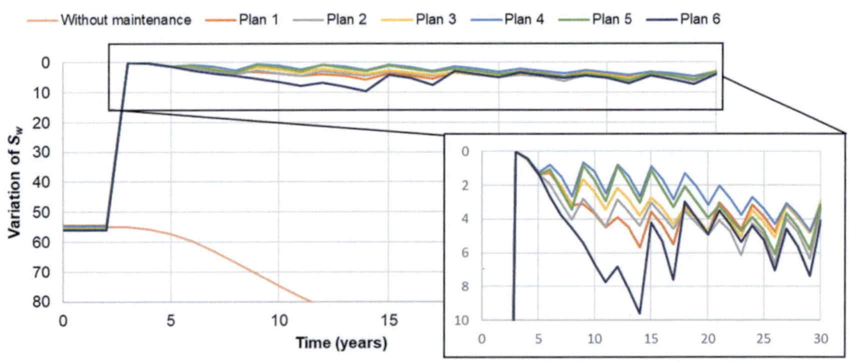

Fig. 11 Degradation Index (S_w) variation for the case study #7

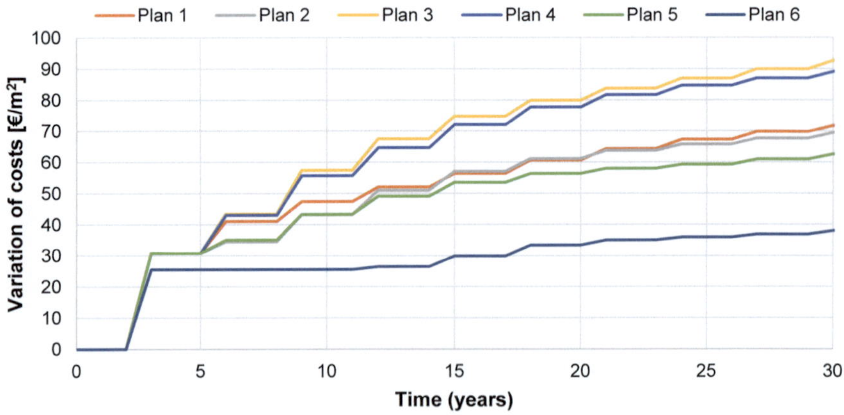

Fig. 12 Cost variation for the case study #7 [€/m^2]

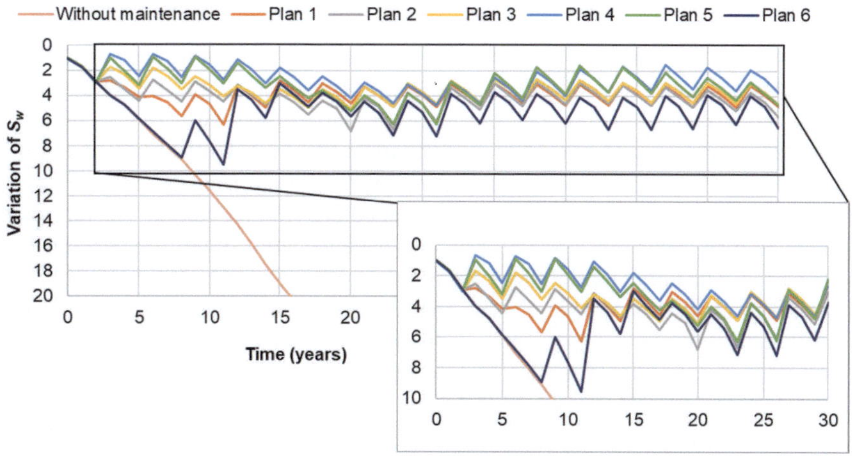

Fig. 13 Degradation Index (S_w) variation for the case study #9

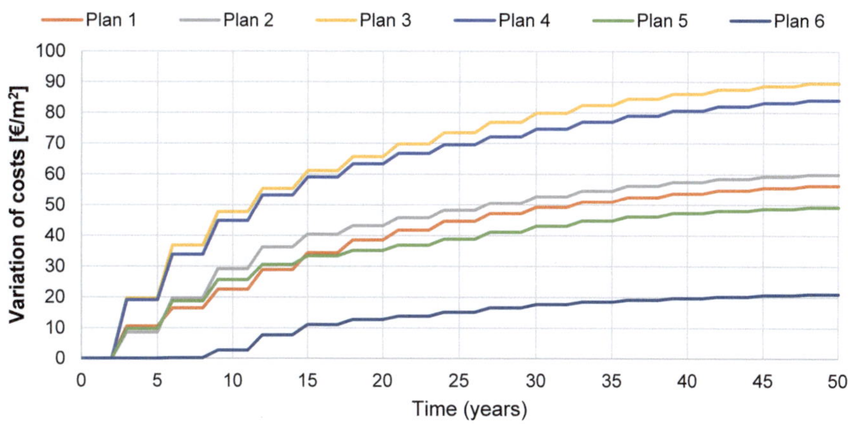

Fig. 14 Cost variation for the case study #9 [€/m^2]

- Plan 1 offers a balanced approach by applying medium-level cleaning at an early stage (condition B) before degradation worsens. By allowing for three cleaning interventions, it delays the need for replacement. This approach ensures that the building maintains a good condition without frequent replacements, leading to moderate maintenance costs over the building's life cycle;
- Plan 2 is like Plan 2, but the medium cleaning is initiated at a later stage (condition C). In this sense, a worse degradation condition is achieved before proceeding to the intervention, possibly leading to higher cumulative maintenance costs due to increased severity of repairs needed by the time cleaning is conducted. However, it still intends to delay the costly replacement stage;

- Plan 3 includes a more intensive cleaning policy, beginning with minimum cleaning early (condition B) and escalating to maximum cleaning at a more severe degradation stage (condition C). This comprehensive maintenance strategy can effectively control degradation but involves higher initial costs due to frequent and intensive cleaning interventions. The trade-off is a potential reduction in the frequency of full replacements, balancing out the life cycle costs;
- Plan 4 encompasses painting as an intermediate step (condition C), this plan intends to increase the protection of the cladding after initial degradation has occurred. The initial minimum cleaning helps to manage early degradation, while painting adds an extra layer of protection before reaching the replacement stage. Although this plan can be costlier due to the painting process, it effectively prolongs the cladding's service life, potentially reducing overall life cycle costs compared to more frequent replacements;
- Plan 5 bounces the early cleaning stages and directly involves painting once moderate degradation is detected (condition C). Painting acts as a significant intervention to halt further degradation and preserve the cladding. This approach might result in higher costs compared to plans with earlier cleaning, but it still intends to prevent the severe degradation that requires immediate replacement;
- Plan 6 is the most affordable plan in terms of initial budget, this strategy involves waiting until severe degradation is reached (condition D or E) before intervening with painting. While it minimises short-term costs, it carries a high risk of accelerated degradation and potential failure of the building cladding due to delayed maintenance. The long-term costs could be significantly higher if premature replacement becomes necessary due to insufficient maintenance.

The analysis from Figures 9, 10, 11, 12, 13 and 14 highlights the importance of proper maintenance for building cladding to prevent rapid deterioration and costly premature replacements. The key points are:

Maintenance versus Replacement Costs

- Routine maintenance, though requiring upfront investment, reduces long-term costs by preserving the cladding's integrity and functionality of the building's cladding over an extended period.
- Premature replacement due to neglect is significantly more expensive that routine maintenance interventions.

Maintenance plans analysis

- Plans 3 and 4 provide comprehensive and intensive maintenance strategies, addressing both moderate and severe degradation conditions effectively. These plans, while potentially more expensive, offer the best protection against an accelerate degradation and can lower long-term costs by extending the cladding's service life.
- Plans 1, 2 and 5 provide balanced approaches with varying levels of intervention, offering cost-effective options for different maintenance needs.

- Plans 1 and 2 offer relatively balanced maintenance approaches, with Plan 1 being slightly more proactive. These plans aim to maintain the building in good condition with moderate maintenance costs over the life cycle.
- Plan 5 strikes a balance between intervention frequency and cost, targeting moderate degradation with painting.
- Plan 6 is the cheapest upfront but carries the highest risk of accelerated degradation if critical maintenance needs are neglected.

Choosing the Best Plan

The choice of the best maintenance plan depends on various factors, including the specific condition of the building facade, available budget, and long-term maintenance goals.

- For buildings that require rigorous protection and have higher budgets, Plans 3 and 4 are more suitable.
- For those seeking a balance between cost and maintenance frequency, Plans 1, 2, and 5 offer viable options. Plan 6 should be considered only when short-term budget constraints are significant, and the risks of accelerated degradation are acceptable.

By carefully evaluating these factors, stakeholders can select a maintenance plan that optimally balances upfront costs, long-term savings, and the building's structural integrity over its life cycle.

4.3 Built Digital Model

The results from the previously two stages are merged into a digital model. In this case, a BIM model of the building was built and then, the maps of stains from the image-based assessment were added to the model. Further, the information of the degradation index and maintenance costs can also be analysed in a final Digitalizing Building Maintenance. Figure 15 presents an example of the actual ongoing layout, with all data compiled for one building, in one time-instant and considering several maintenance plans. The scenario planning provides a detailed understanding of potential future states, enabling better decision-making regarding repairs, upgrades, and investments.

The model can help in long-term strategic planning by identifying future maintenance needs and integrating them into the broader organizational objectives. A well-defined plan allows for flexibility and adaptability in response to unexpected changes or challenges in the building's environment or usage patterns. BIM-Powered Asset Management Solutions enable efficient control of metrics and performance evaluation.

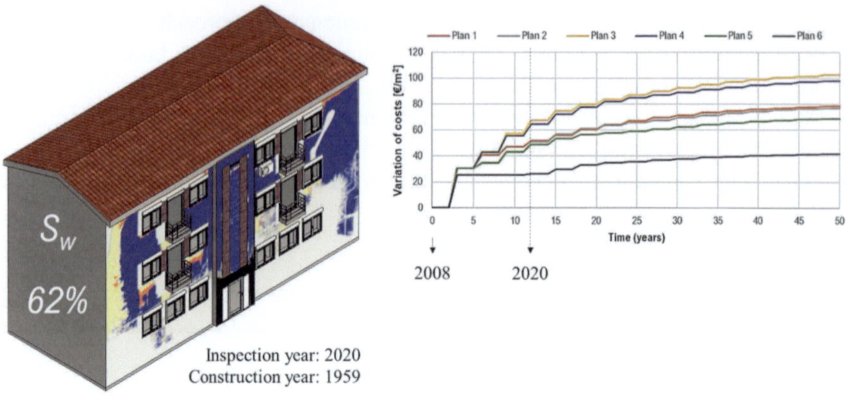

Fig. 15 Example of BIM-powered asset management solution for case study #4

5 Conclusions

The concept of BIM-Powered Asset Management Solution is showcased with real buildings, evaluating the impact of different maintenance strategies in the performance of the case study under analysis. The case study serves as a tangible example of how the methodology can contribute to enhancing asset management practices. The automatic mapping of facades is performed by image-based methods, followed by the calculation of the degradation index, based on the maps obtained. All outputs can be analysed and visualized in BIM environment, enabling a comprehensive analysis of the actual state of conservation on the building as well as its evolution during service life. By analysing and visualizing the data within the BIM framework, decision-makers can gain valuable insights into the condition of the building and formulate informed maintenance strategies to ensure its longevity and sustainability. For facility managers, the BIM-powered approach enables real-time tracking and forecasting of maintenance needs, allowing facility managers to plan resources and budgets more efficiently. This proactive model reduces the likelihood of unexpected repairs and ensures consistent monitoring. For architects, this methodology provides a digital representation of the building's evolving condition, informing future design adjustments and providing data for more resilient building materials and structural elements. Engineers benefit from precise, data-driven insights into the building's state, which supports accurate maintenance schedules and strengthens decision-making for repairs or replacements. The model's integration of condition and cost data helps engineers prioritize interventions, optimize lifecycle management, and improve the reliability of maintenance outcomes.

In summary, BIM-Powered Asset Management Solutions leverage BIM's capabilities to enhance management and maintenance-built assets throughout their lifecycle, improving and facilitating collaboration among project stakeholders, including architects, engineers, contractors, and facility managers. Defining possible scenarios for a building maintenance plan is a strategic approach that enhances efficiency and enables proactive management. The methodology proposed can works with other anomalies besides stains, such as cracking and detachment, which are also used to compute the global degradation index.

As mentioned below, implementing a BIM-Powered Asset Management Solution can bring numerous benefits, but it also comes with several potential challenges. Some of these are related to the resistance to change, since many professionals accustomed to traditional methods may find the new methodologies and technologies complex and resist adopting it. In this case, effective change management and training are crucial to overcome this. On other hand, the high initial investment in software, hardware, and training can be significant, and the organizations often need to explore options and funding strategies to manage these costs. In the future, a clear standardization is also important, since without standardized processes, the implementation of this kind of approach can be inconsistent and without guaranteeing uniformity. This also helps to solve possible interoperability issues related to the fact of different stakeholders using various software, that can lead to data loss or misinterpretation. Ensuring technology and software compatibility and open standards can mitigate this.

Addressing these challenges requires a strategic approach, including robust training, clear communication, and the adoption of standardized processes. By doing so, organizations can fully leverage the potential of the methodology proposed for asset management. To help mitigate some of the challenges mentioned, particularly in terms of communication between all stakeholders, and resistance to change, an Application Programming Interface based on Augmented Reality, is under development to assist inspections during onsite work and the evaluation of maintenance plans and strategies.

Acknowledgements The authors acknowledge the Portuguese Foundation for Science and Technology (FCT) the funding of the project CITIESTWINS: A digital framework to merge durability data, maintenance models and energy retrofitting decisions (2022.15504.MIT) and research unit CERIS (UIDB/04625/2020). J. Valença and A. Silva acknowledge the support of FCT through the individual projects CEECIND/04463/2017 and CEECIND/01337/2017, respectively.

References

Barberousse, H., Lombardo, R. J., Tell, G., Couté, A. (2006). Factors involved in the colonisation of building façades by algae and cyanobacteria in France. *Biofouling, 22*, 69–77, Taylor & Francis

Chen, K., Reichard, G., Xu, X., & Akanmu, A. (2021). Automated crack segmentation in close-range building façade inspection images using deep learning techniques. *Journal of Building Engineering, 43*(2021), Article 102913. https://doi.org/10.1016/j.jobe.2021.102913

Kulinan, A., Park, M., Aung, P., Cha, G., & Park, S. (2024). Advancing construction site workforce safety monitoring through BIM and computer vision integration. *Automation in Construction, 158*, Article 105227. https://doi.org/10.1016/j.autcon.2023.105227

Landgrebe, D., & Biehl, L. (2005). MULTISPEC-A freeware multispectral image data analysis system. https://engineering.purdue.edu/%7Ebiehl/MultiSpec/

Lee, S., Kalos, N., & Shin, D.-H. (2014). Non-destructive testing methods in the US for bridge inspection and maintenance. *KSCE Journal of Civil Engineering, 18*(5), 1322–1331. https://doi.org/10.1007/s12205-014-0633-9

Pantoja-Rosero, B., Achanta, R., & Beyer, K. (2023). Damage-augmented digital twins towards the automated inspection of buildings. *Automation in Construction, 150*, Article 104842. https://doi.org/10.1016/j.autcon.2023.104842

Pourebrahimi, M., Eghbali, S., & Roders, A. (2020). Identifying building obsolescence: Towards increasing buildings' service life. *International Journal of Building Pathology and Adaptation, 38*(5), 635–652. https://doi.org/10.1108/IJBPA-08-2019-0068

Salvador, C., Nieto, R., Linares, C., Díaz, J., Alves, C. A., & Gimeno, L. (2021). Drought effects on specific-cause mortality in Lisbon from 1983 to 2016: Risks assessment by gender and age groups. *Science of the Total Environment, 751*, 142332. https://doi.org/10.1016/j.scitotenv.2020.142332

Santos, B. O., Valença, J., & Júlio, E. (2019). Automatic mapping of cracking patterns on concrete surfaces with biological stains using hyper-spectral images processing. *Structural Control Health Monitoring, 26*, 1–15. https://doi.org/10.1002/stc.2320

Silva, A., Brito, J., & Gaspar, P. (2016). Methodologies for service life prediction of buildings: With a focus on façade claddings. Springer International Publishing.

Silva, A., Brito, J., Thomsen, A., Straub, A., Prieto, A. J., & Lacasse, M. A. (2022). Causal effects between criteria that establish the end of service life of buildings and components. *Buildings, 12*, 88. https://doi.org/10.3390/buildings12020088

Tan, Y., Xu, W., Chen, P., & Zhang, S. (2024). Building defect inspection and data management using computer vision, augmented reality, and BIM technology. *Automation in Construction, 160*, Article 105318. https://doi.org/10.1016/j.autcon.2024.105318

Tuhaise, V., Tah, J., & Abanda, F. (2023). Technologies for digital twin applications in construction. *Automation in Construction, 152*, Article 104931. https://doi.org/10.1016/j.autcon.2023.104931

Torres-González, M., Valença, J., Santos, B. O., Mendes, M. P., & Silva, A. (2023). StainView: A fast and reliable method for mapping stains in facades using image classification in HSV and CIELab colour space. *Remote Sensing, 15* (11), 2895. Special Issue: Remote Sensing-Based Structural Health Monitoring and Damage Assessment. https://doi.org/10.3390/rs15112895

Valença, J., Gonçalves, L. M. S., & Júlio, E. (2013). Damage assessment on concrete surfaces using multi-spectral image analysis. *Construction and Building Materials, 40*, 971–981. https://doi.org/10.1016/j.conbuildmat.2012.11.061

Valença, J., Morin, K., Jouen, N., Olivo, N., Torres-González, M., Mendes, M.-P., & Silva, A. (2024). Feeling-BIM: A digital model to support maintenance decisions, based on automatic inspection and dwellers' feelings. *Journal of Building Engineering, 87*, Article 108937. https://doi.org/10.1016/j.jobe.2024.108937

Watt, D. S. (1999). *Building pathology—principles and practice* (1st ed.). Blackwell Science Ltd.

Yiğit, A. Y., & Uysal, M. (2025). Virtual reality visualisation of automatic crack detection for bridge inspection from 3D digital twin generated by UAV photogrammetry. *Measurement, 242*, Article 115931. https://doi.org/10.1016/j.measurement.2024.115931

Yilmaz, G., Akcamete, A., & Demirors, O. (2023). BIM-CAREM: Assessing the BIM capabilities of design, construction and facilities management processes in the construction industry. *Computers in Industry, 147*, 103861. https://doi.org/10.1016/j.compind.2023.103861Zhang

Zhang, C., Wang, F., Zou, Y., Dimyadi, J., Guo, B. H. W., & Hou, L. (2023). Automated UAV image-to-BIM registration for building façade inspection using improved generalised Hough transform. *Automation in Construction, 153*, 104957. https://doi.org/10.1016/j.autcon.2023.104957

Assessment of the Technical and Functional Performance of Public Buildings

Frederico Hooper, Francielle Santos, Filipa Salvado, and Nuno Almeida

Abstract Integrated in the construction management activity, the concept of performance has been applied to address the suitability for use of attributes of a building, where each specific characteristic must be assessed in terms of satisfying or not the intended performance. Related to technical and functional performance, emphasis should be placed on the international standard ISO 19,208, which establishes regulatory requirements at the level of the methodological framework, and on the international standards ISO 15,928 and ISO 11,863, which establish regulatory requirements at the building's level. Regarding the end users technical and functional requirements, the European standard EN 15,643 has relevant contributions and should be considered. Based on this normative framework, the present research work defines a methodology for assessing the technical and functional performance of buildings. Its performance specifications are framed, to satisfy end-users' requirements and society's expectations. Buildings behaviour in the use phase (e.g., health, safety, convenience, comfort, property protection, contributions to sustainable development) and changes in its performance throughout its life cycle are considered. To apply the developed methodology, a case study composed of a set of existing public buildings in existing in Portugal is used. Thus, demonstrated that the assessment of the technical and functional performance of these buildings (based on the identification of anomalies at various levels), helps in the decision-making process of interventions to be carried out throughout their useful life's. This methodology also contributes to long-term economic sustainability, as it optimizes the costs of using buildings, as well as future investments in rehabilitation interventions.

Keywords Technical performance · Functional performance · Life cycle · Public buildings · ISO (2016)

F. Hooper · N. Almeida
Civil Engineering, Architecture and Georresources, University of Lisbon, Lisbon, Portugal

F. Santos (✉)
Civil Construction Coordination, Federal Institute of Goiás, Jataí, Goiás, Brazil
e-mail: francielle.santos@ifg.edu.br

F. Salvado
Buildings Department, National Civil Engineering Laboratory -LNEC, Lisbon, Portugal

A. Crespo Márquez et al. (eds.), *Case Studies in Digital Transformation*, Engineering Asset Management Review 4, https://doi.org/10.1007/978-3-032-05592-7_10

1 Introduction

Public infrastructure plays a crucial role in society, encompassing sectors such as transportation, health, and education. These assets have a significant impact on social, environmental, and economic aspects such as employment, quality of life, resource consumption, capital investment, and life cycle costs (Salvado, 2019). In addition, public buildings such as schools are an important asset for the development of human well-being (Norazman et al., 2021). Faced with limited resources and emerging ecological challenges, it is imperative to adopt the principles of asset management to monitor the performance and improve the sustainability of public infrastructure (Trindade et al., 2018).

Asset management provides a framework for managing the challenges of aging infrastructure that continues to support communities for long periods of time, and responding to growing end-user demands for reliable and efficient services while minimizing costs and risks (The Institute of Asset Management, 2015). The principles of asset management encompass proactive planning, data-driven decision-making, risk assessment, and performance monitoring. By adopting these principles, organizations can make informed decisions about investments, maintenance strategies, and the use of available resources, ensuring that public infrastructure is resilient, efficient, and capable of meeting the evolving needs of communities (Salvado, 2019).

Despite the growing adoption of information technologies applied to build assets, such as Building Information Modeling (BIM) and its collaborative processes, challenges remain in defining the essential data for the operation and maintenance phase and determining how this data will be reused after the transition to that stage (Brunet et al., 2019). Moreover, although digital transformation reveals significant potential gains for asset owners, there is still a lack of full understanding of these benefits and of the steps required to optimize existing processes and systems (Gurevich et al., 2017).

The availability of comprehensive asset information serves a core role in driving informed decision-making at all stages of the life cycle (Hooper, 2023). This information needs to be collected and analyzed to monitor the state of the assets. However, without effective standardization in management and the associated decisions, managers can stray from the organizational goals, adopting specific management practices for each sector and circumstance. Furthermore, reaching a consensus among these managers, especially on budget-related issues, can be a significant challenge (Crespo et al., 2020).

During the planning stage, this information has a key function in identifying the current state of the infrastructure, assessing its capacity, and determining future needs. It enables proactive planning and effective allocation of resources. During operation and maintenance, the availability of asset information permits organizations to monitor the condition and performance of the infrastructure, implement planned maintenance programmes, schedule inspections, and fix potential problems before they become more serious. Additionally, asset information is of paramount importance for decisions regarding renewal or replacement, which can be based, for example, on the analysis of historical performance data or consideration of the remaining service life of assets.

The digital transformation in the construction and operation of facilities requires the efficient management of information generated throughout the life cycle. Integrating design, construction, operation, and maintenance data into management systems based on consensual naming conventions is necessary to optimize asset managers' work. Implementing technologies such as BIM facilitates this integration, acting as a repository for efficient building management (Brunet et al., 2019).

In that context, building performance assessment appears typically as an input to asset management processes, providing critical data and insights that inform asset management decisions (Hooper, 2023). By evaluating technical-functional factors such as energy efficiency, occupant comfort, and maintenance needs, along with economic factors like Life Cycle Costs (LCC), organizations can forecast, identify improvement areas, and implement strategies to enhance building performance, ensuring sustained value and optimal operation throughout the assets' life cycle. Additionally, public building performance assessments help in meeting regulatory requirements, supporting sustainability goals, and demonstrating a commitment to responsible resource management.

While a building may appear to be in a satisfactory condition without any visible degradation, it may still not meet the performance expectations of its owners, users and facility managers. Owners focus on cost- effectiveness to make investment decisions (Love et al., 2013). Users commonly prioritize a comfortable and safe environment, that contains well-functioning equipment and cleanliness (Ali, 2009), while facility managers focus on ensuring that the built environment functions properly (Cotts et al., 2009). Therefore, assessing a building's performance is crucial not only to determine if it meets requirements, but also to identify if it requires intervention (Talon et al., 2005). Without such an assessment, maintenance efforts may lead to high costs due to unnecessary or urgent repairs (de Brito et al., 2016).

The standard ISO (2016) focuses on establishing a framework for specifying performance in buildings, dealing specifically with in-use behavior, related to the technical-functional fields, for example, concerned with safety, health, comfort, convenience, and property protection. That said, this standard categorizes performance into four types: (1) Reaction to agents; (2) Influence on human activities; (3) Impact on society; (4) Change in performance over time.

Each performance category—stability, fire safety, visual or acoustical—has specified objectives, which may to be determined by the intended use or the way they are related to other parts or the building as a whole. The performance descriptions establish qualitative requirements for an attribute, while performance parameters establish quantitative ones (Table 1). At least, the evaluation of the solution is related to the interpretation of performance data, (ISO 2016).

Those standard lists sixteen categories of requirements commonly required and expected by users and society: Stability; Fire safety; Safety in use; Tightness; Hydrothermal; Air purity; Acoustical; Visual; Tactile; Dynamic; Hygiene; Suitability of spaces for specific users; Durability; Accessibility; and Contributions to sustainable development (ISO, 2016).

Table 1 Description and parameters should be for different types of performance (ISO, 2016)

Types of building performance	Performance description	Performance parameters
Reaction to agents	"In terms of behaviour as the result of external agent or the consequence of such behaviour to fulfil objectives."	"Can be framed around the quantum of the agent."
Influence on human activities	"In terms of the effects on human existence or activities and their consequences."	"Can be framed around the height difference level that is likely to trigger tripping for 95% of average users."
Impact on society	"In terms of the effects on society and their results which may relate to one or more stages of the cycle of a building."	"Can be framed around the level of simulated emission of CO2 per year."
Changes in performance over time	"Typically relate to the durability, fatigue and creep of materials, should be described in terms of the cause of change and the consequences of the change, as well as design life and maintenance schedules, as relevant."	"Can be framed around the expected level of performance after 30 years in use, or years for the performance expected to deteriorate to 70% level immediately after construction."

In fact, the performance of the building can vary from its parts, as well as being impacted by them. Also, as highlighted by ISO (2016), "a part of a building may have multi-faceted objectives, derived from the multi- faceted performance of the building as a whole". Thus, for instance, a wall might be required to satisfy different performance requirements, such as visual, thermal, acoustical, tightness and structural.

Technical-functional performance assessment systematically relates buildings and facilities to users and their needs. It must be noted that there are differences between quantitative and qualitative aspects of building performance, especially concerning their respective performance measures.

Many aspects of building performance are indeed quantifiable, such as lighting, acoustics, temperature and humidity, durability of materials, quantity, and so on. On the other hand, qualitative aspects of building performance concern the perception of the environment of space, involving sensory modes such as touch, hearing, smell, and visual. Both of those aspects are relevant and related to each other for the assessment (Hooper, 2023; Vischer, 2008).

However, one can easily imagine the disruption that would be caused among students, teachers, and parents should the school's infrastructure prove inadequate to withstand a potential earthquake, with exposed electrical wiring, broken windows, unsanitary toilets, decay resulting from insufficient maintenance, or vulnerability to extreme weather events—flooding and wind damage from heavy rains. This makes both teaching and learning difficult.

One way to conduct building performance evaluation is through facility management systems with integrated sensors that monitor energy use, occupancy, lighting, and thermal and climatic conditions. These systems generate databases of actual performance, the analysis of which allows predicted performance to be compared with actual performance. This connectivity facilitates data collection and exchange, promoting efficient analysis and significantly improving asset performance management and operations optimization (Crespo et al., 2020; Gurevich et al., 2017).

These technological support tools play a fundamental role in the asset management process, which needs to be carefully designed and controlled to guarantee significant improvements in outcomes. Furthermore, effective use of the data generated by these tools is crucial to improving decision-making in asset management, boosting its efficiency and effectiveness (Crespo et al., 2020).

Given the complex challenges associated with the organization, production and accessibility of information, this research defines a methodology for assessing the technical and functional performance of buildings (Hooper, 2023; Salvado, 2019). Particularly in the context of our case study, public secondary school buildings in Lisbon, improving the management of these assets can also generate benefits in learning environments, responding to the specific needs of children and teachers, which positively affects child development (Barrett et al., 2019). Therefore, the main objective of this article is to develop a representative methodology to assess the technical-functional performance of a public building portfolio over its life cycle. To achieve this objective, the study relies on several relevant international standards, scientific literature sources and industry guidelines that focus on the analysis of building performance.

2 Methodology

Collecting data on building performance, to be useful to the asset management domain, should enable managers to act on, what can occur at various levels, from portfolio management to building and facilities management. For the management of a specific building and its facilities, there are a range of possible performance indicators that can be used in managing the business and aligning the use of the building. On the other hand, at the portfolio management level, decisions about new actions or investigations are driven by a limited number of key performance indicators that represent the "vital signs" of the "health" of the operational facilities of a cluster of buildings (Vischer, 2008).

EN (2023) outlines a comprehensive framework for evaluating physical assets in the construction industry during their usage phase, from commissioning until they are no longer in service. This overarching standard directs users to more specific methods detailed in ISO (2015) and ISO (2016). In essence, the assessment process is a methodical approach to establishing asset management objectives and requirements, collecting relevant asset information, and making determinations about the present state and performance of individual assets, groups of assets, and the asset portfolio as a whole. The resulting information is then utilized to make informed decisions and confirm that asset management objectives are being met.

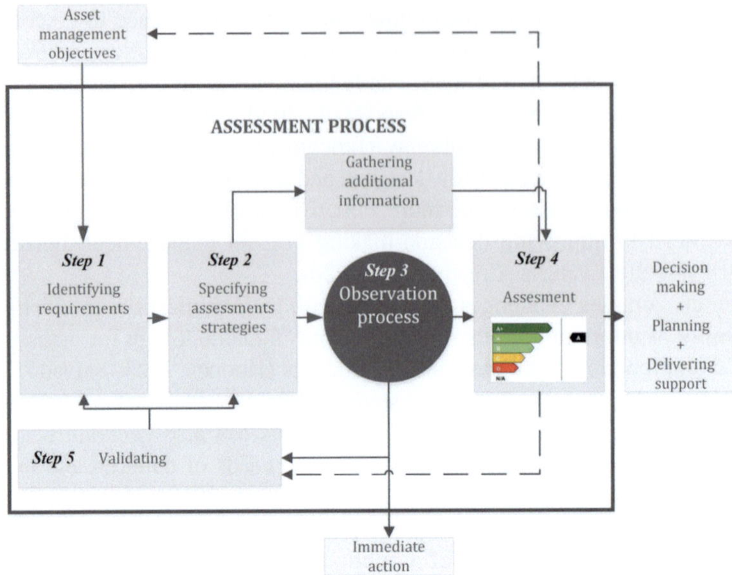

Fig. 1 Assessment process. Adapted from EN (2023)

The assessment process, which adheres to the "Plan-Do-Check-Act" methodology, includes the following steps (see Fig. 1).

2.1 *Step 1: Identifying Requirements*

The initial stage of the assessment process involves identifying the necessary requirements that establish the minimum acceptable level of performance for individual assets, groups of assets, or the asset portfolio as a whole (Hooper, 2023). In the current study, the assessment of the technical-functional performance of the public buildings portfolio is carried out through two distinct approaches, by remaining service life of the systems and by performance indicators of the building as a whole.

2.2 *Step 2: Specifying the Assessment Strategy*

Defined the requirements, the asset or facility manager should specify the assessment strategy, which describes why, how, when and what to observe, as shown in Table 2.

Table 2 Aspects of the assessment strategy (EN, 2023)

Level of assessment	Asset portfolio	Asset system	Asset
Purpose	Future demands	Current status	Validation
	– Future status – Strategic requirements – Modification	– Planning – Maintenance – Improvement – Replacement	– Requirements – Assessment strategies – Asset management objectives
Scope	All assets	Critical assets	Samples
Planning	Scheduled	On request	Continuously
	– Periodic (frequency) – Targeted	– Acute – Not–acute	
Observation category	Global observation	Main observation	Detailed observation
Observation technique	Human sensory perception	Measurements	Continuous monitoring
	– (Visual, touch, hearing and smell) – Focused – Non-focused	– On/Off Site – Destructive or Non-Destructive	– Local – Remote

2.3 Step 3: Observation Process

In the assessment process, the observation of assets and asset groups is a vital step that informs the evaluation of their performance. The collection of performance data can be carried out for the performance categories (fire safety, hygiene, acoustical, accessibility, etc.), the systems (HVAC, roofing, lighting, windows, etc.), or the spaces (corridors, classes, parking, play areas). That process can be done through several methods: a questionnaire survey (including a user satisfaction survey), objective measurements, the walkthrough evaluation, and the analysis of the building design. In order to perform the assessment, sometimes is relevant to gather additional information about the asset itself, for instance: previous assessment results/interventions; age; modification data; BIM (Building Information Modelling); Maintenance costs; and future plans.

2.4 Step 4: Assessment

After collecting the observational data and additional information, the assessment can be performed at different levels, including asset portfolio, aggregated assets or individual assets. In this study, data on assets is reported using a rating tool that complies with applicable standards, legislation or expert/provider guidance. The asset portfolio-level assessment, which is the focus of this study, is intended to support

Table 3 Calibration of rating performance scale (ISO, 2011a)

Rating	General calibration rule
9	Exceptionally demanding or non-applicable
[7,9]	Clearly above average, but not the exceptionally demanding
[5,7]	Typical mid-range or normal
[3,5]	Clearly below average, but acceptable under justified circumstances
[1,3]	Exceptionally below average, but acceptable under exceptional and justified circumstances
0	Unacceptable, not required or non-applicable

Table 4 Correspondence of the numerical scale to the letter scale (class) (Hooper, 2023)

Class	F	E	D	C	B	A	A +	A + +
Rating	[1,2]	[2,3]	[3,4]	[4,5]	[5,6]	[6,7]	[7,8]	[8,9]

various decisions, such as expansion, reduction, innovation, or other approaches that align with asset management objectives.

For this study, the evaluation of performance is carried out through a rating scale, which enables (i) communicating in plain language that the "demand" side can understand without the need for technical judgments; (ii) evaluating the conformity of the "supply-side" during the building design; and (iii) determining the level of effort and resources required to control deviations during the design, construction, and use phases.

ISO (2011a) states that there is no mandatory counting of levels or statements on a pair of scales, but it suggests that there are 5 evaluation levels plus 0. The recommended numbering of statements is expressed as one-digit integers on a scale of 1, 3, 5, 7 and 9 where 1 corresponds to the worst performance of the respective indicator and 9 to the best (Table 3). Following that approach, this study uses the rating system developed by Almeida (2011) to evaluate the structural safety and serviceability of new buildings.

Although the evaluation criteria for the parameters are numerical, it was decided to adopt a final classification with eight categories, transformed into letter classes from F to A + + (Table 4), similarity what is used in "Report Card for American Infrastructure". This classification system, like the one used in the energy efficiency certificate, ensures that the reading is easy, and accessible, which allows the differentiation of the level of performance to become more user-friendly.

2.5 Validation

At the end of the assessment, the assessor reviews the entire process to ensure that the steps have been carried out in accordance with the requirements of the standard and that the results obtained are reliable, and whether further observations are necessary. The objective of the validation step is to confirm the assessed requirements and the valuation strategy so that it can be adjusted according to the asset portfolio and systems. This enables the organization to act proactively and not only reactively in the future (EN, 2023).

3 Results and Discussion

Although the developed model guarantees a generic application in several types of public buildings, the case study chosen is Portuguese school buildings used for secondary education. Such selection is based on several factors. First, there is an extensive and updated database that includes the life cycle costs of 166 of these buildings, as analysed in previous research conducted by Salvado (2019). That sample of school buildings constitutes a significant part of the public-built heritage in Portugal, which directly affects the daily lives of a substantial segment of the population (Hooper, 2023; Salvado, 2019; Parque Escolar, 2011). Furthermore, the Parque Escolar Modernization Program, implemented between 2007 and 2011, with the aim of enhancing and maintaining the public secondary school network in Portugal, has generated a wealth of information and studies specifically related to this type of building through Parque Escolar's initiatives.

3.1 Description of the Case Study

The Parque Escolar Modernization Program, implemented from 2007 to 2011, aimed to revitalize 174 school buildings, covering a total area of 1.2 million m^2 through rehabilitation and 1.3 million m^2 through new construction. The program had an investment of around 2 billion euros. In Fig. 2 is possible to see the comparison between before and after the Parque Escolar Modernization Program for two schools (Hooper, 2023; Salvado, 2019).

The existing Portuguese school portfolio for public secondary education consists of a collective total of 477 school buildings, the construction of which began in the late nineteenth century. Of these, 23% were completed by the 1960s. The remaining 77% were built during the period of expansion of the school network and the implementation of the extension of compulsory schooling to six and nine years, with around 46% of these schools being built in the 1980s.

The methodology for monitoring the economic and technical-functional performance of public buildings focuses specifically on a sub-category: Portuguese secondary school buildings. Within this sample of school buildings, 10 schools were carefully selected to compose the analysis portfolio, with the aim of providing a comprehensive representation of the overall performance of the entire sample. The selection of these 10 schools is of great importance as it allows for the inclusion

Fig. 2 Before and after the Parque Escolar Modernization Program for two schools in Lisbon, Portugal

of a diverse range of characteristics and conditions found in different school environments. Factors such as age, size, geographical location, building systems and facilities are taken into account.

The disclosure of the schools (name and municipality) is confidential, and they are therefore numbered from 1 to 10 and their data are presented with exclusive reference to the identification number, being designated as S1, S2, … S10. However, it may be indicated that the schools are located between the northern, central and west regions, including the districts of Coimbra, Espinho, Figueira da Foz, Lisbon, Leiria, Alcobaça, Guimarães and Guarda. Table 5 presents a concise overview of the pre- and post-rehabilitation information for each school building.

3.2 *Assessment of Technical-Functional Performance*

Step 1: Identtifying requirements

Firstly, the type of building performance based on "changes in performance over time" can be measured through the remaining service lifetime of the building subsystems. As highlighted by Silva et al. (2022), since building service life refers to the period in which it effectively fulfils its purpose and meets various performance standard requirements, its technical and functional performance is closely linked to the state of the physical systems. Accordingly, the physical deterioration over time of the building subsystems compromises its ability to accommodate the functions and activities needed by its users (Hooper, 2023; Salvado, 2019). This approach provides an understanding of the general condition and potential maintenance needs of the buildings, helping in the planning of future rehabilitation interventions.

Table 5 Pre- and post-rehabilitation information for each school building

School	Location	Before rehabilitation (1944–2008)				After rehabilitation (2008–2023)				
		Construction (Year)	Plot Area [m^2]	Built Area [m^2]	Capacity (Students)	Rehabilitation (Year)	Demolition area [m^2]	Rehabilitation Area [m^2]	Built Area [m^2]	Capacity (Students)
S1	North	1975 (3ºP)	21.357	7.570	726	2009–2011	2.113	5.457	9.034	1.390
S2	North	1959 (2ºP)	18.882	8.962	769	2009–2011	4.655	4.307	13.009	1.485
S3	Lisboa	1983 (3ºP)	29.266	9.050	687	2009–2011	858	10.042	6.548	1.260
S4	Center	1964 (2ºP)	26.330	9.831	636	2009–2011	1.907	7.924	7.141	975
S5	Center	1945 (2ºP)	27.647	7.420	451	2009–2011	775	6.645	9.392	975
S6	Center	1966 (2ºP)	23.640	13.688	900	2009–2010	1.145	12.543	2.351	1.015
S7	Lisboa	1956 (2ºP)	46.884	8.630	457	2009–2011	887	7.743	5.490	555
S8	Center	1963 (2ºP)	20.327	8.966	800	2009–2010	1.155	7.811	7.036	1.155
S9	Lisboa	1964 (2ºP)	17.250	12.065	670	2009–2010	1.190	10.875	21.811	1.300
S10	Lisboa	1983 (3ºP)	25.145	8.790	739	2009–2011	2.181	6.609	6.504	1.165

Considering that the focus in this assessment section is the technical-functional aspect, the deterioration over time of the building subsystems in this study is represented by the theoretical concept of functional equivalent depreciation of buildings which encompasses technical depreciation and functional of building assets.

For the technical depreciation of buildings, it is considered that their technical end of life is in line with the minimum legislative and regulatory requirements for buildings, defined in Council Directive 89/106/CEE and EU Regulation No 305/2011, meaning that buildings should be fit for their intended use and should meet the requirements of: (i) mechanical strength and stability; (ii) fire safety; (iii) hygiene, health and environmental protection; (iv) safety in use; (v) noise protection; and (vi) energy saving and thermal insulation. On the other hand, the functional depreciation of a building is characterized by the loss of utility, primarily due to its obsolescence in response to new demands or requirements arising from evolving lifestyles and construction techniques.

Subsequently, a questionnaire is prepared to be filled out by people who know the building, such as its users. This form allows a more detailed assessment of the building's performance regarding the performance requirements based on 18 indicators, most of which are related to the 19,208 or 15,928 standards (Table 6).

Table 6 Building Performance Indicators

Technical-functional performance categories	
Mechanical resistance and stability	1. Structural safety
	2. Structural serviceability
	3. Structural durability
Safety and security	4. Physical safety
	5. Electrical safety
	6. Aggressive agents
	7. Security
	8. Parking safety
	9. Fire safety
Comfort and health	10. Hygrothermal
	11. Air purity
	12. Visual
	13. Acoustical
	14. Hygiene
Appearance	15. Interior appearance
	16. Exterior appearance
Safety in use	17. Accessibility
	18. Contributions to sustainable development

Step 2: Specifying the assessment strategy

As indicated in Fig. 3, this study employs two approaches to assess the technical-functional performance of public buildings. The first approach utilizes a structured bottom-up method, where critical assets or asset systems are evaluated based on their remaining service life. By evaluating a group of assets, the overall performance of the building can be assessed. This process is repeated for each building, allowing for an evaluation of the entire building portfolio. On the other hand, the second approach involves the assessment of each building through performance indicators using a questionnaire, which includes either questions to be answered on a "Satisfaction Scale" or by means of a "Checklist". Each indicator is related to a portfolio of assets. For example, when assessing the thermal comfort category, user satisfaction is assumed to be affected by several assets (envelope, HVAC, roofing, etc.).

Observation process

For the first approach, which is based on asset depreciation, the analysis focused on the residual lifetime of the building's assets. Considering the fact that the buildings in the portfolio were intervened between 2009 and 2011 (Parque Escolar's intervention), the analysis started after that period. Then, based on the service lifetime stipulated by the Ministry of Finance, it became possible to project the depreciation of the assets and therefore of the building over time—a procedure that is detailed later.

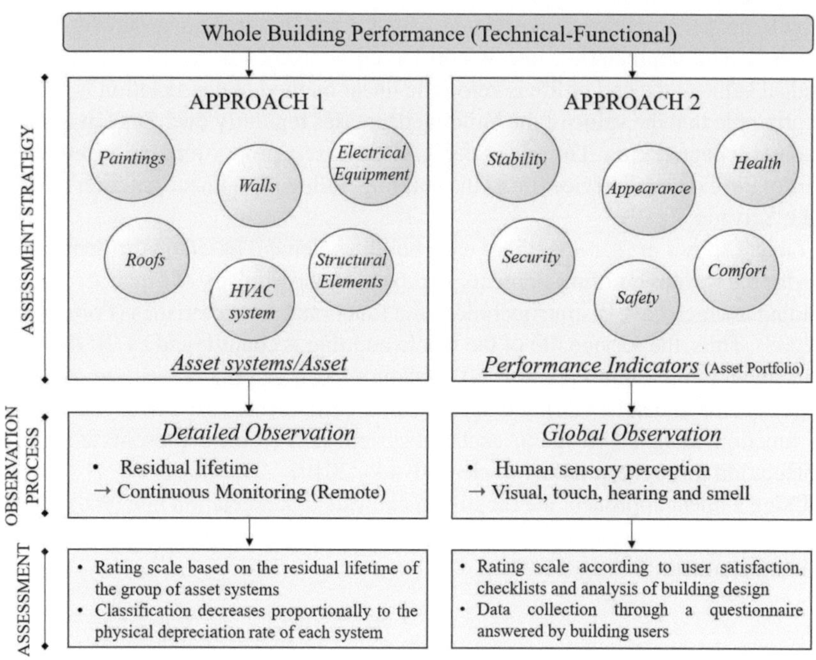

Fig. 3 Assessment strategy carried out

This observation process in fact focuses mainly on technical and financial aspects, such as the lifespan of the building's components and the depreciation forecast. This is crucial for assessing the building's long-term economic sustainability and for helping to make decisions regarding maintenance and future investments.

On the other hand, in the second evaluation approach, observation focused on understanding how users and society in general perceive the building, considering visual, tactile, auditory and olfactory aspects. Just as the analysis of the degradation of the building's assets seeks to represent the overall performance of the building, in this approach, it is considered that the evaluation of various performance indicators by users tends to reflect the complete state of the school building. On this basis, the observation in this approach followed a satisfaction scale/checklist form applied to various actors who use the buildings. This includes more subjective aspects such as comfort, quality of spaces, accessibility and overall satisfaction, helping to capture the practical experience of the people who use the building, which is vital to understanding its real value and the impact it has on the community. The application of a questionnaire was aimed at speeding up and facilitating access to information on the building's performance, making the collection of data related to different indicators for many schools more time efficient.

Step 4: Assessment

Assessment based on service life remaining of building elements:

For the first assessment approach, based on the remaining service life, the decrease of building performance is correlated to the depreciation of a group of building elements. The depreciation rate is considered constant for each element and the residual value at the end of life is zero. The linear method of depreciation is based on the principle that the value of the building decreases regularly over time, in a process of constant degradation. The rate of decline is inversely proportional to the number of years of the expected service life of the building, following a linear function (Hooper, 2023; Salvado, 2019).

Table 7 shows the service life of each building element based on the depreciation plan for the various building elements, approved by the Ministry of Finance for school buildings, which have distinct technical and functional characteristics (Portaria 701-H/2008). Thus, the service life of the whole building is conditioned by the durability of its subsystems (landscaping (LS), structure (ST), external elevations and roofs (ER), interior divisions (ID) and services and equipments (SE)) and, according to the function assigned to them, each subsystem and element presents a different depreciation throughout its life cycle (Salvado, 2019).

Using a linear approach, the functional equivalent depreciation rate (γD_i) for each element is calculated as given in (Eq. 1), where *SL* is the expected service life of a building element *i*:

$$\gamma_{D_i} = \frac{1}{SL_i} \tag{1}$$

Table 7 Service life and functional equivalent depreciation rate (%) for each building element

Subsystem	Element	Service life (years)	Depreciation rate (%)
Landscaping (LS)	Urbanistic arrangements elements	50	2.00
Structure (ST)	Structural elements	50	2.00
External elevations and roofs (ER) and Interior divisions (ID)	Walls	50	2.00
	Coatings	40	4.00
	Paintings	15	2.50
	Glass and mirrors	30	6.67
External elevations and roofs (ER)	Insulation	25	2.00
	Stone elements	50	2.00
	Metal elements	50	2.00
Interior divisions (ID)	Wood elements	50	2.00
	Plastic elements	50	3.33
Services and Equipment (SE)	Waters and sewage	40	2.50
	Electrical	40	2.50
	Communications	50	2.00
	HVAC	30	3.33
	Gas	30	3.33
	Integrated security	30	3.33
	Centralized technical management	30	3.33
	Transport of persons and cargo	40	2.50
	Renewable energy production	30	3.33

In this way, in a scenario of construction or refurbishment of the asset, it is considered a class A++, which corresponds in the numerical scale to 9. This numerical value decreases in a constant manner following the depreciation rate (γD_i), until reaching the minimum value (1; class F) at the end of the service life. To estimate the performance rating of the whole building each year, the arithmetic mean of the numerical scale of all subsystems is performed.

The evaluation of the technical-functional performance of the portfolio by depreciation is applied in this study only to the second reference period, which is post the Parque Escolar Modernization Program. Prior to the renovation phase, when the schools were deteriorating and neglected, a minimum baseline performance score was roughly set (Score 1, class F). After the renovation (around 2011), a maximum score is established (Score 9, class A++). From 2011 onwards, the decline in the assets' condition is factored in, based on the previously determined depreciation rate (outlined in Table 8).

Table 8 Functional equivalent depreciation rate for each subsystem (%)

Subsystem	Functional equivalent depreciation rate (%)
Landscaping (LS)	2.00
Structure (ST)	2.00
External elevations and roofs (ER)	3.21
Interior divisions (ID)	3.08
Services and Equipment (SE)	2.91

Initially, individual depreciation is computed for all elements within a subsystem (solid line). Subsequently, based on the collective performance of these elements (as presented in Table 7), the average depreciation for the subsystem is defined (dashed line). Figure 4, 5, 6 and 7 show the depreciation of each element in each group of subsystems, which helps to understand the assessment process adopted (Hooper, 2023; Salvado, 2019).

To determine the depreciation curve for the building system or portfolio, a simple average of the curves for all the subsystems is applied, obtaining a Class A (Score 6.46) in 2023, as shown in Fig. 8.

Assessment based on Building Performance Indicators:

The second approach for assessing building technical-functional performance is based on the completion of a questionnaire that includes 9 performance indicators,

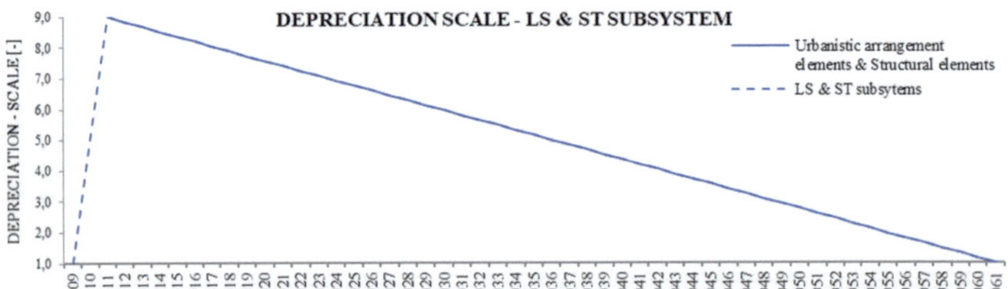

Fig. 4 Linear performance depreciation line for LS and ST elements

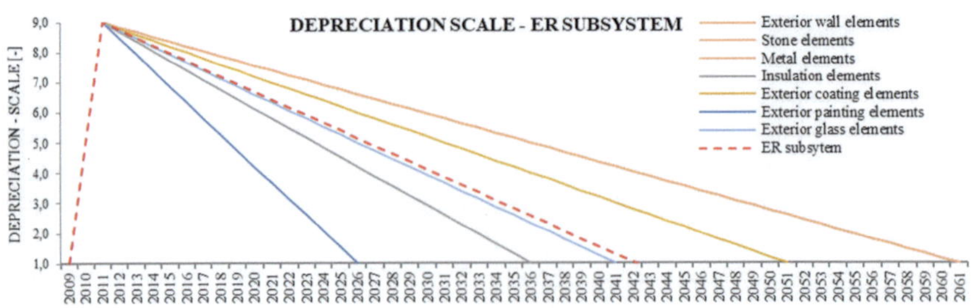

Fig. 5 Linear performance depreciation line for ER elements

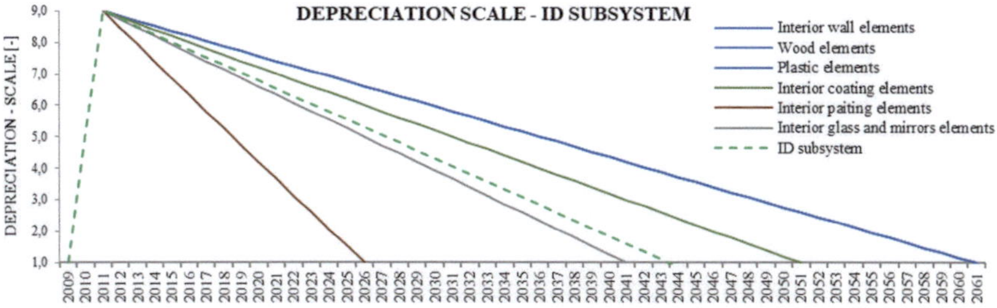

Fig. 6 Linear performance depreciation line for ID elements

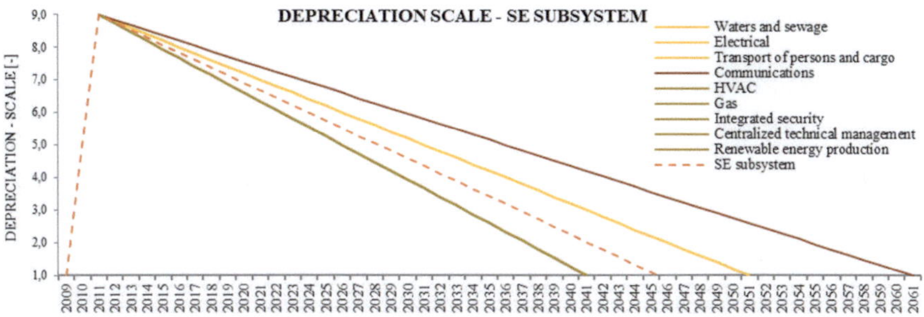

Fig. 7 Linear performance depreciation line for SE elements

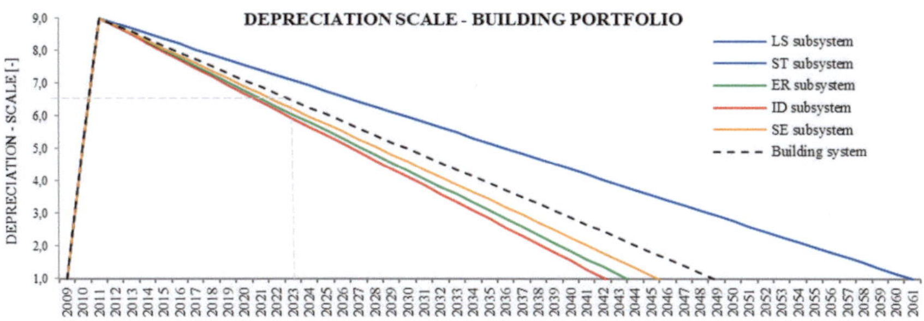

Fig. 8 Linear performance depreciation line for building system

comprising a total of 31 criteria. The survey consists of bipolar descriptive adjectives (e.g., very poor/poor/fair/good/outstanding) and dichotomous checklist questions (yes/no). The performance rating is determined on a numerical scale ranging from 1 (F) to 9 (A++), with higher scores indicating better performance. Similar to the first approach, the overall performance rating of the building is estimated by calculating the arithmetic mean of the numerical scale for all indicators. Somehow, these indicators should reflect the users' satisfaction with them and, therefore, the overall functionality of the building.

The form was implemented virtually using the Microsoft Forms platform and aimed at different users, including students, employees, parents and teachers. Regarding the profile of those interviewed, the majority of participants were students, representing 65% of the total. Regarding the age range of those interviewed, around 71% were between 15 and 36 years old. The schools included in the sample analysis were: S1, S3, S7 and S10, with school S3 accounting for the majority of respondents.

Based on the answers provided by the 17 interviewees with respect to the 9 performance indicators, covering 31 criteria, the following result is reached for the sample composed of 4 school buildings (Table 9).

As a complement to the analysis of user experience in relation to the performance of school buildings, the questionnaire included questions related to satisfaction with the school's main spaces, such as the canteen, library, classrooms, sports areas and corridors, reception and administrative rooms. In Table 10, users' satisfaction scores for these school spaces are shown.

Table 9 Performance Score/Class for each school and for the portfolio by questionnaire approach

Performance indicators	Score/class				
	S1	S3	S7	S10	Portfolio
Fire safety	5.27	6.30	6.00	6.70	6.07 (A)
Thermal comfort	6.00	7.00	8.00	6.75	6.94 (A)
Air purity	5.83	7.31	6.50	7.00	6.66 (A)
Visual	6.17	7.88	7.00	8.25	7.32 (A+)
Acoustical	6.11	7.08	7.00	7.83	7.01 (A+)
Hygiene	5.50	6.94	5.25	6.50	6.05 (A)
Interior appearance	7.00	8.25	8.00	8.00	7.81 (A+)
Exterior appearance	5.44	7.08	5.67	6.83	6.26 (A)
Accessibility	5.80	6.95	6.20	6.90	6.46 (A)
Average	5.90 (B)	7.20 (A +)	6.62 (A)	7.20 (A +)	6.73 (A)

Table 10 Questionnaire results by school and for the portfolio based on school spaces

School space	S1	S3	S7	S10	Portfolio
Canteen	5.67	6.75	9.00	7.00	7.10
Library	5.67	7.25	8.00	7.00	6.98
Classrooms	7.00	8.00	8.00	8.00	7.75
Sports areas	7.67	8.50	7.00	8.00	7.79
Corridors/reception/ administrative rooms	6.33	6.50	5.00	7.50	6.33
Average	6.47 (A)	7.40 (A+)	7.40 (A+)	7.50 (A+)	7.19 (A+)

Table 11 Results of the last question of the questionnaire by school and for the portfolio

	S1	S3	S7	S10	Portfolio
"What overall satisfaction rating would you give the school building?"	6.07 (A)	7.50 (A+)	6.60 (A)	7.40 (A+)	6.89 (A)

To conclude the form, the last question asked to users was: "What overall satisfaction rating would you give the school building?" (Scale between 1 and 9). In Table 11, is the average result for this question per school.

In fact, the positive results shown on the questionnaire are directly related to the recent rehabilitation and modernization process carried out in these schools, which sought to adapt the school environments to the new standards, regulations and new demands from users.

3.3 Validation

In the context of the methodologies adopted to evaluate the performance of public buildings, it should be emphasized that certain validation processes are indispensable to verify the reliability of the data collected and analyzed. Considering, for example, the initial technical-functional approach centered on measuring the performance based on the remaining service life of assets, depreciation alone can inadequately reflect the performance of assets in the real world. Given the heterogeneous nature of assets in a school environment, hiring specialized professionals or consultants to validate the results of the methodology is important, especially for assets that have lower performance classes. Furthermore, in a portfolio made up of several public buildings, the validation of the results can begin with the selection of the most critical buildings.

4 Conclusions

This article represents a significant contribution to the improvement of public asset management, promoting well-informed and effective decision-making throughout the life cycle of public buildings. The methodology employed in this research, which provides a joint assessment of the technical- functional performance of these buildings throughout their life cycle, has been developed to gather useful data that can improve the decision-making process at all stages, regardless of the specific type of public building in question.

Furthermore, the possible impact of this study goes beyond the academia and expert field, made up of engineers and architects, but also extends to a variety of other stakeholders. For facility and asset managers, this information is crucial for optimizing the maintenance and operational efficiency of buildings. For building owners, it supports strategic decisions about investments in renovation and improvements. In parallel, regulatory bodies and authorities can extract valuable insights from a deeper understanding of the performance of public assets in order to design more effective policies and regulations. Banks and insurance companies, on the other hand, can use this data to assess the associated risks and thus influence their financing and insurance policies. Finally, the end users of these buildings, who utilize these spaces, can benefit from safer, more comfortable and efficient environments, thus underscoring the practical relevance and importance of this article.

While the methodology holds relevance for various public buildings, the primary focus of this study has been on a portfolio comprising 10 secondary school buildings situated in diverse regions of mainland Portugal. These structures carry a historical legacy dating back to the 1940s and have experienced substantial modifications as part of the Parque Escolar Modernization Programme, which unfolded between 2009 and 2011.

These public buildings bear immense significance, forming an integral component of the state's overall asset inventory. Beyond representing a significant commitment of financial and investment resources, drawing from both national and EU budgets, their effective management and economic assessment serve as pivotal elements in fulfilling the responsibilities of the Portuguese state. Moreover, secondary school buildings fulfil an irreplaceable social function within society, serving as vital cornerstones for the education and development of the younger generations. These spaces serve as conduits for the transfer of knowledge, nurturing of essential skills, and the active shaping of the nation's future.

In addition to the wide-ranging contributions highlighted previously, the establishment of a classification system for assessing the technical and functional performance of a portfolio of buildings is a profoundly significant collaborative achievement. The act of categorizing buildings using this system provides a framework that greatly improves the understanding of building performance among the various stakeholders, allowing for faster analysis and identification of vulnerabilities. In fact, the classification given to the portfolio of school buildings through the application of the two technical-functional evaluation approaches showed a positive result, with a Class A classification. This result means that, from a general perspective, this portfolio of school buildings has consistently met the requirements of its users. This result can be directly attributed to the intervention process carried out in Portuguese schools, which involved modernizing these buildings to bring them into line with contemporary demands and regulatory standards.

With this in mind, several promising directions for future studies come to light, such as, data validation through statistical analyses, visits to specific schools within the portfolio, and the assignment of weights for calculating the final performance class of the building portfolio represent crucial steps. Determining the weights for each criterion can be established through consultations with experts in the field or by employing the Analytic Hierarchy Process (AHP) (Silva, 2012). AHP is a multi-criteria decision-making technique that aids in decision-making by conducting multiple pairwise comparisons to determine the relative importance of each criterion.

References

Ali, A. S. (2009). Cost decision making in building maintenance practice. *Journal of Facilities Management,7*(4), 298–306

Almeida, N. (2011). Modelo de gestão técnica de edifícios baseada no desempenho e no risco—Concepção, desenvolvimento e exemplo de aplicação a estruturas. s.l.:Tese de Doutoramento em Engenharia Civil, Departamento de Engenharia Civil e Arquitetura, Instituto Superior Técnico, Universidade de Lisboa.

Barrett, P., et al. (2019). *The impact of school infrastructure on learning: A synthesis of the evidence.* International Development in Focus. Washington, DC: World Bank.

Brunet, M., Motamedi, A., Guénette, L.-M., & Forgues, D. (2019). Analysis of BIM use for asset management in three public organizations in Québec, Canada. *Built Environment Project and Asset Management, 9*(1), 153–167.

Cotts, D., Roper, K. O., & Payant, R. P. (2009). *The facility management handbook.* AMACOM.

Council Directive 89/106/EEC of 21 December 1988 on the approximation of laws, regulations and administrative provisions of the Member States relating to construction products.

Crespo Marquez, A., Gomez Fernandez, J.F., Martínez-Galán Fernández, P., & Guillen Lopez, A. (2020). Maintenance management through intelligent asset management platforms (IAMP). Emerging factors, key impact areas and data models. *Energies,13*, 3762.

de Brito, J., Silva, A. & Gaspar P., L. (2016). *Methodologies for Service Life.* Springer International Publishing.

EN 17840:2023—Performance and condition assessment for buildings and civil engineering works—Framework for assessment within physical asset management.

EU Regulation No 305/2011—European Parliament, 2011. Laying down harmonised conditions for the marketing of construction products and repealing.

Gurevich, U., Sacks, R., & Shrestha, P. (2017). BIM adoption by public facility agencies: Impacts on occupant value. *Building Research & Information, 45*(6), 610–630.

Hooper, F. (2023). *A joint approach to the economic and technical-functional life cycle performance of public building portfolios.* Mcs thesis in civil engineering, Instituto Superior Técnico, University of Lisbon (IST-UL).

ISO 11863:2011a—Buildings and building-related facilities—Functional and user requirements and performance—Tools for assessment and comparison.

ISO 15928-1:2015—Houses—Description of performance

ISO 19208:2016—Framework for specifying performance in Buildings.

Love, P. E. D., Simpson, I., Hill, A., & Standing, C. (2013). From justification to evaluation: Building information modelling for asset owner. *Automation in Construction, 35*, 208–216.

Norazman, N., Che-Ani, A., Hussain, A. H., & Ismail, W. (2021). Toward a classroom condition index (CCI) assessment scheme: Assessment categories and their performance indicators. *Journal of Facilities Management, 29*, 10.

Parque Escolar. (2011). *Parque Escolar 2007–2011. Intervenção em 106 escolas.* Lisbon: Parque Escolar EPE, Direção-Geral de Projeto—Área de Edificações.

Portaria, N. (2008). de 29 de julho—Conteúdo obrigatório do programa e do projeto de execução e normas a adotar na elaboração e faseamento de projetos de obras públicas. Diário da República, n.º 145, Série I de 29 de julho de 2008, pp. 5106(37)–5106(80).

Salvado, F. (2019). Custo do ciclo de vida na gestão de edifícios. Modelo de apreciação económica aplicado a portefólios de edifícios escolares públicos. PhD thesis in civil engineering, Instituto Superior Técnico, University of Lisbon (IST-UL).

Silva, A., et al. (2022). Causal effects between criteria that establish the end of service life of buildings and components. *Buidings.* https://doi.org/10.3390/buildings12020088

Silva, V. F. (2012). *Análise de risco na construção—Guia de procedimentos para gestão.* Universidade do Porto, Faculdade de engenharia.

Talon, A., Boissier, D., Chevalier, J. L. & Hans, J., 2005. Temporal quantification method of degradation scenarios based on FMEA. In *Proceedings of 10th International conference on durability of building materials and components. Lyon, France*, pp. TT4–139.

The Institute of Asset Management (2015). *An Anatomy of Asset Management.* Version 3.

Trindade, M., Almeida, N., Finger, M. & Silva, J. (2018). Application of a value-based decision-making process to an industrial water supply system. In *Conference: WCEAM 2018 13th World Congress on Engineering Asset Management.*

Vischer, J. (2008). Towards a user-centred theory of the built environment. *Building Research & Information 36*, 231–240.

Specialized Topics and Emerging Applications

Infodynamic Analysis of Damage Detection on Bridges

Jorge Vieira and Miguel O. Panão

Abstract This study advances Structural Health Monitoring (SHM) by leveraging infodynamics, a novel approach that measures the information extracted from SHM raw data. Unlike conventional methods that rely on distances or statistical moments, this approach uses the information theory to interpret the stochastic nature of data as a key metric for quantifying informational content. Redundant data lack informational value, whereas stochasticity from external events necessitates real-time monitoring to identify structural health changes. A central question in SHM is determining when sufficient information is acquired for reliable damage assessment. This research explores Shannon's formulation for measuring information, termed "informature," which is sensitive to the entire data distribution and lays the foundation for new infodynamic strategies in SHM. To validate this approach, we applied informational analysis to dynamic data from the Z24 Bridge in Switzerland before its demolition, part of the Brite EuRam BE-3157 project "System Identification to Monitor Civil Engineering Structures" (SIMCES). The data included accelerometer readings that reflected the bridge's response to the induced damage. The results demonstrate the effectiveness of "informature" in capturing sudden and gradual changes in the accelerometer data, highlighting the potential for real-time assessment of the correlation between "informature" and structural damage indicators, marking a significant advancement in SHM.

Keywords Structural health monitoring · Bridges · Data · Information · Informature · Infodynamics · Damage detection

J. Vieira (✉)
Matereospace Lda, Coimbra, Portugal
e-mail: jorgealexandrevieira@matereo.com

M. O. Panão
University of Coimbra, Coimbra, Portugal
e-mail: miguel.panao@dem.uc.pt

A. Crespo Márquez et al. (eds.), *Case Studies in Digital Transformation*, Engineering Asset Management Review 4, https://doi.org/10.1007/978-3-032-05592-7_11

1 Introduction

The primary goal of Structural Health Monitoring (SHM) tasks, processes, and methodologies is to convert data into valuable information that can facilitate more effective decision-making concerning the predictive maintenance of bridges or other critical infrastructures. SHM systems gather static or dynamic data via sensors installed on structures, which enables the implementation of data analytics strategies to extract information related to structural behavior and the early detection of structural anomalies/damage. Damage is defined by changes in the material properties and/or geometry of bridge components, which introduce a transformation to the structural system and affect its safety and current and future performance. Bridges can suffer damage owing to extreme events such as earthquakes or gradually over time because of the corrosion of structural elements (e.g., suspension cables), deformation (e.g., creep), or fatigue. Other factors, such as design flaws (e.g., lack of redundancy of structural elements), construction defects, or degradation of expansion joints and bearings, can also contribute to damage development (Meixedo, 2021).

From the point of view of the 1st Law of Thermodynamics, also known as the principle of conservation of energy, in a permanent regime, the energy that enters a structure (loads) is equivalent to the energy that leaves it (energy dissipated through heat due to friction between structural elements or structural deformation). Bridges are subjected to cyclical loads throughout their lifetime, and the energy leaving the bridge system is dissipated through heat, deformation, and cumulative damage owing to fatigue. Vibrations in bridges create dynamic tension and deformation that causes fatigue and eventual premature failure of the structure. In metallic bridges, fatigue corrosion phenomena (fretting corrosion) occur between the elements in contact, which normally impair the structural performance and reduce the useful life of structures. Fatigue cracks normally occur in stress concentration areas of structural elements, particularly where the cross-section is reduced, in notches, and welding joints, among others. The bridge design must consider the impact of cyclic loads and predict the total number of cycles without failure. Regular inspections and predictive maintenance are essential to ensure that a bridge fulfills its function throughout its lifetime.

Since the beginning of the 90s, SHM has been proposed to operators and asset managers as a solution to optimize bridge life cycle management and avoid structural failures based on damage identification strategies. In this context, *Asset Management* is defined as "the coordinated activity of an organization to generate value from its assets" (ISO, 2014) and aims to balance cost, risk, and performance throughout the entire asset lifecycle. With the increasing prevalence of digital engineering in project delivery, along with advancements in the Internet of Things (IoT), sensing technologies, and computational capabilities, it has become advantageous to promote the application of SHM throughout the asset lifecycle. Recent research has strategically employed SHM for efficient and intelligent asset management, both at the project level, to improve individual assets, and at a broader level by transport authorities (Christodoulou et al., 2024). To address the challenges associated with the vast amounts of data collected from assets, Candón et al. (2024) proposed integrating Internet of Things (IoT)-based monitoring models with an Asset Health Index (AHI) model. This approach provides a comprehensive perspective on asset digitization, encompassing various levels of complex asset system management. It also facilitates a stronger link between real-time monitoring and a more profound, long-term comprehension of asset conditions and performance. Recent advancements in software platforms for data visualization and analysis have leveraged the increasing importance and capabilities of cloud computing, making it easier to adopt decision-making tools for predictive maintenance processes based on the real-time monitoring of assets (Crespo et al., 2024).

Concerning damage identification, an SHM system hierarchical classification has a five-level scale depending on the level of information it provides (Rytter, 1993) (Tomé, 2019):

- Level 1—Damage detection: Information about the presence or absence of damage.
- Level 2—Damage localization: Information regarding the probable position of the damage.
- Level 3—Damage classification: Information about the type of damage.
- Level 4—Damage assessment: Information about the severity of the damage.
- Level 5—Remaining useful life (RUL) prediction: Estimation of the residual life of the structure.

There are two main methods for detecting structural damage by using SHM systems. The first is the model-based approach, in which data gathered from the response of the structure is compared with numerical models or experimental data to identify damage. The second is a data-based approach, which uses time-series analysis techniques to analyze trends in the structural response and identify discrepancies or outliers. The model-based approach requires the development of complex numerical models, particularly in the case of bridges. However, once robust and reliable, this approach can not only detect but also locate and identify the type and severity of damage and estimate the remaining useful life. The data-based approach can be implemented with a strategy relying on input–output (based on loads and their structural response) or output-only (based only on the structural response). Data-based solutions have numerous advantages, owing to their simplicity and speed of implementation. However, to date, this approach can only detect the presence of damage and, in some cases, its location (which requires a large number of sensors distributed throughout the structure). It is essential to consider the limitations and disadvantages of each approach when choosing which one to use. In recent years, a hybrid approach combining model-based and data-based approaches has been adopted (Figueiredo & Moldovan, 2023). Data-based damage identification strategies typically involve comparing two condition states using statistical pattern recognition (SPR), which is a branch of artificial intelligence. These strategies involve three main steps. First, sensors are installed to acquire real-time data from the structures, followed by damage indicators (features) extracted from the collected data. Features are the attributes of the data used to differentiate and classify data points. For an efficient analysis, signals can be split into their sub-bands before feature extraction using filters or wavelet transforms. Wavelet transform is a signal analysis technique composed of a family of basic functions that can describe a signal in a localized time and frequency domain (useful for performing local analysis of a signal) (Ren & Sun, 2018). Only sub-bands containing high energy are considered for further analysis to save processing resources. The average power required for each sub-band is calculated using the Power Spectral Density (PSD). PSD shows the distribution of the power of a signal in the frequency domain or the energy of a function as a function of frequency. Signal features can be broadly divided into two categories: statistical (e.g., mean, standard deviation, variance, first difference mean, second difference mean, Hjorth parameter, Kurtosis parameter, etc.) and nonstatistical (PSD, entropy, the average energy of bands of signal, etc.) (Vijay Sanker et al, 2022). In the field of SHM, classic feature extraction involves the use of Power Spectral Density (PSD) and other methods (e.g., peak-picking) to extract modal frequencies from a time series of acceleration data, which are used as indicators sensitive to damage because they correlate with structural stiffness changes (Maeck et al., 2001). Other vibration-based indicators can also be extracted from acceleration time series (e.g., peak-to-peak and vibration intensity) and can be used as damage-sensitive indicators (Moughty & Casas, 2017). Alternatively, parameters from autoregressive models adjusted to acceleration data can be used as damage indicators ((Meixedo, 2021) (Tomé, 2019). Finally, in the last step of the damage identification process, supervised or unsupervised machine learning algorithms were used to classify damage indicators and enable decision-making regarding damage detection. For example, Meixedo et al. (2021) proposed an online procedure for damage detection on railway bridges using exogenous autoregressive models and their parameters as damage indicators, principal component analysis for operational and environmental effect removal, Mahalanobis Distance for data fusion, and k-means algorithms for feature classification and damage detection.

The main purpose of the present study is to explore a simple, fast, and scalable method for damage detection in bridges. To achieve this, complex calculations, data filtering, or transformations (e.g., feature extraction) must be avoided. In this sense, (1) a data-based approach and output-only analysis must be adopted, which excludes the need for numerical modeling; (2) feature extraction must be performed directly from raw data, without the need for data filtering; (3) data analysis must be performed in the time domain, without the need for data transformation; and (4) the solution must have the capacity to provide real-time or near-real-time information. In line with these premises, the concept of informature (misinterpreted as entropy; see Ben-Naim (2008) for more details) has been applied to different domains, including power systems, physics, finance, biology, physiology, and cardiovascular time series. The eighth (and last) axiom of Structural Health Monitoring is the rationale behind using information measurements in SHM. This axiom states that damage increases the complexity of a system related to uncertainties from a dataset collected by sensors installed in a structure. Informature is a measure of the uncertainty of a signal and is proportional to its complexity. The greater the entropy values, the more complexity a message accumulates and the more information it contains (Farrar et al., 2010).

For these reasons, this work explores information-based SHM solutions and a novel concept for damage identification based on the informature determined from sensor data. The applicability of the informature for detecting damage on bridges has been applied to acceleration data from sensors installed on the Z24 bridge. These data are part of the Brite EuRam BE-3157 project, which is one of the few projects that provide real-world data related to bridge damage. This has enabled multiple SHM studies over the last 25 years and has resulted in significant advancements in the scientific community in this field. In the present study, instead of using modal parameters as damage indicators, the evolution of the informature is obtained directly from the acceleration time series, which shows sudden real-time changes resulting from outliers in the data owing to environmental effects or structural damage.

2 New Monitoring Solutions

2.1 General Overview

Traditional bridge maintenance management methods rely on visual inspection to monitor the structural health of bridges. However, over the past 30 years, nondestructive testing (NDE) and SHM systems have been increasingly adopted to overcome the limitations of visual inspection. These systems enable the collection of crucial information regarding the structural integrity of bridges, which cannot be obtained through visual inspection alone. NDE methods encompass various analyses using magnetic fields, radiography, thermal fields, and acoustic or ultrasonic methods. These tests are conducted at specific times to assess the structural integrity of a bridge or its components, requiring the mobilization and demobilization of equipment for the location of interest and subsequent analysis of the tests. By contrast, SHM takes an online, continuous approach, allowing for the ongoing global analysis of a structure with autonomous data extraction (Figueiredo et al., 2022). In this sense, a typical structural health monitoring (SHM) system involves installing a sensor network on a bridge structure and a data transmission system to be fed into a database. This allows for the online processing and visualization of the collected information in real or near real-time. Intelligent wireless sensor technologies offer cost savings and easier implementation than traditional wired solutions. A major drawback of wireless solutions is their reduced energy autonomy owing to battery limitations. Efforts have focused on developing integrated solar/wind energy solutions and operational energy-saving strategies. An alternative to overcome energy issues involves using passive wireless sensors, which do not require a built-in power supply, namely sensors based on passive radio frequency identification (RFID) powered by external exciters. These RFID-based sensors are cost-effective and can operate over the entire lifespan of an infrastructure. Additionally, the design of the antennas can be correlated with the parameters of interest for SHM, such as deformation, humidity, and temperature. Edge computing solutions enable the incorporation of capabilities, such as signal filtering and reducing the burden of data transmission between sensor network nodes, into wireless sensors to process raw data. As sensor networks continue to grow, it is crucial to adopt efficient security measures and secure storage of large volumes of data. This has led to the adoption of "cloud" infrastructure as an analytical and scalable access platform for data processing and visualization. Currently, new types of sensors are available for SHM applications. These include fiber optic sensors (FOS) that can be embedded in a concrete structure during construction or installed on the exterior along the length of a bridge. These sensors allow for the collection of a wide range of parameters, such as deformations, rotations, temperature, and vibrations, with the same sensor. Commercially available sensors are based on microelectromechanical systems (MEMS), including accelerometers and inclinometers (Laflamme et al., 2023). Some promising technologies for SHM include the potential use of smartphones, the development of smart materials, and remote sensing. Smartphones offer computational and communication capabilities, as well as integrated sensors such as accelerometers, simplifying the data collection process for bridges, Research has shown that smartphones can be used to collect the natural frequencies in bridges, producing results consistent with those of conventional accelerometers (differences lower than 2.42%) (Figueiredo et al., 2022). There are also ongoing experiments with smart structural materials, particularly concrete, which incorporate distributed sensory systems for self-monitoring of structural parameters. This involves adding conductive or semiconductor fillers into concrete, allowing it to detect stresses, deformations, damage (e.g., cracks), and environmental loads (e.g., temperature and humidity) while maintaining or even improving mechanical properties and durability (Laflamme et al., 2023).

Despite the limited use of satellite remote sensing with Synthetic Aperture Radar Interferometry (InSAR) for SHM on bridges, this method has been successfully employed to monitor large infrastructures, such as dams and tunnels, especially for tracking vertical displacements. Recently, InSAR was used to monitor the thermal expansion of the Hammersmith viaduct in London. This study introduces an innovative approach for identifying points with strong radar reflection, known as Persistent Scatterers (PS). These points were integrated into Geographic Information Systems (GIS) along with a Building Information Modeling (BIM) model of the viaduct. Additionally, the authors used a Fourier transform, specifically the Fast Fourier Transform (FFT), to identify points exhibiting oscillating behavior over time, which helped in recognizing the thermal expansion and contraction deformations of the structure caused by temperature effects. To validate the obtained results, the authors compared the measurements collected from Linear Variable Differential Transformer (LVDT) sensors installed next to the viaduct bearings with InSAR data. The estimated thermal expansion parameter is 1.07 mm/°C for LVDT and 1.04 mm/°C for InSAR. This confirms that the in situ measurements align with the InSAR measurements, despite different observation geometries, and that the thermal expansion parameter can be estimated using both methods. Additionally, monitoring deformations on this bridge helped identify blocked bearing devices, which significantly limited the horizontal movement of the structure owing to thermal effects. Consequently, these devices were replaced to ensure that the bridge behaved normally under thermal conditions (Selvakumaran et al., 2022).

2.2 *Paso Real Bridge Data Flow Architecture—Colombia*

The Paso Real Bridge, located in Santa Fé de Antioquia, Colombia, crosses the Cauca River and was built in 1965 to connect Medellín to the western part of the country. The bridge has a total length of 426 m, a main span of 216 m, and a deck that is 6.50 m wide. It crossed the river at a height of 16 m. The bridge is a suspended metal structure with two towers: one 35 m high and the other 33 m high. It is composed of two main beams that are 2.5 m high, 83 mm diameter hangings, and a 2–1/2″ cable diameter. The deck floor was made of 200 mm thick reinforced concrete (Fig. 1).

To monitor the evolution of the structural behavior of the Paso Real Bridge, sensors were installed to collect static and dynamic parameters in real-time. The location of the sensors or checkpoints was defined by a simplified analysis of the bridge structure

Fig. 1 Paso real bridge

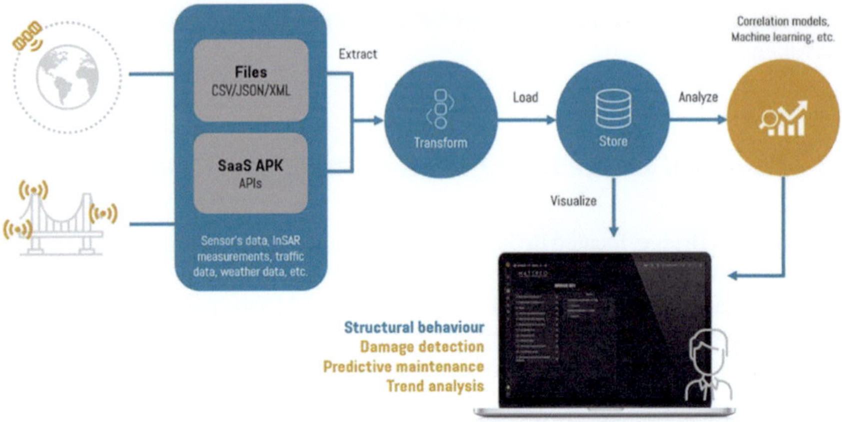

Fig. 2 Paso real bridge high-level SHM system implementation

to identify checkpoints with predictably higher deformations and vibrations. After completing the empirical analysis of the structure, vibration sensors were installed along the main span and suspension cables. Inclinometers were installed along the main span and in the towers, and displacement sensors were implemented to monitor the movement of the expansion joints. Figure 2 represents the high-level architecture of the SHM system used in the Paso Real Bridge, from data acquisition to decision-making. This includes the extract-transform-load (ETL) process, storage, data analysis, and visualization tools.

Regarding vibration sensors installed on the Paso Real Bridge, one of the main purposes is to extract information about the levels of vibration induced by operational (e.g., heavy traffic) and environmental (e.g., wind) effects. For this application, MEMS sensors were adopted, which allow the capture of the maximum accelerations and velocities during each measurement, including dominant frequencies (F_{dom}) extracted from the velocity spectrum, in which only the frequency associated with the peak velocity is transferred to the database, along with top accelerations (A_{top}) and velocities (V_{top}), which ensures the capture of the signal that incorporates the greatest vibrational energy. Figure 3. shows one of the installed vibration sensors. Each vibration sensor had an internal battery powered by a solar panel and a 4G SIM card for direct data transmission to the database. A_{top}, V_{top}, and F_{dom} features and other parameters easily obtained from them (e.g., vibration intensity) were used to analyze the vibrational energy embedded in the structure and its damage potential correlation.

MEMS triaxial tilt sensors and optical displacement sensors were used to collect static data. These sensors are accurate to within a fraction of a millimeter and incorporate long-lasting internal batteries that can last up to 12 years, depending on the acquisition rate. They communicate and transmit data via Wi-Fi to a gateway powered by a solar panel, which then transmits the data in real-time over 4G to the database. The image in Fig. 4 shows one of the tilt sensors installed.

Fig. 3 Vibration sensor installed on Paso real bridge cables

Fig. 4 Tilt sensor installed on Paso real bridge tower

Figure 5 shows the home page of the visualization tool (webapp), which integrates static and dynamic data collected from sensors and InSAR data collected from Sentinel 1. Different decisions were made based on the information extracted from the Paso Real Bridge data regarding vibration control of the structure and maintenance needs.

Fig. 5 Online visualization tool for decision-making

3 Infodynamic Analysis: A Novel Lexicon

When a measurement is subjected to stochasticity, indeterminacy is embedded in the nature of the underlying physical process. Quantifying this uncertainty is equivalent to measuring the amount of information required to understand an outcome. Claude Shannon (1948) began developing a mathematical theory of communication to understand the minimum amount of information that ensures the decoding of a message when affected by noise in the communication channel. The properties of this measure H are as follows.

1. H is continuous in p_i as the probability (frequency) of a particular outcome.
2. Suppose p_i is equal for all possible n values, $p_i = 1/n$, H is equal for all possible n values, and H is a monotonically increasing function of n because, with equally likely events, there is more choice for a higher number of possible events.
3. If one splits the choice phase-space into two, the original H is the weighted sum of the resulting H values of the two groups of choices.

Shannon proved that the only function for H(x) fulfilling these properties was given by,

$$H_b = -K \sum\nolimits_{i=1}^{n} p_i \log_b(p_i) \tag{1}$$

where K is an arbitrary constant, n corresponds to the number of possible configurations, and the unit of this formulation is the *bit*, henceforth referred to as the abbreviation for a binary unit (not digit), because Shannon considers $b = 2$ for the logarithm base.

In his seminal work, Shannon (1948, p. 11) writes — «*The form of H will be recognized as that of entropy, as defined in certain formulations of statistical mechanics, where p_i is the probability of a system being in cell I of its phase space. We shall call $H = -K \sum p_i \log p_i$ the entropy of the set of probabilities p_i, ..., p_n*—Ben-Naim (2008) explained in detail why John von Neumann misled Claude Shannon into naming his function *entropy*. To avoid further misinterpretations and accommodate information theory in engineering, a new lexicon is introduced to perform an infodynamic analysis of the data. First, each diagnostic technique or sensor that captures the stochastic or nondeterministic nature of a certain physical quantity is an *infosensor*.

Similar to a "thermosensor," like a thermocouple that uses the Seebeck effect to measure the temperature of a physical system in Kelvin, Fahrenheit, or Celsius, an *infosensor* uses statistics to measure the *informature* (amount of information) of a complex physical system in *bits* (if the information answers YES/NO binary questions), *nats* (if using $b = e$ and information reports to natural systems), or *dets* (if using $b = 10$ and information reports to systems with values in different orders of magnitude). Therefore, adapting Shannon's formulation to the new lexicon means that

$$H_b = K_c \bullet H_{I,b} \tag{2}$$

with K_c as a scale contextualizing the *informature* given by

$$H_{I,b} = -K_b \sum\nolimits_{i=1}^{n} p_i \log_2(p_i) \tag{3}$$

where K_b denotes the scale setting of the logarithmic base ($K_2 = 1 \Rightarrow$ *bits* for *bi*nary uni*ts*, $K_e = \ln(2) \Rightarrow$ *nats* for *na*tural uni*ts*, and $K_{10} = \log_{10}(2) \Rightarrow$ *dets* for *de*cimal uni*ts*). Instead of Shannon entropy, H_b is a *contextualized informature* that quantifies the degree of transformation (*trope* in Greek) by information of a physical system, thus, an *infotropy*.

If each configuration x_i of the n possibilities has the same probability of occurrence, $p(x_i) = 1/n$, the system is chaotic, and *informature* is maximum and given by,

$$H_{max,b} = \log_b(\mathrm{n}) \tag{4}$$

In this case, reducing the indeterminacy of the physical system decreases the number of possible configurations. Therefore, no information was obtained because the system was predictable. If one normalizes the informature by the maximum value, the result takes the form,

$$H_n = \frac{\mathrm{H}_{I,b}}{H_{max,b}} \tag{5}$$

with values varying between 0 (full certainty) and 1 (full chaos). The complement is the *redundancy*

$$R_n = 1 - H_n \tag{6}$$

indicating that the system with a single possible configuration ($H_n = 0$) is fully redundant. For example, a sensor measuring 10,000 samples of the same value does not need a data file with that value repeated 10,000 times, but a single value and the information of its measurement during the period considered. Otherwise, if $R_n \to 0$ because $H_n \to 1$, the measured values are uniformly distributed within an interval, and every measure counts to understand the information conveyed by the *infosensor*.

Depending on the process and time series, variations in $H_{I,b}$ measurements have been introduced, including, but not restricted to, Approximate $H_{I,b}$ (useful in measuring patterns in time series and uncovering the regularities by extracting the noises from the original data), Sample $H_{I,b}$ (useful in quantifying the fluctuation degree of a time series), Transfer $H_{I,b}$ (useful in measuring the information flow between two time-series and determining whether the variability in one random variable helps explain the variability in a second variable), and Permutation H_n (the normalized form of *informature* over a probability distribution $P = \{p(xi), i = 1, \ldots, n\}$) (Nandari & Li, 2019).

Some authors have explored information-based SHM solutions with different forms of quantifying the *informature* $H_{I,b}$ through the phase-space of specific parameters combined with different techniques. For example, Ren et al. (2018) combined wavelet transform with the informature part of Shannon's formulation to detect structural damage from measured vibration signals. Cui et al. (2022) used the same approach for fatigue breathing cracks detection on structures, in which the wavelet transform is used to amplify irregularities in the signal and *informature* to quantify irregularities and the number of nonlinear patterns in the time series. Moreno-Gomez et al. (2018) combined the Empirical Mode Decomposition (EMD) method (useful in analyzing time signals with non-linear, transient, and non-stationary properties) with Shannon's approach to detecting incipient damages associated with corrosion in a truss-type bridge. Yang et al. (2014) proposed the use of generalized local "entropy"[1] (GLE) (an *infotropy* limited into a local set) for crack fault diagnosis in beam structures. Using the evolution of the *informature*, cracks were detected by the GLE analysis of the fundamental and second mode-shapes of the beam. The word "entropy" is often used in these works. Still, here, one opts to refer to Shannon's formulation for what it is, a measure of information, *informature*, or *infotropy* when contextualized by K_c, avoiding further propagation of misinterpretations.

[1] *Shannon entropy* used by numerous authors is a misleading term because *entropy,* as a neologism invented by Rudolf Clausius, is a word that synthesizes the prefix *en-* (as in *en*ergy) and *trope* (from the Greek that means transformation). In Shannon's formulation, the transformation of information is a general case. When $K_c = k_B$, the Boltzmann's constant, $K_e = \ln(2)$, and $p_i = 1/W$, with W as the total number of microstates in a physical system (*e.g.*, a gas), $H_e = k_B \ln(W) = S$, which is the thermodynamic entropy. Therefore, in *infodynamics*, the term *infotropy* as *contextualized informature* is a more general term than the misleading Shannon entropy.

4 Case Study: Z24 Bridge

4.1 Bridge Description and Damage Scenarios

The Z24 bridge is a post-tensioned concrete two-cell box-girder bridge near Solothurn, Switzerland, connecting the villages of Koppigen and Utzenstorf over the A1 highway between Bern and Zürich. It had a main span of 30 m and two side spans of 14 m, and was a freestanding frame with rotated supports, making it a skew bridge. The bridge was demolished in 1998, because a new railway adjacent to the highway required a new bridge with a larger side span. Data were collected for one year (starting in November 1997) to study the environmental effects on structural response. One month before the demolition of the bridge, progressive damage tests were conducted (starting in August 1998), and 65,536 samples of acceleration data samples were collected at a sampling rate of 100 Hz (Maeck & De Roeck, 2003). Table 1 describes the damage scenarios.

This benchmark case is fascinating because it includes both damage (started on August 10, 1998) and temperature effects on the bridge that caused modal frequency changes (occurring in February 1998), as shown in Fig. 6. The vertical dashed lines represent the damage scenarios.

For a better understanding of the temperature effects, Fig. 7 shows the ambient temperature evolution during the tests, and the peak at -10 °C occurred on February

Table 1 Progressive damage test scenarios

Date (1998)	Scenario
4 August	Undamaged condition
9 August	Installation of the pier settlement system
10 August	Lowering of the pier, 20 mm
12 August	Lowering of the pier, 40 mm
17 August	Lowering of the pier, 80 mm
18 August	Lowering of the pier, 95 mm
19 August	Lifting of pier, tilt of foundation
20 August	New reference condition
25 August	Spalling of concrete at soffit, 12 m2
26 August	Spalling of concrete at soffit, 24 m2
27 August	Landslide of 1 m at abutment
31 August	Failure of the concrete hinge
2 September	Failure of 2 anchor heads
3 September	Failure of 4 anchor heads
7 September	Rupture of 2 out of 16 tendons
8 September	Rupture of 4 out of 16 tendons
9 September	Rupture of 6 out of 16 tendons

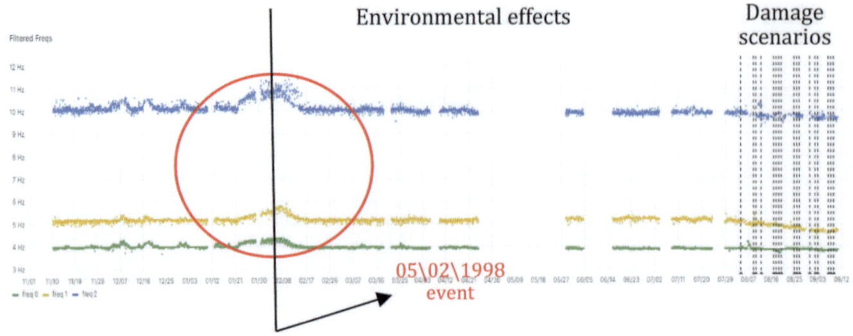

Fig. 6 Z24 bridge modal frequency evolution

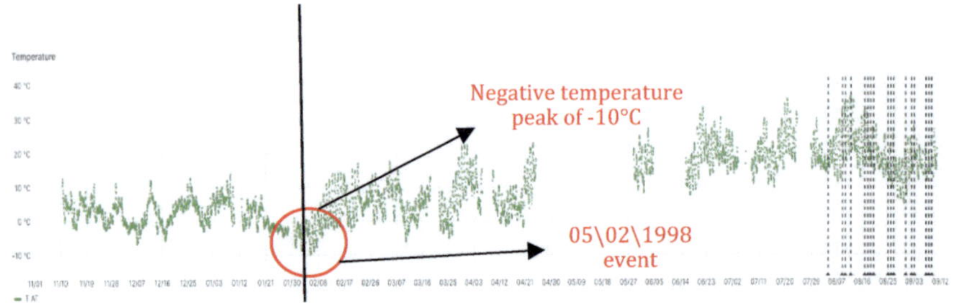

Fig. 7 Ambient temperature evolution

05, 1998, associated with a reversible increase in the natural frequencies due to this extreme event, as clearly shown in Fig. 7. During the progressive damage test scenarios, a gradual decrease in the modal frequencies was observed, which was expected owing to the correlation between the reduction in stiffness and damage. Nonetheless, it is interesting to observe structural changes during the ambient and damage scenarios.

4.2 Z24 Bridge Statistical Pattern Recognition

Figure 8 shows a classical damage-detection approach using Mahalanobis Distance (MD). MD is a statistical distance measure used to identify and analyze patterns. It calculates the difference between the baseline condition of a structure and each new set of the extracted indicators. In this case, the natural frequencies were used as damage indicators. The larger the MD, the more significant the difference between the training data (baseline condition) and the current structural condition. The MD values calculated using Eq. (7) consider X as a potential outlier, $\overline{X}$ as the mean, and [S] as the covariance matrix of the training data.

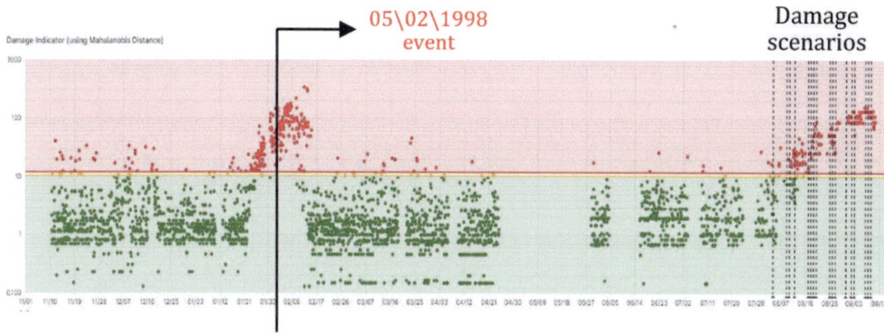

Fig. 8 Damage detection using Mahalanobis distance

$$\mathrm{MD} = \sqrt{(\{\overline{X} - \{X\})^T [S]^{-1} (X - \{\overline{X}\})} \tag{7}$$

In Fig. 8, one observes that the classical approach detected structural changes in January and February 1998 caused by thermal effects and structural changes caused by damage that started on August 10, 1998. It is noteworthy that this conventional approach, based on natural frequencies as damage indicators and a statistical distance to compare a baseline condition with a new dataset, can only indicate global structural changes. However, it does not provide information regarding the location of these changes. The following section presents the results and a preliminary discussion of an alternative approach to statistical pattern recognition based on an infodynamic analysis of the Z24 bridge structure.

4.3 Infodynamic Analysis

Infodynamics is not yet a well-established research field in engineering, and there is no consensus definition of this term (Salthe, 2001; Kåhre, 2002; Ceruti & Rubin, 2007; Dompere, 2018). In this work, one follows Salthe's insight of being a field studying the accumulation of informational constraints during system development because it considers possible limitations to the phase-space (not all imaginable configurations are feasible) and the evolution of information associated with the development of the system. Therefore, an infodynamic analysis of the Z24 bridge structure was performed.

Figure 9 shows the informature determined from the acceleration data collected from sensors 03, 05, 06, 07, 10, 12, 14, and 16.

From the analysis of the evolution of the informature of each sensor, there are different informature signatures but similar behavioral changes on relevant dates during the tests. Except for sensors 10 and 16, it was possible to observe a sudden informature peak from days 100 to 150, in line with the structural changes occurring in January and February 1998. These informature peaks mean that sensors measured

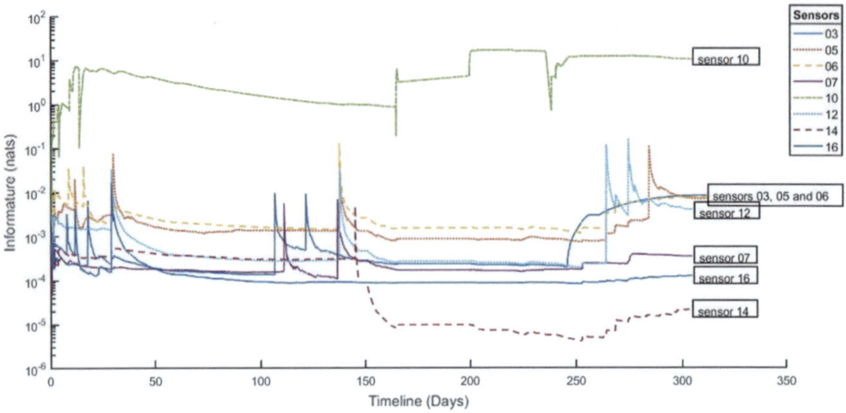

Fig. 9 Z24 bridge informature evolution

acceleration values that were different from the usual measurements. From day 250, sensors 03, 05, 06, and 12 exhibited informature changes, possibly indicating structural damage (damage scenarios started on day 260). The informature trend from day 250 of sensor 03 is interesting to observe, indicating a gradual increase in informature that implies a change in the distribution of the acceleration data. This means that the informature is adapted to the new distribution and updated with the new acceleration values caused by damage. It is also noteworthy that sensor 10 did not exhibit a relevant informature trend during the test duration.

5 Conclusions

This preliminary study of informational analysis applied to SHM data shows that the observation of informature determined from raw acceleration data collected from sensors can detect outliers that represent structural changes due to environmental or damage effects. The different informature signatures observed within the sensors installed on the Z24 bridge may indicate the ability of the proposed approach to detect local structural changes, which may indicate that informature measurements can reach level 2 of SHM (damage localization: information about the probable position of the damage). Further analysis is needed to differentiate structural changes from environmental or operational effects from damage effects. For this purpose, further clarification of the concept of entropy, combined with informature, might uncover correlations between time series (for instance, between acceleration and temperature data). Also, the informature signature may be a feature extracted directly from acceleration data, which, included in machine learning algorithms, could aid in predicting damage in real-time, enable localized damage identification, and establish new criteria for SHM.

The results show how the informature optimizes data flow from acquisition to decision-making, thereby enhancing SHM systems, including the one depicted in Fig. 2. In future work, further analysis is needed to explore the capabilities of informature in the following applications:

1. Explore the capability of the informature to optimize the location of the infosensors in the structure, avoid the installation of redundant infosensors, and reduce the costs of data acquisition.
2. Explore the incorporation of the informature damage detection capabilities directly into the infosensor to drastically reduce the volume of data and equally increase battery longevity, in which one may choose to transmit only the structural changes detected in the infosensor to the database.
3. Explore the capabilities and sensitivity of informature to distinguish structural changes due to environmental and operational effects from damage
4. Explore the agnosticism inherent to informature and test its capabilities in static and dynamic data to enhance the scalability of this new approach to SHM applications.

Finally, it is important to mention that one of the main obstacles to the global adoption of SHM systems is the cost of implementation. Data or Model-based approaches, using static or dynamic data, have produced reliable information for decision-making. However, the central question is how to extract the necessary information at the minimum possible cost. Benchmarking tests and data from progressive damage tests on bridges are essential for this purpose because they facilitate the implementation and comparison of different methodologies to develop a reliable damage detector (that mitigates false positives and false negatives).

As previously mentioned, the scientific community is making significant technological advancements in the field of damage detection in bridges and other critical infrastructures. The objective is to maximize damage identification by accurately predicting the remaining useful life (RUL) of structures. However, forecasting the RUL of bridges is a complex and challenging task that necessitates significant research effort and investment. Despite these challenges, implementing predictive maintenance processes could greatly enhance the industry's efficiency by providing greater certainty about the behavior of critical assets throughout their entire life cycle. Therefore, it is inevitable that the next steps of this study should follow this direction by exploring the potentialities of informature associated with the power of artificial intelligence and machine learning solutions. For example, the infodynamic analysis of benchmarking test data may reveal correlations between informature signature and structure degradation over time. In this case, one can explore an RUL prediction model based on the informature signature as a degradation feature and the improved temporal convolution network (TCN), as proposed by Wenting and Ye, (2024) to predict the RUL of an aero-engine. The validation of this approach could mark a significant advancement in the prediction of Remaining Useful Life (RUL) for bridges. However, given the extensive number of bridges worldwide, it poses both financial and technical challenges for authorities to install Structural Health

Monitoring (SHM) systems or to gather comprehensive datasets from each individual bridge. To address this issue, transfer learning (or knowledge transfer) can be employed for bridges that are structurally similar and widely replicated. This can be achieved through a feature-based transfer learning approach, where classifiers utilize labeled training data from one bridge (the source domain), such as the Z24 test data, along with unlabeled monitoring test data from another bridge (the target domain) that share similar structural characteristics (Yano et al., 2023).

Acknowledgements Z24 long-term monitoring data and short-term progressive damage test data have been used as benchmark information in various scientific studies focusing on system identification methods for modal analysis, data normalization methods for removing the influence of environmental variations on dynamic structural characteristics, and vibration-based damage identification methods (Ku Leuven, 2022). The Z24 data were collected as part of the Brite EuRam Programme BE-3157 SIMCES with financial support from the European Commission. The data were generously provided by the project coordinator, the Structural Mechanics Section of KU Leuven. The authors gratefully acknowledge the Brite EuRam Programme BE-3157 SIMCES, European Commission, and Structural Mechanics Section of KU Leuven for gathering and sharing data on the Z24 bridge.

The authors also thank the team members from the company Matereospace Lda, for their assistance and cooperation, regarding the Paso Real Bridge SHM system planning and implementation.

References

Ben-Naim, A. (2008). *Statistical Thermodynamics Based on Information*. World Scientific.

Candón, E., Crespo, A., Guillén, A., Gómez, J., & López, J. (2024). Asset digitalization strategy using IoT platforms and asset health model. *IFAC-PapersOnLine, 58*(8), 216–221. ISSN 2405-8963. https://doi.org/10.1016/j.ifacol.2024.08.123.

Ceruti, M. G., & Rubin S. H. (2007). Infodynamics: Analogical analysis of states of matter and information. *Information Sciences, 177*(4), 969–87.

Christodoulou, C. (2024). Structural health monitoring for intelligent asset management. *Proceedings of the Institution of Civil Engineers—Bridge Engineering 177*(2), 73–74. https://doi.org/10.1680/jbren.2024.177.2.73.

Crespo, A., Fernandez J., Martínez-Galán, P., & Lopez, A. (2024). Maintenance management through intelligent asset management platforms (IAMP). Emerging factors, key impact areas, and data models. *Energies, 13*, 3762. https://doi.org/10.3390/en13153762

Cui, S., Maghoul, P., Liang, X., Wu, N., & Wang Q. (2022) Structural fatigue crack localization based on spatially distributed entropy and wavelet transform. *Engineering Structures, 266*. https://doi.org/10.1016/j.engstruct.2022.114544.

Dompere, K. K. (2018). *The Theory of Info-Dynamics: Rational Foundations of Information-Knowledge Dynamics*. Springer International Publishing.

Farrar, C. R., Worden, K., & Park, G. (2010). *Complexity: A New Axiom for Structural Health Monitoring?* Los Alamos.

Figueiredo, E., Moldovan, I., Alves, P., Rebelo, H., & Souza, L. (2022). *Smartphone Application for Structural Health Monitoring of Bridges., 22*, 8483. https://doi.org/10.3390/s22218483

Figueiredo, E., Moldovan, I. (2023). *Short Course on Introduction to Structural Health Monitoring*. http://civilresearchgroup.ulusofona.pt

ISO (International Organization for Standardization) ISO 55000:2014 (en). (2014). *Asset Management—Overview, principles and terminology.* International Organization of Standardization, Geneva, Switzerland.

Kåhre, J. (2002). Infodynamics. In *The Mathematical Theory of Information.* The Springer International Series in Engineering and Computer Science, vol 684. Springer, Boston, MA. https://doi.org/10.1007/978-1-4615-0975-2_6.

Laflamme, S., Ubertini, F., Di Matteo, A., Pirrota, A., & Perry, M. (2023). Roadmap on measurement technologies for next generation structural health monitoring systems. *Measurement Science & Technology, 34*, Article 093001.

Leuven, K. (2022). *Z24 Bridge benchmark*. https://bwk.kuleuven.be/bwm/z24

Maeck, J., & De Roeck, G. (2003). Description of Z24 benchmark. *Mechanical Systems and Signal Processing, 17*(1), 127–131. https://doi.org/10.1006/mssp.2002.1548

Maeck, J., Peeters, B., & De Roeck, G. (2001). Damage identification on the Z24 bridge using vibration monitoring. *Smart Materials and Structures, 10*(3), 512–517. https://doi.org/10.1088/0964-1726/10/3/313

Meixedo, A., Santos, J., Ribeiro, D., Calçada, R., & Todd, M. (2021). Damage detection in railway bridges using traffic-induced dynamic responses. *Engineering Structures, 238.* https://doi.org/10.1016/j.engstruct.2021.112189.

Meixedo, A. (2021). *Damage identification in railway bridges based on train-induced dynamic responses.* PhD thesis, University of Porto. UP Library Repository. https://hdl.handle.net/10216/134156

Moreno-Gomez, A., Amezquita-Sanchez, J. P., Valtierra-Rodriguez, M., Perez-Ramirez, C. A., Dominguez-Gonzalez, A., & Chavez-Alegria, O. (2018). EMD-Shannon Entropy-Based methodology to detect incipient damages in a truss structure. *Applied Sciences Switzerland, 8*(11). https://doi.org/10.3390/app8112068.

Moughty, J.J., & Casas, J.R. (2017). Performance assessment of vibration parameters as damage indicators for bridge structures under ambient excitation. In *Procedia Engineering.* Elsevier Ltd, pp. 1970–1975. https://doi.org/10.1016/j.proeng.2017.09.306.

Namdari, A., & Li, A. (2019). A review of entropy measures for uncertainty quantification of stochastic processes. *Advances in Mechanical Engineering, 11*(6). https://doi.org/10.1177/1687814019857350.

Ren, W. X., & Sun, Z. S. (2018). Structural damage identification by using wavelet entropy. *Engineering Structures, 30*(10), 2840–2849. https://doi.org/10.1016/j.engstruct.2008.03.013

Rytter, A. (1993). *Vibrational Based Inspection of Civil Engineering Structures*, PhD Thesis, Aalborg University. Dept. of Building Technology and Structural Engineering, Aalborg University.

Salthe, S. N. (2001). What is Infodynamics? In U. Complexity (Ed.), *Aug 31* (pp. 31–38). Springer, US.

Selvakumaran S., Sadeghi Z., Collings M., Rossi, C., Wright, T., & Hooper, A. (2022). Comparison of in situ and interferometric synthetic aperture radar monitoring to assess bridge thermal expansion. In *Proceedings of the Institution of Civil Engineers—Smart Infrastructure and Construction.* ICE Publishing.

Shannon, C. E. (1948). A mathematical theory of communication. *The Bell System Technical Journal, 27*(3), 379–423.

Tomé, E. (2019). *Smart structural health monitoring applied to management and conservation of bridges.* PhD thesis, University of Porto. UP Library Repository. https://hdl.handle.net/10216/121877

Vijay Sanker, S., Ramya Sri Bilakanti, N.B., Thomas, A., Gopi, V.P., & Palanisamy P. (2022). Emotion-recognition-based music therapy system using electroencephalography signals. In *Edge-of-Things in Personalized Healthcare Support Systems.* Elsevier, pp. 217–235. https://doi.org/10.1016/B978-0-323-90585-5.00009-6

Wenting, Z., & Ye, Y. (2024). An aero-engine remaining useful life prediction model based on feature selection and the improved TCN. *Franklin Open, 6*, Article 100083.

Yang, Z., Chen, X., Jiang, Y., & He, Z. (2014). Generalised local entropy analysis for crack detection in beam-like structures. *Nondestructive Testing and Evaluation.*

Yano, M., Figueiredo, E., Silva, S., & Cury, A. (2023). Foundations and applicability of transfer learning for structural health monitoring of bridges. *Mechanical Systems and Signal Processing, 204*, 110766. ISSN 0888-3270. https://doi.org/10.1016/j.ymssp.2023.110766.

Early Failure Detection in Secondary Cryogenic Pumps Through Machine Learning Techniques in the Context of Industry 4.0

Sonia Liñán García, Antonio de la Fuente Carmona, Javier Serra Parajes, and Adolfo Crespo Márquez

Abstract The paper presents a new approach to Asset Management that utilizes Industry 4.0 techniques and Artificial Intelligence (AI), specifically Machine Learning (ML). The research emphasizes early anomaly detection and failure mode classification in operating equipment in dynamic ranges. The study is based on the secondary cryogenic pumps of a Liquefied Natural Gas (LNG) regasification plant, which operate in a highly dynamic environment with rapid changes in pressure. Traditional condition monitoring methods, which rely on monitoring operational parameters and physical measurements, are contrasted with the proposed ML-based approach. ML models aim to detect early-stage issues and forecast critical failures by exploiting complex and nonlinear relationships among multiple operational variables. For the study, six years of historical data gathered by the different sensors of the 4 pumps have been used.

Keywords Artificial intelligence · Failure mode classification · Cryogenic equipment · Prognosis · Diagnosis

S. Liñán García (✉) · J. Serra Parajes
Enagás S.A., Madrid, Spain
e-mail: aslinan@enagas.es

J. Serra Parajes
e-mail: jserra@enagas.es

A. de la Fuente Carmona · A. Crespo Márquez
Department of Industrial Management, Universidad de Seville, Seville, Spain
e-mail: antoniodela84@gmail.com

A. Crespo Márquez
e-mail: adolfo@us.es

A. Crespo Márquez et al. (eds.), *Case Studies in Digital Transformation*, Engineering Asset Management Review 4, https://doi.org/10.1007/978-3-032-05592-7_12

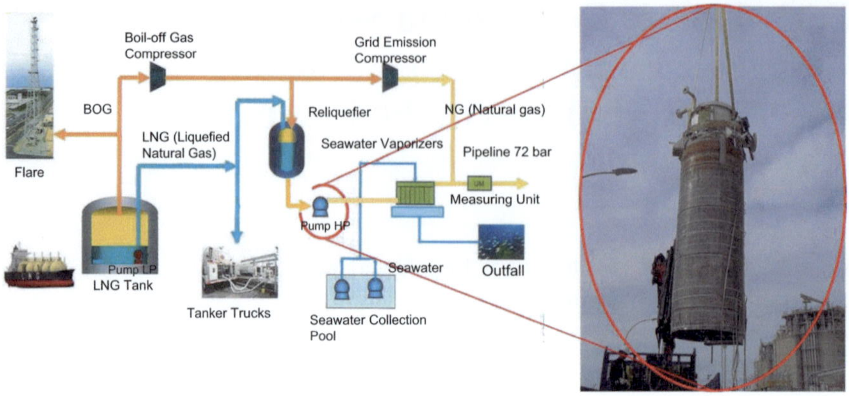

Fig. 1 LNG regasification process

1 Introduction

Enagás is a leading Spanish company in natural gas (NG) transportation, contributing to the development of the Spanish Gas System, recognized for its safety and diversified supply. The company faces the challenge of ensuring the proper operation of all its assets, including secondary pumps, essential for the regasification process of LNG, which operate in cryogenic conditions, adding complexity and risk of failures (Fig. 1). Therefore, it is important to monitor their operation regularly to detect possible anomalies (Collart et al., 2022).

The purpose of this research is to develop a tool that can identify secondary pumps with anomalous operation before incidents occur (Dutta et al., 2021). Additionally, the study aims to address key questions about the parameters and patterns associated with the normal operation of these pumps.

However, the study has limitations due to the fact that it was conducted on a limited number of Enagás pumps, which may affect the generalization of the results to all cryogenic secondary pumps. Additionally, the study is focused on a limited number of operating parameters, there is the possibility that there are other unidentified normal patterns (Fuente et al., 2020).

2 Literature Review

The study at Enagás focuses to enhance the efficiency and predictive maintenance of cryogenic pumps using advanced ML and deep learning (DL) techniques within the industry 4.0 framework. This involves real-time data collection and analysis from Enagás' SCADA system to identify patterns and anomalies, predicting failures and improving preventive maintenance. Recent research highlights the effectiveness of transfer learning and meta-learning models in improving anomaly detection accuracy in cryogenic pumps, offering faster and more efficient solutions (Fengqian et al., 2022).

Cryogenic pumps are crucial in the LNG industry due to their ability to handle fluids at extremely low temperatures. The literature emphasizes their specialized design and the challenges in their operation and maintenance, particularly the importance of reliability and energy efficiency (Cui et al., 2024). Significant challenges in maintaining cryogenic pumps include mechanical wear and adverse operating conditions, which affect performance and longevity (Adumene et al., 2023). Energy efficiency is also critical, as optimal design and operation can lead to significant energy savings.

The SCADA system at Enagás provides a robust platform for real-time data collection from cryogenic pumps, including variables such as pressure, temperature, flow, and vibration, which are crucial for predictive analysis. Integrating SCADA data with ML techniques enhances early fault detection and reduces downtime (Ehu, 2021; Fernandes et al., 2022).

DL techniques, such as Convolutional Neural Networks (CNNs) and Recurrent Neural Networks (RNNs), have shown promising results in fault prediction for cryogenic pumps by analyzing time series data and identifying complex patterns (Hewamalage et al., 2020; Zhang & Li, 2021). These techniques improve early fault detection and optimize predictive maintenance.

Viswanathan et al. (2023) suggest that ML-based anomaly detection can enhance industrial pumps, including cryogenic ones, by identifying issues early. Studies comparing ML techniques for fault prediction in LNG pumps at regasification plants show these models outperform traditional methods in accuracy and efficiency.

Moreover, Implementing ML models for the predictive maintenance of cryogenic pumps can help reduce operational and maintenance costs, improve energy efficiency, and extend equipment lifespan. This is primarily due to these models' ability to identify failures before they become critical issues, thereby avoiding unplanned downtime and costly maintenance interventions (Achouch et al., 2022).

Finally, tools like RapidMiner (RM) have also been identified as essential for applying ML and real-time data analysis due to their ease of use, versatility, and ability to integrate with SCADA systems (Apriade, 2023).

3 Methodology

The methodology employed in the study comprises two major blocks, each designed to address specific aspects of the analysis of Enagás' secondary pumps:

Data Preprocessing:

- Historical operation data of the pumps are collected over a 6-year period, from 2013 to 2020, with a data extraction granularity of one minute.
- This data is sourced from sensors located on the pumps and stored in the PI osisoft (PI) software.

- It is complemented with information on the maintenance history and redesigns of each equipment, vital for determining suitable periods for model training and interpreting production results.

Comparison and Selection of ML Models:

- The RM tool is utilized, previously proven in similar studies, for its versatility and ease of use.
- Different ML models are explored to select the most suitable for the analysis of the secondary pumps' data.

The methodology used in the study consists of three main blocks. The RM tool is used, which has been previously tested in similar studies for its versatility and ease of use (Apriade, 2023).

3.1 Data Processing

The data processing begins with the consolidation of historical PI files to form a coherent and complete database. This data ingestion is carried out using RM Studio.

Files are grouped together; missing data and outliers are removed. The operational signals collected from PI are:

- Date [dd.mm.aaaa hh:mm:ss]
- Flow rate
- Aspiration Temp
- Discharge Temp
- Operating state
- Operating hours since the last major maintenance
- Total operating hours
- Intensity
- Power
- Aspiration Pressure
- Discharge Pressure
- Pot Level
- Performance
- Number of stars

The process of extraction, chronological sorting, and storage is carried out with the assistance of RM, thus generating a unique database covering the period from 2013 to 2020, with approximately 4 million records.

Data Cleansing involves removing lines without information for any of the signals and identifying and eliminating outliers using boxplot representation and the interquartile range. For instance, in the case of discharge Tª, the lower and upper limits are calculated based on the interquartile range, and any outliers beyond these limits are removed from the study (Fig. 2).

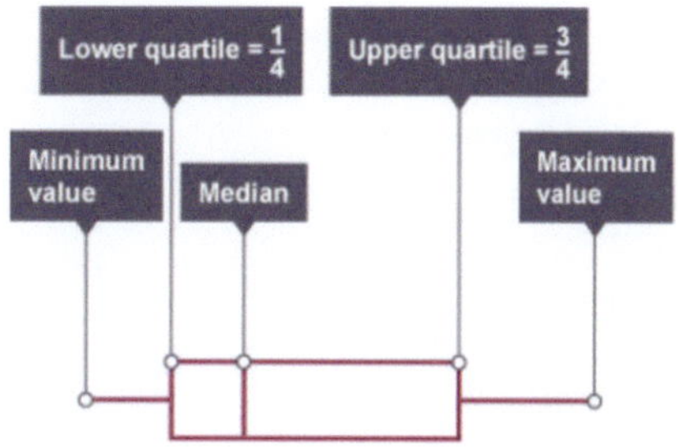

Fig. 2 Interpretation of the box plot representation

Example: Discharge Temp

Thus, the outliers for the Discharge Tª would be:

- Lower Q1: -128,54°C –(**1,5** × L) = **< -149,50°C**
- Uper Q3: -114,57 + (**1,5** × L) = **> -93,62°C**

3.1.1 Study of Variable Correlation

In the selection of variables to obtain a consistent model that replicates the normal behavior of secondary cryogenic pumps and detects anomalies, a study of the correlation matrix is conducted. Since these pumps are rotating equipment with constant operation, the goal is to identify representative variables capable of discriminating different behaviors based on condition or operating modes.

The correlation matrix is obtained using RM, and variables with 100% correlation with power are discarded.

In the resulting correlation table, variables with less than 100% correlation with power are identified as candidates for the consumed power prediction model (Table 1).

In the following figure (figure 3), the correlation of variables with the pump's point power is ordered from smallest to largest.

These variables are:

- Discharge Pressure
- Pot Level
- Discharge Tª
- Aspiration Tª
- Aspiration Pressure
- Start count → It is excluded due to the lack of information regarding this variable in many cases.
- Power

The consumed power variable will be used as the target variable because it is closely correlated with flow rate, current, and discharge pressure, which accurately

Table 1 Correlation matrix

Attributes	Flow rate	Aspiration Tª	Discharge Tª	Current	Power	Discharge pressure	Pot level	Start count	Aspiration pressure
Flow rate	1	– 0.258	– 0.277	0.996	0.997	0.985	0.970	– 0.076	0.248
Aspiration Tª	– 0.258	1	0.986	– 0.222	– 0.220	– 0.334	– 0.923	0.278	– 0.911
Discharge Tª	– 0.277	0.986	1	– 0.239	– 0.239	– 0.349	– 0.928	0.252	– 0.892
Current	0.996	– 0.222	– 0.239	1	1.000	0.987	0.970	– 0.058	0.205
Power	0.997	– 0.220	– – 0.239	1.000	1	0.990	0.975	– 0.012	0.202
Discharge pressure	0.985	– 0.334	– 0.349	0.987	0.990	1	0.975	– 0.099	0.325
Pot level	0.970	– 0.923	– 0.928	0.970	0.975	0.975	1	– 0.209	0.847
Start count	1	– 0.258	– 0.277	0.996	0.997	0.985	0.970	– – 0.076	0.248
Aspiration pressure	– 0.258	1	0.986	– 0.222	– 0.220	– 0.334	– 0.923	0.278	– 0.911

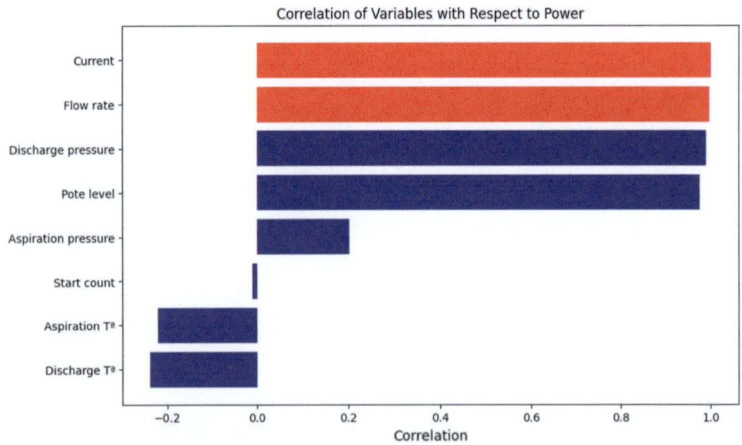

Fig. 3 Graphical representation of the correlation of variables with the pump's consumed power

represent the behavior of the operating conditions. As such, it provides a simplified representation of the pump's performance. This approach helps reduce multicollinearity, enhancing the robustness and generalization of the model by avoiding redundancies.

This technique of using power as a target variable in predictive maintenance is commonly applied in the industry due to its strong relationship with other key operational metrics (Zhang & Wang, 2021).

3.2 *Comparison and Selection of ML Models*

To compare models in RM the steps to follow are: Upload the training data, select the input variables, select the variable to predict, select the algorithms to compare and run and analyze the results.

3.2.1 Comparison of ML Algorithms

To compare ML algorithms in predicting the power consumed in secondary cryogenic pumps, RM's Automodel option is used. The algorithms evaluated include Generalized Linear Model, DL, Decision Tree, and Random Forest.

Linear models, such as the Generalized Linear Model (GLM), are known for their simplicity and computational efficiency. These models assume a linear relationship between the input variables and the target variable, making them highly interpretable and quick to train. However, their ability to capture complex relationships in the data is limited, which can result in suboptimal performance in problems where the relationships are nonlinear (Dalatu et al., 2016). Nonlinear models, such as DL and Random Forest, are capable of capturing complex and nonlinear patterns in the data; they can handle more intricate relationships between variables (Giudici et al., 2024).

The results of the comparison*, RM's Automodel, are presented in Table 2. It is observed that the best performance is achieved with the Random Forest and Deep Leaning** models, which have a time-efficient performance.

Table 2 Results of the comparison of the different algorithms

Model	Correlation	Standard desviation	Total time	Training time	scoring time
Generalized linear model	0.998	±0	3 s	2 ms	1 ms
Deep learning	0.999	±0.001	1 min 14 s	495 ms	18 ms
Decision tree	0.999	±0.001	8 s	2 ms	1 ms
Random forest	1	±0	1 min 11 s	110 ms	89 ms

* RM's Automodel uses cross-validation to evaluate the model's accuracy. This process is repeated multiple times, and the results are averaged to obtain a robust estimate of the model's performance. It compares the models using various performance metrics, such as mean squared error (MSE), mean absolute error (MAE), and the coefficient of determination (R^2)

** En RM, Deep Learning is based on a multi-layer feed-forward artificial neural network that is trained with stochastic gradient descent using backpropagation

The choice of model is based on a balance between precision, efficiency, and complexity of the problem. Although Random Forest excels in correlation between real power and prediction power and efficiency, the DL model is chosen due to its high correlation, consistency, ability to capture complex patterns, and its potential for improvement with additional data. The original and more simplified variant of RNNs is chosen (LeCun et al., 2015).

3.2.2 Comparing Different Variants of the RNNs Algorithm

The next step consists of a more detailed study of the different variants of the RNN model, for this, different alternatives will be designed and compared to use the most powerful and most accurate in the study.

A custom-tailored process is designed for the secondary pumps, with the purpose of training the model using a portion of the dataset and subsequently deploying it in production with another dataset before the failure recorded in the Maintenance Management System (MMS). However, this is detailed in the following section.

Now the study is focused on analyzing which configuration of the RNN algorithm is most suitable for this use case.

For the initial model, the standard configuration of RM is chosen, and the remaining models will be variations where the hidden layers and neurons are modified. Some notable configurations include RN-7–5-1, RN-7–8-1, RN-7–8-4–1, and RN-7–5-2–1.

Metrics such as Root Mean Square Error (RMSE), t penalizes larger errors more heavily due to the squaring of errors before averaging; Mean Absolute Error (MAE), this makes it more interpretable as it reflects the average prediction error in a linear fashion; Relative Root Mean Square Error (R-RMSE), expresses the error as a percentage of the actual value, providing a relative view of the error concerning the actual values; and Correlation, measures the strength and direction of the relationship between the model predictions and the actual values. A value closer to 0 suggests no linear relationship between them. This are employed to evaluate the models.

Formula RMSE: $\sqrt{\frac{1}{n}\sum_{i=i}^{n}(y_i - \hat{y}_i)^2}$ Where y_i is the actual value and $\hat{y}_i$ is the predicted value.

Formula MAE: $\frac{1}{n}\sum_{i=i}^{n}|y_i - \hat{y}_i|$ Where y_i is the actual value and $\hat{y}_i$ is the predicted value.

Formula MER: $\frac{1}{n}\sum_{i=i}^{n}\frac{|y_i - \hat{y}_i|}{y_i} \times 100$.

Correlation (R): $\frac{\sum((y_i - \hat{y}_i)\cdot\hat{y}_i - \bar{\hat{y}})}{\sqrt{\sum(y_i - \hat{y}_i)^2 \cdot \sum(\hat{y}_i - \bar{\hat{y}})^2}}$ Where $\overline{y}$ and $\bar{\hat{y}}$ are the means of the actual and predicted values, respectively.

The results are presented in Table 3:

The RMSE is the most appropriate metric for selecting the best model, as it penalizes larger errors, which is crucial in systems where minimizing prediction failures is essential. The RN- 7-5-1 model provides a good balance between simplicity, low

Table 3 Comparing results of different neural network architectures for secondary pumps

Model	RMSE	MAE	MER	Correlation
RN (7- 5–1) default	6.236	4.727 ± 4.067	0.52% ± 0.45%	0.994
RN (7–8-1)	6.337	4.853 ± 4.075	0.53% ± 0.45%	0.994
RN (7–8-4–1)	6.32	4.811 ± 4.098	0.53% ± 0.45%	0.993
RN (7–5-2–1)	6.137	4.719 ± 3.923	0.52% ± 0.43%	0.994
Deep learning	7.247	5.821 ± 4.315	0.69% ± 0.94%	0.994

error (as indicated by RMSE and MAE), and high correlation, making it the best option. It is decided to continue the study with a neural network having an input layer with 7 neurons, a hidden layer with 5 neurons, and an output layer with 1 neuron, architecture RN-7-5-1, although performance metrics indicate that the RN-7-5-2-1 model would be the best, this model adds complexity to the architecture and increases computational cost, which is considered not to provide a differentiating value to the result (Hodson, 2022).

The chosen neural network architecture for further study consists of the following layers:

- Input layer: 7 neurons, which receive input data corresponding to the number of features.
- Hidden layers: These layers, located between the input and output layers, extract relevant features from the input data. In deep neural networks, there can be multiple hidden layers, each composed of neurons.
- Output layer: 1 neuron, responsible for producing the final model output (Power).

This architecture, denoted as RN-7-5-1, strikes a balance between simplicity, computational efficiency (due to fewer neurons), and the ability to learn complex patterns while controlling model complexity through regularization.

4 Model Training and Validation

A custom-tailored process is designed for the secondary pumps.

This process involves data preparation to validate, train, and test the RNN model with the RN- 7–5-1 architecture in two distinct contexts: before and after failure. The temporal subdivision and the validation and testing approach allowed for the evaluation of the model's performance under simulated conditions (before failure) and on future data (both before and after failure), enhancing the model's generalization capability (Crespo et al., 2024).

Different scenarios were defined according to the operational phases of a secondary pump, from startup to the end of its operational life. Five specific scenarios were identified:

- **Equipment started up after a new installation or following major maintenance (E0):** corresponds to the initial hours of operation, during which the equipment is expected to undergo a running-in period to assess its performance. This scenario varies depending on each manufacturer and equipment; in this case, it is considered to be the first 200–300 h of operation.
- **Equipment as new scenario (E1):** corresponds to the initial hours of operation of the equipment following major maintenance or replacement, approximately constituting 20% of the equipment's total lifespan, around 3,500–4,000 first hours of operation.
- **Normal operation scenario of the equipment (E2**): corresponds to the majority of the equipment's lifespan, between 20 and 80% of the time since startup, i.e., between 4,000 and 16,000 h of operation.
- **End-of-life operation scenario (E3):** corresponds to the final period, from 80% of the equipment's lifespan until the next major maintenance.
- **Pre-failure operation scenario (E4):** this less common scenario in equipment corresponds to the period before failure, which will depend on each equipment and each failure mode. To analyze the behavior, a temporal window of 3,000 h of operation prior to the failure will be used.

The following figure (Fig. 4) depicts a representation of the temporal evolution of the operating hours of a secondary pump, the percentages of time over the total lifespan, the different time periods, and the identification of the scenarios.

From scenario E1, information is obtained regarding how far the pump's consumption or performance is from ideal behavior. With this idea, this information can be used to assign different risk levels to the different scenarios, as will be seen later. A scenario exhibiting behavior deviating more significantly from the optimal is deemed to possess a higher risk profile (Marti-Puig et al., 2021).

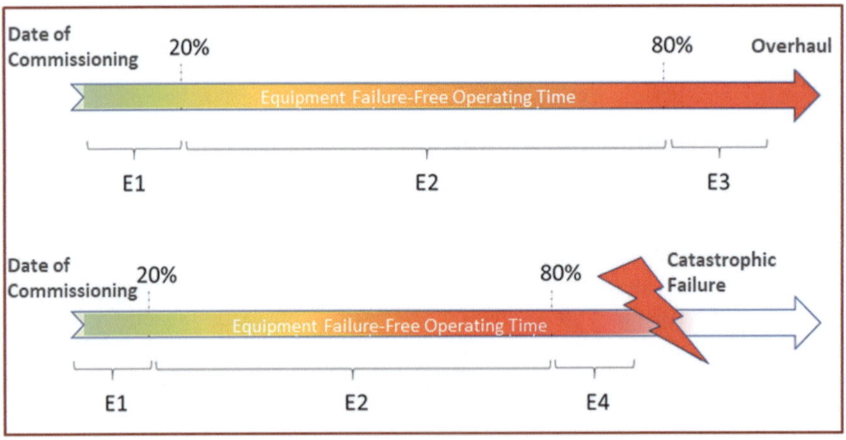

Fig. 4 Scenarios for the study of behavior patterns with a ML model

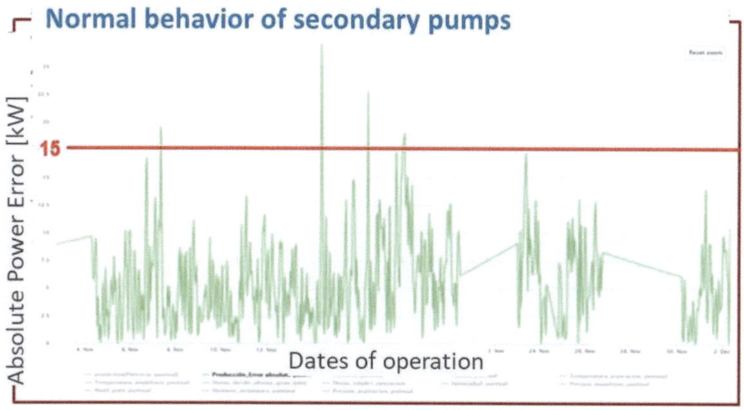

Graph 1 Absolute error plot of a faultless pump over a specified time period

In our analysis, the GA-115-H pump from Huelva is a pump that has not experienced any failures. Specifically, it has passed through scenario E1 and remains in scenario E2.

For this pump, **with no detected failure mode**, the Absolute Power Error (EA) [kW] **is less than 15 kW, and the mean value is 5 kW ± 5 kW** (Graph 1).

A new variable is generated, ***Absolute Power Error (AE) [kW]***, which is nothing more than the absolute difference between the actual Power and the Power Prediction at each time instant. This variable will give an idea of how far or close the pump's consumption is from the consumption when it is in a "like-new" state, corresponding to what it would have in an E1 scenario. The characteristic AE of a pump in the different scenarios is:

- **Scenario E1:** The **AE** should be minimal, characterized by having an average value distribution equal to 5 kW ± 5 kW, and **less than 15 kW**.
- **Scenario E2:** AE behavior similar to E1, where high values will not appear until reaching the end of E2, due to the aging of the pump or premature deterioration.
- **Scenario E3:** The AE begins to accumulate operating hours at higher values, but in a smoothed and sustained manner.
- **Scenario E4:** The AE frequently spikes, in an exponential manner.

5 Results Analysis (Prognosis)

5.1 Application to the P-2003-A Secondary Pump, in Barcelona, in Scenarios E2, E3 and E4

From the historical data available for this pump, it is known that a major maintenance was performed, and an inverter was also installed. Shortly after, the failure occurred.

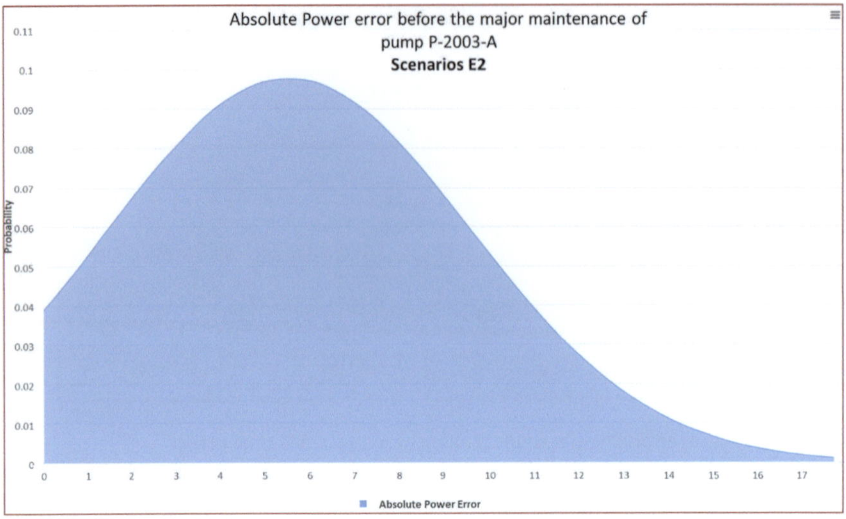

Graph 2 Distribution plot of the Absolute Power Error behavior before the inverter installation and major maintenance with 21,099 h of operation

The previous process from Fig. 6 is executed, and the behavior of the new AE variable is observed before and after the inverter installation.

Graph 2 shows the behavior of the Absolute Error (AE) of the power before the inverter installation and the major maintenance with 21,099 h of operation.

The mean value of AE before the major maintenance is 5.5 kW ± 4 kW with a maximum of 27.1 kW.

Graph 3 shows the behavior of the Absolute Power Error just before the failure on May 8, but after the major maintenance, with 888 h of operation and 12 starts (E3 and E4).

maintenance

The mean value of AE before the failure, but after the major maintenance, is 12.5 kW ± 12.9 kW with a maximum of 85.1 kW.

It is clearly observed that the Absolute Error behavior before the major maintenance is completely different from before the failure. Before the failure, more minutes accumulate at higher absolute error values, as reflected in the distribution plots of the Absolute Error (Figs. 52 and 53).

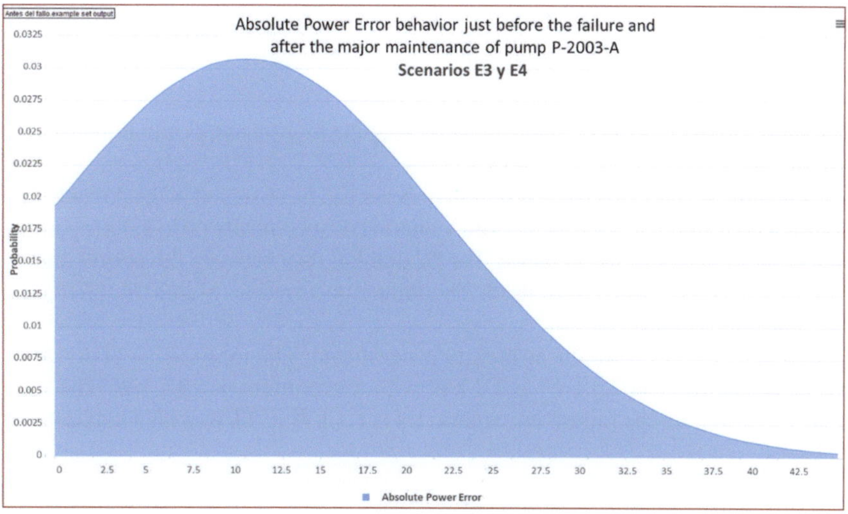

Graph 3 Distribution plot of the Absolute Power Error behavior just before the failure and after the major

5.2 *Application to the P-2003-B Secondary Pump, in Barcelona, in Scenarios E2 Y E4*

From the historical data available for this pump, it is known that the pump degraded until the major maintenance was performed, after which the failure occurred.

The training was conducted with data available from the period ranging from 13,000 to 15,500 operating hours. The E4 corresponds to the hours leading up to the failure, which occurred before the major maintenance was carried out.

Similar to the previous case, different patterns can be observed in the AE behavior. For E2, the data between the period from 15,700 to 16,200 operating hours were used. Meanwhile, for E4, the data between the period from 16,200 up to the failure were used. The failure occurred on February 18th with 16,837 operating hours and 234 starts.

In this pump, the differences are not as significant as in the previous case. The mean value of AE at the end of the E2 scenario is 7.1 kW $\pm$ 5 kW with a maximum of 25.4 kW. The mean value of AE before the failure, in the E4 scenario, is 7.6 kW $\pm$ 6.2 kW with a maximum of 39.8.

5.3 Application to the GA-115-I Secondary Pump, in Huelva, in Scenarios E1, E2 Y E4

The study of the pump was conducted in three of the four scenarios mentioned earlier, specifically, scenarios E1, E2, and E4.

Similar to the previous case, different patterns can be observed in the AE behavior. Training was conducted with data from scenario E1, specifically up to 2,000 operating hours, after the major maintenance. For E2 and E4, data between the period ranging from 2,300 to the failure were used. The failure occurred on March 14, 2016, with 7,605 operating hours.

In this pump, the differences are quite significant. The mean value of AE at the end of scenario E1 is 2.9 kW ± 2.7 kW with a maximum of 29.7 kW. The mean value of AE before the failure in scenario E4 is 8.4 kW ± 7 kW with a maximum of 139 kW.

5.4 Application to the GA-115-I Secondary Pump, in Huelva, in Scenarios E1 Y E2

The study of the pump was conducted in two of the four scenarios mentioned earlier, specifically, scenarios E1 and E2.

The GA-115-H pump is a case very similar to the previous one (GA-115-I). However, unlike the GA-115-I pump, the GA-115-H pump has not experienced any failures up to the date of the study in 2022.

Unlike the previous pumps, the accumulation of minutes at higher values is less pronounced, with AE values of smaller magnitude than in the previous cases.

Similar to the previous case, different patterns can be observed among them. Training was conducted with data from scenario E1, with approximately 3,500 operating hours. For E2, data were used from around 3,500 to 10,000 operating hours.

In this pump, the differences are not as noticeable. The mean value of AE at the end of scenario E1 is 2.56 kW ± 2.4 kW with a maximum of 60 kW. The mean value of AE during scenario E2 is.

1. 1 kW ± 5 kW with a maximum of 106 kW.

Table 4 summarizes the results of the Absolute Error (AE) of power in different scenarios and situations of the pumps, providing a comparative view of their performance under various conditions.

For faulty pumps, in scenario E2, the probability distribution concentrates around 5.5 kW, with a very sharp-shaped distribution; reaching maximum values of just over 17 kW.

Table 4 Results of the Absolute Error (AE) of power in different scenarios and situations of the pumps

Pump	E1 (kW)	E2 (kW)	E4 (kW)	Situation
P-2003-A		5,5 ± 4	12,5 ± 12,9	Failure Post-Overhaul
P-2003-B		7,1 ± 5	7,6 ± 6,2	Failure Pre-Overhaul, in End-of-Life Failure
GA-115-I	2,9 ± 2,7		8,4 ± 7	Failure Pre-Overhaul
GA-115-H	2,6 ± 2,4	6,1 ± 5		No Failure

In scenario E4, the probability distribution centers around 12.5 kW, and the distribution is already quite flat, reaching considerably higher values, close to 45 kW (Graph 4).

The variability, after overhaul (E2) and before failure (E4), along with the highest values of absolute error (kW), suggest potential operational issues. This pattern could serve as an early indicator of failures, emphasizing the importance of continuous monitoring and analysis for anomaly detection.

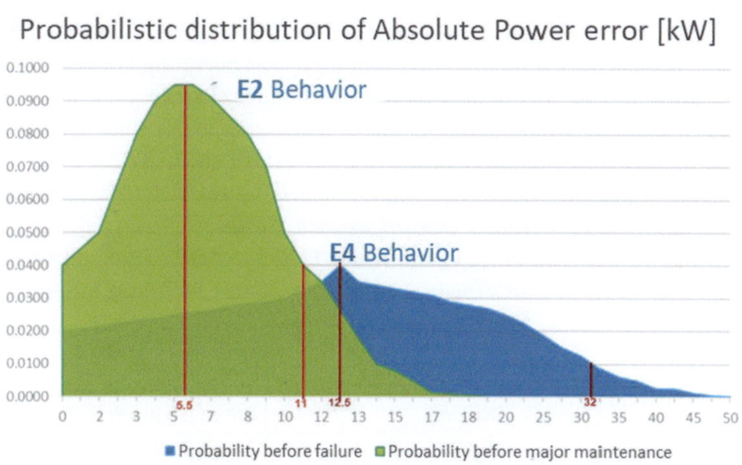

Graph 4 Probability distribution of the absolute power error (kW), in scenario E2 and just before failure (E4)

6 Definition of the Classification Model Based on Risk Levels (Diagnosis)

6.1 Definition and Analysis of Risk Levels

In this section, we commence with the risk analysis for each of the previously identified scenarios.

To enhance the precision of the analysis and to enable a comparative assessment of different equipment across various scenarios, we employ the descriptor **Cumulative Operating Time** at risk level i (TRi), where i ranges from 0 to 6. Each level of the descriptor corresponds to a distinct risk level for the occurrence of a failure mode. As the accumulation of operating hours increases at higher risk levels (3, 4, 5, and 6), the likelihood of pump failure also escalates. In this instance, it is not feasible to provide a failure probability value associated with each risk level; a statistical study involving a larger number of equipment failures prior to major maintenance would be required (González et al., 2023; Chelmiah et al., 2022).

Table 5 defines these TRi descriptors based on the Absolute Error (AE) of power:

Furthermore, for each of the use cases, an analysis of the percentage of operating time at each risk level, TRi, is also conducted.

Graph 5 depicts the evolution of the various TRi as operating hours accumulate.

It is noteworthy that, in pumps experiencing failures (P-2003-A, P-2003-B, GA-115-I), the accumulation of operating time at higher risk levels is more pronounced compared to the pump without failures (GA-115-H) (Li et al., 2022).

Table 6 quantitatively compares the accumulated time at each risk level (TRi) and the percentage of total operation time for the four pumps.

The objective of this phase is to define and model a classification algorithm that allows for the establishment of action recommendations based on the state of the failure mode.

Table 5 Definition of TRi descriptors

TRi level	Range AE in kW
TR0*	$AE < 15$
TR1	$15 \leq AE < 20$
TR2	$20 \leq AE < 25$
TR3	$25 \leq AE < 30$
TR4	$30 \leq AE < 35$
TR5	$35 \leq AE < 40$
TR6	$45 < AE$

* For TR0, the 15 kW limit is chosen based on observations of the neural network behavior in fault-free pumps, increasing by 5 kW increments according to the average value of such pumps

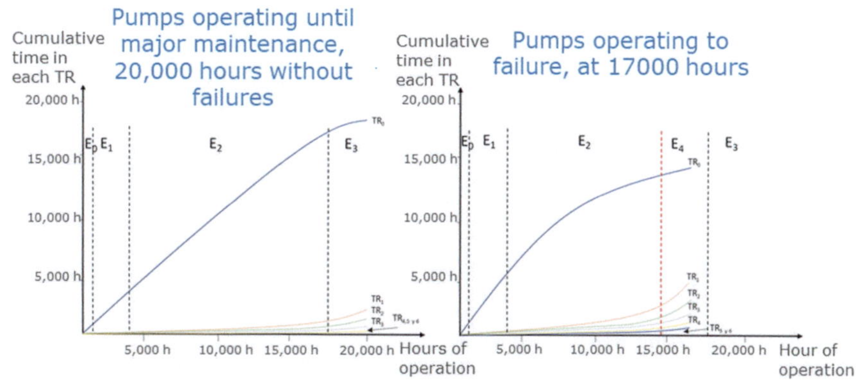

Graph 5 Analysis of TRi levels for pumps P-2003-A (left) and P-2003-B (right)

Table 6 Comparative analysis of accumulated time percentages at each risk level TRi

	TR_0 (%)	TR_1 (%)	TR_2 (%)	TR_3 (%)	TR_4 (%)	TR_5 (%)	TR_6 (%)
PA-2003A	73.39	11.95	5.86	3.16	0.68	0.79	4.17
PA-2003B	69.22	18.06	8.08	2.84	1.55	0.09	0.17
GA-115I	84.73	7.63	4.36	2.14	0.81	0.25	0.09
GA-115H	94.46	3.65	0.92	0.61	0.30	0.04	0.02

A classification algorithm is defined, and training and validation are conducted using the RM class prediction tool.

The following three Class are defined:

- **Class 1:** Corresponds to a failure mode of a piece of equipment that has not yet begun to manifest, thus it can be considered that there is no failure mode detectable through the prediction of the power consumed by the pump. In this case, all operating minutes are accumulated in TR0, TR1, and TR2.
- **Class 2:** Corresponds to a latent failure mode that begins to manifest, detectable by the prediction of consumed power. It is assumed that this rule applies for an accumulation of more than 10 consecutive minutes of operation at risk level TR3.
- **Class 3:** Corresponds to the final stage of the asset before failure, when it has been confirmed that the equipment exhibits behavior deviating from normal, verified through condition inspections, such as vibration measurements, performance tests, etc.

Table 7 represents the accumulated % of time in each of the following classes: Class 1 (no failure mode), Class 2 (latent failure mode), and Class 3 (existing failure mode).

In this table, it's evident that for the fault-free pump, the accumulated % of time in high-risk values doesn't exceed 0.5% (GA-115-H; 0.36%). However, for

Table 7 Cumulative percentage of time in each class

Classification	C1 (%)	C2 (%)	C3 (%)
PA-2003A	91.20	3.16	5.64
PA-2003B	95.36	2.84	1.81
GA-115I	96.72	2.14	1.15
GA-115H	99.03	0.61	0.36

faulty pumps, it already surpasses 1%, with some pumps exceeding 5% (PA-2003-A: 5.64%).

At this point, using RM's Auto Model class prediction tool.

Table 8 presents a comparison of class prediction models, highlighting that the algorithms with the least error are Gradient Boosted Tress, DL, Decision Tree, and Random Forest. Based on the results, the Decision Tree algorithm is the most practical option. Compared to other algorithms, it stands out for its efficiency in processing time (training, evaluation, and total). It is a simple and easily interpretable model. Regarding classification error, or accuracy, its error rate is quite low (5.4%) and minimal compared to the most accurate algorithm, Gradient Boosted Tress (4.4%).

The results suggest distinctive patterns in pumps experiencing failures; one of these observed patterns is that the pumps operated under more severe conditions before failing, accumulating more operating time at higher risk levels.

Table 8 Results of the comparison of class prediction models

Model	Classification error (%)	Standard deviation (%)	Gains	Total time	Training time (1,000 Rows) (ms)	Scoring time (1,000 Rows) (ms)
Naive Bayes	6.6	±0.0	9,384	35 s	4	283 ms
Generalized linear model	12.9	±0.1	− 2,504	1 min 54 s	153	310 ms
Logistic regression	11.5	±2.0	0	1 min 18 s	33	536 ms
Fast large margin	11.5	±0.0	2	1 h 5 min 58 s	734	556 ms
Deep learning	5.4	±0.0	8,822	2 min 3 s	256	355 ms
Decision tree	5.4	±0.0	8,710	30 s	9	248 ms
Random forest	5.5	±0.1	2,136	2 min 49 s	42	613 ms
Gradient boosted trees	4.4	±0.0	2,538	3 min 49 s	209	1 s
Support vector machine	10.6	±0.2	84	46 min 7 s	492	1 s

7 Recommendations for Operation and Maintenance

The objective of this phase is to define action recommendations based on the state of the failure mode.

Figure 5 represents a proposal for event and action planning based on the equipment's condition, prediction algorithms, and classification algorithms.

Events can be of two types: detection events (1 and 2) that are automatically activated upon the fulfillment of a rule, and scheduled events (3, 4, and 5) programmed based on the former, which are used for state verification and operation and maintenance actions.

The proposed sequence of events is as follows.

1. Prior to the occurrence of the first event, the pump is operating normally, with only the power prediction algorithm in use.
2. Event 1 occurs, and the neural network detects, for the first time, a prediction error greater than 25 kW. At this moment, the following analyses are initiated:

    a. Accumulated minutes counter at risk level TR3 (25 kW $\leq$ AE < 30 kW).
    b. Diagnosis by the classification algorithm of the pump's state.

3. Event 2 occurs, and the automatic classification-based diagnosis predicts that the pump's failure mode is state 2, with a probability greater than 60% that this is the case. The following actions are initiated at this event:

    a. The pump is set to a non-priority startup state.
    b. Event 3 for vibration diagnosis is scheduled.
    c. The failure mode state transitions to a medium risk level.

4. Execution of Event 3, vibration diagnosis. At this moment, two outcomes are possible: either it is verified that the pump has high vibrations, associated with a particular failure mode, or the pump shows no anomalies in the vibration analysis.

If the former occurs, Event 4 is planned, and the pump's state transitions to a high-risk level. If, on the contrary, the pump does not exhibit high vibrations, the pump remains at the medium risk level and is put under monitoring.

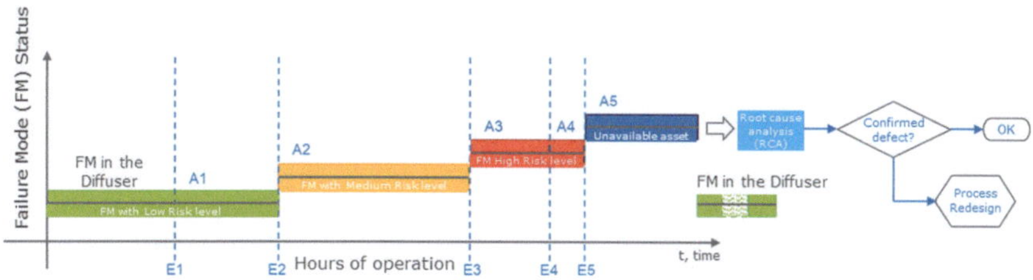

Fig. 5 Proposed state, events, and actions diagram for a specific failure mode of the pump

5. Execution of Event 4 involves diagnosing the pump through inspection and examination. If a failure mode is confirmed in the pump, maintenance intervention or replacement is scheduled depending on the state.
6. Execution of Event 5 involves maintenance intervention based on condition, preventing the onset of the failure mode. Subsequently, a Corrective Action Request (CAR) is carried out for the identified failure mode.

If necessary, and based on the results of the previous analysis, it is advisable to retrain the automatic classification-based diagnosis for the failure modes that have occurred. This helps to achieve a more precise adjustment of the diagnosis.

8 Conclusions

The paper focuses on the early identification of anomalies (prognosis) and the classification of failure modes in secondary pumps (diagnosis).

The prognosis part aids in failure prevention, enabling actions to be taken prior to failure; in maintenance planning, either reducing or increasing the frequency of scheduled maintenance to mitigate the risk of failure; and enhancing safety to prevent accidents and injuries by isolating the pump if necessary.

The identification of the occurring failure mode or diagnosis of the failure mode assists technicians in determining the causes of the failure and making decisions about the repair or replacement of the equipment or its parts; identifying the most probable failure modes; and focusing on the failure modes that require priority attention.

This document presents an analysis method based on the condition state of the secondary pumps, with four different scenarios through which a pump can pass or has passed, for prognosis. It also defines risk levels based on AE, in which the accumulated times at each level are measured, for the diagnosis of failure modes.

Nine ML algorithms were compared for prediction or prognosis, and another nine for classification or diagnosis, with the aim of ensuring the selection of the best model depending on the balance between accuracy, efficiency in training and evaluation time, and above all, the complexity of the problem.

For prediction, a Neural Network algorithm (RNN-7–5-1) was chosen and validated with four pumps, three of which experienced failures in different scenarios and one without a failure. It is clearly observed that in all pumps during scenarios E1/E2, they exhibit behavior that is completely different than before the failure, in scenarios E3/E4. In scenarios E3/E4, more minutes accumulate in higher absolute error values. Meanwhile, in the pump without failures, the AE trend does not change.

For the classification model, three stages were defined: Stage 1, when the failure mode has not yet begun to manifest, corresponding to risk levels TR0, TR1, and TR2; Stage 2, where the failure mode begins to manifest, accumulating more than 10 consecutive minutes at risk level TR3; and Stage 3, which corresponds to before the failure, where the pump's behavior deviates from its normal behavior and more times accumulate at risk levels TR4, TR5, and TR6. Based on this classification, the Decision Tree algorithm was chosen, where it is observed that for the three pumps that experienced failures, the prediction of their stage was 3, with a greater accumulation of time at risk levels TR4, TR5, and TR6, at approximately 5%; whereas for the pump without failure, the accumulation of times at risk levels TR4, TR5, and TR6 was approximately 1%, demonstrating the importance of diagnostic methods in maintenance management.

Lastly, maintenance recommendations are provided based on the analyses conducted.

It is concluded that the application of ML to identify malfunction patterns in cryogenic pumps is a significant advancement for these types of hard-to-access assets. With the technology used so far and the maintenance plans, there was still uncertainty, leading to either over-maintenance or under-maintenance, depending on the strategies.

9 Implications for Future Studies

It is necessary to extend the study to encompass the entire pump fleet at Enagás to demonstrate the scalability of the model and validate it across different operational scenarios. Moreover, as data collection expands, it will be essential to enhance and refine the models through retraining with new data, thereby optimizing them and enabling comparisons with new models.

Additionally, a relevant analysis would be to investigate less frequent failure scenarios, specifically identifying the "rarest" failures using anomaly detection techniques or other existing methods. Furthermore, it is crucial to assess the economic impact to analyze the costs associated with corrective actions versus those incurred with predictive models. This evaluation would include assessing the reduction in downtime and the increase in equipment lifespan, as well as optimizing maintenance plans to balance maintenance frequency and reduce the risk of failure.

The comparison between the most advanced DL models and traditional methods for predictive maintenance has demonstrated that DL models are more effective. Incorporating these alternative approaches could facilitate a broader discussion of the findings and enhance the overall effectiveness of the predictive maintenance framework.

References

Achouch, M., Dimitrova, M., Ziane, K., Sattarpanah Karganroudi, S., Dhouib, R., Ibrahim, H., & Adda, M. (2022). On predictive maintenance in Industry 4.0: Overview, models, and challenges. *Applied Sciences, 12*(16), 8081. https://doi.org/10.3390/app12168081.

Adumene, S., Khan, F., Adedigba, S., Mamudu, A., & Rosli, M. I. (2023). Offshore oil and gas development in remote harsh environments: Engineering challenges and research opportunities. *Safety in Extreme Environments, 5*(1), 17–33. https://doi.org/10.1007/s42797-022-00057-1

Apriade, V. (2023). Implementasi rapidminer dengan metode clustering k-means untuk analisa penjualan pada toko oj cell. *JATI (Jurnal Mahasiswa Teknik Informatika), 7*(1), 101–104. https://doi.org/10.36040/jati.v7i1.6094.

Collart, E., Longley, A., Gordon, D., Nordquist, J., & Matthews, P. (2022). Predictive maintenance practices for cryogenic pumps in semiconductor manufacturing. In *2022 33rd Annual SEMI Advanced Semiconductor Manufacturing Conference (ASMC)* (pp. 1–6). Saratoga Springs, NY, USA. https://doi.org/10.1109/ASMC54647.2022.9792482.

Crespo, A., Seecharan, T. S., Abdul-Nour, G., & Amadi-Echendu, J. (Eds.). (2024*). Advances in asset management: Strategies, technologies, and industry applications.* Springer Cham. https://doi.org/10.1007/978-3-031-52391-5.

Cui, B., Ye, Z., An, Y., & Zhang, Z. (2024). Analysis of internal flow and energy loss in a LNG cryogenic submerged pump. *AIP Advances, 14*(8), Article 085218. https://doi.org/10.1063/5.0220920

Chelmiah, E. T., McLoone, V. I., & Kavanagh, D. F. (2022). Remaining useful life estimation of rotating machines through supervised learning with non-linear approaches. *Applied Sciences, 12*(4136). https://doi.org/10.3390/app12094136.

Dalatu, P. I., Fitrianto, A., & Mustapha, A. (2016). A comparative study of linear and nonlinear regression models for outlier detection. In *Recent Advances on Soft Computing and Data Mining* (pp. 316–326). Springer. https://doi.org/10.1007/978-3-319-51281-5_32

Dutta, N., Palanisamy, K., & Umashankar, S. (2021). *Application of Machine Learning Algorithm for Anomaly Detection for Industrial Pumps*, pp 237–263. https://doi.org/10.1007/978-3-030-50641-4_14.

Ehu, A. (2021). Sensors data analysis in supervisory control and data acquisition (SCADA) systems for fault diagnosis. *Sensors, 21*(8), 2762. https://doi.org/10.3390/s21082762

Fengqian, Z., Shengtian, S., Ming, J., Xiaoming, L., & Haifeng, Z. (2022). Few-shot pump anomaly detection via Diff-WRN-based model-agnostic meta-learning strategy. *Structural Health Monitoring-an International Journal.* https://doi.org/10.1177/14759217221132114

Fernandes, M., Corchado, J. M., & Marreiros, G. (2022). Machine learning techniques applied to mechanical fault diagnosis and fault prognosis in the context of real industrial manufacturing use- cases: A systematic literature review. *Applied Intelligence, 52*(6), 14246–14280. https://doi.org/10.1007/s10489-022-03344-31

Fuente, A., de la, Márquez, A., Crespo, E., Candón, J., Gómez, J., & Serra, J. (2020). A comparison of machine learning techniques for LNG pumps fault prediction in regasification plants. *IFAC-PapersOnLine, 53*(3), 125–130. https://doi.org/10.1016/J.IFACOL.2020.11.020.

Giudici, P., Raffinetti, E., & Riani, M. (2024). Robust machine learning models: Linear and nonlinear. *International Journal of Data Science and Analytics.* https://doi.org/10.1007/s41060-024-00512-1

González, J., & Pérez, M. (2023). Análisis de riesgos y clasificación de modos de falla en sistemas de suministro de agua: Una revisión exhaustiva.*Revista de Ingeniería y Gestión del Agua, 15*(2), 123–145. Recuperado de https://www.redalyc.org/pdf/482/48215094003.pdf

Hewamalage, H., Bergmeir, C., & Bandara, K. (2020). Recurrent Neural Networks for Time Series Forecasting: Current Status and Future Directions. *Journal of Computational Intelligence.* https://doi.org/10.48550/arXiv.1909.00590.

Hodson, T. O. (2022). Root-mean-square error (RMSE) or mean absolute error (MAE): When to use them or not. *Geoscientific Model Development, 15*(14), 5481–5487. https://doi.org/10.5194/gmd-15-5481-2022

LeCun, Y., Bengio, Y., & Hinton, G. (2015). Deep learning. *Nature, 521*(7553), 436–444. https://doi.org/10.1038/nature14539

Li, Q., Yan, C., Chen, G., Wang, H., Li, H., & Wu, L. (2022). Remaining useful life prediction of rolling bearings based on risk assessment and degradation state coefficient. *ISA Transactions, 129*(Part B), 413–428. https://doi.org/10.1016/j.isatra.2022.01.031.

Marti-Puig, P., Blanco-M, A., Serra-Serra, M., & Solé-Casals, J. (2021). Wind Turbine Prognosis Models Based on SCADA Data and Extreme Learning Machines. *Applied Sciences, 11*(2), 590. https://doi.org/10.3390/app11020590

Viswanathan, P. C., Venkatesh, S. N., Dhanasekaran, S., Mahanta, T. K., Sugumaran, V., Lakshmaiya, N., Paramasivam, P., & Ramasamy, S. N. (2023). Deep learning for fault prediction in cryogenic pumps. *Journal of Mechanical Systems, 11*(9), 874. https://doi.org/10.3390/machines11090874

Zhang, Y., & Li, X. (2021). Smart predictive maintenance for high-performance computing systems: A comprehensive overview and comparative analysis on deep learning and traditional methods. *Journal of Supercomputing, 77*(4), 17473–17493. https://doi.org/10.1007/s11227-021-03811-7

Zhang, Y., & Wang, L. (2021). Machine fault detection methods based on machine learning algorithms: A comprehensive review. *Mathematical Biosciences and Engineering, 18*(5), 6345–6362. https://doi.org/10.3934/mbe.2022534

Statistical Modelling of Digital Capture Data of Water Assets: Principal Components and Cluster Analyses of Water Tanks in Brazilian Municipalities

Wagner Oliveira de Carvalho, Nuno Marques de Almeida, Rui Cunha Marques, and Marta Castilho Gomes

Abstract Access to clean drinking water remains a global challenge, impacting 2 billion people. Additionally, the water distribution sector experiences substantial financial losses, estimated at $14 billion annually due to high water loss. The digital transformation heralded by Industry 4.0 promises significant enhancements in water service efficiency. The Digital Water program launched by IWA in 2022 highlights the several benefits of digitalization in operational efficiency and water resource management. This study investigates the application of digital reality capture technologies to improve asset information for water supply services. Using statistical modelling techniques of principal components and cluster analyses, this research analyzes a database comprising 2,584 physical assets from water tanks in Brazil. The data analysis, conducted using IBM SPSS and visualized in PowerBI, demonstrates the potential of these technologies as a robust decision-making support tool for the Asset Management System (AMS).

Keywords Water supply services · Digitalization · Asset management system · Reality Capture · Principal components Analysis · Cluster

1 Water Asset Management

Organizations are increasingly required to adopt multidisciplinary and proactive approaches to managing their built assets, especially the critical infrastructures that serve communities and the functioning of society. This is the case for water

W. Oliveira de Carvalho (✉) · N. Marques de Almeida · M. Castilho Gomes
Instituto Superior Técnico, Lisbon, Portugal
e-mail: wagner.carvalho@tecnico.ulisboa.pt

R. C. Marques
Universidade Lusófona, Lisbon, Portugal
e-mail: rui.marques@ulusofona.pt

A. Crespo Márquez et al. (eds.), *Case Studies in Digital Transformation*, Engineering Asset Management Review 4, https://doi.org/10.1007/978-3-032-05592-7_13

supply services, which manage systems with tens of thousands of infrastructure assets, involving significant resources in their creation, operation, renewal, and rapid adaptation to unforeseen situations (Almeida, 2023).

Urban water services manage critical infrastructures of high public interest, and–still today–access to reliable and safe water remains a significant challenge in many developing countries, particularly as populations grow and urbanize (UNICEF 2023). The social value of the water infrastructure significantly exceeds their economic value, therefore international organizations are concerned with promoting greater efficiency in management and supporting regulation in this sector (Institutions and Regulation 2022; Marques, 2005). The contemporary scenario is even more challenging due to conflicting factors such as urban growth, natural resource limitations, and climate change, making it even more complex to ensure system resilience, promote service sustainability, and adopt principles of the circular economy.

The way an organization manages its assets determines its success in addressing the challenges of providing water services (Asian Development Bank, 2013).

Water utility managers often inherit infrastructures composed of physical assets in varying conditions and stages of their life cycles. Some are linear and buried, such as pipe networks, while others are above ground, including treatment plants, pumping stations, and storage structures–commonly referred to as 'vertical assets' in some countries (Alegre et al., 2014). Mature organizations in asset management discipline are raising the importance of the information about each asset that makes up the systems they operate (Institute and of Asset Management (IAM), 2024).

This work is motivated by the potential of asset digitalization to increase the operational efficiency of the water service industry in Brazil (International Water Association (IWA), 2022). Despite the country's global significance in water resource availability, the reality is that around 32 million Brazilians still lack access to potable water (approximately 14% of the population), which conflicts with the sector's low efficiency, recording losses of more than 1 L of water for every 3 L produced for the supply system. This translates to a loss rate of 37.78%, placing the country at 78th out of 139 nations analyzed (no Brasil, 2024).

Structured digitalization processes can increase the reliability and quality of the informational pillar of asset management. To confirm this potential, a sample of data from the physical assets of a Brazilian water utility was selected for the application of advanced statistical modelling methods. The data were collected through the application of innovative digital reality capture technologies in the field, meaning the organization invested in the physical base of the operation to create a more accurate representation of actual conditions and to expand knowledge about the facilities (Niles et al., 2022).

However, the scenario is still very challenging to increase the reliability of the informational base of physical assets. According to the report by the Reliability Leadership Foundation–a world leader in asset management reliability–the current average knowledge of assets by operators is below 50% and rarely exceeds 70% (O´Hanlon & Gulati & 2020).

2 Literature Review

(Grosch & Bilot, 2002) study conducted at the beginning of the century for water systems already indicated the potential for digital era transformation in organizations, in response to the challenge of adapting to the expected demands amidst rapid changes in environmental conditions and operational assets. The approach called "digital nervous system" aimed to achieve high efficiency in the management processes of water and wastewater stations. Technologies integrated the systems for information collection, management, structuring, and dissemination throughout the organization.

According to Helfert & Ge (2007), numerous business management losses and failures are caused by problems with low Information Quality (IQ). In this state-of-the-art research, IQ is defined as the information's ability to meet users' needs and system specifications. IQ research is divided into three main aspects: IQ assessment, IQ management, and contextual IQ.

The topic of the informational pillar of physical assets has gained relevance in water asset engineering, thus Amadi-Echendu (2012) conducted a study on the state of practice in information quality management with several organizations. The benchmarking study was conducted with asset-intensive water organizations in the United Kingdom and revealed challenges in the three areas of information quality management: information management, quality management, and knowledge management (Fig. 1).

The Information Quality Management Capability Maturity Model (MMC-QGI) was developed and validated with ten water asset management organizations. These organizations were classified according to their adherence to Critical Success Factors (CSFs) at different levels of information management maturity: optimising, managed, measuring, reactive, and chaotic. The research results are presented in Table 1, which references the first column with maturity levels, the second row with organizations analysed by letters A to J, and the third row with the percentage values for total (F) or partial (PF) adherence to CSFs. The last row shows that none of the analysed water utilities, at the time, achieved the maximum maturity level of 5 (optimising); eight organizations were classified as level 2 (reactive), and only one organization reached level 4 (managed).

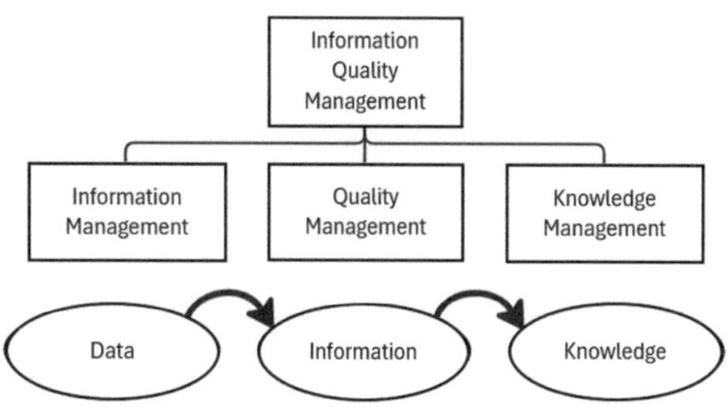

Fig. 1 Information quality management *Source* adapted from Amadi-Echendu (2012)

Table 1 Final maturity level of each organization for total (F) and partial (PF) adherence at each maturity level *Source* adapted from Amadi-Echendu (2012)

Maturity level	Organization																			
	A		B		C		D		E		F		G		H			I	J	
	F	PF	F	PF	F	PF	F	PF	F	PF	F	PF	F	PF	F	PF	F	PF	F	PF
5	0	0	0	0	0	25	0	0	0	0	0	0	0	25	0	0	0	0	0	0
4	0	23	8	62	54	92	0	46	0	46	0	15	15	54	15	46	8	46	0	23
3	7	33	13	67	73	100	20	47	7	53	0	20	53	87	33	73	7	47	13	47
2	100	100	100	100	100	100	93	100	100	100	93	93	93	100	93	100	93	100	64	100
1	100	100	100	100	100	100	100	100	100	100	100	100	100	100	100	100	100	100	100	100
Final maturity level	2		2		4		2		2		2		3		2		2		2	

The advancement of digitalization in organizations has raised awareness about the need for more qualified and structured information management. Nevertheless, besides the investments in technology, it is imperative to train and qualify human resources and develop processes integrated with the management of their informational assets.

In this new digitalization perspective many questions emerge from water managers, such as: what effort and investment are required to collect structured information from assets? What is the "tangible" benefit of asset information quality in the organization?

Investments in data management and collection can be very costly, and evaluating the generated benefits is not always straightforward and easy to prove. Essentially, the water sector requires Infrastructure Asset Management (IAM) to provide services to the population, and good results depend on governance and the effective use of data to support their processes.

Rokstad et al. (2016) developed a methodology based on IAM tools to quantify the costs of data collection and the informational benefits provided in the water sector. Costs were accounted in hours of work invested, including base costs (acquisition, configuration, and maintenance of tools) and data recording costs (collection and processing). The benefits are defined as informational results that support decision-making processes in IAM. The analysis is consolidated in a structured spreadsheet to organize data, calculate costs and benefits of tool combinations, and evaluate the cost–benefit ratio for different data classes.

The practical application of this methodology is demonstrated in a European water utility, anonymously named Utility X. The cost–benefit analysis of real data collection and informational use revealed opportunities to maximize benefits through the IAM tools implemented in this organization. The results were summarized in a structured table highlighting possibilities for improving decision-making processes, resource allocation, and overall efficiency.

Digital transformation adds new dimensions to asset information management, particularly in the field of inspections, where new processes and technologies for data collection, called reality capture (Niles et al., 2022), are being applied. In this context, digitalization in Industry 4.0 was a major topic at the 16th World Congress on Engineering Asset Management Proceedings (Alonso et al., 2022).

Alonso et al. (Alonso et al., 2022) studied various asset digitalization approaches (BIM, AIM, AAS, and different Digital Twins), revealing the current complexity of Industry 4.0 and the potential benefits of new approaches, provided they are adequately selected in a structured asset management process within the organization. The investigation revealed low adherence to new trends, such as Digital Twins, in asset maintenance management. These professionals make complex decisions (planning and executing maintenance) daily and continue to use traditional methods because they still have low confidence in technology results.

Digitalization is reshaping the nature of assets, but methods and strategies must be developed to standardize asset modelling in each industry and/or sector. The management model should consider structured asset data in an architecture that facilitates the development and use of more sophisticated digital solutions (Alonso et al., 2022).

Balogun et al. (2024) developed a systematic literature review of Artificial Intelligence (AI) and its subfields, including reality capture advancements to various industries. The study highlighted the transformative changes of AI-driven tools but also identified some limitations and challenges related to data collection for deconstruction planning.

AI is promising to be the new transformative strand to improve reality capture processes (Balogun et al., 2024). The primary asset data can become more detailed and structured, enhancing information quality (IQ) management.

AI categories such as Machine Learning (ML), Deep Learning (DL) and Computer Vision (CV) are increasingly being applied to Automated Data Analysis of images captured by various devices (drones, cameras) to extract meaningful data about physical assets: location, measurements, structural and condition understanding, for instance (Balogun et al., 2024; Rani et al., 2024).

The Point Cloud Classification has been widely used with the advancements of 3D sensing technologies (3D scanners and LiDARs), and their applications range from classification tasks in robotics, autonomous driving, shape analysis, remote sensing, etc. (Feng et al., 2025).

The Object Detection and Recognition AI algorithms are used to detect and identify specific objects within the physical environment. These systems use techniques like Convolutional Neural Networks (CNNs) and DL to recognize buildings, equipment, machinery, or other relevant assets from images or video streams (Goodfellow et al., 2018).

Despite significant advancements in Machine Learning (ML) and Deep Learning (DL) for tasks like recognition, detection, and segmentation, material audits and inventory management still face challenges. These include limited training data and a lack of technical expertise for accurately annotating and preparing captured data (Balogun et al., 2024).

Data management became so relevant to the organizational activities that the International Organization for Standardization recently published the ISO 55013:2024 Asset management – Guidance on the management of data assets (ISO, 2024a, 2024b). Its main objective is to help organizations manage their data effectively thus supporting informed decision-making to achieve organizational strategy goals. The most relevant contribution of this new standard is addressing data management as an organizational asset, offering guidelines for data collection, analysis, storage, protection, and use, ensuring its reliability, traceability, and alignment with strategic objectives (Fig. 2).

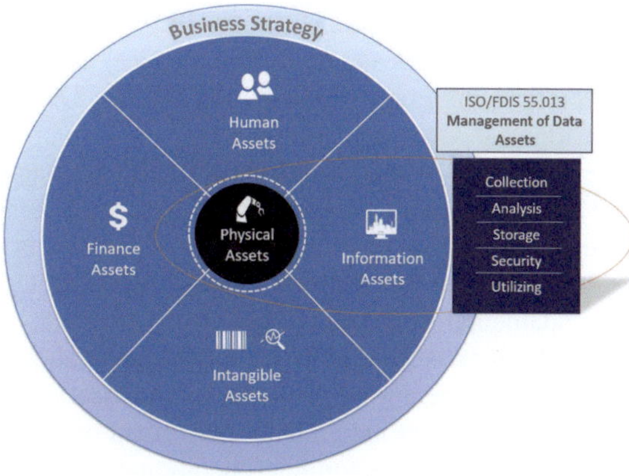

Fig. 2 Asset management Mandala. *Source* Adapted from ISO 55001 and ISO 55013

3 Methodology

The methodology applied in this work involved advanced statistical modelling on a sample of the physical asset database of a water service provider in Brazil. The data originates from digital collection applying a structured process of asset identification and verification, called AIV (Asset Identification and Verification) by the organization (Carvalho, 2020), which is a combination of advanced reality capture technologies (Niles et al., 2022).

The statistical modelling sought to characterize quantitative and qualitative aspects of the data collected in the sample in relation to the information required in the organization's OIR model (Organization Information Requirements) (ISO, 2024a).

The OIR model of the studied water utility is presented in Fig. 3, and is based on the following dimensions:

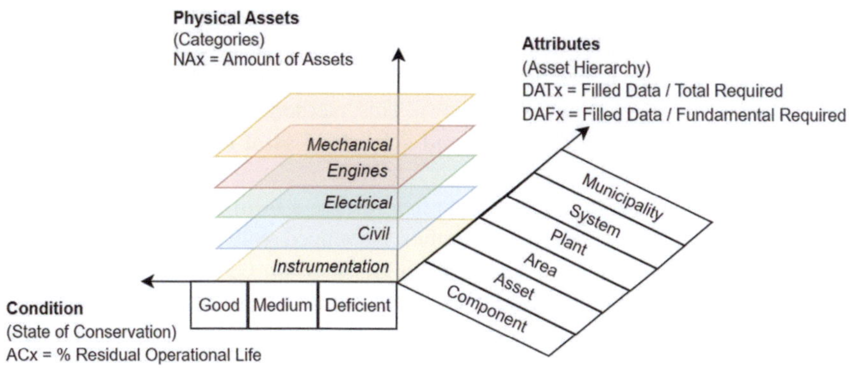

Fig. 3 Dimensions of the organization information requirements model (OIR)

- Physical Assets: classifies the specific typology (more than 300 distinct types) and quantifies in the category of the physical asset discipline in mechanical, motor, electrical, civil or instrumentation (NAx = Quantity of Assets);
- Attributes: asset information requirements vary according to their hierarchical level (Order of the organization's strategic, tactical and operational levels are Municipality, System, Plant, Area, Asset and Component). More technical details are required for operational and tactical levels (DATx = Filled Data / Total Required) and less technical details for the strategic level (DAFx = Filled Data / Fundamental Required);
- Condition: it is the evaluation of the conservation status to estimate the remaining or residual operational useful life of the asset. The result is the combination of the visual inspection individually performed on the asset by the specialist added to the available data recording (operational data, maintenance history, performance records, among others). According to the remaining useful life, the classification can be good, medium or deficient in terms of conservation, and depending on the criticality of the asset, it can mean a high exposure to risk for the organization, since the low conservation condition can indicate an imminent operational failure (ACx = % of Residual Operational Useful Life).

The study also analysed possible correlations between these variables of quantity, information (attributes) and condition of assets with context variables in municipalities that have different population densities and distinct socioeconomic characteristics in Brazil.

4 Database Analysis

4.1 Qualitative Analysis

Data acquisition is a key stage of the digitalization process used to capture the reality of water assets in the field (Niles et al., 2022). According to Carvalho (2020), the data collection method, developed by the Infra Inteligente program (Aegea), is known as AIV (Asset Identification & Verification). This method leverages BIM (Building Information Modelling) technologies and adheres to asset management standards outlined in ISO 55001 (2024b).

Multidisciplinary professionals in the field utilize a form application to classify assets by typologies, categories, and families. Advanced reality capture technologies such as drones, 360-degree cameras, and high-precision GPS (Niles et al., 2022) generate high-resolution images and 3D digital meshes of the assets. This approach ensures that the technical attributes are accurately documented, as illustrated in Fig. 4.

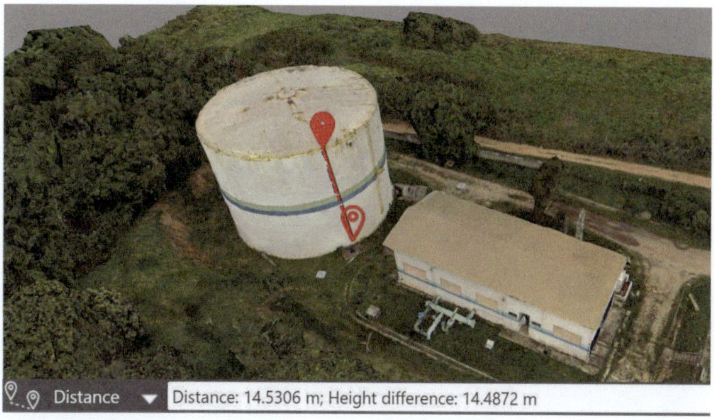

Fig. 4 Digital 3D model (3D Plant Mesh)

The AIV process aims to reliably answer essential questions for operational effectiveness as outlined in the Asset Information Requirements (AIR): What are the physical assets of the water system? Where are they located with geolocation precision? What condition are they in, including their remaining useful life?

After the collection and processing stages, the asset database is stored in the Oracle Spatial platform (Murray et al., 2024). This processed data is then shared with the Key Performance Areas (KPA) through various visualization formats on the organization's asset management platforms (Fig. 5).

The reliable asset data/information captured in the field is a key enabler for asset management thus the organization digitalization strategy includes Digital Models, Digital Shadows, and Digital Twins for decision-making lifecycle. The corresponding framework is linked to the level of automation in data transfer between physical and virtual assets (Kritzinger et al., 2018; Vieira et al., 2022).

The Fig. 6 highlights the integration of graphic and non-graphic data that resulted in the Digital Twin of the ETR plant (water tank and pumping station) developed by the organization. This Digital Twin is a faithful digital replica of the plant, incorporating static and real time attributes collected from the assets (Bolton, 2018). It

Fig. 5 Asset organization database

Fig. 6 Digital twin (Water Tank and Pumping Station) *Source* XRProj platform https://www.xrproj.com/

can also be virtually explored in an immersive environment using multiple platforms such as laptops, smartphones, tablets or virtual reality glasses (Vive Pro or Oculus Quest) (XRProject 2016).

4.2 Quantitative Analysis

The selected sample encompasses 19 municipalities in Brazil, covering 2,584 assets distributed across 106 entities (plants), specifically water storage plants known as ETR (Water Tank and Pumping Station). For the statistical modelling 2 non-metric variables (municipality and operational status), 2 context variables (population density and human development index) and 24 additional metric variables were established. These metric variables are derived from the dimensions of the organization information requirements model presented in Chapt. 3 which include variables related to quantity, condition, and technical attributes for the five categories of physical assets: mechanical, motors, civil, electrical, and instrumentation. The Table 2 summarizes the selected variables containing the name (abbreviation), the variable description, the unit of measurement and the specific source.

5 Results and Discussion

The study involved statistical modelling of the database highlighted in the previous chapter, which was developed in the software IBM SPSS (Cronk, 2018). In the first stage uni- and bivariate analyses were performed, and the correlation matrix

Table 2 Variable description

Variables	Description	Unit
Mun	Municipality of Brazil	Nominal
SituaOper	Plant Operational Status (1)	Nominal
DensPop	Population Density (2)	People/km^2
IDHM	Municipal Human Development Index (L = Longevity, E = Education and R = Income) (2)	$\frac{IDHM(L)+IDHM(E)+IDHM(R)}{3}$
NAm,n,e,c,i	Number of Assets by Category (*) in the Plant (1)	$\frac{NAm,n,e,c,i}{Plant}$
NTme	Total Number of Assets per Plant (1)	$\frac{NT}{Plant}$
ACm,n,e,c,i	Average Condition Index of Assets, or remaining useful life, by Category (*) in the Plant (1)	$\frac{ACm,n,e,c,i}{Plant}$
ACme	Average Condition Index of Assets, or average remaining useful life in the Plant (1)	$\frac{AC}{Plant}$
DATm,n,e,c,i	Data Index of Filled Attributes by Category (*) in the Plant (Entity) in relation to the total required (1)	$\frac{(Filled\ Data)m,n,e,c,i}{Total\ Required}$
DATme	Data Index of Filled Attributes per Plant in relation to the total required (AIR) (1)	$\frac{Filled\ Data}{Total\ Required}$
DAFm,n,e,c,i	Data Index of Filled Attributes by Category (*) in the Plant in relation to the fundamental required (AIR) (1)	$\frac{(Filled\ Data)m,n,e,c,i}{Fundamental\ Required}$.
DAFme	Data Index of Filled Attributes per Plant in relation to the fundamental required (AIR) (1)	$\frac{Filled\ Data}{Fundamental\ Required}$

Sources (1) Physical Asset Inventory (Carvalho, 2021); (2) Brazilian Institute of Geography and Statistics–IBGE (2010 Census); Legend of the categories: m (Mechanical), n (Motor), e (Electrical), c (Civil) and i (Instrumentation)

is presented in appendix 1. Few pairs of variables have significant values of linear correlation coefficients, which are marked in yellow (above 0.4) and red colour (above 0.6) in the correlation matrix.

5.1 Principal Component Analysis

Principal component analysis (PCA) is commonly applied in data exploration and predictive model construction. The objective of this study was to condense various variables into a reduced number of new variables, called components, with minimal loss of information, in order to facilitate the understanding and interpretation of the data (Márquez, 2022).

The Fig. 7 presents a partial extract of the database.

Before performing the principal component analysis, the data were processed because there were missing values in some condition and technical information

Entidade	Mun	DensPop	IDHM	NAm	NAn	NAe	NAc	NAi	NTme
Descrição	Nome do município (Brasil)	Medida da densidade populacional no município	Índice estatístico composto de expectativa de vida, educação e renda per capta	Número de Ativos Mecânicos por Planta	Número de Ativos Motores por Planta	Número de Ativos Elétricos por Planta	Número de Ativos Civis por Planta	Número de Ativos de Instrumentação por Planta	Número Total de Ativos por Planta
Entidade	Nominal	Pessoas/km²	0 - 1	NAm/Plant	NAn/Plant	NAe/Plant	NAc/Plant	NAi/Plant	NTme/Plant
Planta	Município	DensPop	IDHM	NAm	NAn	NAe	NAc	NAi	NTme
PL-PRO-ETR2250	Arraial do Cabo	172.91	0.733	8	1	2	1	6	18
PL-PRO-ETR2262	Arraial do Cabo	172.91	0.733	7	4	3	1	5	20
PL-PRO-ETR3094	Búzios	392.16	0.728	35	3	24	4	17	83
PL-PRO-ETR3096	Búzios	392.16	0.728	15	2	19	4	8	48
PL-PRO-ETR3154	Búzios	392.16	0.728	4	1	2	1	3	11
PL-PRO-ETR4095	Cabo Frio	453.75	0.735	49	2	24	11	15	101
PL-PRO-ETR4129	Cabo Frio	453.75	0.735	13	2	4	1	5	25
PL-PRO-ETR4138	Cabo Frio	453.75	0.735	21	3	3	2	10	39
PL-PRO-ETR4207	São Pedro da Aldeia	264.05	0.712	2	1	1	2	3	9
PL-PRO-ETR4208	São Pedro da Aldeia	264.05	0.712	0	0	0	1	0	1
PL-PRO-ETR4219	Cabo Frio	453.75	0.735	20	2	3	5	2	32
PL-PRO-ETR4241	Cabo Frio	453.75	0.735	3	0	2	1	3	9
PL-TMN-ETR0051	Timon	89.18	0.649	6	1	5	1	5	18
PL-RJA-ETR0001	Cachoeiras de Macacu	56.9	0.7	4	0	0	0	0	4
PL-RJA-ETR0002	Cachoeiras de Macacu	56.9	0.7	6	0	1	1	0	8
PL-RJA-ETR0003	Cachoeiras de Macacu	56.9	0.7	8	0	1	4	0	13
PL-RJA-ETR0024	Cachoeiras de Macacu	56.9	0.7	4	0	0	0	0	4
PL-RJA-ETR0029	São Sebastião do Alto	22.35	0.646	1	1	1	1	0	4
PL-RJA-ETR0111	São Francisco de Itabapoana	36.84	0.639	25	7	18	2	1	53

Fig. 7 Partial extract of the database

variables of the assets. The incomplete data pertain to inaccessible assets, and for proper technical treatment, the missing values for each entity in this condition were filled using the mean of the observations.

In Table 3 of eigenvalues generated from the data of the 26 variables, the Kaiser criterion (eigenvalues greater than (1) identifies that 7 components should be adopted, and by the retained, or explained, variance criterion, 5 components are necessary, as they retain 73% of the total variance (70% is a commonly used cumulative variance value for this criterion).

In the scree plot (Fig. 8) there are variations in inclination (elbows) for 2, 4 and 6 components.

Given the indications of the number of components to retain by the aforementioned criteria, the table of communalities was subsequently analyzed for the extraction of 3, 4, 5, 6, and 7 components (Table 4). Communality is the percentage of the variance of a variable retained when extracting a given number of principal components.

In Table 4, values of communalities above 0.6 (indicating 60% of retained variance) are highlighted in red, and values between 0.4 and 0.6 are highlighted in yellow. Thus, it is observed that with the extraction of 3 components, only a minority of variables show communalities above 0.6, while with 7 components, all variables surpass this threshold. The columns of extraction of 4 and 5 components indicate high communalities, however the latter value was chosen because it includes the contextual variables (DensPop and IDHM), which are highly relevant in this study.

The Table 5 presents the factorial weights matrix or "factor loadings" obtained through Varimax rotation, a method that focuses on simplifying the columns of the

Table 3 Eigenvalue table

Total variance explained						
Components	Initial eigenvalue			Extraction sums of squared loads		
	Total	% variance	% cumulative	Total	% variance	% cumulative
1	8.061	31.002	31.002	8.061	31.002	31.002
2	3.960	15.230	46.232	3.960	15.230	46.232
3	3.581	13.772	60.004	3.581	13.772	60.004
4	1.949	7.494	67.499	1.949	7.494	67.499
5	1.585	6.097	73.596	1.585	6.097	73.596
6	1.021	3.928	77.524	1.021	3.928	77.524
7	1.007	3.874	81.398	1.007	3.874	81.398
8	0.893	3.436	84.834			
9	0.729	2.803	87.636			
10	0.582	2.237	89.874			
11	0.523	2.012	91.886			
12	0.431	1.658	93.544			
13	0.421	1.619	95.163			
14	0.360	1.386	96.549			
15	0.309	1.187	97.735			
16	0.190	0.729	98.465			
17	0.176	0.676	99.141			
18	0.095	0.367	99.508			
19	0.055	0.210	99.717			
20	0.034	0.132	99.849			
21	0.025	0.096	99.945			
22	0.014	0.053	99.998			
23	0.000	0.001	99.999			
24	0.000	0.001	100.000			
25	7.031E-09	2.704E-08	100.000			
26	–5.578E-16	–2.145E-15	100.000			
Extraction Method: Principal Component Analysis						

factorial weights matrix. Factor loadings represent the coefficients of linear correlation between each variable and the respective component; the higher (in magnitude) the loading, the more a component explains or is related to a given variable. To facilitate the analysis of the table, factor loadings above 0.6 are highlighted in red and those between 0.4 and 0.6 (in magnitude) are highlighted in yellow.

The analysis of the highest factorial weights in each column (component) shows that principal component analysis allows summarizing the variables into technical dimensions of interest for asset management, as presented in Table 6.

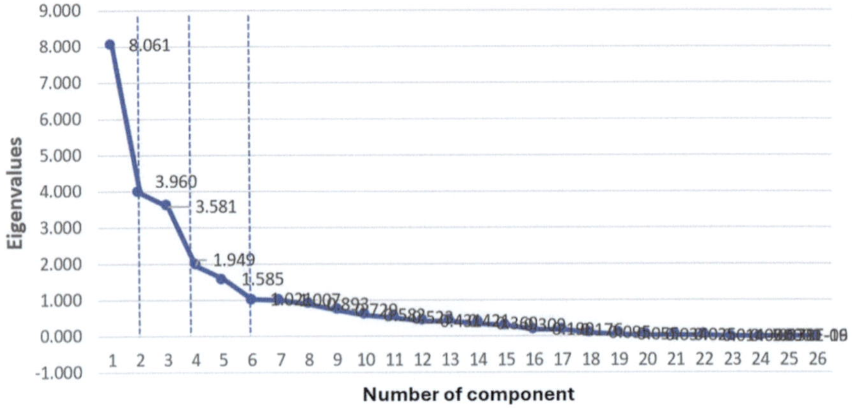

Fig. 8 Scree plot

5.2 *Cluster Analysis*

The main objective of cluster analysis is to group entities into clusters with homogeneous characteristics, based on the analysis and observation of their similarities and dissimilarities (King, 2015). In this study, both hierarchical and non-hierarchical methods were applied, beginning with the standardization of the 26 variables. This standardization involves subtracting the mean and dividing by the standard deviation for each variable, making the variables dimensionless and comparable in magnitude.

Hierarchical Method

In cluster analysis using the agglomerative hierarchical method, the algorithm gradually merges pairs of clusters until all entities form a single cluster (group). In the agglomeration method, Ward's and centroid criteria were applied (using Euclidean distance).

Ward's method produced more balanced results in terms of cluster composition. From the analysis of the respective dendrogram and agglomeration plot (Fig. 9), the division into 4 or 5 clusters emerged as the most significant. The decision was made to divide the entities into 5 clusters because the group dimensions are more similar and represent a greater diversity of entities according to the dendrogram analysis, although the results from the agglomeration plot coefficients (Fig. 10) did not show significant changes in slope ("elbows").

Result of clustering of entities by the Ward method was also displayed in PowerBI software (Fig. 11).

Table 4 Communalities for the extraction of 3–7 components

	Communalities					
Variables	**Initial**	**Extraction 3**	**Extraction 4**	**Extraction 5**	**Extraction 6**	**Extraction 7**
DensPop	1,000	0,473	0,479	0,941	0,946	0,958
IDHM	1,000	0,448	0,453	0,887	0,909	0,923
NAm	1,000	0,802	0,802	0,806	0,806	0,826
NAn	1,000	0,504	0,556	0,568	0,659	0,665
NAe	1,000	0,780	0,815	0,822	0,862	0,862
NAc	1,000	0,320	0,320	0,326	0,595	0,622
NAi	1,000	0,576	0,608	0,679	0,705	0,706
NTme	1,000	0,953	0,959	0,960	0,963	0,969
ACm	1,000	0,558	0,654	0,676	0,700	0,731
ACn	1,000	0,575	0,632	0,669	0,673	0,759
ACe	1,000	0,438	0,443	0,517	0,521	0,624
ACc	1,000	0,482	0,500	0,561	0,562	0,647
ACi	1,000	0,764	0,764	0,794	0,796	0,801
ACme	1,000	0,900	0,915	0,989	0,990	0,992
DATm	1,000	0,614	0,618	0,619	0,748	0,868
DATn	1,000	0,384	0,902	0,913	0,938	0,939
DATe	1,000	0,620	0,710	0,710	0,716	0,716
DATc	1,000	0,537	0,721	0,769	0,837	0,883
DATi	1,000	0,639	0,641	0,654	0,654	0,738
DATme	1,000	0,919	0,947	0,948	0,950	0,950
DAFm	1,000	0,542	0,543	0,566	0,714	0,824
DAFn	1,000	0,420	0,871	0,888	0,921	0,922
DAFe	1,000	0,531	0,607	0,616	0,637	0,659
DAFc	1,000	0,468	0,689	0,732	0,830	0,870
DAFi	1,000	0,446	0,493	0,586	0,586	0,766
DAFme	1,000	0,908	0,909	0,938	0,938	0,944
	Extraction Method: Principal Component Analysis					

Table 5 Factorial weight matrix ("factor loadings") obtained by varimax rotation

Matrix of rotating component[a]					
	Component				
	1	2	3	4	5
DensPop	-0.018	-0.271	0.020	0.043	0.930
IDHM	0.038	-0.247	0.049	0.057	0.905
Nam	0.054	-0.017	0.884	0.066	0.134
NAn	0.072	0.087	0.654	0.308	0.183
NAe	0.069	0.082	0.888	-0.136	0.056
NAc	-0.223	0.049	0.501	-0.063	-0.136
NAi	0.188	0.101	0.725	-0.049	-0.326
NTme	0.066	0.035	0.975	0.005	0.059
ACm	0.168	0.730	0.043	0.321	-0.103
ACn	-0.038	0.792	-0.007	0.131	-0.153
Ace	0.134	0.701	0.080	0.039	-0.015
ACc	0.256	0.684	-0.057	-0.140	-0.067
ACi	0.201	0.810	0.257	0.009	-0.178
ACme	0.171	0.965	0.064	0.074	-0.136
DATm	0.720	0.105	0.076	0.256	0.133
DATn	0.250	0.119	-0.005	0.912	0.066
DATe	0.789	0.289	0.025	0.004	-0.053
DATc	0.782	0.239	-0.196	-0.171	0.180
DATi	0.746	-0.005	-0.025	0.309	0.032
DATme	0.787	0.191	-0.029	0.533	0.083
DAFm	0.631	0.031	0.200	0.355	-0.028
DAFn	0.302	0.127	-0.035	0.882	0.030
DAFe	0.744	0.177	0.142	0.043	-0.096
DAFc	0.747	0.253	-0.190	-0.234	0.139
DAFi	0.709	-0.026	0.128	0.136	-0.218
DAFme	0.868	0.139	0.086	0.391	-0.069
Extraction Method: Principal Component Analysis.					
a. Converged rotation in 6 iterations.					

5.3 *Non-Hierarchical Methods*

Non-hierarchical methods are iterative processes based on the grouping of units into a predefined number of clusters, therefore they are more complex to apply in computational terms than hierarchical methods. The K-Means method was used

Table 6 Colour legend of components and their summarized variables

(blue)	Component 1: Asset information excluding engines. Refers to the attributes data filled in for assets, apart from motor category.
(green)	Component 2: Condition of assets. This component refers to the analysis of individual inspections of the condition of each asset.
(yellow)	Component 3: Quantity of assets. Represents the result of the quantity of assets identified in the ERT (plant).
(grey)	Component 4: Engine information. Refers to the attributes data completed from the motor category assets.
(orange)	Component 5: Context variables.

which aims to minimize the sum of intragroup quadratic errors (so that the groups become internally homogeneous) thus maximizing the sum of intergroup deviations and consequently promoting more heterogeneity between groups.

Five clusters were defined (result of the Ward method) considering all standardized variables. Once the cluster centres were obtained for each variable the cluster profile was graphically represented in Fig. 12.

Appendix 2 includes the ANOVA table, which evaluates whether the differences in cluster centres are statistically significant. The clusters are indeed distinct across all variables (significance level less than 0.001), except for population density and human development index.

The Fig. 12 allows visualizing the heterogeneous groupings of plants based on the characteristics of metric and strategic context variables important for the organization:

- Profiles on the left: Cluster 4 stands out with high values for population density, IDHM, number of mechanical, motor, electrical assets, instrumentation, and total assets (C4: Plants in densely populated areas with high IDHM, and a large quantity of assets). Cluster 5 has the lowest values for population density and IDHM, and the highest value for civil assets (C5: Plants in regions with lower population density and IDHM).
- Profiles on the right: Cluster 1 stands out with the best condition and filled attributes indexes for different categories (C1: Plants with the highest condition and information levels).

As a final step, the K-means method was applied again (with 5 clusters), but this time considering the entities represented by the 5 components obtained in the principal component analysis, i.e., considering the synthesis of the original variables in these 5 components.

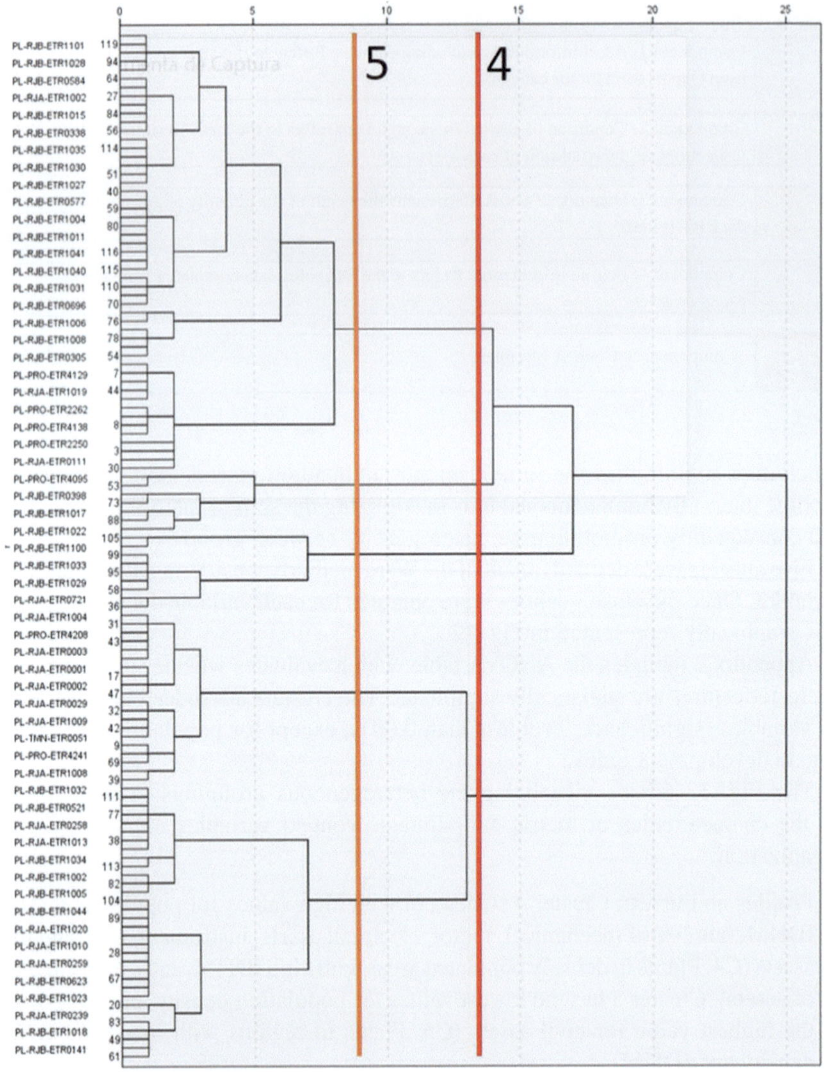

Fig. 9 Dendrogram obtained by Ward's method

The ANOVA table (Appendix 3) allows to conclude that the cluster centres are distinct (significance level less than 0.001) for components 1–4, but not for component 5, which is highly correlated with population density and human development index. This result is consistent with the findings considering all variables.

The Fig. 13 presents the profiles of the clusters obtained in terms of the components. Each cluster is distinguished by one or more "peaks" in the component values. If the peak is positive, it means that the average of that component in the cluster is above the overall mean (the overall mean, considering all entities, is zero because

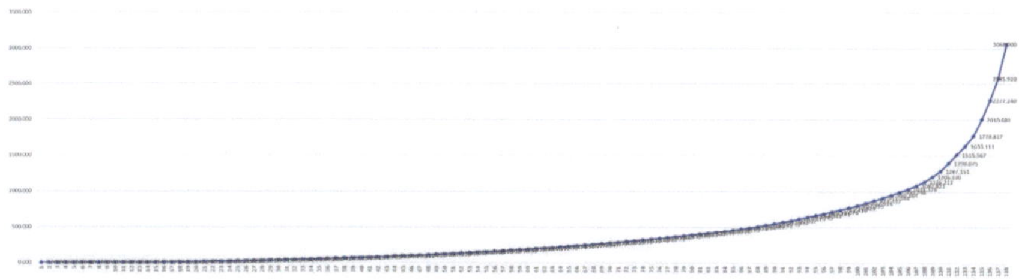

Fig. 10 Clustering planning coefficients (Ward method)

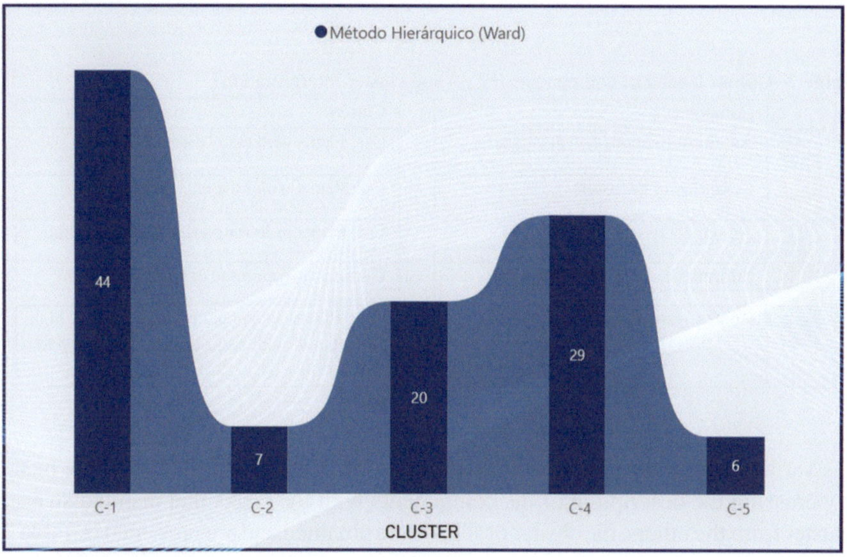

Fig. 11 Hierarchical method (Ward)

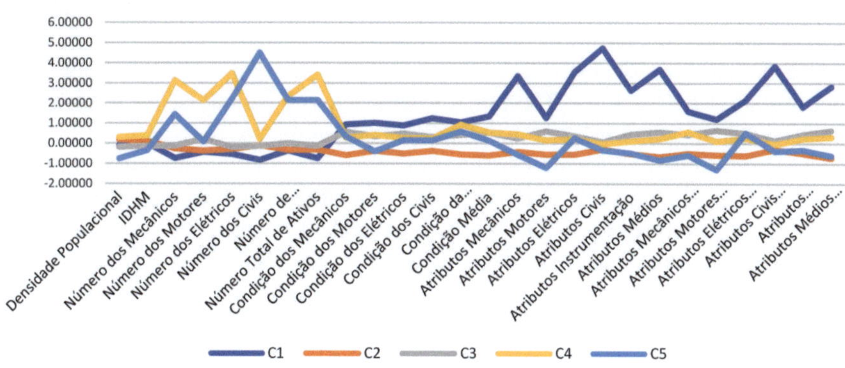

Fig. 12 Cluster profiles (K-Means method with the original variables)

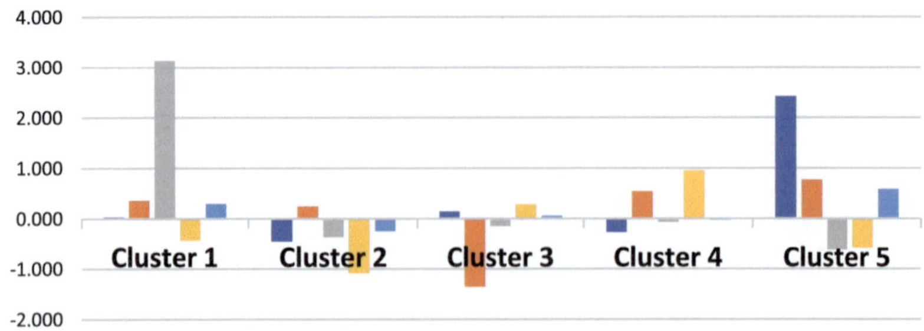

Fig. 13 Cluster profiles (K-Means with PCA)

Table 7 Colour legend of components (PCA) and cluster interpretation

	Components:	Cluster:
	Asset information, except engines	C-1: Plants with many assets
	Condition of the assets	C-2: Plants with little engine information
	Amount of assets	C-3: Plants in lower conservation condition
	Information of motor assets	C-4: Plants with more engine information
	Context variables	C-5: Plants in populated regions and high MHDI, and with more information of the assets

the variables were standardized); conversely, if it is negative, it is below the mean. By crossing the description of the components with the peaks that distinguish each cluster from the others, the cluster profiles were obtained and are presented in Table 7.

As a synthesis of the analysis, the non-hierarchical K-means method with PCA was chosen for clustering entities since it showed to be more effective than Ward's hierarchical method. Therefore, this statistical modelling result was integrated into the business intelligence software PowerBI (Ferrari et al., 2016) enabling asset management decisions through a structured view of geo-spatialized, graphical and tabular data in digital perspectives. The Fig. 14 demonstrates the interactive selection of Cluster 3 (plants with low asset maintenance condition).

This digital integration with statistical modelled data simplifies the comprehension of technical and contextual asset information, enabling more informed management decisions regarding these critical water supply plants. Thousands of assets, with hundreds of technical data points and over two dozen variables, were combined in advanced statistical analyses, structuring complex data and information into the dimensions of the organization information requirements model (Fig. 3, Chap. 3).

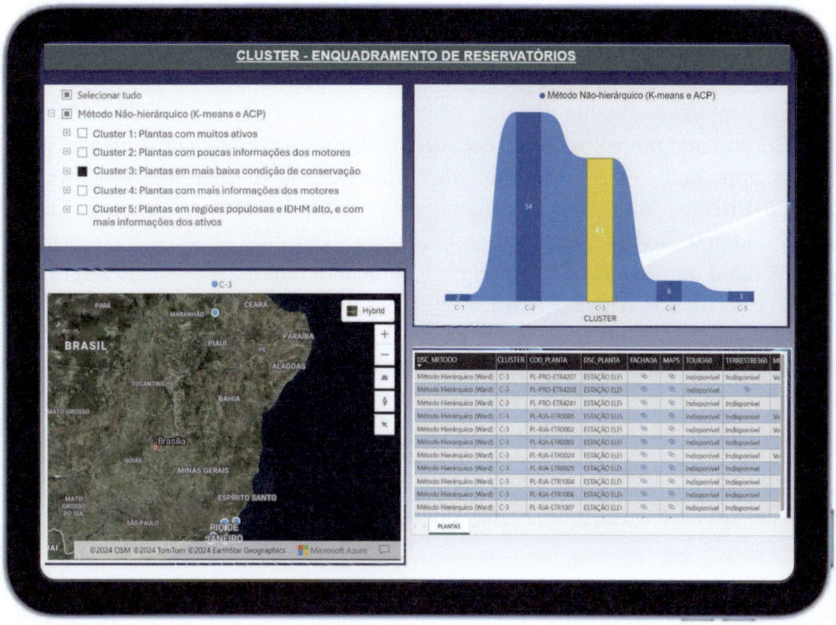

Fig. 14 Dashboard ETR water tanks in powerBI (Cluster profiles obtained by K-Means method with PCA)

6 Conclusion

This study was motivated by the challenges of the asset digitalization process in the water industry to enhance operational efficiency and increase the level of service. It was grounded in previous research questioning the quality of asset information (IQ) and their impacts in water infrastructure management.

The study contributes by applying advanced statistical modelling methods to assess the reliability of a sample from a water utility's database in Brazil, where the asset data were collected through digital the reality capture process (Niles et al., 2022).

Qualitatively, it demonstrated that digitalization processes provide a robust asset data management from traceability until the information reliability into the organization's AMS (ISO, 2024a).

The application of cluster analysis and principal components analysis to the 106 reservoirs resulted in a new "tool" for the organization, enabling a broader view of the asset "health" in managing the critical water supply infrastructure. These methods provided valuable insights, offering opportunities for resource allocation prioritization and more structured decision-making for strategic governance.

This approach not only verified the effectiveness of digitalization processes through statistical modelling but also highlights the benefits of increasing investment in advanced data collection technologies. The case study with water tanks demonstrated improvement in accuracy, technical detailing, and integration of more reliable information with the AMS.

Future studies could encompass expanding this data analysis to other typologies of infrastructure assets. It is also recommended to research on the impact of AI algorithms to extract more valuable information for decision making and risk management in the organization´s asset management activities.

Acknowledgements The author is grateful for the Foundation for Science and Technology's support through funding UIDB/04625/2020 from the research unit CERIS.

Appendix 1–Correlation Matrix

Matriz de correlações

Correlação	DensPop	IDHM	NAm	NAn	NAe	NAc	NAi	NTme	ACm	ACn	ACe	ACc	ACi	ACme	DATm	DATn	DATe	DATc	DATi	DATme	DAFm	DAFn	DAFe	DAFc	DAFi	DAFme
DensPop	1.000																									
IDHM	0.936	1.000																								
NAm	0.113	0.120	1.000																							
NAn	0.134	0.115	0.553	1.000																						
NAe	0.042	0.038	0.713	0.551	1.000																					
NAc	-0.087	-0.039	0.352	0.077	0.328	1.000																				
NAi	-0.310	-0.209	0.489	0.379	0.675	0.301	1.000																			
NTme	0.044	0.063	0.950	0.613	0.880	0.428	0.673	1.000																		
ACm	-0.273	-0.247	0.054	0.142	0.062	0.034	0.118	0.077	1.000																	
ACn	-0.348	-0.332	0.014	0.039	0.037	0.008	0.125	0.038	0.608	1.000																
ACe	-0.208	-0.185	0.064	0.129	0.109	0.069	0.110	0.098	0.462	0.335	1.000															
ACc	-0.256	-0.191	-0.097	0.018	0.030	0.025	0.126	-0.033	0.398	0.368	0.441	1.000														
ACi	-0.346	-0.312	0.179	0.213	0.280	0.112	0.347	0.258	0.609	0.636	0.600	0.549	1.000													
ACme	-0.376	-0.333	0.040	0.123	0.121	0.058	0.207	0.098	0.763	0.795	0.707	0.731	0.865	1.000												
DATm	0.066	0.115	0.186	0.127	0.027	-0.071	0.104	0.138	0.326	0.107	0.154	0.159	0.227	0.233	1.000											
DATn	0.051	0.084	0.049	0.309	-0.054	-0.107	0.068	0.031	0.339	0.174	0.138	0.066	0.119	0.203	0.361	1.000										
DATe	-0.133	-0.043	-0.004	0.106	0.066	-0.089	0.275	0.051	0.315	0.238	0.290	0.372	0.377	0.406	0.597	0.260	1.000									
DATc	0.014	0.018	-0.090	-0.030	-0.018	-0.280	0.017	-0.080	0.214	0.160	0.198	0.307	0.219	0.284	0.555	0.150	0.614	1.000								
DATi	0.065	0.082	0.058	0.118	-0.013	-0.143	0.056	0.035	0.238	-0.018	0.161	0.186	0.169	0.169	0.559	0.433	0.480	0.531	1.000							
DATme	0.021	0.071	0.051	0.222	-0.013	-0.181	0.135	0.044	0.401	0.190	0.245	0.255	0.276	0.337	0.755	0.749	0.717	0.653	0.785	1.000						
DAFm	-0.039	0.041	0.271	0.205	0.105	-0.048	0.174	0.229	0.370	0.062	0.093	0.085	0.251	0.194	0.809	0.372	0.424	0.307	0.437	0.605	1.000					
DAFn	0.009	0.044	0.047	0.254	-0.066	-0.147	0.044	0.018	0.340	0.188	0.173	0.074	0.127	0.221	0.352	0.967	0.285	0.189	0.441	0.748	0.395	1.000				
DAFe	-0.105	-0.020	0.082	0.179	0.152	-0.026	0.287	0.140	0.272	0.114	0.273	0.307	0.317	0.318	0.474	0.239	0.868	0.403	0.434	0.600	0.484	0.284	1.000			
DAFc	-0.019	-0.009	-0.076	-0.066	-0.004	-0.320	0.020	-0.071	0.221	0.171	0.192	0.333	0.228	0.298	0.405	0.077	0.532	0.918	0.409	0.524	0.320	0.164	0.431	1.000		
DAFi	-0.124	-0.098	0.119	0.163	0.129	-0.074	0.182	0.139	0.159	-0.031	0.174	0.216	0.294	0.190	0.373	0.227	0.422	0.345	0.761	0.542	0.455	0.275	0.489	0.371	1.000	
DAFme	-0.080	-0.014	0.135	0.227	0.094	-0.158	0.204	0.138	0.379	0.129	0.256	0.276	0.342	0.335	0.666	0.573	0.696	0.560	0.728	0.862	0.745	0.637	0.753	0.590	0.771	1.000

Appendix 2–ANOVA Matrix (k-Means)

ANOVA

	Cluster Quadrado Médio	df	Erro Quadrado Médio	df	Z	Sig.
Zscore(DensPop)	1,454	4	0.984	114	1,478	0.214
Zscore(IDHM)	0.725	4	1,010	114	0.718	0.581
Zscore(NAm)	17,838	4	0.409	114	43,593	<0.001
Zscore(NAn)	9,501	4	0.702	114	13,539	<0.001
Zscore(NAe)	23,776	4	0.201	114	118,392	<0.001
Zscore(NAc)	16,150	4	0.486	114	34,539	<0.001
Zscore(NAi)	13,400	4	0.565	114	23,720	<0.001
Zscore(NTme)	23,003	4	0.228	114	100,904	<0.001
Zscore(ACm)	9,765	4	0.692	114	14,102	<0.001
Zscore(ACn)	4,682	4	0.871	114	5,377	<0.001
Zscore(ACe)	7,242	4	0.781	114	9,273	<0.001
Zscore(ACc)	4,453	4	0.879	114	5,067	<0.001
Zscore(ACi)	8,870	4	0.724	114	12,254	<0.001
Zscore(ACme)	10,337	4	0.672	114	15,374	<0.001
Zscore(DATm)	12,343	4	0.602	114	20,503	<0.001
Zscore(DATn)	11,237	4	0.641	114	17,535	<0.001
Zscore(DATe)	15,620	4	0.487	114	32,073	<0.001
Zscore(DATc)	18,245	4	0.395	114	46,202	<0.001
Zscore(DATi)	11,705	4	0.624	114	18,745	<0.001
Zscore(DATme)	20,993	4	0.298	114	70,335	<0.001
Zscore(DAFm)	8,608	4	0.733	114	11,744	<0.001
Zscore(DAFn)	12,437	4	0.599	114	20,774	<0.001
Zscore(DAFe)	12,186	4	0.608	114	20,059	<0.001
Zscore(DAFc)	12,819	4	0.585	114	21,901	<0.001
Zscore(DAFi)	8,535	4	0.736	114	11,602	<0.001
Zscore(DAFme)	18,980	4	0.369	114	51,421	<0.001

Appendix 3–ANOVA Matrix (k-means with ACP)

ANOVA

	Cluster Quadrado Médio	df	Erro Quadrado Médio	df	Z	Sig.
REGR factor score 1 for analysis 2	10,454	4	0.455	101	23,479	<0.001
REGR factor score 1 for analysis 2	15,748	4	0.389	101	40,513	<0.001
REGR factor score 1 for analysis 2	21,433	4	0.274	101	78,344	<0.001
REGR factor score 1 for analysis 2	17,890	4	0.329	101	54,438	<0.001
REGR factor score 1 for analysis 2	0.700	4	1.045	101	0.670	0.614

OS Testes-F devem ser usados apenas para finalidades descritivas porque os cluster foram escolhidos para maximizar as differencas entire os casos em clusters diferentes os níveis de significância observados não estão corrigidos para issoe, dessa forma, não podem interpretados como testes da hipótese de que as médias de cluster são iguais

References

Alegre, H., Vitorino, D., & Coelho, S. (2014). Infrastructure value index: A powerful modelling tool for combined long-term planning of linear and vertical assets. In *Procedia Engineering*. Elsevier Ltd.

Almeida, N. M. (2023). Estrutura e Conteúdos de um Plano de Gestão de Ativos. ed. RAE–Revista de Gestão de Ativos de Engenharia.

Alonso, P. J., Guillén, A. J., Gómez, J. F., & Candón, E. (2022). Review of asset digitalization models in the context of ıntelligent asset management and maintenance. *In 16th WCEAM Proceedings, Review of Asset Digitalization Models in the Context of Intelligent Asset Management and Maintenance*. Seville: Springer International Publishing, (pp. 87–97). *Lecture Notes in Mechanical Engineering*. https://link.springer.com/https://doi.org/10.1007/978-3-031-25448-2

Amadi-Echendu, J. E., Brown, K., Willett, R., & Mathew, J. (2012). Asset condition, ınformation systems and decision models, approaches to ınformation quality management: state of the practice of UK asset-ıntensive organisations, Springer London. *In: Engineering Asset Management Review* (vol. 2, pp.1–17) (EAMR). http://link.springer.com/https://doi.org/10.1007/978-1-4471-2924-0

Asian Development Bank. (2013). Water utility asset management: a guide for development practitioners.

Balogun, H., Alaka, H., Demir, E., Egwim, C. N., Olu-Ajayi, R., Sulaimon, I., & Oseghale, R. (2024). Artificial intelligence for deconstruction: Current state, challenges, and opportunities. https://www.sciencedirect.com/science/article/pii/S0926580524003777
Bolton, A. (2018). The gemini principles. *Centre for Digital Built Britain.* https://doi.org/10.17863/CAM.32260
Carvalho, W. O. (2021). BIM and AM to manage critical and relevant water and wastewater utilities assets. In *Proceedings of the 18th International Conference on Computing in Civil and Building Engineering–ICCCBE 2020* (pp. 697–720). https://link.springer.com/chapter/https://doi.org/10.1007/978-3-030-51295-8_49
Cronk, B. C. (2018). *How to Use SPSS® a Step-by-step Guide to Analysis and Interpretation, 10th Edition. Taylor & Francis Group, ed. Routledge.* https://routledgetextbooks.com/textbooks/9781032582351/
Feng, Y., Lin, S., Tang, X., Wang, M., Zheng, J., He, Z., Pang, Z., Yang, J. Chen, M., & Wei, X. (2025). Hyperbolic prototype rectification for few-shot 3D point cloud classification. *In Pattern Recognition*, Vol. 158.
Ferrari, A., & Russo, M. (2016). Introducing Microsoft Power BI, ed. Microsoft. https://a.co/d/7bkPqXE
Goodfellow, I., Bengio, Y., & Courville, A. (2018). Deep learning: Genetic programming and evolvable machines, pp. 305–307. https://doi.org/10.1007/s10710-017-9314-z
Grosch, R., & Bilot, P. (2002). A simple strategy for integrated plant management and control. In *ISA Instrumentation, Systems, and Automation Conference Proceedings*, pp. 13–23. https://www.scopus.com/record/display.uri?eid=2-s2.0-0036972664&origin=resultslist
Helfert, M., & Ge, M. (2007). A review of ınformation quality research: develop a research agenda. https://www.researchgate.net/publication/220918901
International Water Association (IWA). (2022). Digital Water Programme: A Strategic Digital Transformation for the Water Industry. IWA Publishing. https://iwa-network.org/publications/operational-digital-twins-in-the-urban-water-sector-case-studies/
ISO 55013:2024. (2024). Asset management–guidance on the management of data assets. https://www.iso.org/standard/82455.html
ISO 55001:2024. (2024). Asset management–management systems–requirements. https://www.iso.org/standard/83054.html
King, R. S. (2015). Cluster analysis and data mining: an ıntroduction. *Mercury Learning and Information, ed. David Pallai.* https://a.co/d/hiw8CGv
Kritzinger, W., Karner, M., Traar, G., Henjes, J., & Sihn, W. (2018). Digital twin in manufacturing: a categorical literature review and classification, *IFAC (International Federation of Automatic Control).* Elsevier B.V.
Marques, R. C. (2005). Regulação de Serviços Públicos, ed. Sílabo. Lisboa. https://silabo.pt/
Márquez, F. P. G. (2022). *Advances in Principal Component Analysis. London, ed. IntechOpen.* https://www.intechopen.com/books/11201
Murray, C., Anderson, R., Ravada, S., Hu, Y., Abugov, D., & Alexander, N. (2024). Oracle® Spatial and Graph Developer's Guide. https://docs.oracle.com/en/database/oracle/oracle-database/19/spatl/spatial-and-graph-developers-guide.pdf
Niles, J., McClure, S., & Pouliquen, D. (2022). Reality capture: A digital twin foundation. https://www.digitaltwinconsortium.org/wp-content/uploads/sites/3/2022/06/Reality-Capture-A-Digital-Twin-Foundation.pdf
O´Hanlon, T., & Gulati, R. (2020). 10 Rights of asset management. https://a.co/d/cT8G2Wm
Rani, A., Ortiz-Arroyo, D., & Durdevic, P. (2024). A survey of vision-based condition monitoring methods using deep learning: A synthetic fiber rope perspective. In *Engineering Applications of Artificial Intelligence*, Vol. 136.
Rokstad, M. M., Ugarelli, R. M., Sægrov, S. (2016). Improving data collection strategies and infrastructure asset management tool utilisation through cost benefit considerations. In: Urban Water Jornal, Taylor and Francis Ltd, pp. 710–26.

Sistema Nacional de Informações sobre o Saneamento (SNIS) e Trata-Brasil: Estudo de Perdas de Água de 2024: Desafios na Eficiência do Saneamento Básico no Brasil (2024). www.goassociados.com.br

The Institute of Asset Management (IAM). (2024). Asset Management–an anatomy. 4th ed. IAM. www.theIAM.org

United Nations Children's Fund (UNICEF) and World Health Organization (WHO). (2023). Progress on household drinking water, sanitation and hygiene 2000–2022. New York. https://washdata.org

Vieira, J., Martins, J. P., Almeida, N. M., Patrício, H., & Morgado, J. G. (2022). Towards resilient and sustainable rail and road networks: A systematic literature review on digital twins. *In: Sustainability (Switzerland), 14*. https://www.mdpi.com/journal/sustainability

World Bank Group. (2022). Water supply and sanitation: policies, institutions, and regulation. https://www.worldbank.org

XRProject. (2016). *Immersive Data Visualization, All Rights Reserved by FormulaXR*. https://www.xrproj.com/

The Synergy Between Lean Philosophy and Value Engineering for New Product Development

André Guimarães, Daniel Gaspar, Pedro Reis, and Antonio J. Marques Cardoso

Abstract Organizations worldwide consistently strive to eliminate waste through approaches like Lean and adopting core functions through concepts such as Value Engineering (VE). Several sources affirm that integrating VE with Lean can enhance, streamline, and amplify efforts to implement Lean principles within an organization. Conversely, Lean can improve the effectiveness of VE initiatives. Based on a comprehensive literature review utilizing a natural language processing algorithm, this study focuses on understanding the intersection between these concepts. The review identified eight main sub-topics across three key areas: Lean Healthcare and Performance, Customer Value Improvement, and Process and Product Optimization. The practical implications of integrating Lean and VE in product development include faster time-to-market, enhanced manufacturability, and improved product quality while reducing start-up issues and development costs. This integration fosters a more collaborative environment, aligning teams with customer needs and expectations. The unique contribution of this study lies in demonstrating how Lean and VE, when applied together, form a holistic and robust framework that optimizes efficiency and ensures superior functionality and cost-effectiveness throughout the product development lifecycle.

Keywords Lean production · Lean tools · Value engineering · Customer value

---

A. Guimarães (✉) · D. Gaspar · A. J. Marques Cardoso
CISE, Electromechatronic Systems Research Centre, University of Beira Interior, Covilhã, Portugal
e-mail: andre.m.guimaraes@ubi.pt

D. Gaspar
e-mail: danigaspar@estgv.ipv.pt

A. J. Marques Cardoso
e-mail: ajmcardoso@ieee.org

A. Guimarães · D. Gaspar · P. Reis
CISeD, Research Centre for Digital Services, Polytechnic Institute of Viseu, Viseu, Portugal
e-mail: pedroreis@estgv.ipv.pt

A. Crespo Márquez et al. (eds.), *Case Studies in Digital Transformation*, Engineering Asset Management Review 4, https://doi.org/10.1007/978-3-032-05592-7_14

1 Introduction

The Lean philosophy has been widely adopted to optimize processes by minimizing waste. Its positive impact on enhancing productivity and various other aspects is well-recognized. Initially associated with manufacturing, lean practices have shown significant potential in diverse areas, including developing products and services (Karlsson & Ahlstrom, 1996; Acur et al., 2012). However, despite substantial resources allocated to implementing lean on the manufacturing shop floor, fewer resources are devoted to those other areas (Marodin et al., 2018). Implementing Lean principles in the new product development process (NPD) is known as Lean Product Development (Karlsson & Ahlstrom, 1996; Salgado & Dekkers, 2018). According to various authors, lean product development promises to expedite the product development process, enhance manufacturability, elevate product quality, reduce production start-up issues, and achieve a quicker time to market (Karlsson & Ahlstrom, 1996; Khan et al., 2013; Meybodi, 2013).

Furthermore, it is well-known that a substantial portion of the costs incurred in product development are often spent on waste during the NPD process. Therefore, it is crucial to implement mechanisms to improve it. In this regard, methodologies such as Value Engineering (VE) have been applied to support the creation of new products by pinpointing chances to eliminate extra costs. This approach ensures quality, reliability, and performance, among other factors, aligning with customer expectations (AbdAllah et al., 2021; Adnan et al., 2018; Ekanayake & Sandanayake, 2017; Gumede & Hattingh, 2020; Ni et al., 2011). In addition to cost reduction, VE can improve communication, teamwork and knowledge sharing (Ganiyu et al., 2015). Integrating Lean practices with VE into the new product development process can further amplify these benefits, fostering a holistic approach to efficiency and cost-effectiveness from ideation to the final product delivery. While Lean is acknowledged as an operational philosophy capable of influencing organizational strategy, VE is characterized as an analytical tool commonly applied for tactical activities (Cell & Arratia, 2003; Musa et al., 2016; Nayak, 2006); they present two distinct approaches.

Although Lean Philosophy and Value Engineering (VE) have been widely studied independently, they were not initially intended to be integrated. Therefore, they require investigations to understand how to overcome the challenges in implementing this hybrid methodology. There is a lack of comprehensive studies investigating the integration of these methodologies in developing new products. Most existing research focuses on isolated approaches, which limits understanding of how these tools can be used together to maximize efficiency and added value.

The essential integration of these two concepts can yield superior outcomes, but it necessitates further comparative studies compared to their implementation. These studies should explore the synergy between the two concepts and assess the feasibility of an integrated approach in the industry. The decision-making framework is a crucial element for the successful implementation of Lean and VE, and it remains an area that requires further research.

Given this gap in the literature, the primary objective of this study is to explore how the integration of Lean and Value Engineering (VE) can enhance the product development process, particularly in terms of efficiency, cost-effectiveness, and product quality. Specifically, the research seeks to answer the following question: How can Lean tools be optimally integrated with VE methodologies to overcome current challenges in new product development? By addressing this question, the study aims to provide a practical framework that demonstrates the benefits of this integration, offering valuable insights for academia and industry on maximizing efficiency and delivering added value through a hybrid Lean-VE approach.

Furthermore, with increasing market pressures to reduce development time and costs while maintaining high quality, the need for a combined approach that effectively responds to these challenges is more relevant than ever. This study fills this gap by exploring the synergies between Lean and VE, offering an updated and practical perspective on how this integration can transform product development processes. The study contributes significantly to the body of knowledge by providing a detailed analysis and a helpful model, highlighting the applicability of this integration and the tangible benefits in the current industrial context.

This raises the question of how lean tools can be optimally integrated with the methodologies and tools of Value Engineering to enhance the process of developing new products. A literature review was conducted using the Latent Dirichlet Allocation (LDA) natural language processing algorithm to explore this. This algorithm enables the examination of article abstracts, pinpointing the key topics encompassing lean philosophy and value engineering.

The remaining sections are organized as follows. First, the study begins with a theoretical background section, with a literature review of the main concepts. In Sect. 3, the methodological steps are explained. In Sect. 4, the analysis and findings are presented. Finally, in Sect. 5, the conclusions are given, and the future research directions are proposed.

2 Literature Review

2.1 Lean Philosophy

The Lean philosophy has been extensively adopted to optimize processes by minimizing waste, with its positive impact on productivity and various other aspects being well-recognized. Originally associated with manufacturing, Lean practices have demonstrated significant potential across diverse areas, including product and service development (Karlsson & Ahlstrom, 1996; Acur et al., 2012). Lean principles help streamline operations, reduce costs, and enhance quality. However, despite substantial investments in implementing Lean on the manufacturing shop floor, a lack of equivalent focus and resources are often dedicated to product development processes (Marodin et al., 2018). This disparity suggests a missed opportunity to leverage Lean's full potential in creating more efficient and innovative product development cycles, ultimately leading to quicker time-to-market and improved competitive advantage.

According to Tauriainen et al. (2016), Lean, in its simplest form, concentrates on providing superior value to customers by eradicating waste from every stage of the work process. Mandujano et al. (2016) state that Lean is a management philosophy that centers around recognizing and minimizing waste using its tools and principles. Womack & Jones (1997) emphasize the pivotal role of value in Lean thinking, stating that value is determined by the end customer when a particular product or service satisfies their requirements at a specific price and within a specific timeframe.

Lean Philosophy in New Product Development

There is a rising concern regarding the rapid pace of developing and launching new products to keep up with dynamic market changes. However, speed alone is insufficient and inadequate if it compromises quality or fails to provide value to consumers. In that sense, Morgan (2002) suggests that expediting the launch of new products involves optimizing efficiency in both product development processes (PDP) and manufacturing stages.

Applying lean principles to new product development could have a more profound impact on lean enterprises than lean production (Morgan & Liker, 2020). Marodin et al. (2018) illustrated that companies achieving superior operational performance adopt lean manufacturing (LM) and product development. A lean approach to new product development is valuable, effectively integrating people, processes, tools, and technologies to deliver value to consumers and society (Morgan & Liker, 2020). The authors contend that lean concepts give companies more opportunities to gain a competitive advantage in product development than other industrial processes. In Reinertsen (2005) point of view, Lean Development (LD) aims to use Lean Manufacturing (LM) principles in product development. This is done to create efficient processes that lead to quicker launches of new products in the market, enhancing a company's responsiveness. According to Womack et al. (1990), Lean Manufacturing tools can be adapted for application in new product development. Moreover, Ward and Sobek (2014) propose that Lean Development (LD) can reduce the time and resources needed for new product development by up to four. Moreover, it can decrease quality and deadline risks by up to ten.

2.2 *Value Engineering*

Value Engineering is a systematic problem-solving approach that examines various aspects, including systems, facilities, services, and supplies, to accomplish essential functions at the lowest life cycle cost (LCC) without compromising quality. It aims to minimize unnecessary costs and, at the same time, improve or maintain quality, applying to different areas such as products, services, processes, methods, materials, and programs. Chen et al. (2010) defined VE as a systematic method that combines practical insight and technical knowledge to identify and eliminate unnecessary project costs, ensuring optimal value for money. According to Zhang et al. (2009), VE is a management tool that attains the essential functions of a product, service, or project at the lowest possible cost. Additionally, Male et al. (2007) described VE as a methodological management style focused on enhancing value. By promoting teamwork, VE facilitates innovative cost-reduction techniques, contributing to improving project value, quality, and risk reduction (Adnan et al., 2018).

Expanding on the findings of Perera et al. (2011), it is crucial to emphasize that VE goes beyond cost reduction; its primary aim is to achieve the best value or ensure cost-effectiveness in a project. Beyond cost savings, VE can yield additional advantages such as enhanced communication, improved teamwork, shared understanding among key stakeholders, higher project quality, more precise design definition, and increased innovation (Amuda Yusuf et al., 2015).

Value Engineering in New Product Development

Due to the expansion and growth of competition, companies must strive to meet customer demands and expectations. Therefore, there is a need to develop new products that meet customer expectations, applying diverse techniques to enhance the efficiency, value, and reliability of products and services while reducing costs. An indispensable technique for achieving these goals is VE (Adnan et al., 2018; Gambhir & Belokar, 2015).

Engaging with potential customers during product development and consistently verifying results are essential to ensure the product's competitiveness (Gruner & Homburg, 2000; Hoyer et al., 2010). Another significant task is cutting production costs and meeting the product's target cost (Murukina et al., 2020). The VE method is employed to determine the worth or value of a product during its development stage (Abdullah & Adesta, 2015). Value Engineering reduces the time required to develop a new product and increases competitiveness. Diversification and development of new products become essential for business adaptation in a constantly changing economic environment (Murukina et al., 2020). Value engineering can enhance a new product's development or redesign by increasing its value and cutting costs (Kiran, 2016). It enables the perspective of viewing the product as a collection of functions it must fulfill, thereby creating value for the consumer.

2.3 *Integration of Lean Philosophy and Value Engineering*

Lean and VE provide systematic methods to reduce unnecessary costs, time, and waste while ensuring project functionality and value for the client's money. While both share the goal of achieving value, it is important to note that Lean is a philosophy, and VE is an analytical tool. Despite Lean's effectiveness, it doesn't solve all problems (Cell & Arratia, 2003), necessitating additional efforts to overcome associated drawbacks (Garbie, 2010). The primary aim of Lean is to eliminate non-value-adding activities in all processes, whereas VE focuses on enhancing project functionality at a minimal cost. Despite their different approaches, Lean and VE converge on a shared goal: delivering value for the customer's money (Ekanayake & Sandanayake, 2017).

Lean and VE were originally designed separately, with no intention of combining their theoretical concepts, tools, and techniques (Nayak, 2006). Both methodologies frequently utilized common elements such as: Value Stream Mapping, Waste elimination, Function analysis, Failure mode effect analysis (FMEA) (Gumede & Hattingh, 2020).

The literature investigates different ways to implement the Lean and VE hybrid methodology, examining approaches such as concurrent and integrated use models (Cell & Arratia, 2003; Nayak, 2006). Some sources suggest exclusively using integrated use models (Ekanayake & Sandanayake, 2017; Mandelbaum et al., 2017; Shekari & Fallahian, 2007), believing that the similarities between Lean and VE can justify their interchangeable use (Musa et al., 2016; Nayak, 2006). Hybrid methodologies that combine Lean and VE typically follow the following development approaches (Cell & Arratia, 2003; Ekanayake & Sandanayake, 2017; Mandelbaum et al., 2017; Musa et al., 2016; Nayak, 2006; Shekari & Fallahian, 2007):

- Reviewing Lean and VE theories and practices.
- Analyzing Lean and VE comparatively to assess strengths, weaknesses, advantages, and disadvantages, considering organizational factors like products, processes, and system objectives.
- Concluding a decision-making process.
- Implementing a hybrid Lean and VE methodology based on the chosen model type.

Several terms have been used to characterize the implementation models of hybrid Lean and VE methodologies. According to the study by Gumede & Hattingh (2020), to minimize confusion, three primary models for Lean and hybrid VE methodology are suggested:

- **Interchangeable Use Models**: Employing either Lean or VE (or their components) interchangeably. Lean and VE are applied separately and are mutually exclusive (Musa et al., 2016; Nayak, 2006);
- **Concurrent Use Models**: Simultaneously applying individual Lean and VE (or their components). Lean and VE are applied separately and are mutually inclusive (Cell & Arratia, 2003; Nayak, 2006);
- **Integrated Use Models**: Sequentially implementing amalgamated Lean and VE (or their combined components). Lean and VE are connected and interdependent, forming a cohesive whole. They are applied together through a merged structure (Cell & Arratia, 2003; Ekanayake & Sandanayake, 2017; Mandelbaum et al., 2017; Nayak, 2006).

Considering the strengths and weaknesses of Lean and Value Engineering (VE), integrating these two methodologies has been emphasized as crucial for addressing fundamental issues that lead to poor industry performance and high costs. The primary goal is to enhance customer value by optimizing costs, quality, and delivery.

A seamless implementation of Lean and VE has been suggested as beneficial. Furthermore, it has been noted that Lean and VE concepts can complement each other in manufacturing. The essential integration of these concepts has been highlighted to achieve superior results compared to separate implementations. An algorithm, presented as a flowchart, was proposed to integrate Lean and VE concepts, thereby realizing benefits and solving challenges that may not be addressed individually in manufacturing. Additionally, synergies between Lean Six Sigma and VE have been explored, identifying opportunities for combined applications to enhance overall benefits beyond the capabilities of individual approaches.

3 Method

This study used a comprehensive literature review utilizing a natural language processing model. The literature review attempts to identify what has been written about a particular subject to provide a broad and thorough understanding of the current state of knowledge in a given area (Paré et al., 2015). It provides the theoretical foundations and context for the research question, thus serving as an essential starting point in the research process.

Seven main steps were followed to conduct the literature review, as illustrated in Fig. 1.

The following sections outline the methodological steps undertaken during the research process.

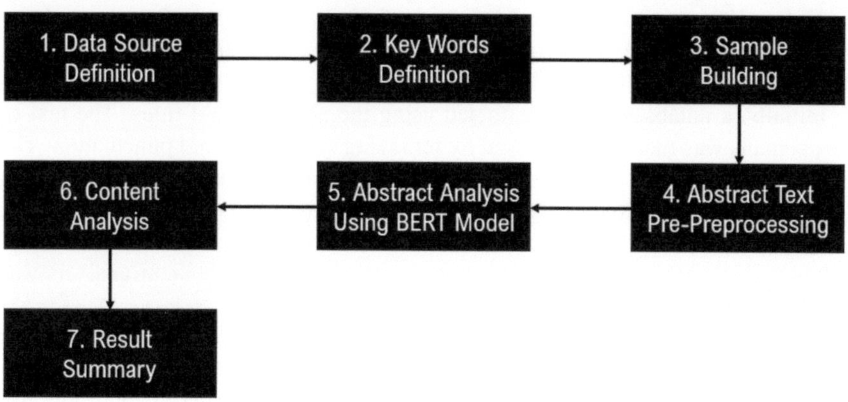

Fig. 1 Methodological steps

3.1 Data Source

The Scopus database was utilized for gathering data because it is recognized as a trustworthy source for research projects involving literature reviews. Scopus offers an Application Programming Interface (API) that enables researchers at different levels to conduct automated and effective searches, making it easier to retrieve articles.

3.2 Data Collection

The keywords employed were: ("lean philosophy" OR "lean production" OR "lean manufacturing" OR "lean start-up" OR "lean product" OR "lean innovation" OR "Lean thinking") AND ("Value Engineering" OR "Value Analysis" OR "Value Identification" OR "Customer Value"). The research was restricted to articles published in English.

3.3 Model Building

A natural language processing model known as BERTopic (Wang et al., 2023) was used to analyze abstracts and identify the main intersection topics between Lean and Value Engineering (VE). The choice of BERTopic over other NLP methods is due to its ability to generate easily interpretable topics while preserving important word descriptions, thanks to combining transformers and c-TF-IDF to create dense clusters. This approach allows for a richer and more contextualized analysis of the themes addressed, facilitating the identification of significant patterns in the data.

Initially, a database was constructed using the abstracts and titles. The text of the abstracts was then pre-processed by removing stop words and punctuation. The BERT model was run in the next stage, classifying articles based on their abstract content. The words with the highest scores were analyzed to understand each topic better. Additionally, the correlation between issues was analyzed using a heatmap. Following selecting articles based on the code execution, a content analysis was conducted by reading and summarizing each article.

However, it is essential to note that using BERTopic has some limitations. One of the main limitations is its dependence on abstract text rather than complete articles. This can limit the depth of the analysis, as abstracts often do not capture the full complexity and nuances of the content discussed in the articles. Consequently, the interpretation of the topics may not fully reflect the ideas and themes explored in the analyzed publications. These limitations should be considered when interpreting the analysis results and considering future investigations in this area.

4 Results and Discussions

A total of 457 articles were obtained. Utilizing the BERT model, eight primary topics associated with Lean and Value Engineering were identified, as illustrated in Fig. 2. Upon closer examination of Figs. 2 and 3, it became evident that specific topics exhibited high correlation. Consequently, these topics were consolidated into three major themes.

The first major topic is related to Lean Healthcare and Lean Performance: This topic covers articles mainly focused on Lean Healthcare and how to improve the patient experience. It also includes articles that studied the concept of Lean startup and metrics to measure lean performance.

The second major topic pertains to Customer Value Improvement. Studies within this theme primarily focus on Customer Requirements Identification, Value Creation, Value Design in the construction sector, and Cost Reduction.

The third major topic pertains to Process and Product Optimization, encompassing articles examining strategies for enhancing manufacturing quality and productivity across various stages, from the new product development process to production and distribution. In Fig. 3, it is possible to observe how sub-topics group the articles.

In Fig. 4, it is possible to observe how the articles are grouped by sub-topics.

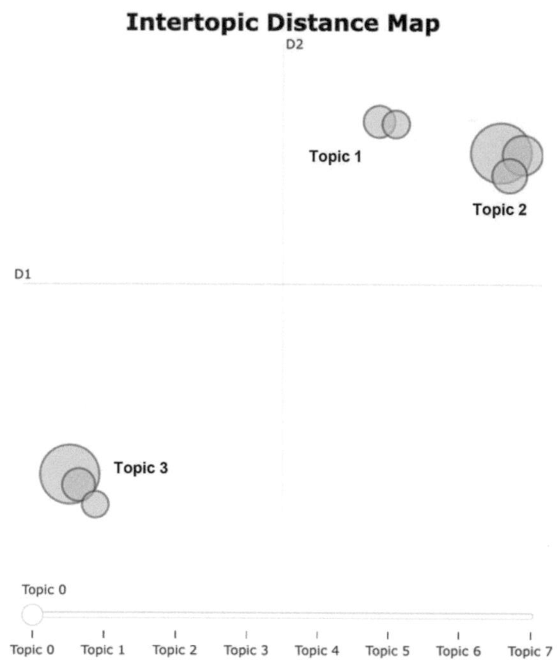

Fig. 2 Number of topics

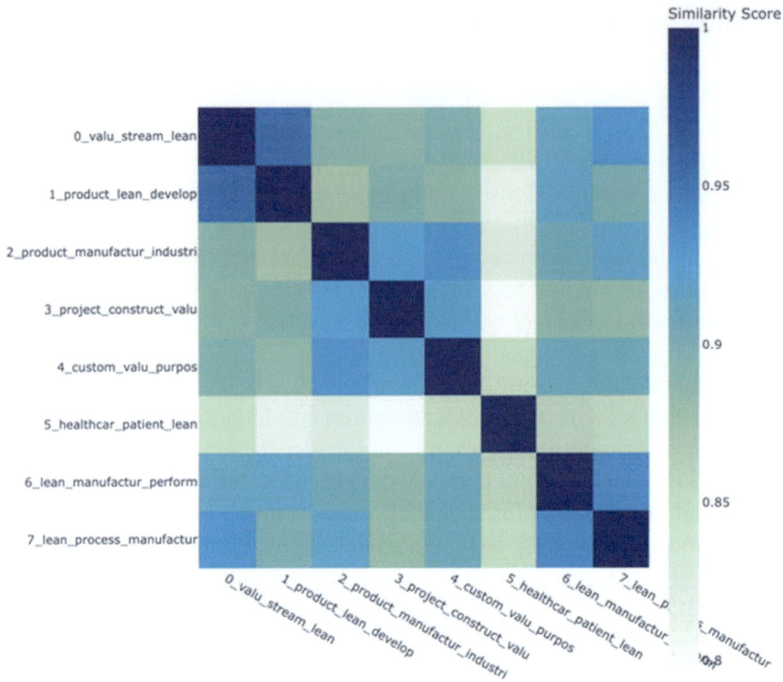

Fig. 3 Correlation between topics

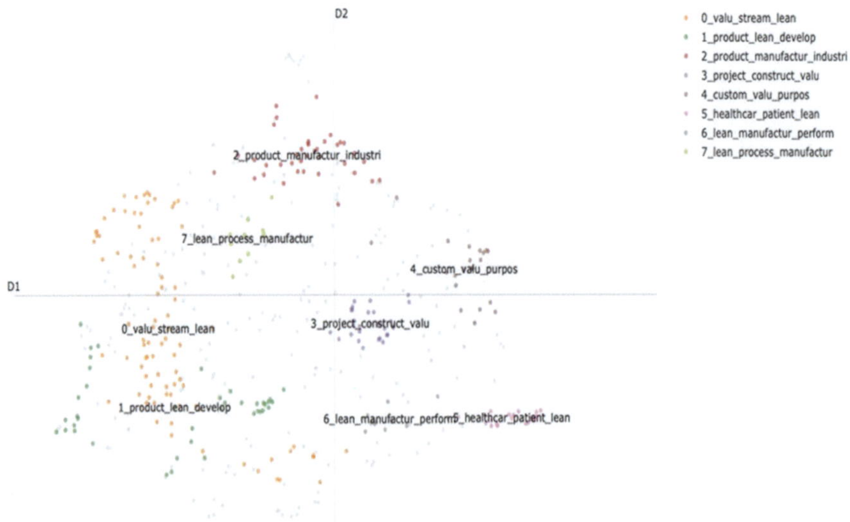

Fig. 4 Clusters representation

Studies on Lean Healthcare have primarily concentrated on optimizing and enhancing service delivery while improving the patient experience. These studies have utilized lean methodologies such as Value Stream Mapping, one-piece flow, and root-cause analysis to streamline operations, reduce cycle times, and identify inefficiencies to enhance patient care (Amati et al., 2022; Kim et al., 2007). However, no studies have been identified that explored the integration of value engineering with lean principles in this domain. Hence, this represents a potentially promising avenue for future research.

Moreover, within the scope of Topic 1, there has been significant academic interest in understanding how to measure the implementation of Lean methodologies. Various studies have concentrated on developing indicators and performance evaluation models to assess the effectiveness of Lean practices (Ruben et al., 2017). Within this subtopic, Lermen et al. (2023) specifically explored evaluating the implementation of Lean Startup Agile UX methods within digital startups, including Design Thinking, Lean Startup, and Lean User Experience. Aligned with the Value Engineering (VE) methodology, the Lean Startup approach facilitates testing the generated value and implementing incremental enhancements to the product before its introduction to the market. This is achieved through a systematic, iterative process of innovation creation.

As for Topic 2, most studies have focused on tools and methodologies to identify customer requirements to enhance product functionalities, reduce production costs, and improve overall customer value. Authors in this context have explored Design for Manufacturing, Engineering Change, and Lean Product Development (Gudem et al., 2013; Lodgaard et al., 2018). Additionally, some researchers have examined digital technologies like Virtual Reality and Information Modeling for product customization (Zhang et al., 2022). Notably, most of these studies have applications in the construction sector.

Furthermore, various articles have explored the joint application of methodologies such as Lean Six Sigma, Value Engineering (VE), Lean Production, and Quality Function Deployment (QFD) in product design and testing to optimize processes and minimize costs (Pries & Quigley, 2012; Gavareshki & Rostamkhani, 2017).

Finally, the Process and Product Optimization topic encompasses studies exploring concepts such as Lean Design, Lean Product Development, Lean Innovation, Cost Value Stream Mapping, and the use of Simulation as a complementary tool to support Value Stream Mapping (Gudem & Welo, 2010; Gudem et al., 2014; Rajesh et al., 2019). These studies focus on strategies for enhancing manufacturing quality and productivity across various stages, from new product development to production and distribution. Researchers have examined integrating these lean methodologies to optimize processes, reduce costs, and improve overall efficiency, showcasing how such tools can significantly contribute to better performance in manufacturing environments.

Figure 5 summarizes the main results found.

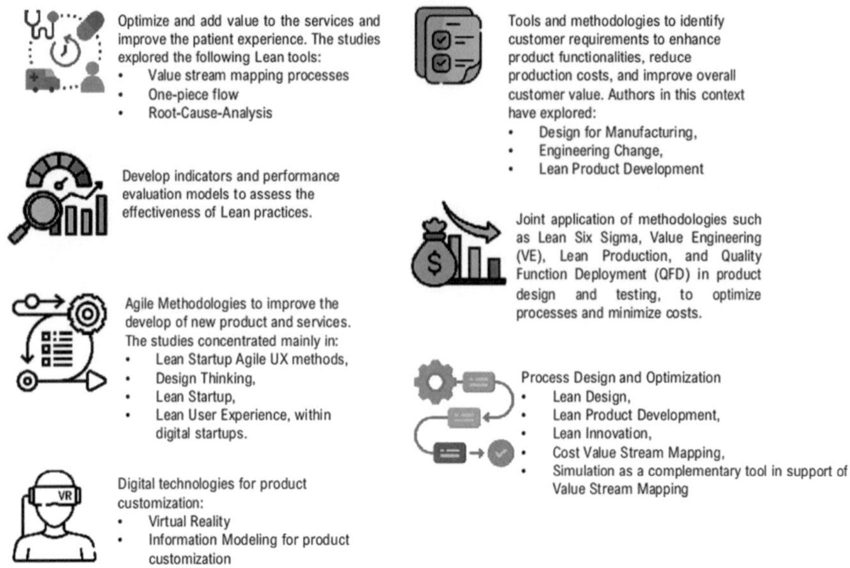

Fig. 5 Results summary

5 Conclusion

This article comprehensively overviews the critical domains in integrating Lean Manufacturing and Value Engineering (VE). Three principal areas have been identified: Lean Healthcare and Lean Performance, Customer Value Improvement, and Process and Product Optimization. Studies on Lean Healthcare have focused on improving the patient experience and suggest a promising future for implementing VE alongside Lean in this sector. Despite the intrinsic differences between Lean and VE methodologies, this study has uncovered substantial potential for their combined application in product development and reengineering. This integration fosters a holistic framework and comprehensive paradigm that enhances operational efficiency, reduces costs, and improves product quality, offering significant value throughout the entire product development lifecycle, from conception to final product delivery.

In practical terms, this integration holds particular promise for healthcare, construction, and manufacturing industries, where cost reduction and high-quality levels are critical. The Lean-VE synergy can help these industries streamline processes, minimize waste, and deliver customer value efficiently. For example, Lean and VE could lead to shorter lead times in patient care delivery while maintaining high-quality standards. In manufacturing, this integration may accelerate the time-to-market of products while controlling production costs.

Future studies should focus on empirical research and case studies that explore the practical application of Lean and VE in various sectors. Such studies would provide deeper insights into how these methodologies can be effectively implemented, assess their effectiveness, and measure their impact on industry-specific outcomes. Comparative analyses across different sectors could also help identify unique challenges and best practices, offering valuable lessons for academic research and real-world applications. Emphasizing practical benefits in specific industries will further demonstrate the applicability of the Lean-VE hybrid approach, enhancing its relevance in today's competitive market environment.

Acknowledgements This work is funded by National Funds through the FCT–Foundation for Science and Technology, I.P., within the scope of the project Ref. UIDB/05583/2020. Furthermore, we would like to thank the Research Centre in Digital Services (CISeD) and the Polytechnic Institute of Viseu for their support. This work was also supported by the Foundation for Science and Technology (FCT), funded by the research grant with the reference UI/BD/154507/2022.

References

AbdAllah, E., Mostafa, N., Gamila, M. A., & Elawady, H. (2021). Value engineering and cost of quality: An integrated framework. *International Journal of Productivity and Quality Management, 33*(3), 407–419.

Abdullah, A., & Adesta, E. (2015). Implementation of functional analysis using value analysis value engineering (VAVE). *ARPN J. Eng. Appl. Sc, 10*(21), 10072–10076.

Acur, N., Kandemir, D., & Boer, H. (2012). Strategic alignment and new product development: Drivers and performance effects. *Journal of Product Innovation Management, 29*(2), 304–318.

Adnan, T. M., Hasan, S., Rahman, M. S., & Das, A. (2018). An analytical way to reduce cost of a product through value engineering employment (case study: Walton). *International Journal of Scientific Engineering and Research, 9*(2), 527–533.

Amati, M., Valnegri, A., Bressan, A., La Regina, D., Tassone, C., Lo Piccolo, A., & Saporito, A. (2022). Reducing changeover time between surgeries through lean thinking: An action research project. *Frontiers in Medicine, 9*, Article 822964.

Amuda Yusuf, G., Sanni, A. O., & Olowa, T. O. (2015). Appraisal of application of value engineering methodology in mechanical and electrical services installations.

Cell, C. L., & Arratia, B. (2003). Creating value with lean thinking and value engineering. In *43rd Annual Society of American Value Engineers International Conference* (pp. 7–11).

Chen, W. T., Chang, P. Y., & Huang, Y. H. (2010). Assessing the overall performance of value engineering workshops for construction projects. *International Journal of Project Management, 28*(5), 514–527.

Ekanayake, E. M. A. C., & Sandanayake, Y. G. (2017). LiVE approach: lean integrated value engineering for construction industry. *Built Environment Project and Asset Management, 7*(5), 518–533.

Gambhir, A. S., & Belokar, D. (2015). Review and illustrates the value engineering technique. *International Journal of Engineering Technology, Management and Applied Sciences, 3*, 406–413.

Ganiyu, A. Y., Sanni, A. O., & Olowa, T. O. (2015). Appraisal of application of value engineering methodology in mechanical and electrical services installations. *J Teknol, 77*, 85–93.

Garbie, I. H. (2010). Enhancing the performance of industrial firms through implementation of lean techniques. In *IIE Annual Conference. Proceedings. Institute of Industrial and Systems Engineers* (IISE) (p. 1).

Gavareshki, M. K., Abbasi, M., & Rostamkhani, R. (2017). Application of QFD & VE & lean approach for control tests in a product design. *Archives of Materials Science, 66*, 66.

Gruner, K. E., & Homburg, C. (2000). Does customer interaction enhance new product success? *Journal of Business Research, 49*(1), 1–14.

Gudem, M., & Welo, T. (2010). From lean product development to lean innovation: finding better ways of satisfying customer value. In New World Situation: New Directions in Concurrent Engineering: In *Proceedings of the 17th ISPE International Conference on Concurrent Engineering* (pp. 347–355). Springer London.

Gudem, M., Steinert, M., & Welo, T. (2014). From lean product development to lean innovation: Searching for a more valid approach for promoting utilitarian and emotional value. *International Journal of Innovation and Technology Management, 11*(02), 1450008.

Gudem, M., Steinert, M., Welo, T., & Leifer, L. (2013). Redefining customer value in lean product development design projects. *Journal of Engineering, Design and Technology, 11*(1), 71–89.

Gumede, N. P., & Hattingh, T. S. (2020). Establishing a selection framework for a lean and value engineering hybrid methodology. *South African Journal of Industrial Engineering, 31*(4), 32–45.

Hoyer, W. D., Chandy, R., Dorotic, M., Krafft, M., & Singh, S. S. (2010). Consumer cocreation in new product development. *Journal of Service Research, 13*(3), 283–296.

Karlsson, C., & Ahlström, P. (1996). The difficult path to lean product development. *Journal of Product Innovation Management, 13*(4), 283–295.

Khan, M. S., Al-Ashaab, A., Shehab, E., Haque, B., Ewers, P., Sorli, M., & Sopelana, A. (2013). Towards lean product and process development. *International Journal of Computer Integrated Manufacturing, 26*(12), 1105–1116.

Kim, C. S., Hayman, J. A., Billi, J. E., Lash, K., & Lawrence, T. S. (2007). The application of lean thinking to the care of patients with bone and brain metastasis with radiation therapy. *Journal of Oncology Practice, 3*(4), 189–193.

Kiran, D. R. (2016). Total quality management: Key concepts and case studies. Butterworth-Heinemann.

Lermen, F. H., de Moura, P. K., Bertoni, V. B., Graciano, P., & Tortorella, G. L. (2023). Does maturity level influence the use of Agile UX methods by digital startups? Evaluating design thinking, lean startup, and lean user experience. *Information and Software Technology, 154*, Article 107107.

Lodgaard, E., Ringen, G., & Larsson, C. E. (2018). Viewing the engineering change process from a Lean product development and a business perspective. *Journal of the Knowledge Economy, 9*, 1374–1390.

Male, S., Kelly, J., Gronqvist, M., & Graham, D. (2007). Managing value as a management style for projects. *International Journal of Project Management, 25*(2), 107–114.

Mandelbaum, J., Hermes, A., Parker, D., & Williams, H. (2017). *Value engineering synergies with lean six sigma: Combining methodologies for enhanced results.* CRC Press.

Mandujano, R. M. G., Alarcón, L., Kunz, J., & Mourgues, C. (2016). Identifying waste in virtual design and construction practice from a lean thinking perspective: A meta-analysis of the literature. *Revista de la Construcción, 15*(3), 107–118.

Marodin, G., Frank, A. G., Tortorella, G. L., & Netland, T. (2018). Lean product development and lean manufacturing: Testing moderation effects. *International Journal of Production Economics, 203*, 301–310.

Meybodi, M. Z. (2013). The links between lean manufacturing practices and concurrent engineering method of new product development: an empirical study. *Benchmarking: An International Journal, 20*(3), 362–376.

Morgan, J. M. (2002). High performance product development: a systems approach to a lean product development process. University of Michigan.

Morgan, J., & Liker, J. K. (2020). *The Toyota product development system: Integrating people, process, and technology.* CRC Press.

Murukina, A. D., Tipner, L. M., Prilutskaya, M. A., & Kalinina, N. A. (2020). Marketing aspect in the 'Value Engineering' in the new products development of machine-building enterprises. *In IOP Conference Series: Materials Science and Engineering, 966*(1), 012097

Musa, M. M., Pasquire, C., & Hurst, A. (2016). Where lean construction and value management meet.

Nayak, B. (2006). Lean manufacturing and value management convergence of divergent tools. In *46th Annual Society of American Engineers: Managing Projects to Maximize Value, Savannah,* Georgia, USA, pp. 342–359.

Ni, Y., Fan, F., Zheng, Y., & Zhang, Y. (2011). Value engineering-driven lean product development. *Advanced Science Letters, 4*(6–7), 2440–2445.

Paré, G., Trudel, M. C., Jaana, M., & Kitsiou, S. (2015). Synthesizing information systems knowledge: A typology of literature reviews. *Information & Management, 52*(2), 183–199.

Perera, S., Hayles, C. S., & Kerlin, S. (2011). An analysis of value management in practice: The case of Northern Ireland's construction industry. *Journal of Financial Management of Property and Construction, 16*(2), 94–110.

Pries, K. H., & Quigley, J. M. (2012). *Reducing Process Costs with Lean, Six Sigma, and Value Engineering Techniques*. CRC Press.

Rajesh, M. B., Shalij, P. R., Kiron, K. R., Sajith, V. S., & Sreejith, J. (2019). Methodology for preparing a cost-value stream map. *In Journal of Physics: Conference Series, 1355*(1), 012021.

Reinertsen, D. (2005). Let it flow: How lean product development sparked a revolution. *Industrial Engineer, 37*(6), 40–46.

Ruben, R. B., Asokan, P., & Vinodh, S. (2017). Performance evaluation of lean sustainable systems using adaptive neuro fuzzy inference system: A case study. *International Journal of Sustainable Engineering, 10*(3), 158–175.

Salgado, E. G., & Dekkers, R. (2018). Lean product development: Nothing new under the sun? *International Journal of Management Reviews, 20*(4), 903–933.

Shekari, A., & Fallahian, S. (2007). A new approach to linking value engineering and lean methodology. In *19th International Conference on Production Research, Valparaiso, Chile* (Vol. 29).

Tauriainen, M., Marttinen, P., Dave, B., & Koskela, L. (2016). The effects of BIM and lean construction on design management practices. *Procedia Engineering, 164*, 567–574.

Wang, Z., Chen, J., Chen, J., & Chen, H. (2023). Identifying interdisciplinary topics and their evolution based on BERTopic. *Scientometrics*, 1–26.

Ward, A. C., & Sobek II, D. K. (2014). Lean product and process development. Lean Enterprise Institute.

Womack, J. P., & Jones, D. T. (1997). Lean thinking—banish waste and create wealth in your corporation. *Journal of the Operational Research Society, 48*(11), 1148–1148.

Womack, J. P., Jones, D. T., & Roos, D. (1990). The machine that changed the world. *Rawson Associates. New York, 323*(1), 273–287.

Zhang, X., Mao, X., & AbouRizk, S. M. (2009). Developing a knowledge management system for improved value engineering practices in the construction industry. *Automation in Construction, 18*(6), 777–789.

Zhang, Y., Wang, J., Ahmad, R., & Li, X. (2022). Integrating lean production strategies, virtual reality technique and building information modeling method for mass customization in cabinet manufacturing. *Engineering, Construction and Architectural Management, 29*(10), 3970–3996.

Business and Organizational Perspectives

An Asset Management Approach to Beekeeping for Enhanced Pollination and Agriculture Sustainability

Azucena Marques, Miguel Vilas-Boas, and Nuno Marques de Almeida

Abstract Intensive agriculture has led to increasingly homogenous landscapes in Europe and North America, decreasing the biodiversity of rural areas. Plant-pollinator interactions are affected by crop diversification, flower availability, and environmental conditions. Pollinators are crucial in maintaining the ecosystem, responsible for about 70% of crop species worldwide and approximately 35% of total food production. The decline in insect pollination can result in significant economic losses, food shortages, and the extinction of several species. In the European Union, almost four-fifths of wildflowers and crops in temperate regions depend to some extent on insect pollination. Among more than 200,000 known species of pollinators, the honeybee *Apis mellifera* is one of the most efficient and essential pollinators. Bees can carry many pollen grains and are highly dependent on floral resources, making them necessary and effective service providers. Beekeeping offers invaluable benefits to agriculture by supporting crop production, thereby increasing the yields of pollinator-dependent crops. Beekeeping is a source of income for millions worldwide, and pollination services are worth over $215 billion annually. In the United Kingdom, *Apis mellifera* provides pollination for approximately 34% of commercial crops and plays a fundamental role in supporting biodiversity. In 2007, the value of pollination as a contribution to the UK agricultural market was £430 million. Honeybees provides different products such as honey, beeswax, pollen, honeydew, and propolis. The beekeeping activity contributes to biodiversity and forest conservation. Bees are a natural asset and a key to sustainability and life on earth; however, they are at risk, and action is needed to protect them and optimize the value they can derive from them. This paper discusses the opportunities for approaching this complex problem using asset management principles and techniques.

Keywords Asset management · Honeybees · Beekeeping · *Apis mellifera* · Sustainable farming · Pollination services

---

A. Marques (✉) · N. Marques de Almeida
CERIS, Instituto Superior Técnico, Universidade de Lisboa, Lisboa, Portugal
e-mail: azucena.marques@tecnico.ulisboa.pt

A. Marques · M. Vilas-Boas
CIMO, LA SusTEC, Instituto Politécnico de Bragança, Bragança, Portugal

A. Crespo Márquez et al. (eds.), *Case Studies in Digital Transformation*, Engineering Asset Management Review 4, https://doi.org/10.1007/978-3-032-05592-7_15

1 Introduction

Pollinators, particularly bees, play an essential role in pollination and the ecosystem. These natural assets yield approximately 70% of crop species worldwide, accounting for around 35% of total food production (Wood et al., 2015). Of this service, 80% was attributed to *Apis mellifera L.* (Potts et al., 2010; Wood et al., 2015).

Agricultural intensification has resulted in increasingly less heterogeneous landscapes across Europe and North America, the main driver of the decline in farmland biodiversity. While there is evidence that wild bee decline rates are slowing, the truth is that they have been negatively affected (Centeno-Alvarado et al., 2023; Wood et al., 2015). The decrease in insect pollination can result in enormous economic, social, and environmental impacts due to the disappearance of several species and, consequently, a food shortage (Centeno-Alvarado et al., 2023).

Pollinator loss will impact wildflowers and cultivated crops (Potts et al., 2010). Plant-pollinator interactions are affected by crop diversification, i.e., flower availability, environmental conditions, and vegetation composition (Centeno-Alvarado et al., 2023). The current agricultural production system, with the excessive use of pesticides, fertilizers, and monocultures, has caused a drastic decrease in pollinators (Hipólito et al., 2016). Beekeeping can act in the opposite direction, promoting biodiversity and supporting forest conservation (Abro et al., 2022).

Bees depend highly on floral resources (nectar and pollen) and can transport many pollen grains, making this species one of the most essential and effective pollinators (Patel et al., n.d.). In the European Red List assessment, from the 1965 species of European bees, 9,2% were threatened. Still, much data was unavailable to effectively assess the conservation status of almost 57% of European species, so many may also be threatened.

In recent years, there has been an increased demand for pollinators due to the increase in global agriculture. Growing pollinator dependence does not appear to increase with crop diversification but rather due to the rise of large-scale pollinator-dependent monocultures such as soybeans. Unfortunately, while pollinator dependence has increased, agricultural practices that undermine pollination services have also increased. As a result, there has been an effective reduction of pollinators in agricultural fields (Mashilingi et al., 2022).

The decline of pollinators worldwide has severe consequences, not only for crop yields but also for human health. Pollinator-dependent crops are the primary sources of many essential micronutrients, including vitamins A and C, calcium, and folic acid (Bartholomée et al., 2020; Potts et al., 2016). Those policies were designed to implement different interventions such as: (i) knowledge exchange, advisory, training, and technical assistance; (ii) investments for combatting beehive diseases and invaders, preventing climate damage and adaptation, restocking of beehives and breeding or rationalizing transhumance; (iii) improvement and control of apiculture products; (iv) preserving and increase the number of beehives; (v) cooperation for research in beekeeping and products; (vi) promotion, communication and marketing and; (vii) enhancing product quality (Union European, 2024). These measures offer opportunities to preserve and improve the sector and ensure the survival of bees.

In the European Union, nearly four-fifths of wildflowers and crops in temperate regions depend to varying degrees on insect pollination. The annual contribution of pollinating insects to European agriculture is around €15 billion.

Of over 200.000 known pollinator species, the honeybee *Apis mellifera* remains the most important pollinator. Beekeeping is a source of income for millions worldwide, and pollination services are worth more than €196 billion annually (Abro et al., 2022).

In the UK, *Apis mellifera* provides pollination for approximately 34% of cash crops and plays a crucial role in supporting biodiversity. The value of pollination as a contribution to the UK agricultural market was £430 million in 2007 (approximately 408 million euros) (Maderson & Wynne-Jones, 2016).

The global population is expected to increase by 50–70% over the next 25 years, placing immense pressure on the agricultural sector to provide sufficient food. Balancing the need for increased food production while maintaining healthy ecosystems and habitats is one of the most pressing challenges of the twenty-first century (Thorn et al., 2015).

It is essential to determine and understand how much the honeybee, *Apis mellifera*, contributes to the ecosystem's sustainability, what it can provide to the family income, and the value of improving the quality of crops.

According to the ISO 55000, asset management could be defined as an essential activity that involves various disciplines and is applied throughout the organization, contributing to generating value from the asset portfolio. It requires resolving conflicting objectives and making decisions that balance risks, costs, and opportunities to maximize value over the asset life cycle (ISO/FDIS 55000:2024, 2024).

The bee hive, viewed as an asset, requires careful management to maximize its value over time. This management involves balancing resources, risks, and benefits to ensure the hive thrives despite challenges and changes. Keeping the hive in good condition requires a long-term vision and coordinated actions that ensure its continuity and sustainability. Applying ISO 55000 to beekeeping can bring numerous benefits, especially in organizing and managing hives as productive assets. Like industrial assets, hives have a life cycle that needs to be monitored and optimized. By following ISO 55000, beekeepers can implement continuous monitoring and preventive strategies, such as regular pest and disease control, to ensure the longevity and productivity of hives while managing risk factors like Varroa infestation, climate change, or hive losses, all while maximizing production.

The Institute of Asset Management (IAM) provides a detailed framework for applying asset management and optimizing its performance and value throughout the life cycle. They recently published "Nature-based Solutions," highlighting the potential of applying asset management principles to natural assets. This model can enhance hive management by treating them as assets in the studied context. It includes strategic planning to monitor environmental conditions and bee health, aiming for productivity and disease prevention. It emphasizes the importance of a structured organizational culture, promoting a more scientific and professional management approach (IAM, 2015; Nature-Based Solutions for Asset Management, 2024).

This paper explores ways asset management can help beekeepers effectively control their production, decreasing unexpected losses and increasing productivity. This improvement leads to more excellent economic stability for beekeepers and their families, strengthening the resilience of farming communities that depend on these services. Beekeeping is a source of income for many families, and the diversification of activity, such as producing other hive-derived products or implementing pollination services, can provide new revenue opportunities. Enhanced management facilitates activity diversification, helping beekeepers adapt to market fluctuations and seasonal variations.

The first phase of the manuscript describes the methodology and procedure applied for selecting the articles under analysis. In the second phase, the results are presented, first showing the percentage of articles in each category using the conceptual model of asset management approached by the IAM, followed by an analysis of each group. It ends with a more in-depth discussion of the subject under study and the conclusion.

2 Methodology

2.1 Methods and Eligibility Criteria

The study presents the results of a systematic literature review following the PRISMA method to extract insights on the importance of honeybees in pollination and agricultural sustainability, analyzing the findings through the lenses of asset management.

Inclusion criteria required explicitly mentioning the following themes: *Apis mellifera*, risk assessment, beekeeping management, environmental management, management practices, agriculture management, and risk factors).

All articles included in this study meet three eligibility criteria: (i) publications in English; (ii) articles published or at the final stage of publication to ensure that all candidate records have been peer-reviewed; (iii) no restrictions were placed on the year of publication, journal title, number of citations or otherwise.

Following the analysis, some articles were excluded if they corresponded to (i) review and research articles, (ii) non English articles, (iii) non open access, (iv) topics other than Apis, risk assessment, beekeeping management, environmental management, management practices in general, agriculture management, risk factors; (v) incomplete articles; (vi) comments on other articles or scientific opinion; (xvi) different subject (Fig. 1).

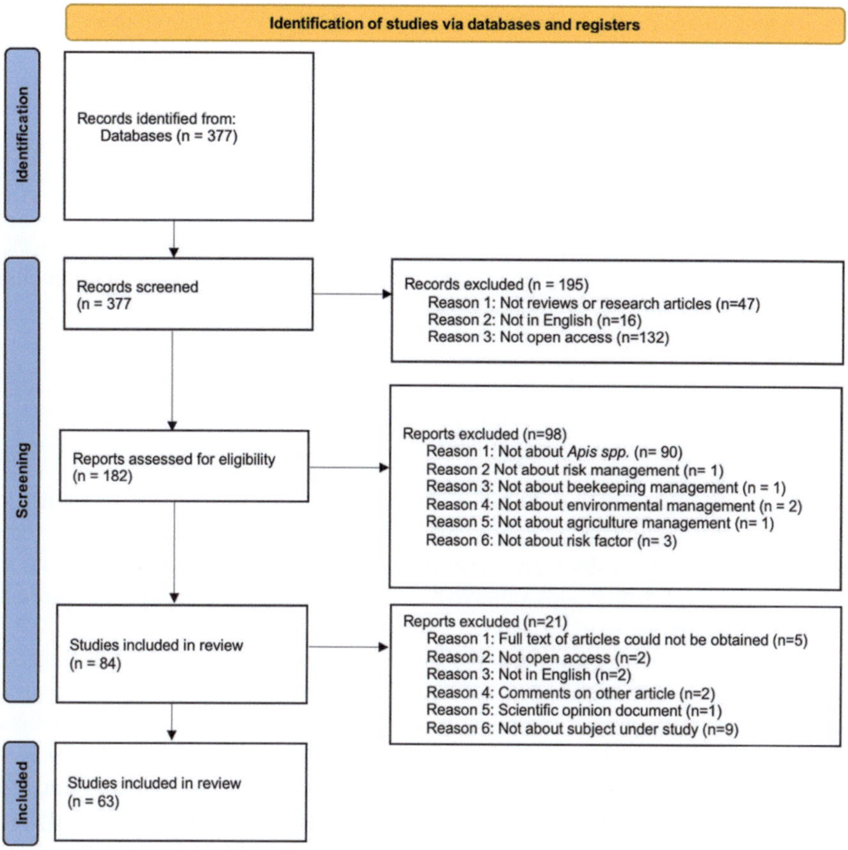

Fig. 1 PRISMA flow diagram illustrating the literature search and selection process

2.2 *Study Selection*

As can be observed in Fig. 1, and according to the methodology mentioned above in the first phase of the study, 377 articles were considered based on title, abstract, and keywords. Of those, 195 articles were excluded for not meeting the selection criteria (revision, language, and access). In the second phase, 98 articles were excluded based on the themes they addressed in the abstract.

For the final stage, the entire paper was evaluated to assess its suitability for analysis. It turned out that some lacked some essential parameters for analysis, leading to disregard. The reasons for rejecting the articles involve: (i) not fully accessible; (ii) not possible to extract the complete articles; (iii) language rather than English; (iv) not scientific; (v) not related to the topic under study. In the first phase, 52% of the articles were removed, leaving 48% (n = 182) for further evaluation. In the second phase, an additional removal of 26% was applied, resulting in 22% (n = 84) of the articles remaining. By the end of the third phase, another 6% were excluded, leaving 17% (n = 63) of the selected articles for complete analysis (see Fig. 1).

2.3 *Risk of Bias*

This literature review presents a few sources of bias risk. The reviewing process was conducted by a single person, which entails the risk of affecting the general quality of the study since there is no redundancy for conflict resolution.

3 Results

The sources of information used in the research, including data for the bibliometric study, were collected from the Scopus database. This search engine provides instant bibliometric analysis of the results obtained (distribution of publications by author, country, year, etc.), which adds value to the search and supports the iterative process of choosing a suitable search string.

Each selected article was duly read and categorized under different areas of beekeeping: hives, genetics, migration, beekeeping practice, feeding, disease control, pollination, bee products, knowledge, hive monitoring, procurement needs, winter hive losses, hive losses due to disease, climate change, pesticides, agriculture intensification. Table 1 and Fig. 2 show the matching between each category and the groups of the asset management body of knowledge (IAM, 2015). For the study, we select the conceptual asset management model addressed by IAM (Institute Asset Management). This model comprises a set of 6 classes (groups) interconnected in the organization's overall objective in an asset management Landscape.

With a percentage (Fig. 2) above 10%, we found only 4 categories of beekeeping studies: hive monitoring (16%), disease control (14%), hive losses due to disease (13%), and beekeeping practice (11%). Considering that the most significant cause of hive death is varroa, a parasite mite that worldwide contributes to introducing diseases to honeybees, it would be expected that this would also be found at a higher percentage. These four categories are interconnected, and it is interesting to note that they fall under different group areas of asset management. Following the disease control category, 7% of studies deal with pollination within the life cycle delivery area.

3.1 *Group 1: Strategy and Planning*

This group, aligned with an organization's asset management activities, allows individuals to carry out their day-to-day asset management, including planning

Table 1 Groups for asset management and their correspondence with each category

Groups	Categories
Strategy & planning	Hives Genetics
Decision-making	Migration Beekeeping practice
Life cycle delivery	Feeding Disease control Pollination Bee products
Asset information	Knowledge Hive monitoring
Organization & people	Procurement needs
Risk & review	Winter hive losses Hive losses due to disease Climate change Agriculture intensification Pesticides

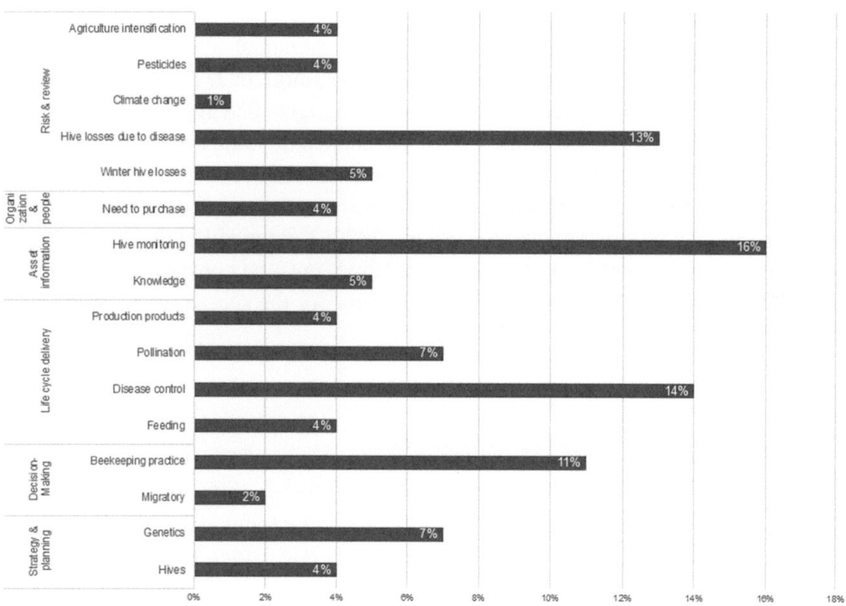

Fig. 2 Percentage of articles by categories

to improve an organization's asset management capabilities and the management system for asset management (IAM, 2015). The type of hive, the number of hives, and the kind of bee used are essential factors in strategy and planning. Small and medium-sized beekeepers, in addition to honey production, must look for other sources of income to make production profitable. The smaller the number of hives, the greater the diversification of production and sources of income. Small-medium beekeepers have an interest in local pollination, providing additional revenue streams for beekeepers who wish to sell their honey and other value-added products or pollination services, invoke pleasure, personal development, and well-being, and produce environmental benefits on a smaller scale.

Another important factor when choosing the type of hive is its weight; different hives have different weights and are more expensive to transport than others. A small-scale beekeeper may not find the weight of the hives relevant as they are unlikely to focus on making extensive trips. On the other hand, a large-scale beekeeper can prefer hives that are lighter to transport or have higher yields, for example, in the case of honey extraction. For the professional beekeeper, optimized management of his livestock and an improvement in livestock health are essential (Kady et al., 2021; Velardi et al., 2021). This can be decisive in determining what type of exploration beekeepers want. If you wish to carry out transhumance, you must consider the logistics of this service, such as the hive's weight, transportation, and costs associated with transportation. Besides the types, determining the number of hives will regulate the associated costs and working time. The greater the number of hives, the more time the beekeeper needs on the farm.

Honeybee genetics can determine better environmental adaptation or greater production yield, so beekeepers are expected to use more or less advanced genetic selection practices to guarantee greater hive yield or higher bee hygiene capacity. The choice of the sub-species can influence the prevalence of some diseases/pests or the requirements for care and management. The most successful approaches frequently focused on native species and local ecotypes as those are usually better adapted to the environmental conditions (Bieńkowska et al., 2020; Korená Hillayová et al., 2022).

In the planning and strategy phase, these factors must be considered as an initial investment, which is necessary and can be decisive for the success of the beekeeper activity.

3.2 Group 2: Decision Making

Effective asset management decision-making is essential for an organization to maximize the value realized over the lives of its assets. Decisions made at each stage impact subsequent stages (IAM, 2015). Within this asset group, we considered two categories: migration and beekeeping practice.

The first, migration, is mentioned to contribute to the pollination needs of many cropping systems, resulting in an additional income for beekeepers. However, the use of this practice may cause stress to bees due to the confinement period and transport distance, environmental changes, intensive management, and poor nutrition, among other factors, which can be associated with the weakening of bees' immune systems, making colonies more susceptible to disease and potential collapse (Guimarães-Cestaro et al., 2017; Mazur et al., 2022). Migration is considered when pollination services are required when the beekeeper plans to obtain a monofloral honey characteristic of a specific area or even in the event of nutritional problems due to nectar or pollen lack.

The other category of this group, beekeeper's practice, can be influenced by numerous factors, the beekeeper's knowledge and experience, the environmental conditions, intended business goal (e.g., pollination or honey production), the number of hives, equipment type, pests and diseases, queen replacement, feeding practices, and others (Kady et al., 2021; Kulhanek & Steinhauer et al., 2021a, 2021b; Sperandio et al., 2019). Varroa monitoring is one of the practices that requires the most attention. Being responsible for the death of countless hives around the world every year, treatments and control must be continuous and highly successful. In temperate climates, there is a greater risk due to the presence of brood all year round. Consequently, high levels of Varroa infestation can be reached very quickly, requiring a higher number of treatments (Giacobino et al., 2014).

Identifying risk factors is essential to define and apply good beekeeping management practices (Kulhanek & Steinhauer et al., 2021a, 2021b; Tubene et al., 2023). Honey bee's health and production levels are critically affected by management practices. Beekeepers need to understand the honeybee behavior, climate, flora, and other factors relevant to the colony's survival. For example, beekeepers can provide supplemental food to colonies when natural pollen or nectar is reduced or absent, guaranteeing a strong colony when the flux of nectar begins. Different types of beekeepers (hobbits, professionals), or regions (temperate, Mediterranean, tropical, etc.) require different approaches, so beekeepers need to adapt to the needs and adjust the corresponding management (El Agrebi et al., 2021; Oberreiter & Brodschneider, 2020; Steinhauer et al., 2021a, 2021b). Good practice and management can guarantee the success and survival of the colony, but poor management can lead to the death of the bees. This group is fundamental, as a wrong decision could jeopardize the entire asset. The decision taken must always aim at the success of the organization and must consider that the decision can influence the other phases of the asset.

3.3 *Group 3: Life Cycle Delivery*

This group intends to implement the asset management plans developed in the first point, Strategy and Planning. Organizations incur most of their asset-related expenditure through the activities in Life Cycle Delivery (IAM, 2015), where we consider categories such as supplementary feeding, disease control, pollination, and bee products.

Supplementary food includes several products such as honey, sugar syrup, sugar paste, multivitamin syrup, and protein paste. Each must be selected depending on the objectives and needs, e.g., lack of pollen or nectar, brood development, winter preparation (Clair et al., 2022; Olate-Olave et al., 2021). In the larval stage or for the development of the honeybee, food supplements rich in protein are essential;

however, for feeding foraging bees, the food must have a more significant amount of carbohydrates.

Virus, bacteria, fungi, and mites constantly put pressure on honeybees, demanding the use of external inputs to prevent and control diseases, (Clair et al., 2022; De Carolis et al., 2023; Dynes et al., 2020; Giacobino et al., 2014; Hernandez et al., 2022; Kulhanek & Garavito et al., 2021a, 2021b; Roberts et al., 2020; Thoms et al., 2019), increasing the costs of the activity. The Varroa mite remains the leading cause of death in thousands of worldwide colonies. Varroa is a native ectoparasite of the *Apis cerana* that transferred to *Apis mellifera.* Due to the inability of *Apis mellifera* to adapt to this mite, the studies on the Varroa are immense due to the impact on the survival of honeybees. High varroa infestation rates in spring/summer can result in massive colony losses in the following winter. Every year, more than 30% of colonies die due to Varroa or associated diseases (Genersch et al., 2010; Kady et al., 2021; Kulhanek & Steinhauer et al., 2021a, 2021b; Steinhauer et al., 2021a, 2021b; Van Esch et al., 2020). Correct and careful monitoring of Varroa infestation can significantly improve colony survival. Nosema has also been a cause of death, due to the energetic stress it causes to honey bees. Usually, bees die in the presence of more than one stress and risk factor, so it is essential to identify and prevent them.

Honeybees are one of the most important pollinators of crops consumed by humans, so the third category focused on this topic. The greater the global growth, the greater the need for pollinators. Landscapes are being changed to intensively managed monocultures, contributing to the decline of the natural habitat of wild pollinators. This increases the need to place beehives on crops to ensure correct pollination, as with almond trees (Dufour et al., 2020). Beekeepers providing pollination services must guarantee the profitability of hives for correct pollination in the agricultural field, but farmers must preserve the pollination service without applying, for example, phytochemicals (Decourtye et al., 2010; Maderson, 2023). This type of service will be increasingly demanded as the world population increases, intensive agriculture increases, and pollinators decrease.

The fourth category is bee products. Honey continues to be the main bee product from which the beekeeper obtains his income (Gratzer et al., 2021; Guzman-Novoa et al., 2020; Kady et al., 2021; Olate-Olave et al., 2021). However, beekeepers can increase profitability by exploring other products from the hive, such as beeswax, pollen, propolis, queen trade, swarms, etc. Product diversification may require additional materials and equipment and some adaptation to the hive management. Still, it is becoming an alternative to face productivity fluctuation due to climatic variability or market instability and increase the resilience of the activity.

3.4 Group 4: Asset Information

Organizations rely on data and asset information as essential enablers across the full breadth of asset management activities. They are usually an input to processes and will be an output of a process (IAM, 2015). We fitted the knowledge and hive monitoring categories in this group.

Knowledge is commonly passed from generation to generation. The beekeeper must know the life cycle of honey bees, the adequate management procedures, the surrounding floral diversity and their flowering periods, the nutritional needs, what diseases affect honeybees, and how to prevent and treat them, among many others. Not all this information is continuously acquired from family, and so it is necessary to obtain additional knowledge throughout life (De Carolis et al., 2023; Maderson, 2023; Van Espen et al., 2023). The direct observation of bees is knowledge-empowering, but this alone is insufficient. Attending training on different topics, watching debates, or even talking to other beekeepers is essential to increase the beekeeper's knowledge and improve his exploitation.

Constant monitoring of the hives and the surrounding environment allows decisions to be made at the right time, avoiding the death of the hive (e.g., hunger, diseases, pesticides), bringing the hives forward to flowering (e.g., stimulating the queen) or migration (Kulhanek & Garavito et al., 2021a, 2021b; Lecocq et al., 2015; Pernal et al., 2008; Siede et al., 2017). Correct and constant monitoring allows you to mitigate risk factors leading to the colony's death.

3.5 Group 5: Procurement Needs

An asset management approach leads organizations to question traditional thinking and working methods. This highly interdependent group strongly influences the organization's ability to adopt and incorporate successful asset management. Sometimes, it is necessary to restructure the organization to achieve success, requiring investment (IAM, 2015). The procurement needs category fits in this group.

Over time, it is necessary to acquire material for the survival of the colony (e.g., new queens, artificial food, treatment), for the maintenance of the business (e.g., vans, warehouse), for the maintenance of the beekeeper and hive (e.g., suit, hives) or professional help (Bieńkowska et al., 2020; Pettis et al., 2016; Steinhauer et al., 2021a, 2021b). Over time, increasing exploration and money for investment may be necessary. Good property management can mean that it is not required to apply for a large bank loan. European financing can also be requested, requiring viable and economically profitable exploration. There are aids for the beekeeping sector in Portugal that cover different parameters, such as transhumance, treatments against varroa, and combating the Velutina wasp, among others (Union European, 2024).

The beekeeper needs to understand the costs and profits he must determine to assess the viability and profitability of the exploration. To set the price for honey sale, it is necessary to consider all the costs involved, such as transportation, supplementary food, treatments, materials, etc., and only then can a fair price per kg of honey be established.

3.6 Group 6: Risk and Review

This group contains the activities associated with identifying, understanding, and managing risks, which supports continuous improvement of asset management activities and ensures the objectives are achieved (IAM, 2015). The categories such as winter colony loss, colony loss due to disease, agriculture intensification, pesticides, and climate change deal with those questions. Winter colony losses and colony losses due to disease are related since the first are commonly caused by the impact of Varroa mites. Here, we consider two different categories because, in the loss of a colony due to disease, we include all the diseases that bees suffer from, not just varroa.

The highest mortality rate of honeybee colonies has been found during wintering and can reach up to 30%. In this period, the colony reduced its population and became more compact inside the hive to control the temperature, facilitating the transmission of diseases. Besides, food availability is lower during winter, reducing the immune system. At this stage, the beekeeper cannot open the hives with the risk of sudden cooling or moisture entry, so he must foresee and guarantee the best conditions (Brodschneider et al., 2019; Genersch et al., 2010; Steinhauer et al., 2021a, 2021b; van Engelsdorp et al., 2008; Van Esch et al., 2020). Varroa destructor is the dominant cause of honeybee colony loss during the winter. Still, different infections in autumn caused by the *Deformed Wing virus* or *Acute bee paralysis virus*, the presence of old queens heading overwintering colonies, and colony weakness may additionally lower the winter survival of honeybee colonies (Genersch et al., 2010; Hernandez et al., 2022; Mazur et al., 2022; Steinhauer et al., 2021a, 2021b).

The losses of colonies due to the Varroa and virus are not exclusively of winter; they can occur during all seasons, particularly after periods of intense colony development where the higher amount of brood may exponentially increase the mite infestation levels (Kulhanek & Steinhauer et al., 2021a, 2021b).

The combination of several pathogenic factors often causes honeybee colony disease mortality. Although the presence of nosema alone is unlikely to cause the death of a colony when in the presence of other stress factors, it can cause the colony to collapse (Gilioli et al., 2019; Matović et al., 2020; Van Esch et al., 2020). Beekeepers must identify risk factors and develop preventive strategies through adequate beekeeping management (Genersch et al., 2010; Kulhanek & Steinhauer et al., 2021a, 2021b).

Agriculture intensification was considered a third category: a poor diet, a lack of pollen and/or nectar, can lead to problems in larval development, communication between bees, less vigor, and increased disease susceptibility. Pollen is rich in protein and thus supports larval and tissue development, while nectar is rich in carbohydrates and responsible for providing energy. Some plants are more abundant in pollen and others in nectar, so it is essential to ensure the presence of both types of plants around the apiaries to guarantee a balanced bee' diet. Monocultural crops can cause nutritional deficits for honeybees (Dufour et al., 2020; Kulhanek & Steinhauer et al., 2021a, 2021b). Striking a balance between intensive agriculture and ensuring the survival of honey bees is crucial and urgent (Vandame & Palacio, 2010). For example, allowing the vegetation surrounding crops to grow, thus allowing greater flowering diversity and nutritional availability.

Pesticides are considered a category risk since their presence in the honeybee food reduces the bee's immune system. The use of pesticides in intensive agriculture has been one of the factors contributing to the disappearance of bees around the world. In places with intensive agriculture and high use of pesticides, greater mortality is found for honeybees (Decourtye et al., 2010; Lunardi et al., 2017; Smart et al., 2016; Van Esch et al., 2020). Pesticides can alter bee development, adult longevity, mobility, navigation, orientation, feeding behavior, or learning ability, which could explain the common observation of forager bees not returning to their nest (Gilioli et al., 2019; Vandame & Palacio, 2010). Furthermore, with the frequent use of pesticides, hive products are compromised with potential contamination by chemicals (Dixon et al., 2021; Velardi et al., 2021).

Finally, climate change has/will have several interlinked impacts on beekeeping (Van Espen et al., 2023) predominantly negative but not exclusively. Hence, some beekeepers may 'win', and some may 'lose'. Honeybees, as a species, are deemed resilient and, therefore, believed to be able to cope with the challenges imposed by climate change, at least if properly managed. Climate change is perceived as a main challenge for beekeepers, who must demonstrate a certain degree of flexibility, adaptability, and resilience. While Northern Europe is faced with better temperatures and better conditions for the survival of honeybees, Southern Europe is faced with very high temperatures, drought, and less favorable conditions for the survival of bees (Clair et al., 2022; Gilioli et al., 2019; Pohorecka et al., 2014; Van Espen et al., 2023).

Identifying all the risk factors that can lead to failure in beekeeping organizations is difficult, as many variables and factors can be found. However, we identified some risk factors we found during the research study.

4 Discussion

Diseases in the lifecycle of bee assets, namely varroa, are a significant concern because they cause the death of countless colonies worldwide. Knowledge and learning from the beekeeper are also essential for the sector, colonies' survival, and profitability. Constant monitoring can act promptly and mitigate problems. The risks have been increasing, with the use of pesticides and climate change demonstrating a discrepancy between flowering and pollinators, also increasing the death of colonies.

The sector's pollination management service still has a lot to evolve, perhaps due to the concern in agriculture about obtaining quality and quantity of food enough for the world population. There is a lack of comprehensive research on asset management for honeybees, indicating significant room for improvement. This improvement could lead to increased profitability, specifically in beekeeping, but broadened in agriculture.

Isolated risk factors do not usually cause colony death, but a combination of stress factors can cause bee colonies to die. It is essential to identify the stress and risk factors and address them so that risks can be reduced and the survival of honeybees can be increased. By increasing the survival of honeybees and the profitability of beekeepers, the risk of bees and beekeepers disappearing may be diminished.

Approaching bees as a natural asset is possible, and asset management discipline can be further explored and applied in this space. This will allow us to understand risk factors and mitigate risk and stress factors as much as possible. Understand the life cycle of bees as a natural asset and maximize the value that can be extracted from it, including the increase of the profitability of beekeeping and the survival rates of bees as the most crucial pollinator in crops consumed by humans, ultimately leading to greater food security.

Beekeeping study covers all six groups of the body of knowledge in asset management. This shows that it is possible to approach the beekeeping sector using asset management, with the honeybee being considered a natural asset.

Applying asset management in beekeeping can generate significant environmental and economic impacts. Asset management can help mitigate biodiversity loss by ensuring that colonies are kept in optimal conditions to support pollination services. More effective hive management, through disease control and proper nutrition, increases the ability of bees to perform their functions. Strategically locating hives in areas with greater floral diversity can restore degraded ecosystems and increase the resilience of pollinator populations, which have been severely affected by pesticides, agricultural intensification, and climate change. Asset management helps address the challenges posed by climate change, such as seasonal variability and extreme weather events. A robust management system can monitor and adjust beekeeping practices as climatic conditions change, ensuring the survival of hives even in adverse conditions. This contributes to global climate adaptation, as bees play a vital role in food security by pollinating crops. Adopting asset management allows beekeepers to gain better control over production, reducing unexpected hive losses and increasing productivity. Better management facilitates the diversification of activities and improves beekeepers' ability to cope with market fluctuations and seasonality. Efficient hive management improves bee health, increasing the quality and quantity of pollination services. This directly benefits farmers by increasing the yields of crops that depend on pollination by bees, such as fruit and vegetables, which positively impacts food security. In addition, high-quality pollination produces food with more excellent economic value, generating additional income for farmers and beekeepers. The synergy between beekeeping and agriculture strengthens economic resilience in farming communities, particularly in regions where agriculture is the primary source of livelihood.

Introducing asset management tools would mean using more advanced technologies (sensors, monitoring software) to monitor the condition of the hives. This may require initial investment and training but would bring long-term benefits. The traditional approach based on empirical experience could be complemented or even replaced by a practice based on data and analysis. This would boost the professionalization of the sector, helping to overcome the resistance of small beekeepers to new practices. As well as improving hive health, asset management would enable more sustainable beekeeping practices with a lower environmental impact. Beekeepers could become essential agents in the conservation of agricultural biodiversity.

Adopting an asset management approach helps beekeepers anticipate and reduce operational costs. Continuous monitoring enables quick responses to problems, avoiding high expenditures on corrective solutions. Improvements in the efficiency of beekeeping processes free up time and resources that beekeepers can use for innovations or expanding their operations, further increasing their competitiveness in broader markets. This approach aligns with the United Nations' Sustainable Development Goals (SDGs), including food security (SDG 2), economic growth for rural communities (SDG 8), and sustainable agricultural practices (SDG 12) (UNRIC, 2018).

Implementing asset management concepts in beekeeping will improve operational efficiency, profitability, and resilience, strengthening the beekeeping sector while aligning with global sustainability and economic resilience objectives.

5 Conclusion

From the study carried out, we can conclude that the top 5 concerns by the scientific community include disease control (14%), hive losses due to disease (13%), hive monitoring (16%), beekeeper practice (11%) and pollination (7%). These five categories fall under four (out of six) different group areas of asset management: life cycle delivery, decision-making, risk and review, and asset information. Strategy and Planning: Genetics (3%) and hive types (4%) are rarely addressed but could enhance bees' adaptability to climate change, diseases, and pesticide resistance. Asset Management Decisions: Beekeeping practices (11%) and migration (2%) are essential. Proper management and controlled migration reduce risks, though transhumance can cause stress on bees. Life Cycle Delivery: Disease control (14%) is the top concern, particularly regarding the Varroa mite, a significant cause of honeybee mortality. Pollination (7%) is also crucial for biodiversity and food security, while supplemental nutrition is increasingly necessary for bees' survival. Hive Monitoring and Knowledge: Effective monitoring (16%) helps prevent honeybee deaths, but lacking emphasis on knowledge (5%) could hinder beekeepers' ability to meet increasing demands. Organization and People: A lack of financial management in beekeeping reflects a gap in sector management, particularly among smaller beekeepers. Risk and Review: Hive losses due to diseases (13%), pesticides (4%), and agricultural intensification are critical concerns. Climate change (1%) receives little attention despite its growing impact. The study concludes that an asset management approach could improve pollination sustainability and profitability for beekeepers, enhancing bee survival.

Acknowledgements The authors are grateful to FCT Portugal for financial support from national funds, such as FCT/MCTES to CIMO (UIDB/00690/2020 and UIDP/00690/2020). SusTEC (LA/P/0007/2021) and to CERIS (UIDB/04625/2020 https://doi.org/10.54499/UIDB/04625/2020). Thanks to the Next Generation EU recovery funds, through the scope of Project BeeLand PRR-C05-i03-I-000081.

References

Abro, Z., Kassie, M., Tiku, H. A., Taye, B., Ayele, Z. A., & Ayalew, W. (2022). The impact of beekeeping on household income: Evidence from north-western Ethiopia. *Heliyon, 8*(5), Article e09492. https://doi.org/10.1016/J.HELIYON.2022.E09492

El Agrebi, N., Steinhauer, N., Tosi, S., Leinartz, L., de Graaf, D. C., & Saegerman, C. (2021). Risk and protective indicators of beekeeping management practices. *Science of the Total Environment, 799*. https://doi.org/10.1016/j.scitotenv.2021.149381

Bartholomée, O., Aullo, A., Becquet, J., Vannier, C., & Lavorel, S. (2020). Pollinator presence in orchards depends on landscape-scale habitats more than in-field flower resources. *Agriculture, Ecosystems and Environment, 293*. https://doi.org/10.1016/j.agee.2019.106806

Bieńkowska, M., Łoś, A., & Węgrzynowicz, P. (2020). Honey bee queen replacement: an analysis of changes in the preferences of polish beekeepers through decades. *Insects, 11*(8), 1–13. https://doi.org/10.3390/insects11080544

Brodschneider, R., Brus, J., & Danihlík, J. (2019). Comparison of apiculture and winter mortality of honey bee colonies (Apis mellifera) in Austria and Czechia. *Agriculture, Ecosystems and Environment, 274*, 24–32. https://doi.org/10.1016/j.agee.2019.01.002

Centeno-Alvarado, D., Lopes, A. V., & Arnan, X. (2023). Fostering pollination through agroforestry: A global review. *Agriculture, Ecosystems & Environment, 351*, Article 108478. https://doi.org/10.1016/J.AGEE.2023.108478

Clair, A. L. St., Beach, N. J., & Dolezal, A. G. (2022). Honey bee hive covers reduce food consumption and colony mortality during overwintering. *PLoS ONE, 17*. https://doi.org/10.1371/journal.pone.0266219

De Carolis, A., Newmark, A. J., Kim, J., Cazier, J., Hassler, E., Pietropaoli, M., Robinette, C., Formato, G., & Song, J. (2023). Results of an ınternational survey for risk assessment of honey bee health concerning varroa management. *Applied Sciences (Switzerland), 13*(1). https://doi.org/10.3390/app13010062

Decourtye, A., Mader, E., & Desneux, N. (2010). Landscape enhancement of floral resources for honey bees in agro-ecosystems. *Apidologie, 41*(3), 264–277. https://doi.org/10.1051/apido/2010024

Dixon, D. J., Zheng, H., & Otto, C. R. V. (2021). Land conversion and pesticide use degrade forage areas for honey bees in America's beekeeping epicenter. *PLoS ONE, 16*. https://doi.org/10.1371/journal.pone.0251043

Dufour, C., Fournier, V., & Giovenazzo, P. (2020). The impact of lowbush blueberry (Vaccinium angustifolium Ait.) and cranberry (Vaccinium macrocarpon Ait.) pollination on honey bee (Apis mellifera L.) colony health status. *PLoS ONE, 15*(1). https://doi.org/10.1371/journal.pone.0227970

Dynes, T. L., Berry, J. A., Delaplane, K. S., de Roode, J. C., & Brosi, B. J. (2020). Assessing virulence of Varroa destructor mites from different honey bee management regimes. *Apidologie, 51*(2), 276–289. https://doi.org/10.1007/s13592-019-00716-6

Genersch, E., Von Der Ohe, W., Kaatz, H., Schroeder, A., Otten, C., Büchler, R., Berg, S., Ritter, W., Mühlen, W., Gisder, S., Liebig, G., & Rosenkranz, P. (2010). The German bee monitoring project: A long term study to understand periodically high winter losses of honey bee colonies. *Apidologie, 41*(3), 332–352. https://doi.org/10.1051/apido/2010014

Giacobino, A., Cagnolo, N. B., Merke, J., Orellano, E., Bertozzi, E., Masciangelo, G., Pietronave, H., Salto, C., & Signorini, M. (2014). Risk factors associated with the presence of Varroa destructor in honey bee colonies from east-central Argentina. *Preventive Veterinary Medicine, 115*(3–4), 280–287. https://doi.org/10.1016/j.prevetmed.2014.04.002

Gilioli, G., Sperandio, G., Hatjina, F., & Simonetto, A. (2019). Towards the development of an index for the holistic assessment of the health status of a honey bee colony. *Ecological Indicators, 101*, 341–347. https://doi.org/10.1016/j.ecolind.2019.01.024

Gratzer, K., Wakjira, K., Fiedler, S., & Brodschneider, R. (2021). Challenges and perspectives for beekeeping in Ethiopia. A review. *Agronomy for Sustainable Development, 41*(4). https://doi.org/10.1007/s13593-021-00702-2

Guimarães-Cestaro, L., Alves, M. L. T. M. F., Message, D., Silva, M. V. G. B., & Teixeira, E. W. (2017). Honey bee (Apis mellifera) health in stationary and migratory apiaries. *Sociobiology, 64*(1), 42–49. https://doi.org/10.13102/sociobiology.v64i1.1183

Guzman-Novoa, E., Morfin, N., De la Mora, A., Macías-Macías, J. O., Tapia-González, J. M., Contreras-Escareño, F., Medina-Flores, C. A., Correa-Benítez, A., & Quezada-Euán, J. J. G. (2020). The process and outcome of the africanization of honey bees in mexico: lessons and future directions. *Frontiers in Ecology and Evolution, 8*. https://doi.org/10.3389/fevo.2020.608091

Hernandez, J., Hattendorf, J., Aebi, A., & Dietemann, V. (2022). Compliance with recommended Varroa destructor treatment regimens improves the survival of honey bee colonies over winter. *Research in Veterinary Science, 144*, 1–10. https://doi.org/10.1016/j.rvsc.2021.12.025

Hipólito, J., Viana, B. F., & Garibaldi, L. A. (2016). The value of pollinator-friendly practices: Synergies between natural and anthropogenic assets. *Basic and Applied Ecology, 17*(8), 659–667. https://doi.org/10.1016/J.BAAE.2016.09.003

IAM. (2015). An anatomy of asset management asset management-an anatomy. www.theIAM.org

ISO/FDIS 55000:2024. (2024).

Kady, C., Chedid, A. M., Kortbawi, I., Yaacoub, C., Akl, A., Daclin, N., Trousset, F., Pfister, F., & Zacharewicz, G. (2021). Iot-driven workflows for risk management and control of beehives. *Diversity, 13*(7). https://doi.org/10.3390/d13070296

Korená Hillayová, M., Korený, Ľ., & Škvarenina, J. (2022). The local environmental factors impact the infestation of bee colonies by mite Varroa destructor. *Ecological Indicators, 141*. https://doi.org/10.1016/j.ecolind.2022.109104

Kulhanek, K., Garavito, A., & vanEngelsdorp, D. (2021). Accelerated Varroa destructor population growth in honey bee (Apis mellifera) colonies is associated with visitation from non-natal bees. *Scientific Reports, 11*(1). https://doi.org/10.1038/s41598-021-86558-8

Kulhanek, K., Steinhauer, N., Wilkes, J., Wilson, M., Spivak, M., Sagili, R. R., Tarpy, D. R., McDermott, E., Garavito, A., Rennich, K., & vanEngelsdorp, D. (2021). Survey-derived best management practices for backyard beekeepers improve colony health and reduce mortality. *PLoS ONE, 16*. https://doi.org/10.1371/journal.pone.0245490

Lecocq, A., Kryger, P., Vejsnæs, F., & Jensen, A. B. (2015). Weight watching and the effect of landscape on honeybee colony productivity: Investigating the value of colony weight monitoring for the beekeeping industry. *PLoS ONE, 10*(7). https://doi.org/10.1371/journal.pone.0132473

Lunardi, J. S., Zaluski, R., & Orsi, R. O. (2017). Evaluation of motor changes and toxicity of insecticides Fipronil and imidacloprid in Africanized Honey bees (Hymenoptera: Apidae). *Sociobiology, 64*(1), 50–56. https://doi.org/10.13102/sociobiology.v64i1.1190

Maderson, S., & Wynne-Jones, S. (2016). Beekeepers' knowledges and participation in pollinator conservation policy. *Journal of Rural Studies, 45*, 88–98. https://doi.org/10.1016/J.JRURSTUD.2016.02.015

Maderson, S. (2023). There's more than one way to know a bee: beekeepers' environmental knowledge, and its potential role in governing for sustainability. *Geoforum, 139*. https://doi.org/10.1016/j.geoforum.2023.103690

Mashilingi, S. K., Zhang, H., Garibaldi, L. A., & An, J. (2022). Honeybees are far too insufficient to supply optimum pollination services in agricultural systems worldwide. *Agriculture, Ecosystems & Environment, 335*, Article 108003. https://doi.org/10.1016/J.AGEE.2022.108003

Matović, K., Vidanović, D., Manić, M., Stojiljković, M., Radojičić, S., Debeljak, Z., Šekler, M., & Ćirić, J. (2020). Twenty-five-year study of Nosema spp. in honey bees (Apis mellifera) in Serbia. *Saudi Journal of Biological Sciences, 27*(1), 518–523. https://doi.org/10.1016/j.sjbs.2019.11.012

Mazur, E. D., Czopowicz, M., & Gajda, A. M. (2022). Two faces of the screened bottom boards—an ambiguous ınfluence on the honey bee winter colony loss rate. *Insects, 13*(12). https://doi.org/10.3390/insects13121128

Nature-based Solutions for Asset Management. (2024).

Oberreiter, H., & Brodschneider, R. (2020). Austrian COLOSS survey of honey bee colony winter losses 2018/19 and analysis of hive management practices. *Diversity, 12*(3). https://doi.org/10.3390/d12030099

Olate-Olave, V. R., Verde, M., Vallejos, L., Raymonda, L. P., Cortese, M. C., & Doorn, M. (2021). Bee health and productivity in apis mellifera, a consequence of multiple factors. *Veterinary Sciences, 8*(5). https://doi.org/10.3390/vetsci8050076

Patel, V., Pauli, N., Biggs, E., Barbour, L., & Boruff, B. (n.d.). Why bees are critical for achieving sustainable development. https://doi.org/10.1007/s13280-020-01333-9

Pernal, S. F., Albright, R. L., & Melathopoulos, A. P. (2008). Evaluation of the shaking technique for the economic management of american foulbrood disease of honey bees (Hymenoptera: Apidae). *Journal of Economic Entomology, 101*(4), 1095–1104. https://doi.org/10.1603/0022-0493(2008)101[1095:EOTSTF]2.0.CO;2

Pettis, J. S., Rice, N., Joselow, K., Van Engelsdorp, D., & Chaimanee, V. (2016). Colony failure linked to low sperm viability in honey bee (Apis mellifera) queens and an exploration of potential causative factors. *PLoS ONE, 11*(2). https://doi.org/10.1371/journal.pone.0147220

Pohorecka, K., Bober, A., Skubida, M., Zdańska, D., & Torój, K. (2014). A comparative study of environmental conditions, Bee management and the epidemiological situation in apiaries varying in the level of colony losses. *Journal of Apicultural Science, 58*(2), 107–132. https://doi.org/10.2478/JAS-2014-0027

Potts, S. G., Biesmeijer, J. C., Kremen, C., Neumann, P., Schweiger, O., & Kunin, W. E. (2010). Global pollinator declines: Trends, impacts and drivers. *Trends in Ecology & Evolution, 25*(6), 345–353. https://doi.org/10.1016/J.TREE.2010.01.007

Potts, S. G., Imperatriz-Fonseca, V., Ngo, H. T., Aizen, M. A., Biesmeijer, J. C., Breeze, T. D., Dicks, L. V., Garibaldi, L. A., Hill, R., Settele, J., Settele, J., & Vanbergen, A. J. (2016). Safeguarding pollinators and their values to human well-being. *Nature, 540*(7632), 220–229. https://doi.org/10.1038/nature20588

Roberts, J. M. K., Schouten, C. N., Sengere, R. W., Jave, J., & Lloyd, D. (2020). Effectiveness of control strategies for Varroa jacobsoni and Tropilaelaps mercedesae in Papua New Guinea. *Experimental and Applied Acarology, 80*(3), 399–407. https://doi.org/10.1007/s10493-020-00473-7

Siede, R., Faust, L., Meixner, M. D., Maus, C., Grünewald, B., & Büchler, R. (2017). Performance of honey bee colonies under a long-lasting dietary exposure to sublethal concentrations of the neonicotinoid insecticide thiacloprid. *Pest Management Science, 73*(7), 1334–1344. https://doi.org/10.1002/ps.4547

Smart, M. D., Pettis, J. S., Euliss, N., & Spivak, M. S. (2016). Land use in the Northern Great Plains region of the U.S. influences the survival and productivity of honey bee colonies. *Agriculture, Ecosystems and Environment, 230*, 139–149. https://doi.org/10.1016/j.agee.2016.05.030

Sperandio, G., Simonetto, A., Carnesecchi, E., Costa, C., Hatjina, F., Tosi, S., & Gilioli, G. (2019). Beekeeping and honey bee colony health: A review and conceptualization of beekeeping management practices implemented in Europe. *Science of the Total Environment, 696*. https://doi.org/10.1016/j.scitotenv.2019.133795

Steinhauer, N., vanEngelsdorp, D., & Saegerman, C. (2021). Prioritizing changes in management practices associated with reduced winter honey bee colony losses for US beekeepers. *Science of the Total Environment, 753*. https://doi.org/10.1016/j.scitotenv.2020.141629

Thoms, C. A., Nelson, K. C., Kubas, A., Steinhauer, N., Wilson, M. E., & vanEngelsdorp, D. (2019). Beekeeper stewardship, colony loss, and Varroa destructor management. *Ambio, 48*(10), 1209–1218. https://doi.org/10.1007/s13280-018-1130-z

Thorn, J., Snaddon, J., Waldron, A., Kok, K., Zhou, W., Bhagwat, S., Willis, K., & Petrokofsky, G. (2015). How effective are on-farm conservation land management strategies for preserving ecosystem services in developing countries? A systematic map protocol. *Environmental Evidence, 4*(1). https://doi.org/10.1186/s13750-015-0036-5

Tubene, S., Kulhanek, K., Rennich, K., & vanEngelsdorp, D. (2023). Best management practices increase profitability of small-scale US beekeeping operations. *Journal of Economic Entomology, 116*(1), 47–55. https://doi.org/10.1093/jee/toac174

Union European, F. F. (2024). CAP Strategic Plan–Portugal.

UNRIC. (2018). Guia sobre Desenvolvimento Sustentável. http://www.un.org/ga/search/view_doc.asp?symbol=A/RES/70/1&Lang=E

Van Esch, L., De Kok, J.-L., Janssen, L., Buelens, B., De Smet, L., de Graaf, D. C., & Engelen, G. (2020). Multivariate landscape analysis of honey bee winter mortality in Wallonia. *Belgium. Environmental Modeling and Assessment, 25*(3), 441–452. https://doi.org/10.1007/s10666-019-09682-w

van Engelsdorp, D., Hayes Jr., J., Underwood, R. M., & Pettis, J. (2008). A survey of honey bee colony losses in the U.S., Fall 2007 to Spring 2008. *PLoS ONE, 3*(12). https://doi.org/10.1371/journal.pone.0004071

Van Espen, M., Williams, J. H., Alves, F., Hung, Y., de Graaf, D. C., & Verbeke, W. (2023). Beekeeping in Europe facing climate change: A mixed methods study on perceived impacts and the need to adapt according to stakeholders and beekeepers. *Science of the Total Environment, 888*. https://doi.org/10.1016/j.scitotenv.2023.164255

Vandame, R., & Palacio, M. A. (2010). Preserved honey bee health in Latin America: A fragile equilibrium due to low-intensity agriculture and beekeeping? *Apidologie, 41*(3), 243–255. https://doi.org/10.1051/apido/2010025

Velardi, S., Leahy, J., Collum, K., McGuire, J., & Ladenheim, M. (2021). "You treat them right, They'll treat you right": Understanding beekeepers' scale management decisions within the context of bee values. *Journal of Rural Studies, 81*, 27–36. https://doi.org/10.1016/j.jrurstud.2020.12.002

Wood, T. J., Holland, J. M., & Goulson, D. (2015). Pollinator-friendly management does not increase the diversity of farmland bees and wasps. *Biological Conservation, 187*, 120–126. https://doi.org/10.1016/J.BIOCON.2015.04.022

Overview of the Use of Data Assets in the Context of Portuguese Companies: Comparison Between Micro, SMEs and Large Companies

André Guimarães, Daisy Enrique, Daniel Gaspar, Pedro Reis, and Antonio J. Marques Cardoso

Abstract In the digital age, data has become a crucial asset for businesses, serving as a valuable resource for production and decision-making. Effective data management is essential for enhancing companies' competitiveness and operational efficiency. While big data holds the potential to drive innovation, particularly for small and medium-sized companies (SMEs), many companies struggle to leverage this digital capability effectively. This article examines the nuances of data management practices in Portugal, highlighting the differences between micro, small, medium, and large companies. To achieve this, data were collected from 390 Portuguese companies, and a Kruskal–Wallis Test was conducted to determine if significant differences exist in data utilization across company sizes. The results indicate substantial disparities in the use of data for developing new services and in the application of technologies for Data Storage Security, Security for Data Exchange with Partners, and Cloud Computing Security among micro, small, medium, and large companies. These findings underscore the importance of tailored strategies to improve data management practices and enhance the digital capabilities of companies of all sizes.

A. Guimarães (✉) · D. Gaspar · A. J. Marques Cardoso
CISE, Electromechatronic Systems Research Centre, University of Beira Interior, Covilhã, Portugal
e-mail: andre.m.guimaraes@ubi.pt

D. Gaspar
e-mail: danigaspar@estgv.ipv.pt

A. J. Marques Cardoso
e-mail: ajmcardoso@ieee.org

A. Guimarães · D. Gaspar · P. Reis
CISeD, Research Centre for Digital Services, Polytechnic Institute of Viseu, Viseu, Portugal
e-mail: pedroreis@estgv.ipv.pt

D. Enrique
NEO, Organizational Engineering Group, Federal University of Rio Grande do Sul, Porto Alegre, Brazil
e-mail: daisy.v.enrique@ubi.pt

A. Crespo Márquez et al. (eds.), *Case Studies in Digital Transformation*, Engineering Asset Management Review 4, https://doi.org/10.1007/978-3-032-05592-7_16

Keywords Data management · Asset management · Micro · SMEs · Large companies

1 Introduction

In the digital age, data has become a crucial asset for companies, serving as a valuable resource for production (Erel et al., 2021). With the rapid integration of digital technologies such as the Internet of Things (IoT), Cloud Computing, Big Data and Artificial Intelligence, there has been an exponential increase in the volume of data collected and the corresponding processing capabilities. Strategic data analysis has emerged as a powerful tool for diagnosing issues, identifying problems, and facilitating informed decision-making in the dynamic landscape of modern businesses (Wirtz & Wirtz, 2021; Zheng et al., 2024). Data and information, once mere byproducts of business operations, have become indispensable assets for companies across all sectors (Sen et al., 2016).

Data assets are defined by Fleckenstein et al. (2018) as valuable data that, like other business assets, possess both actual and potential value, contributing to supporting strategic decisions and promoting innovation. Data asset management refers to protecting, monitoring, and optimizing the use of these data throughout their lifecycle, ensuring their integration and security. For this management to be effective, a coordinated strategy between different company departments is required to transform data into valuable insights that drive operational efficiency and innovation.

Data management has evolved significantly by adopting advanced digital technologies such as the Internet of Things (IoT) and Artificial Intelligence (AI). These tools enable the continuous collection of real-time data and its predictive analysis, improving operational efficiency and maintenance processes. The field of data management is transitioning from manual and fragmented methods to more integrated and automated solutions, with a growing focus on the use of digital twins and BIM models. This evolution allows real-time monitoring of assets and facilitates strategic decision-making based on more accurate and up-to-date data (Koumou & Isafiade, 2024).

Despite the well-documented benefits of effective data management, countless companies face formidable challenges in fully leveraging these advantages (Zheng et al., 2023). Obstacles such as the shortage of specialized and competent personnel in data collection, processing and analysis, the prohibitive costs associated with implementing specific technologies and widespread concerns about data security are significant. These challenges are particularly pronounced for small and medium-sized companies (SMEs), which often face resource constraints, impeding their ability to harness the full potential of available data (Nasrollahi et al., 2021).

In the Portuguese business landscape, initiatives such as Portugal 2020 and the Digital Transition Action Plan have played a fundamental role in promoting the digital transformation of the business sector. The Industry 4.0 Program, integrated into the National Strategy for the Digitalization of the Economy, aims to accelerate the adoption of Industry 4.0 technologies, promoting Portuguese technological suppliers and making Portugal an attractive hub for I4.0 investment. Launched in 2017, this program seeks to position the country at the forefront of the Fourth Industrial Revolution, focusing on digitalization, innovation, and internationalization, particularly for SMEs. However, due to budget constraints, many SMEs hire generalist professionals, resulting in a lack of specialized knowledge and insufficient skills in Information and Communication Technologies (ICT), which remains a significant obstacle (Faria et al., 2021).

Despite numerous vital initiatives at both national and European levels, SMEs face persistent challenges in integrating and using data, especially in specific sectors. This discrepancy in data usage persists when compared to its larger counterparts. Organizations are integrating emerging digital technologies to streamline business processes, cut costs, retain customers and remain competitive against rivals (Martin & Leurent, 2017).

Studies like Cenamor et al. (2019) highlight that digitalization is crucial for the competitiveness of SMEs, particularly in asset and data management. However, many companies struggle to invest in digital platforms and align these technologies with their operational and financial needs, which affects how they manage assets and utilize data (Cernamor et al., 2019).

Gradual digital transformation allows SMEs to adapt slowly and acquire digital skills over time. This approach is more suitable for companies with limited resources, as it facilitates the adoption of asset management technologies, reducing financial and operational impact and improving data-driven decision-making (Sagala & Őri, 2024).

Effective data management plays a crucial role in companies' competitiveness and operational efficiency. Considering this context, the main objective of the study is to empirically analyze the data use practices of Portuguese companies and discern whether there are noticeable differences in data management between micro, small, medium and large companies in Portugal. In that sense this study has as main research question: What is the difference in data management between micro, small, medium, and large companies?

In order to answer these research questions, a survey of 390 Portuguese companies was conducted. A non-parametric test was applied to understand the differences in data implementation among Portuguese companies. Additionally, a qualitative analysis was carried out to complement our main objective and understand how these companies are applying data management.

The article is organized as follows. Section 2 presents the Theoretical Background. Section 3 outlines the Methodology used to examine the correlation between different forms of data utilization and the variations across company sizes. Section 4 presents the results, followed by a discussion of the main findings in Sect. 5. Finally, Sect. 6 offers the conclusions, addresses the study's limitations, and suggests directions for future research.

2 Theoretical Background

2.1 Data Assets and Data Asset Management

The growing need to manage data and expand businesses has led many companies to adopt a comprehensive data management strategy using digital technologies such as cloud computing, artificial intelligence (AI), the Internet of Things (IoT), and Business Intelligence tools (Tan, et al., 2015). Data assets refer to systematically documented data resources, whether physical or electronic, that have the potential to provide future economic benefits to their owners and improve companies' decision-making processes (Li et al., 2022; Hu et al., 2022).

It is essential to distinguish between data assets and data asset management. Data assets are valuable organizational resources, such as customer information, sales data, or financial records. These are raw data elements that hold value when used effectively. In contrast, data asset management refers to the comprehensive process of organizing, storing, protecting, and strategically utilizing these resources to unlock their full potential and maximize their benefits (Chisholm, 2001). This includes safeguarding the data, ensuring regulatory compliance, and using it to inform decision-making processes that drive business value.

Effective data asset management transforms raw data into actionable insights, helping organizations optimize resource usage. Without this distinction, businesses risk data overload or underutilization, impairing decision-making and operational efficiency (Fleckenstein et al., 2018; Xu et al., 2023). The primary goal of data asset management is to ensure that data assets are utilized to support organizational objectives, enabling better decision-making and improving overall operational performance.

Companies that adopt digital technologies face various challenges, such as the effective management of data assets, security, and privacy, as well as the shortage of interdisciplinary talent capable of maximizing data value. To overcome these obstacles, companies must develop dynamic capabilities to adapt to the rapid technological evolution. Strategies such as using Big Data and establishing partnerships with digital ecosystems are essential to transform data into valuable assets and ensure the successful integration of digital technologies (Xu et al., 2023).

2.2 Data Asset Management Benefits

In today's digital economy, researchers study the impact of big data (Erel et al., 2021), and digital transformation on business operations (Wu et al., 2022). However, the success of big data depends on its organized use as an asset, as not all big data automatically yields superior results (Ghasemaghaei & Calic, 2020). Scholars like Hu et al. (2022) have emphasized that the efficiency of data assets, rather than just the volume of data, is critical to enhancing business operational efficiency.

Implementing an effective data asset management strategy provides several critical benefits to companies, helping them become more competitive. Among the key advantages are:

- **Improved decision-making**: Access to accurate and relevant data enables businesses to make strategic decisions based on robust and reliable information (Li et al., 2022). This is essential in a data-driven business environment.
- **Cost reduction**: Efficient data management helps identify and eliminate unnecessary expenses, such as redundant data storage and excessive processing costs (Chisholm, 2001).
- **Business innovation and agility**: Leveraging data assets allows companies to identify emerging market trends and opportunities, enhancing their ability to innovate and adapt quickly to changes. Improving data processing efficiency and reducing coordination costs are achieved by providing systematic and organized digital resources, thereby promoting innovation efficiency (Zheng et al., 2023).
- **Long-term strategic planning**: Aligning company objectives with insights derived from data enables more effective future planning. Companies with solid data asset management practices are better positioned for sustainable growth as data volumes and market demands evolve (Li & Zhang, 2023).
- **Data security**: A robust data management strategy includes essential security measures such as encryption and access controls, protecting valuable data assets from external threats (Chisholm, 2001). The data infrastructure allows companies to grow sustainably, adapting to increasing data volumes and the ever-evolving market demands (Chisholm, 2001; Li & Zhang, 2023). Although, it is essential to emphasize that a data management strategy is a crucial differentiator for companies, especially those aiming to excel in a data-driven business environment.

An effective data asset management strategy improves internal efficiency and empowers companies to excel in a competitive, data-driven environment (Tan, et al., 2015). Its implementation fosters innovation, cost savings, security, and adaptability to emerging challenges and market opportunities. Organizations can significantly enhance their processes and outcomes by adopting robust practices in this domain.

2.3 Data Asset Management: Difference Between Micro, Small, Medium and Large Companies

Several studies have explored the impact of digital transformation on sustainable development and competitiveness, particularly in SMEs. The role of Industry 4.0 technologies enables SMEs to achieve sustainable growth by improving operational efficiency, reducing resource dependency, and boosting innovation capacity. However, the challenges associated with adopting these technologies vary according to the size and resources of the company, with SMEs often encountering more significant barriers due to resource limitations, lack of technical expertise, and the complexity of integrating advanced digital solutions (Beier et al., 2021; Müller & Voigt, 2018).

Several authors have studied the differences in technology adoption, particularly in data management, across companies of different sizes (Low et al., 2011; Raguseo et al., 2018; Pollák et al., 2019). The literature points out the advantage for large companies, which have more resources to invest in that kind of technology. For example, Low et al. (2011) note that large companies are more likely to adopt cloud computing because they possess the financial capacity to support risks associated with new technologies.

While large companies have the advantage of resources, small and medium-sized companies (SMEs) tend to adopt flexible and cost-efficient technologies, such as cloud computing. According to Horváth and Szabó (2019), small businesses use cloud computing more frequently (60%) due to its affordability and flexibility but struggle with adopting advanced robotics (2%) due to high costs. Medium-sized companies with more investment capacity adopt both cloud computing (49%) and advanced robotics (9%), indicating a higher need for automation to remain competitive (Zolas et al., 2021). Large companies, on the other hand, use cloud computing (41%) to complement their already robust infrastructures, which allows them to implement advanced robotics (13%) more efficiently, as they have the financial and technological resources for complex automation (Martinelli et al., 2021).

Large companies typically have more complex and sophisticated data management systems, including advanced data analytics, cybersecurity, and dedicated IT departments (Zheng et al., 2023). These companies often invest in customized solutions that offer greater control and integration capabilities, benefiting from improved efficiency and competitiveness through more effective data management (Orzes et al., 2018). Large companies also extensively adopt technologies such as IoT, Big Data, and analytics to build comprehensive Cyber-Physical Systems, and they widely adopt sensors and integrated engineering systems to improve operational efficiency (Benitez et al., 2020; Dalenogare et al., 2018; Schwab, 2017). Moreover, according to Brender and Markov (2013), large companies have an advantage because of their resources and expertise, while SMEs may find migration more challenging and require additional support to manage risks effectively.

Medium-sized companies, although more limited than large companies, possess more significant financial resources and a more robust organizational structure than smaller companies. This enables them to adopt a broader range of Industry 4.0 technologies, including additive manufacturing and cloud services (Masood & Sonntag, 2020; Müller & Voigt, 2016; Rüttimann & Stöckli, 2016; Wang et al., 2016). These companies are better equipped to implement technologies that connect products and systems, such as IoT, Big Data, and analytics (Müller et al., 2018). However, they still face challenges, particularly in workforce qualification and management (Huang et al., 2009).

Implementing robust data management strategies for micro and small businesses presents significant challenges due to the required resource investments (Caputo et al., 2020). These businesses often encounter barriers related to the high costs of traditional data storage and the complexities of Big Data adoption (Shabbir &

Gardezi, 2020). As Coleman (2016) highlighted, resistance to Big Data adoption among SMEs stems from difficulties in managing knowledge, resources, and data. Financial limitations and a shortage of time and qualified personnel are common challenges when adopting Big Data (Shah et al., 2017). Besides, SMEs often face challenges in obtaining and processing data, particularly in tracking and reporting real-time data from multiple locations, mainly due to the absence of a centralized policy (Alam & Marwah, 2023). However, when SMEs successfully collect detailed and segmented data, they can leverage these insights to identify market opportunities and conduct more comprehensive risk analyses (Sen et al., 2016).

Companies of different sizes face distinct challenges in digital adoption. Small and medium-sized companies often struggle with financial constraints and a lack of qualified human resources, limiting their ability to implement advanced technologies such as the Internet of Things (IoT) and Artificial Intelligence (AI). To overcome these limitations, SMEs can adopt more accessible solutions, like cloud-based data infrastructures, which enhance efficiency without requiring significant upfront investments. On the other hand, larger companies benefit from more substantial financial resources and robust infrastructures, making it easier to integrate advanced technologies. However, they face the challenge of integrating data across departments and managing operational complexity. Regardless of size, strategic coordination between IT and business departments is essential for maximizing the value generated by data, promoting operational efficiency, and ensuring a successful and sustainable digital transformation (Baars et al., 2022; Fleckenstein et al., 2018).

Although SMEs have been slower to adopt Big Data than larger companies (Selamat et al., 2019), the increasing demand for data management has driven many small and medium-sized businesses to implement these technologies. By utilizing Big Data, SMEs can better understand consumer behavior, identify new business opportunities, and remain competitive (Sen et al., 2016). Due to resource constraints, SMEs often develop specific capabilities that provide a competitive edge by being more agile and adaptable. In contrast, large companies benefit from greater financial capacity and more advanced infrastructure (Molodchik et al., 2016).

Analyzing differences in data asset management among micro, small, medium, and large companies reveal distinct challenges and opportunities each category faces. Understanding these nuances is essential for developing effective strategies that promote technological integration and maximize the benefits of digital transformation at all business levels. In this context, the following hypothesis is proposed for testing:

Hypothesis 1. There are differences in Data Management between Micro, Small, Medium, and Large companies.

3 Methodology

This section outlines the data collection method used in the empirical analysis. The methodology consisted of four stages: (1) data collection, (2) qualitative analysis, (3) sample characterization and (4) data analysis.

The data collection phase involved the collection of comprehensive information from a diverse set of Portuguese companies of different sizes. Various data collection methods were used, including surveys, interviews and secondary data sources. This multifaceted approach ensured a robust dataset that could accurately reflect practices and trends in data usage across different industries and company sizes.

During the data analysis phase, collected data was systematically processed and examined to identify patterns and correlations. Advanced statistical techniques and analytical tools were used to ensure accurate and meaningful insights. The analysis focused on distinguishing differences in data management practices between micro, small, medium and large companies, as well as identifying the maturity levels of these practices across various sectors and geographic locations.

The final step involved interpreting the results of the data analysis. This included an in-depth discussion of the findings, highlighting key trends and significant differences in data usage practices among Portuguese companies. The results were contextualized within the broader landscape of digital transformation and data management, providing a comprehensive understanding of how companies of different sizes approach the use and management of data.

Overall, this methodology provided a structured and systematic approach to investigating the research questions, ensuring that the results are reliable and relevant to the current state of data use practices in Portugal.

3.1 Data Collection

The data collection process was carried out by distributing questionnaires to Portuguese companies between 2021 and 2023 via email with a link for completion on the online platform Shift2Future. Methodologically, a quantitative study was conducted, incorporating selected questions from the questionnaire developed by the Shift2Future consortium, focusing on using data assets in Portuguese companies. This Shift2Future questionnaire was derived from an adapted version for the Portuguese context, based on the "Industry 4.0 Readiness" self-assessment methodology developed by the IMPULS Foundation of the German Engineering Federation (VDMA) (Lichtblau et al., 2015). The choice of this model adapted to the reality of Portuguese companies, was due to the clarity of its well-defined dimensions and subdimensions, the convenience of being an online questionnaire, and its alignment and applicability to the reality of Portuguese companies (Guimarães et al., 2023).

The quantitative research was conducted anonymously, and participation was voluntary. A facilitator completed the questionnaires, clarifying and validating any doubts about interpretation.

To understand how companies utilize data assets, three critical variables were measured: Data Collection (DC), Digital Services (DS), and Information Technology (IT). Accordingly, a question was formulated for each variable, and all responses were measured on a 5-point Likert scale. Question 1 (see Appendix) evaluates the variable DC, "*How do you collect data?*". Question 2 (see Appendix) evaluates the variable DS, "*What is the importance of data-driven services in the company's revenue?*". Question 3 (see) evaluates the variable IT, "*How is the Information Technology (IT) department organized in your company*?".

In addition to these variables, a fourth variable called "security" was also measured, reflecting the growing concern for data security within companies. In this context, this variable was divided into four main sub-variables: Security for Data Exchange with Partners (SDP), Security for Internal Data Exchange (SDI), Security for Cloud Computing (CCS), and Security for Data Storage (DSS). These sub-variables were derived from the responses to Question 4 (see), "What is the state of your IT security solutions?" and were measured on a 4-point scale.

Table 1 presents the vital technological dimensions analyzed in this study, highlighting the role and importance of each variable in data management and security. These variables encompass various aspects of data collection, the relevance of digital services, and the security measures applied internally and externally. Each variable is critical in evaluating how companies organize, manage, and secure their data infrastructure.

3.2 Sample Characterization

The sample for this study consisted of 559 companies from various regions of Portugal, covering different sizes and sectors of economic activity. After data cleaning and preprocessing, 390 valid responses were obtained. The number of employees and annual turnover were also used to measure the company's size.

This sample is statistically valid, following the sampling technique proposed by Etikan et al. (2016) and Mishra et al. (2021). Academic studies suggest a sample size greater than 100 is statistically valid (Sreedharan & Raju, 2018; Mishra et al., 2021).

It is essential to highlight, as previously mentioned, that the entire research process was supervised and validated by the presence of the authors and some facilitators in the various specific sectors of the companies. The responses obtained were subsequently analyzed using a quantitative methodology.

The presented sample is characterized by significant heterogeneity in terms of size, encompassing approximately micro (28%), small (35%), medium (33%), and 4% large companies (according to the EU classification methodology). The companies involved in this study belong to different economic sectors, as illustrated in Table 2.

Table 1 Variables description

Acronyms	Names of variables	Description
DC	Data collection	This variable measures how companies collect data. It assesses the extent to which data is gathered in various company areas, manually or digitally, and how comprehensively data collection is implemented across the organization
DS	Digital services	This variable evaluates the importance of data-driven services to a company's revenue. It measures how much the company relies on digital services powered by data in its business model and overall operations
IT	Information technology	This variable refers to the organization and management of the company's IT department. It assesses the presence and structure of IT resources within the company, whether localized, centralized, or outsourced
SDP	Security for data exchange with partners	This variable measures the security protocols for data exchange between a company and its external partners. It reflects how companies manage communications security and data sharing with external stakeholders to ensure data integrity and confidentiality
SDI	Security for internal data exchange	This variable focuses on the internal security measures that protect data exchange within the organization. It evaluates how secure internal communications and data transfers are, ensuring data is safely transmitted between departments or internal systems
CCS	Security for cloud computing	This variable assesses the security measures to protect data stored or processed in cloud computing environments. It covers the company's policies and technologies to secure its cloud-based operations from potential threats
DSS	Security for data storage	This variable addresses the company's security protocols for storing data. It evaluates the measures to protect stored data from unauthorized access or breaches, ensuring long-term data integrity and security

Table 2 Samples description

Sector	%	Region	%	Company size	%
Textile	8.71	North	27.43	Micro = < 9 employees	27.94
Metal-mechanics	16.92				
Tourism	11.79				
Ceramics	7.17	Center	58.20	Small < 50 employees	34.87
Agri-food	9.48				
Stone	6.92				
Footwear	5.89	Alentejo	8.46	Medium 50 = < employees < 250	33.58
Automotive	4.35				
Glass	1.53	Lisboa & Vale do Tejo	4.61		
Aerospace	0.51				
Molds	1.79	Algarve	1.02	Large > = 250 employees	3.58
Other	24.87				

Table 2 also presents the distribution of the participating companies in the study, segmented by sector, region, and company size. The analysis of the results reveals various insights about the sample.

Regarding economic activity sectors, the metal-mechanic sector represents the largest proportion with 16.92% of the companies, indicating a strong presence of this sector in the sample. The "Others" category includes a variety of unspecified sectors, totaling 24.87%, the largest individual category. Tourism accounts for 11.79%, highlighting the importance of this sector in the Portuguese economy, followed by the agri-food sector with 9.48%, reflecting the relevance of agriculture and food. The textile sector includes 8.71% of the companies, showing its importance in manufacturing. Traditional sectors like ceramics and stone represent 7.17% and 6.92%, respectively. The footwear sector, known for its exports, covers 5.89%. More specialized sectors such as automotive (4.35%), glass (1.53%), aerospace (0.51%), and molds (1.79%) have smaller proportions.

The regional distribution shows that the Centro region represents 58.20% of the sample, being the area with the highest number of participating companies. The Norte region follows with 27.43%, the second largest representation. Alentejo has 8.46%, showing a significant participation, while Lisbon and Vale do Tejo include 4.61% of the companies, being less represented in comparison. The Algarve has the lowest regional representation with only 1.02%.

Regarding company size, micro companies (< = 9 employees) constitute 27.94% of the sample, reflecting the relevance of small business units. Small companies (< 50 employees) represent 34.87%, being the largest category in terms of size. Medium-sized companies (50 < = employees < 250) account for 33.58%, indicating a robust presence of medium-sized companies. Large companies (> = 250 employees) represent only 3.58%, the smallest proportion, indicating a lesser presence of large corporations in the sample.

The sample is considered diverse as it includes companies from various sectors, regions, and sizes. The predominance of companies in the metal-mechanic sector, as well as the significant representation of micro and small companies, reflects the economic structure of Portugal, characterized by a strong presence of small and medium-sized companies (SMEs). The concentration of companies in the Centro region may indicate an important industrial or commercial hub. This diversity of sectors and sizes offers a comprehensive view of business practices and possible regional variations, which is essential for understanding productivity and innovation dynamics in the Portuguese context.

3.3 Response Bias and Common Method Variance

Since bias can be a potential issue in survey design, we implemented several procedures and statistical measures to mitigate it, as recommended by Podsakoff et al. (2012). Given that our survey involved single respondents, common method variance (CMV) was a potential concern. To address this, we randomized the order of the questionnaire blocks to prevent potential associations between variables and reduce social desirability bias. Additionally, a consultant was present during the survey administration to assist respondents with any questions or clarifications needed while completing the questionnaire.

To assess the magnitude of CMV, we applied Harman's single-factor test, where a single factor is tested for its influence on all measured items. If the total variance extracted by one factor exceeds 50%, it suggests the presence of common method bias (Podsakoff et al., 2012). In our study, the single factor explained 31.48% of the total variance, indicating that CMV is not a concern.

3.4 Data Analysis

To perform data analysis, a statistical tool was used using the IBM SPSS software version 29.0.1.0. Before determining the appropriate statistical test, normality and homogeneity of variances of the dependent variables were assessed. The Shapiro–Wilk test examined normality, revealing that the variables did not adhere to a normal distribution. However, the normality of the sample was assumed due to its size exceeding 30. The Levene test was employed to assess homogeneity, indicating a lack of homogeneity as the p-value exceeded 0.05 for nearly all variables. Based on the outcomes of both tests, the decision was made to employ a non-parametric method the Kruskal–Wallis test. This test compares two or more independent samples and serves as the non-parametric equivalent of ANOVA. Data collection enables a wide range of analyses, but this article only addresses a subset of them and provides a general treatment of the data.

Various approaches were used to achieve the objectives of this study concerning thc treatment of the research.

3.5 *Qualitative Analysis*

In addition to the quantitative analysis explained a qualitative approach was adopted to better understand Portuguese companies data asset utilization landscape. This decision was driven by the need to capture more profound insights into the patterns of data asset utilization in Portuguese companies, particularly in areas that might not be fully explored through quantitative measures alone. By adding an open-ended question, the study aimed to uncover the nuanced ways companies use data.

The extra question used was Question 5 (see) "*What is the use of the collected data?*", with the following response options: (a) Does not use data; (b) Creating transparency of production processes; (c) management; (d) Optimization of the logistics process; (e) Optimization of resource consumption (material, energy); (f) Predictive maintenance; and (g) Automatic production control through the use of real-time data.

This qualitative question provided essential insight into how companies across different industries and sizes use data in their operations. While quantitative data offers a broad view of data use, qualitative responses highlight specific practices and challenges, such as preferences for certain uses of data (e.g., transparency in production processes) and difficulties small businesses face with predictive maintenance or real-time data control.

Qualitative analysis also explored why some companies do not fully utilize data, helping to better understand barriers to adopting advanced data-driven processes. By focusing on these responses, the analysis gave a more complete picture of data management, adding value to the overall conclusions.

Therefore, this qualitative analysis deepens the study, highlighting areas for further exploration and shaping recommendations to meet the specific needs of different company profiles.

4 Results

Table 3 summarizes the outcomes of the Kruskal–Wallis Test. It is possible to observe that the test was significant for DS, SDP, DSS. This means that there is a difference in the use of data to develop new Digital Services (DS), the integration of Security for Data Exchange with Partners (SDP), and the application of Data Storage Security (DSS) technologies among micro, small, medium, and large companies.

Digital Services (DS) show statistical significance ($p = 0.006$), with a significance level of 1%, suggesting that larger companies have a more advanced digitalization in implementing digital services. Moreover, there is a growing emphasis on data security, encompassing internal and external sharing and storage. The integration of

Table 3 Kruskal–Wallis test result

	DC	IT	DS	SDP	SDI	CCS	DSS
Chi-Square	3.410	1.837	12.559	10.636	5.798	2.945	8.466
df	3	3	3	3	3	3	3
Asymp. Sig	0.333	0.607	0.006***	0.014**	0.122	0.400	0.037**

[a]Kruskal Wallis Test: * $p < 0.1$; ** $p < 0.05$; *** $p < 0.01$
[b]Grouping Variable: Size

security for data exchange with partners (SDP) shows statistical significance ($p = 0.014$), with a significance level of 5%, indicating that larger companies emphasize data security more during external exchanges. The application of data storage security (DSS) also shows statistical significance ($p = 0.037$), with a significance level of 5%, indicating that larger companies have more advanced data storage security measures.

Surprisingly, significant differences were not found for the variables Data Collection (DC) and Information Technology (IT). This could mean that overall, micro, SMEs, and large companies are concerned about data collection and the establishment of IT infrastructures for this purpose.

These results highlight the relevance of company size in influencing certain data management practices while also showing areas where practices are uniformly adopted regardless of company size. Larger companies tend to have more advanced approaches in digital services, data exchange security, and data storage security due to their more excellent resources and structured processes. In contrast, data collection and IT usage practices appear consistent across companies of all sizes.

In Fig. 1, we can observe the data distribution for DS across different company sizes. It is evident that the median is at the lower limit and is similar across all company sizes. This figure also shows a distribution in the upper values, suggesting more variability or higher values in the micro and large companies compared with SMEs.

Figure 2 presents an analysis of the Kruskal–Wallis test applied to companies of different sizes, with the variable SDP referring to the integration of security for data exchange with partners on the vertical axis and the size of the companies on the horizontal axis.

Regarding data distribution, the values of the SDP variable range approximately from 1.00 to 4.00 for all company sizes. The median SDP appears lower for small companies than for medium, medium, and large ones.

The Kruskal–Wallis test statistic 10.636 with a p-value of 0.014 suggests a statistically significant difference in SDP among different company sizes. The test result for the sample of 390 companies leads to rejecting the null hypothesis that there are no significant differences between the groups.

Micro companies tend to have a higher median SDP, indicating greater security integration, compared to small companies, which show a lower median SDP, indicating lesser security integration than other company sizes. Medium and large

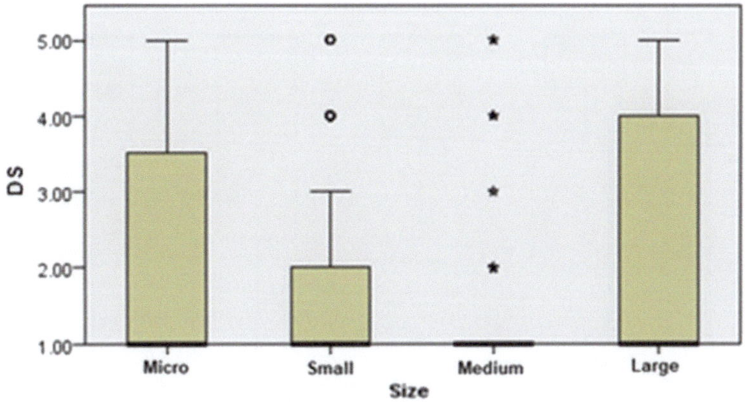

Fig. 1 Independent-samples Kruskal–Wallis test for DS variable

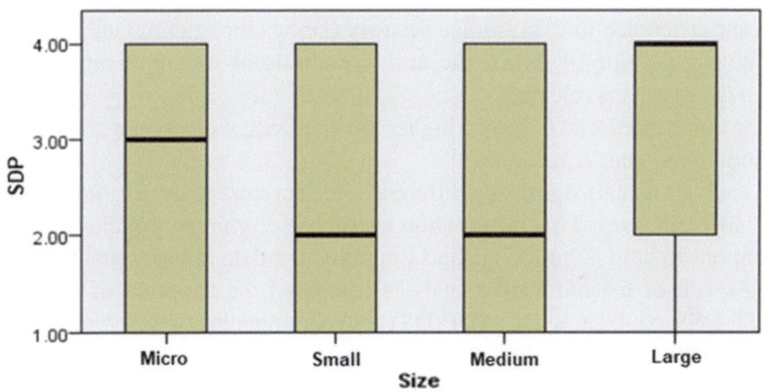

Fig. 2 Independent-samples Kruskal–Wallis test for SDP variable

companies also show a relatively high median, suggesting that these companies have more robust security practices for data exchange with partners.

Notably, there are significant differences in the integration of security for data exchange with partners among companies of different sizes. This information is crucial for directing policies and specific interventions that can help smaller companies improve their data security practices, aligning them with the practices observed in larger companies.

Similarly to the analysis of Figs. 2 and 3 presents an analysis of the Kruskal–Wallis test applied to companies of different sizes, with the variable DSS, which refers to data storage security. The data distribution also ranges between 1.00 and 4.00 for all company sizes. The median DSS appears to be higher for micro and small companies than for medium and large ones.

The Kruskal–Wallis test shows a test statistic of 8.466, 3 degrees of freedom, and an asymptotic significance (p-value) of 0.037. This result suggests a statistically

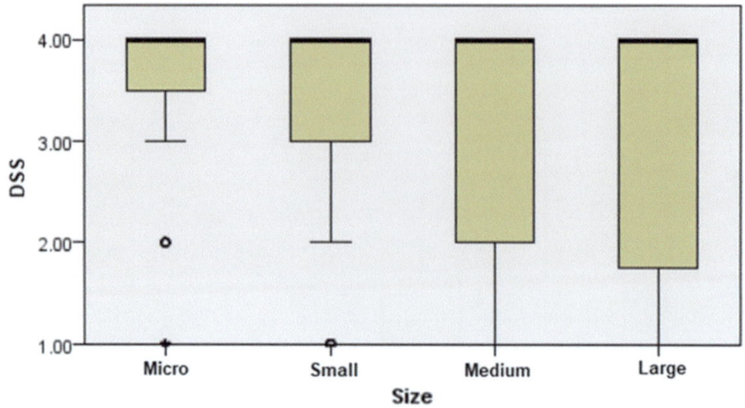

Fig. 3 Independent-samples Kruskal–Wallis test for DSS variable

significant difference in data storage security (DSS) among companies of different sizes. With a p-value of 0.037, the null hypothesis of no significant differences between the groups is rejected.

Micro companies tend to have a higher median DSS, indicating a greater security integration than other companies.

The analysis reveals significant differences in data storage security among companies of different sizes. This information is crucial for guiding policies and specific interventions to help larger companies improve their data security practices.

As a result of the qualitative analysis compared the adoption of various variables (IT, DSS, SDI, CCS, DC, SDP, DS) across companies of different sizes: large, medium, small, and micro (Fig. 4).

The analysis shows that large companies tend to lead in the adoption of more advanced technologies, such as IT and SDP, while micro companies excel in the

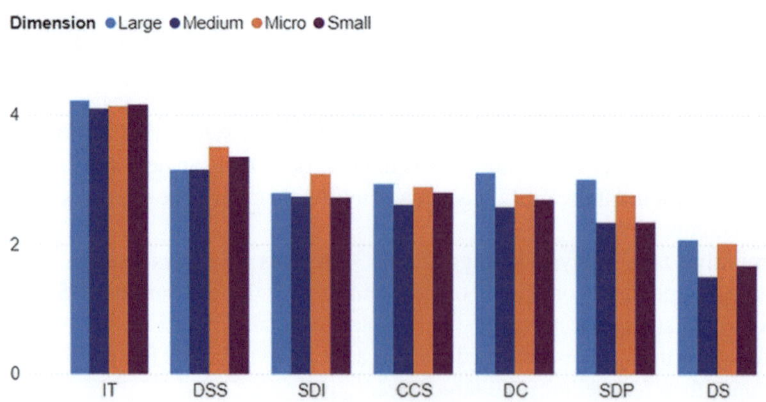

Fig. 4 Comparison of technology adoption by company size

adoption of DSS. The adoption of SDI, CCS, and DC is relatively uniform across different company sizes, indicating that these technologies are widely used regardless of company size. This diversity in technology adoption reflects the different needs and investment capacities among companies of various sizes.

Figure 5 shows the average values of several variables related to the use of technologies and data security (such as CCS, DC, DS, DSS, IT, SDI, and SDP) across different regions of Portugal (Alentejo, Algarve, Lisbon & Vale do Tejo, Center, and North) and four company size categories (large, medium, small, and micro). Larger companies, especially in Lisbon and North, display more variability in IT and DS, indicating more robust adoption of these technologies. Smaller companies, like micro and small-sized businesses, show more uniform values across regions, facing similar challenges in adopting IT and data security technologies. Alentejo and Algarve have lower averages in areas such as cloud security, while Lisbon and North demonstrate more advanced digital technology adoption.

Figure 6 illustrates the response rate to the qualitative question regarding how companies of different sizes use collected data. Portuguese companies strongly focus on data collection for Quality Management, Process and Resource Optimization, and Process Transparency. Categories analyzed include automatic process control, predictive maintenance, resource consumption optimization, logistics process optimization, quality management, and companies that do not use data.

Small companies (38.5%) lead in the use of automatic process control, followed closely by medium and micro companies (both at 29.2%), while large companies show less adoption (3.1%). Predictive maintenance is most prevalent in micro companies (34.9%), with medium (31.7%) and small companies (27.0%) following, and

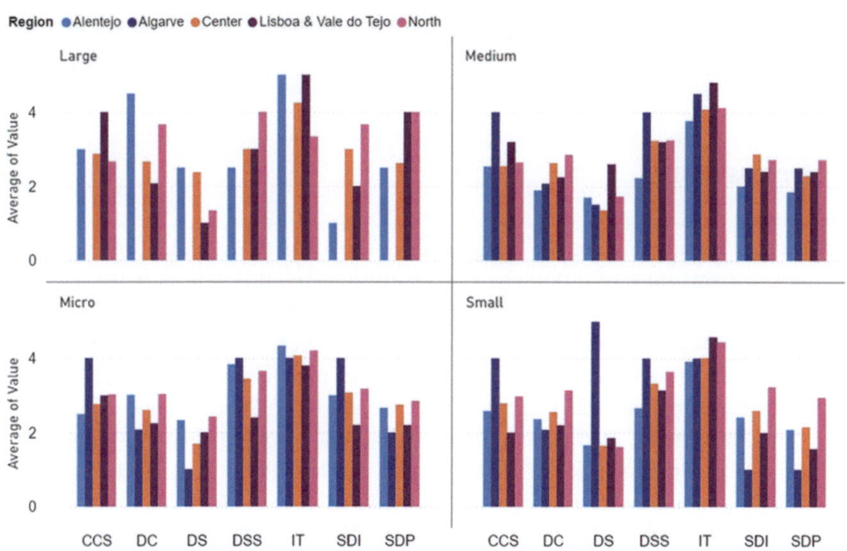

Fig. 5 Average of value by variables, region and dimension

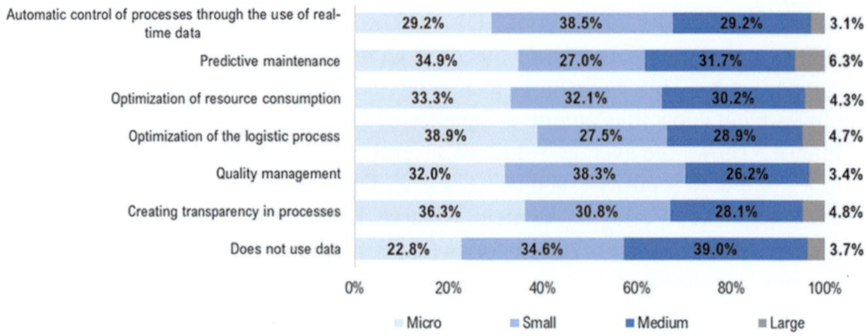

Fig. 6 Use of the collected data by dimension of companies for each topic

large companies accounting for only 6.3%. Micro (33.3%) and small companies (32.1%) exhibit similar usage rates for resource consumption optimization, while medium (30.2%) and large companies (4.3%) lag.

Micro companies (38.9%) also lead in logistics process optimization, followed by medium (28.9%) and small (27.5%), with large companies showing lower usage (4.7%). In terms of quality management, small companies are at the forefront (38.3%), followed by micro (32.0%), medium (26.2%), and large companies (3.4%). For process transparency, micro companies lead (36.3%), followed by small (30.8%), medium (28.1%), and large companies (4.8%). Lastly, medium companies are the most represented (39.0%) among those that do not utilize data, followed by small (34.6%), micro (22.8%), and large companies (3.7%).

These results highlight that smaller companies focus on efficiency-driven data use, while larger companies may already have these practices in place and are focusing on other innovations.

5 Discussion

This study provides valuable insights into the data management practices of Portuguese companies of different sizes, identifying key differences in the adoption of advanced data technologies and security protocols across micro, small, medium, and large companies. These differences are partly attributed to a varied understanding of the tangible impacts of data assets within companies (Zheng et al., 2023).

The findings indicate that large companies tend to have more advanced data asset management systems, particularly in areas like data storage security, secure data exchange, and digital services. Their financial and technical capacity enables them to invest in sophisticated technologies, such as AI, IoT, cloud computing, and big data analytics (Frank et al., 2019). These investments help improve operational efficiency and ensure compliance with stricter regulatory requirements, giving larger companies an edge in the digitalization process. For instance, IoT devices in these companies monitor equipment in real time, allowing AI systems to predict maintenance needs, thus reducing operational costs and enhancing efficiency (Frank et al., 2019). Cloud computing provides flexible storage solutions, enabling secure data access and collaboration, while encryption ensures data protection.

Regarding data security, large companies place a stronger emphasis on securing external data exchanges due to higher regulatory demands and greater risk exposure (Vega et al., 2021). These companies have historically made significant investments in security, driven by competitive pressures and the need to protect sensitive data (Hallová et al., 2019). Large companies often maintain dedicated teams focused on information security (Khan et al., 2020), implementing blockchain, multi-factor authentication (MFA), and encryption technologies to safeguard data integrity and confidentiality. For example, Zhang & Zhang (2021) demonstrated how blockchain can securely manage IoT data in the electricity sector, enhancing data reliability and security in asset management.

In contrast, small and medium-sized companies (SMEs) face greater challenges in adopting advanced data solutions due to resource constraints. While SMEs are focused on building basic IT infrastructure for data collection, they struggle to fully implement technologies like predictive maintenance and real-time process control (Gläser et al., 2023). SMEs also tend to lack robust data security systems, exposing them to potential risks in data exchange and storage.

To address these challenges, SMEs should prioritize investments in affordable technologies such as cloud computing and outsourced IT services to enhance data management without significant financial strain. Additionally, skills development is crucial, as the lack of qualified personnel limits the adoption of advanced data technologies.

The study suggests that a more strategic approach to data utilization in SMEs, such as embracing automation and predictive technologies, could improve efficiency, reduce costs, and foster innovation. Policymakers and industry associations can play a key role by offering incentives and guidance tailored to the specific needs of smaller businesses, helping them reach a level of data management maturity comparable to that of larger companies.

Moreover, skills development and a strong focus on data governance are essential for SMEs to fully benefit from digital transformation (Hannila et al., 2022). By fostering a culture that values and trusts data, SMEs can integrate data from various sources, uncover new business opportunities, and improve decision-making capabilities.

Ultimately, companies that invest in a well-structured data strategy, secure data infrastructure, and skills development are better positioned to harness the full potential of digital technologies. These strategies enable companies to stay competitive in an increasingly dynamic market, where technological advancements and evolving customer demands drive the need for continuous adaptation.

6 Conclusion

Data management in Portugal varies significantly across micro, small, medium, and large companies. Understanding these differences is crucial for developing more effective data management strategies and fostering innovation in the Portuguese business landscape. The primary distinctions among companies involve how they utilize data assets and address data security, with a particular emphasis on data collection for quality management, process optimization, and transparency.

The findings show that larger companies adopt more advanced data security protocols and benefit from technological advantages. In contrast, smaller companies primarily focus on data collection for quality management, process optimization, and transparency. These insights are vital for shaping future strategies to improve data management practices and enhance the Portuguese business environment.

These conclusions offer valuable insights into current data management practices and highlight areas for improvement. By understanding the dynamics of data management in Portuguese companies, it becomes possible to develop policies and interventions that support the efficient use of data assets, irrespective of company size. This knowledge is key to creating strategies that improve operational efficiency and promote a culture of innovation and data security.

The study's findings provide a foundation for future research to explore these factors in greater depth, aiming to develop actionable strategies that enhance data asset management practices across companies. By addressing these critical areas, future research can contribute to a better understanding of how technological advancements and evolving data management practices can be leveraged to strengthen the competitiveness of Portuguese businesses.

7 Limitations and Future Research

A limitation of this study lies in the formulation of the data collection questions. To address this, it is recommended that future research employ more detailed case studies to comprehensively understand data usage and variations across companies. Future research should also explore the factors driving these differences to inform strategies that can improve data management practices across companies.

While the current focus is on data utilization and security within the data asset management process, future studies should investigate other critical steps, such as planning, acquisition, storage, processing, analysis, and disposal. Understanding these dynamics is essential for developing policies and interventions that support the efficient and effective use of data assets in companies of all sizes in Portugal. Additionally, continuous exploration and adaptation of data management practices are necessary to keep pace with technological and regulatory changes, ensuring that companies are prepared for future challenges.

Besides, it is recommended that future studies delve deeper into specific aspects of data asset management that have not been fully explored in this work. For example, future studies could investigate the role of emerging technologies like Artificial Intelligence (AI) and IoT (Internet of Things) in small and medium-sized companies (SMEs), examining how these technologies can improve data management processes, including predictive maintenance, process automation, and advanced analytics.

Another critical area for future research would be to explore the barriers to technology adoption in SMEs, such as financial limitations and lack of skilled personnel, and how these barriers can be overcome through policy interventions or tailored support systems. Additionally, further research should consider a more detailed exploration of the entire data lifecycle, including planning, acquisition, storage, processing, analysis, and disposal, to provide a more comprehensive understanding of how companies handle data across different industries.

To address the limitations identified in this study, future research should utilize case studies to gain a comprehensive understanding of data usage across companies of different sizes. This will allow for more nuanced insights into the variations in data management practices and help tailor recommendations for improving data utilization and security.

Acknowledgements This work is funded by National Funds through the FCT - Foundation for Science and Technology, I.P., within the scope of the project Ref. UIDB/05583/2020. Furthermore, we thank the Research Centre in Digital Services (CISeD) and the Polytechnic Institute of Viseu for their support. This work was also supported by the Foundation for Science and Technology (FCT), funded by the research grant with the reference UI/BD/154507/2022.

Appendix

Survey: Evaluation of Digital Maturity Level for Industry 4.0

Q1 (DC): How do you collect data?

Please select only one option:

- Does collect data.
- Relevant data is collected digitally in at least one area.
- Mainly in manual mode.
- All data is collected digitally, automatically, in all areas.
- All data is collected digitally in multiple areas.

Q2 (DS): What is the importance of data-driven services in the company's revenue?
Please select only one option:

- None
- Contribute less than 1%.

- Contribute less than 2.5%.
- Contribute less than 7.5%.
- Significant contribution, less than 10%.
- Important contribution, over 10%.

Q3 (IT): How is the Information Technology (IT) department organized in your company?

Please select only one option:

- There are local IT departments in each operational area (production, product development, sales, etc.).
- There are IT specialists allocated to each operational area.
- The IT resources are centralized.
- There are no IT resources.
- There are no internal IT resources (an external service provider is used).

Q4 (Security): What is the status of your IT security solutions?

Please select only one option:

	Not planned	Planned	In development	Implemented
(DSS) Security in internal data storage	☐	☐	☐	☐
(CCS) Security of data through cloud services	☐	☐	☐	☐
(SDI) Security of communications for internal data exchange	☐	☐	☐	☐
(SDP) Security of communications for data exchange with business partners	☐	☐	☐	☐

Survey: Informational Question

Q5 (Informational Question): What is the use of the collected data?

Please select only one option:

- Does not use data.
- Creating transparency of production processes.
- Quality management.
- Optimization of the logistics process.
- Optimization of resource consumption (material, energy).
- Predictive maintenance.
- Automatic production control through the use of real-time data.

References

Alam, E. G., & Marwah, K. (2023). Design and evaluation of a data management solution for a small to medium sized enterprise using cloud simulator. In *2023 International Conference on Computational Intelligence and Knowledge Economy (ICCIKE)* (pp. 426–431). IEEE.

Baars, H., Weber, P., & Tank, A. (2022). Institutionalizing analytic data sharing in SME ecosystems–a role-based perspective.

Beier, G., Niehoff, S., & Hoffmann, M. (2021). Industry 4.0: a step towards achieving the SDGs? A critical literature review. *Discover sustainability, 2*(1), 22.

Benitez, G. B., Ayala, N. F., & Frank, A. G. (2020). Industry 4.0 innovation ecosystems: An evolutionary perspective on value cocreation. *International Journal of Production Economics, 228*, 107735.

Brender, N., & Markov, I. (2013). Risk perception and risk management in cloud computing: Results from a case study of Swiss companies. *International Journal of Information Management, 33*(5), 726–733.

Caputo, F., Mazzoleni, A., Pellicelli, A. C., & Muller, J. (2020). Over the mask of innovation management in the world of big data. *Journal of Business Research, 119*, 330–338.

Cenamor, J., Parida, V., & Wincent, J. (2019). How entrepreneurial SMEs compete through digital platforms: The roles of digital platform capability, network capability and ambidexterity. *Journal of Business Research, 100*, 196–206.

Chisholm, M. (2001). *Managing Reference Data in Enterprise Databases*. Morgan Kaufmann.

Coleman, S. Y. (2016). Data-mining opportunities for small and medium enterprises with official statistics in the UK. *Journal of Official Statistics, 32*(4), 849–865.

Dalenogare, L. S., Benitez, G. B., Ayala, N. F., & Frank, A. G. (2018). The expected contribution of Industry 4.0 technologies for industrial performance. *International Journal of Production Economics, 204*, 383–394.

Erel, I., Stern, L. H., Tan, C., & Weisbach, M. S. (2021). Selecting directors using machine learning. *The Review of Financial Studies, 34*(7), 3226–3264.

Etikan, I., Musa, S. A., Alkassim, R. S., et al. (2016). Comparison of convenience sampling and purposive sampling. *American Journal of Theoretical and Applied Statistics, 5*(1), 1–4.

Faria, B. S., Simões, A. C., & Rodrigues, J. C. (2021). Impact of governmental support for the implementation of industry 4.0 in Portugal. In *International Conference Innovation in Engineering* (pp. 108–120). Cham: Springer International Publishing.

Fleckenstein, M., Fellows, L., & Ferrante, K. (2018). *Modern data strategy* (pp. 63–76). Springer International Publishing.

Frank, A. G., Cortimiglia, M. N., Ribeiro, J. L. D., & de Oliveira, L. S. (2016). The effect of innovation activities on innovation outputs in the Brazilian industry: Market-orientation versus. technology-acquisition strategies. *Research Policy, 45*(3), 577–592.

Frank, A. G., Dalenogare, L. S., & Ayala, N. F. (2019). Industry 4.0 technologies: Implementation patterns in manufacturing companies. *International Journal of Production Economics, 210*, 15–26.

Ghasemaghaei, M., & Calic, G. (2020). Assessing the impact of big data on firm innovation performance: Big data is not always better data. *Journal of Business Research, 108*, 147–162.

Gläser, U., Morgado, J., & Holfeld, D. (2023). Strategical and tactical asset management for the North Line in Portugal. *Transportation Research Procedia, 72*, 1723–1730.

Guimarães, A., Reis, P., & Charrua-Santos, F. (2023). Industry 4.0-assessment of digital readiness of manufacturing companies in Portugal. In *2023 IEEE International Conference on Industrial Engineering and Engineering Management (IEEM)* (pp. 0557–0561). IEEE.

Hallová, M., Polakovič, P., Šilerová, E., & Slováková, I. (2019). Proteção e segurança de dados em PMEs no âmbito da infraestrutura empresarial. *Artigos on-line AGRIS em Economia e Informática, 11* (665–2019–3992).

Hannila, H., Silvola, R., Harkonen, J., & Haapasalo, H. (2022). Data-driven begins with DATA; potential of data assets. *Journal of Computer Information Systems, 62*(1), 29–38.

Horváth, D., & Szabó, R. Z. (2019). Driving forces and barriers of Industry 4.0: Do multinational and small and medium-sized companies have equal opportunities? *Technological Forecasting and Social Change, 146*, 119–132.

Hu, C., Li, Y., & Zheng, X. (2022). Data assets, information uses, and operational efficiency. *Applied Economics, 54*(60), 6887–6900.

Huang, X. (2009). Strategic decision making in Chinese SMEs. *Chinese Management Studies, 3*(2), 87–101.

Khan, M. I., Tanwar, S., & Rana, A. (2020). The need for information security management for smes. In *2020 9th International Conference System Modeling and Advancement in Research Trends (SMART)* (pp. 328–332). IEEE.

Koumou, K. O., & Isafiade, O. (2024). Asset management trends in diverse settings involving immersive technology: A systematic literature review. *IEEE Access*.

Li, X., & Zhang, S. (2023). Management mode and path of digital transformation of power grid enterprises based on artificial intelligence algorithm. *International Journal of Thermofluids, 100552*.

Lichtblau, K., Stich, V., Bertenrath, R., Blum, M., Bleider, M., Millack, A., & Schröter, M. (2015). IMPULS, Industry 4.0 readiness. Impuls-Stiftung des VDMA, Aachen-Kölb (pp. 1–76).

Low, C., Chen, Y., & Wu, M. (2011). Understanding the determinants of cloud computing adoption. *Industrial Management & Data Systems, 111*(7), 1006–1023.

Martin, C., & Leurent, H. (2017). Technology and innovation for the future of production: Accelerating value creation. *In World Economic Forum* (pp. 1–38).

Martinelli, A., Mina, A., & Moggi, M. (2021). The enabling technologies of industry 4.0: examining the seeds of the fourth industrial revolution. *Industrial and Corporate Change, 30*(1), 161–188.

Masood, T., & Sonntag, P. (2020). Industry 4.0: Adoption challenges and benefits for SMEs. *Computers in industry, 121*, 103261.

Mishra, M. N., Mohan, A., & Sarkar, A. (2021). Role of lean six sigma in the indian msmes during covid-19. *International Journal of Lean Six Sigma, 12*(4), 697–717.

Molodchik, M., Fernandez-Jardon, C., & Barajas, A. (2016). Intangible-driven performance: Company size matters. *International Journal of Knowledge-Based Development, 7*(3), 225–239.

Müller, J. M., & Voigt, K. I. (2018). Sustainable industrial value creation in SMEs: A comparison between industry 4.0 and made in China 2025. *International Journal of Precision Engineering and Manufacturing-Green Technology, 5*, 659–670.

Müller, J. M., Buliga, O., & Voigt, K. I. (2018). Fortune favors the prepared: How SMEs approach business model innovations in Industry 4.0. *Technological Forecasting and Social Change, 132*, 2–17.

Müller, J., & Voigt, K. I. (2016). Industry 4.0 for small and medium-sized enterprises [Industrie 4.0 für kleine und mittlere unternehmen]. *Product. Manag, 21*, 28–30.

Nasrollahi, M., Ramezani, J., & Sadraei, M. (2021). The impact of big data adoption on SMEs' performance. *Big Data and Cognitive Computing, 5*(4), 68.

Orzes, G., Rauch, E., Bednar, S., & Poklemba, R. (2018). Industry 4.0 implementation barriers in small and medium sized enterprises: A focus group study. In *2018 IEEE International Conference on Industrial Engineering and Engineering Management (IEEM)* (pp. 1348–1352). IEEE.

Podsakoff, P. M., MacKenzie, S. B., & Podsakoff, N. P. (2012). Sources of method bias in social science research and recommendations on how to control it. *Annual Review of Psychology, 63*(1), 539–569.

Pollák, M., & Tkáč, J. (2019). Enterprise information data management system for small manufacturing company. *TEM Journal, 8*(4), 1169–1175.

Raguseo, E. (2018). Big data technologies: An empirical investigation on their adoption, benefits and risks for companies. *International Journal of Information Management, 38*(1), 187–195.

Rüttimann, B. G., & Stöckli, M. T. (2016). Lean and industry 4.0—twins, partners, or contenders? A due clarification regarding the supposed clash of two production systems. *Journal of Service Science and Management, 9*(6), 485–500.

Sagala, G. H., & Őri, D. (2024). Toward SMEs digital transformation success: a systematic literature review. *Information Systems and e-Business Management*, 1–53.
Schwab, K. (2017). The fourth industrial revolution. Crown Currency.
Selamat, S. A. M., Prakoonwit, S., Sahandi, R., & Khan, W. (2019). Big data and IoT opportunities for small and medium-sized enterprises (SMEs). *In Handbook of Research on Big Data and the IoT* (pp. 77–88). IGI Global.
Sen, D., Ozturk, M., & Vayvay, O. (2016). An overview of big data for growth in SMEs. *Procedia-Social and Behavioral Sciences, 235*, 159–167.
Shabbir, M. Q., & Gardezi, S. B. W. (2020). Application of big data analytics and organizational performance: The mediating role of knowledge management practices. *Journal of Big Data, 7*(1), 47.
Shah, S., Soriano, C. B., & Coutroubis, A. D. (2017). Is big data for everyone? The challenges of big data adoption in SMEs. In *2017 IEEE International Conference on Industrial Engineering and Engineering Management (IEEM)* (pp. 803–807). IEEE.
Sreedharan, V., & Raju, R. (2018). Development of a green lean six sigma model for public sectors. *International Journal of Lean Six Sigma, 9*(2), 238–255.
Tan, K. H., Zhan, Y., Ji, G., Ye, F., & Chang, C. (2015). Harvesting big data to enhance supply chain innovation capabilities: An analytic infrastructure based on deduction graph. *International Journal of Production Economics, 165,* 223–233.
Vega, D., Lozano, A., Blanco, F., & Simanca, F. (2021). Model for the implementation of security in wi-fi networks for SMEs. *In Journal of Physics: Conference Series, 1828*(1), 012105.
Wang, S., Wan, J., Li, D., & Zhang, C. (2016). Implementing smart factory of industrie 4.0: an outlook. *International Journal of Distributed Sensor Networks, 12*(1), 3159805.
Wirtz, B. W., & Wirtz, B. W. (2021). Artificial intelligence, big data, and cloud computing. *Digital Business and Electronic Commerce: Strategy, Business Models and Technology*, (pp. 217–258).
Wu, K., Fu, Y., & Kong, D. (2022). Does the digital transformation of enterprises affect stock price crash risk? *Finance Research Letters, 48*, Article 102888.
Xu, T., Shi, H., Shi, Y., & You, J. (2023). From data to data asset: Conceptual evolution and strategic imperatives in the digital economy era. *Asia Pacific Journal of Innovation and Entrepreneurship, 18*(1), 2–20.
Zhang, X., & Zhang, J. (2021). Research on data asset management of electricity industry based on blockchain. In *2021 2nd Asia Service Sciences and Software Engineering Conference* (pp. 28–33).
Zheng, M., Li, T., & Ye, J. (2024). The confluence of AI and big data analytics in industry 4.0: Fostering sustainable strategic development. *Journal of the Knowledge Economy*, 1–37.
Zheng, X., Zhang, X., & Yang, G. (2023). Can data assets spur corporate R&D investment? *Applied Economics Letters*, 1–8.
Zolas, N., Kroff, Z., Brynjolfsson, E., McElheran, K., Beede, D. N., Buffington, C., & Dinlersoz, E. (2021). Advanced technologies adoption and use by us firms: Evidence from the annual business survey (No. w28290). National Bureau of Economic Research.

Correction to: Case Studies in Digital Transformation

Adolfo Crespo Márquez, Turuna Seecharan, Georges Abdul-Nour, Joe Amadi-Echendu, and Jay Lee

Correction to:
A. Crespo Márquez et al. (eds.), Case Studies in Digital Transformation, Engineering Asset Management Review 4, https://doi.org/10.1007/978-3-032-05592-7

The original version of this book was published with an incorrect author name 'Pablo Duque' in the Table of Contents for Chapter 7. In addition, the affiliations and email addresses of the authors were published incorrectly in Chapters 7 and 8. These have now been corrected. The book has been updated with the changes.

The updated versions of these chapters can be found at
https://doi.org/10.1007/978-3-032-05592-7_7
https://doi.org/10.1007/978-3-032-05592-7_8

A. Crespo Márquez et al. (eds.), *Case Studies in Digital Transformation*, Engineering Asset Management Review 4, https://doi.org/10.1007/978-3-032-05592-7_17

MIX
Papier aus verantwortungsvollen Quellen
Paper from responsible sources
FSC® C105338

If you have any concerns about our products,
you can contact us on
ProductSafety@springernature.com

In case Publisher is established outside the EU,
the EU authorized representative is:
Springer Nature Customer Service Center GmbH
Europaplatz 3, 69115 Heidelberg, Germany

Printed by Libri Plureos GmbH
in Hamburg, Germany